RELIGIOUS CONTROVERSY IN BRITISH INDIA

SUNY Series in Religious Studies
Harold Coward, Editor

RELIGIOUS CONTROVERSY IN BRITISH INDIA

Dialogues in South Asian Languages

Edited by

Kenneth W. Jones

State University of New York Press

Published by
State University of New York Press, Albany

Printed in the United States of America

For information, address State University of New York
Press, State University Plaza, Albany, N.Y. 12246

Production by Ruth East
Marketing by Bernadette LaManna

Library of Congress Cataloging-in-Publication Data

Religious controversy in British India : dialogues in South Asian
languages / edited by Kenneth W. Jones.
p. cm. — (SUNY series in religious studies)
Includes bibliographical references and indexes.
ISBN 0–7914-0827–2 (alk. paper) — ISBN 0–7914-0828–0 (pbk. :
alk. paper)
1. India—Religion. I. Jones, Kenneth W. II. Series.
BL2007.5.R44 1992
291.2'0954—dc20

90–24210
CIP

10 9 8 7 6 5 4 3 2 1

This volume is dedicated to the memory of
John Greenfield Leonard (March 18, 1936—November 9, 1985)
A colleague whom we shall not soon forget

CONTENTS

Part Two:
Internal Polemics: Religious and Social Reform

Part Three:
In Summary

PREFACE

This volume will explore forms of internal and external religious controversy. External disputations took place between contesting individuals or movements within different religions; internal discussions occurred in a single religious community. The former were sparked often by Christian missionaries and proponents of new, aggressive religious movements in combat with other religions; the latter were generated by religious reformers who attacked orthodoxy or even by social reformers who did not see themselves as especially religious in their actions and ideology. Until the arrival of purely secular ideologies, an event that took place primarily in the twentieth century, exponents of social and cultural reform drew on religious authority for the legitimization of change even if it was limited to such doctrine as a rationalistic theism. Reformers found their efforts brought them into conflict with members of the religious establishment, which had long defined "proper" human activities as sanctioned by religion or custom.

Research for this volume is based on literature used to express differing opinions in tracts, journals, and plays that were generally issued in small numbers, but widely read as they passed from hand to hand. Even debates that used the well-established oral tradition were put into print after the event had taken place: thus their influence was magnified, because followers and opponents of a particular leader or society read them avidly. Since printing was inexpensive, anyone or any group with an ideology to expound, a position to attack, a leader to support or condemn, could publish works on their ideas. Sacred texts that supported a movement or ideology were translated and made available through inexpensive editions, as were the writings of self-proclaimed advocates of differing religious movements. As the nineteenth century progressed, polemical religious literature and those who wrote it mobilized groups to support their doctrines. These polemicists entered into religious combat as they led their followers forward through a return to what was defined as the "true" religion or attempted to defend established religion against the advocates of change. This collection of nine studies and one analytic chapter opens a window to a world expressed in South Asian languages hitherto closed to many scholars and students of the subcontinent.

The first part of this volume examines external controversy as it developed between proponents of one religious sect or community and was opposed by other religions. We open with three chapters that focus on Hindu-Christian polemics. Frank F. Conlon begins with a study of Swami Vishnubawa Brahmachari, who met Christian missionaries in debate on the beaches of Bombay and sought to condemn Christianity as well as to revive Hinduism through his writings. D. Dennis Hudson follows with the career of Arumuga Navalar, who linked both the northern peninsula of Jaffna and the Hindus of Tamilnad in his attempt to revive Shaiva Siddhanta and to defend it from Christian attacks. Both men were active in the mid-nineteenth century. Kenneth W. Jones turns to the writings of Swami Dayananda Saraswati and to the arguments that he developed to destroy all Christian credibility and at the same time to provide a basis for the one true faith, his own Vedic Hinduism.

In the second section we move on to explore two examples of Muslim-Christian polemics of the nineteenth and early twentieth centuries. A. A. Powell begins with the decade before the Revolt of 1857, when Dr. Wazir Khan entered into controversy with Christian missionaries, particularly the acerbic Reverend C. G. Pfander. Their struggles brought a round of religious polemics to the Agra—Delhi area in the 1840s and early 1850s. Rafiuddin Ahmed takes us to Bengal with a discussion of Islamic reform and the career of Munshi Meheru'llah, who attempted to defend Islam from criticism by Christian missionaries. Here we see the writings of the Reverend Mr. Pfander once more a catalyst for religious conflict.

Not all religious controversy took the form of theological polemics, as shown by Christopher King in the final look at external polemics. He examines two polemical plays that pitted Queen Devanagari against Begum Urdu in a contest between Muslims, who struggled to maintain the dominance of Urdu, and Hindus, who sought equal or if possible superior status for Hindi. In these contexts, language was associated with script and, in turn, with religion. Urdu was written in a modified form of the Arabic script and thus symbolized the Qur'an, the core of Islam, while Devanagari was associated with Sanskrit and the Hindu scriptures.

Part 2 turns to internal religious polemics that pitted social and religious reformers against defenders of orthodoxy. Proponents of new forms of thought and social behavior attempted to redefine acceptable or unacceptable customs as they fought for change within their religious community. The chapter by John and Karen Leonard examines the career of Viresalingam, a social reformer and theistic Hindu influenced by the Brahmo Samaj doctrines, who came into conflict with orthodox authority as he advocated dramatic changes in customary behavior centering around the issue of widow remarriage. Following similar themes Gail Minault writes of Sayyid Mumtaz 'Ali's efforts to defend Islam from external criticism. These efforts became fused with the struggles of 'Ali and his wife, Muhammadi Begum, to reform the role of women in Muslim society. The third chapter of this section, by N. G. Barrier, turns to the internal struggles that developed within the Sikh community as different groups sought religious reform, redefinition of Sikh identity, and standardization of Sikh practices as well as defense of Sikhism from other religions. This is, then, a combination of both internal and external polemics, with the major thrust on internal issues. The final chapter, by Barbara Metcalf, examines the impact of these writings on concepts of religion and communal identity as polemics both internal and external acted to define the religious community.

Together these studies depict a mosaic of religious conflict, reform, and defense that expanded during the nineteenth century and were expressed in South Asian languages. The widespread use of printing provided a technique that made religious polemics all the more influential among a growing audience of literates. Overall the positions articulated in polemical literature were uncompromising, as each writer spoke of the superiority of his religion and the inferiority of his opponents' beliefs. Hindus did not talk of ethical equivalence or of all religions being true as each sought the supreme deity according to one's individual path. The goal repeatedly articulated was one of defeating all opponents and, in that process, of establishing the superiority of a particular religious doctrine—of truth as each defined it. Later religious conflict and the rise of communalism that still haunts independent India are understandable in terms of such ideological positions and polemical techniques. The techniques, organizational base, and attitudes that supported communalism were forged in the nineteenth century and led to politicized expression of religion in the twentieth century. During the years after independence new "enemies" replaced the Christian missionaries as prime targets of religious conflict.

This volume has been the creation of a variety of individuals. We must thank Professor Gail Minault who, while in India, organized a panel for the Twentieth Meeting of the Association for Asian Studies in Philadelphia, April 1986. Success of that panel led to the decision to create a volume on religious controversy and social change, a project joined by several other scholars. The editing was supported through research funds from Kansas State University. I also wish to thank my wife, Marguerite, for her aid in typing the manuscript into our computer, in editing, and in proofreading. She provided crucial help in preparing the final manuscript.

Kenneth W. Jones

PART ONE

External Polemics

SECTION ONE

Hindu-Christian Polemics

One

The Polemic Process in Nineteenth-century Maharashtra: Vishnubawa Brahmachari and Hindu Revival

Frank F. Conlon

The Setting

Bombay city's Hindu society was astir during the autumn of 1856.[1] Reports spread rapidly of a series of meetings, some public, some private, which featured religious discourses delivered by a "new champion of Hinduism," known as Vishnubawa Brahmachari. This thirty-one year old Brahman, it was said, possessed commanding insight into Vedic traditions and, more significantly, such a keen mind and sharp wit as to be able to defeat Christian missionaries in debate and thus to protect, preserve, and promote the ancestral Hindu *dharma*.[2]

During the following months, this Brahmachari Bawa, as he was sometimes called, followed the principle that the best strategy for the defense of his faith was to go on the attack against Hinduism's missionary antagonists.[3] In so doing, he opened a new chapter in religious polemics within Maharashtrian society and clearly touched a responsive chord in many of his fellow Indians, both Hindus and others, as they struggled with the perplexing challenges of separating the persuasive claims of European civilization's material superiority from those of Christianity's spiritual preeminence.

Of the many nineteenth-century Indo-Western cultural confrontations, none was more troublesome than that of evangelical Christianity's challenge to indigenous religious beliefs and practices. The British political conquest of most of the subcontinent had thrust aside the indigenous rulers and their patterns of rule, yet British dominance had little impact upon the daily life of most of their subjects. Indians adapted to the new forms and opportunities of colonial administration with relative ease, particularly in the areas of earliest colonial conquest and administration. The study of English and the spread of Western-style education was slow and geographically restricted. Clearly during the first half of the nineteenth century, the overwhelming majority of the Indian people had little or no direct experience of the new phenomena of Western rule or culture. The minority who did, discovered new ideas and types of association; in places like Calcutta or Bombay they began to generate a process which historians have called the Indian renaissance—a revitalization of their own society and culture.[4] Still, the imposition of a fundamentally alien domination inevitably eroded the prestige and influence of indigenous cultural values and practices. Accompanying the excitement of renewal and discovery, whether of new knowledge from the West or of classical traditions of India's ancient heritage, there remained for educated Indians a sense of ambivalence and vulnerability.[5] These sentiments were further intensified by the challenges of an increasingly aggressive propagation of the Christian gospel by Western missionaries.

As most every student of Indian history knows, the East India Company's initial policies toward Christian missionaries were at best ambivalent. The Honorable Company pursued a strategy of pragmatic neutrality toward the religions of their Indian subjects and sought to keep European Christian missionaries out of company territories altogether. Whether these policies were rooted in an enlightenment era sympathy for the attainments of Indian civilization or a hard-eyed concern to avoid the potential costs of conflict with Indian society, the effects would have been similar. Until pressure at home was created by the evangelical Christian interests, the Company kept mission stations out of its territories and tried to limit the entry of missionaries thereto. The British parliament eliminated these restrictions in the charter renewals of 1813 and 1833, opening British India to missionary endeavor.[6]

The encounter of the new Christian initiatives with India and Indians was often perceived on both sides as a meeting of religions and respective civilizations. Within the debates over the issue of missionary activities in India, advocates of the missions not only spoke of the imperative to spread the Christian faith, but also stressed the view that Indian society and culture required a thorough regeneration under British guidance. While some Britons admired the achievements of Indian civilization, others, including the evangelical Charles Grant, believed that India was a backward place, stagnated by Hindu beliefs and practices. If Britain was obligated to uplift India, then surely Hinduism, which Grant conceived as the ultimate source of India's many social evils, must be undermined.[7] Grant asserted that it was essential to bring the Gospel to the East since Indians were capable of a transformation: "the Hindoos err because they are ignorant; and their errors have never fairly been laid before them."[8] While the linkage of Christianity and the secular European civilization was not inevitable, certainly many Europeans took it as a given. Furthermore, it appears that Indians also perceived this relationship and found it troubling. They searched for the means by which they could avoid the dilemma by accommodating the best fruits of the West's material achievements while preserving their own religious and cultural identity.

Among the sources of external culture, surely the Christian missionaries offered the most highly visible, if not inherently attractive, external messages to Indian audiences. As in the case of other aspects of Western influence, the initial stage for missionary activities was to be found in colonial cities and towns, but even as early as the 1830s Christian representatives were visiting towns in the remote corners of the countryside. As these endeavors became more widespread, so too did popular antipathy and antagonism. In all localities missionaries faced an initial problem of finding an audience for their message and a means of attracting some intellectual and emotional engagement as a prelude to encouraging conversions. In this work they built upon the ancient legacies of their own faith, taking a leaf from the pages of the apostles, going and preaching to "the heathen."

Proponents of the Christian gospel sought contact with the widest range of the Indian population. They practiced attention-getting techniques of street preaching. The novelty of a European speaking on a street corner in broken Marathi was itself an attraction. Street preaching was a form of public propaganda which might draw a substantial audience from among those who were not literate. On another level much missionary energy was invested in education and the consequent spread of literacy. Education was an inherently useful product which might attract Indians, but literacy could be the path to knowledge of scripture. The pioneering work of the British Baptist mission at Serampore in Bengal in developing typefaces for the printing of Bibles and inexpensive Christian tracts in Indian languages is well known.[9]

In the contexts of tract printing and public preaching, the missionary challenge to Indian belief repeatedly returned to themes of religious polemic. Initial response was often mixed. Audiences often simply dismissed the missionary messages. Some street preachers who sought to stimulate their listeners, only aggravated them, prompting their audience to counter with abuse and, sometimes, even physical violence.[10] The polemic process, however, did not remain a one-sided affair. Ultimately the missionary challenge forced Hindus to defend their faith. Indeed the process contributed to the very conception of Hinduism as a concrete thing, a religion possessed of an ideology. This new perspective would be in itself unsettling, yet its impact was magnified by its coincidence in time with the overall claims of the superiority of Europe over India.

While an exceedingly small proportion of the missionaries' listeners embraced Christianity, others did give consideration to the missionary critiques of Hinduism and put forward their own observations critical of Hindu belief and practice. For example, Lokahitawadi, Gopal Hari Deshmukh (1823–1892), propounded severe strictures against conventional Hindu customs and urged the need for reform from within.[11]

Most Maharashtrian Hindus were not prepared to accept such propositions. A strong counterthrust of explicitly anti-Christian polemic also arose. Practitioners of this response attempted to shift the ground of debate to familiar territory of Indian tradition. Some polemicists, including the subject of this essay, Vishnubawa Brahmachari, went on to launch stinging counterassaults upon the *Khristi lok* and their religion. These efforts were reinforced by the application of the new printing technology to the production of Hindu religious tracts and broadsides.

Religious polemic was not an altogether new phenomenon in nineteenth-century India. Brahmanic tradition had long encompassed erudite debate on philosophical or theological subjects. Hindu philosophy contained a legacy of arguments against the views of Buddhists, Jains, and materialists. In the nineteenth-century confrontations, however, these traditions were only of limited use to the defenders of Hindu *dharma.* Unlike the traditional debates which had been conducted by India's religious elites among their own ranks, the modern discussions were of a public nature. Street preaching and broadcasting of tracts potentially introduced an unprecedented force, the general audience. As we shall see below, an "audience effect" clearly conditioned the shape and direction of public debate. Also, the ambivalence of many Indians toward their colonial rulers' culture affected the discourse. In the course of debates, the role of Western material superiority as the great prop to the claims of the Christian religion was weakened by the emergence of the argument that Europe's material greatness was offset by India's inherent spiritual superiority. Thus even before the time of the British assumption of direct rule in 1858, Hindu religious polemics already had generated one of the most potent and enduring articles of faith underlying India's modern Indian national identity. Among the voices which raised this new rejoinder to the claims of the West was the subject of this essay, an unusual Maharashtrian who combined the characters of traditional divine and modern publicist.

Vishnubawa Brahmachari was an ascetic defender of Hindu *dharma* in mid-nineteenth-century Maharashtra. Although often overlooked in general histories written by Indian and non-Indian alike, Vishnubawa has remained honored in the memory of Maharashtra.[12] He has been described variously: "the first great revivalist of modern Maharashtra,"[13] the author of "the Marathi *avatār* of *The Communist Manifesto,*"[14] "predecessor of the two great swamis of modern times, Dayananda and Vivekananda,"[15] and "a queer bird."[16]

Vishnubawa, from his arrival in Bombay in 1856 until his death there in 1871, developed a reputation for witty repartee and vigorous argument in confrontations with Christian missionaries and, occasionally, with other Hindus. His debates in Bombay in 1857 were widely publicized in Marathi and English, and at least nine books were published either by him or containing extracts of his writings.[17] He was not the first Marathi polemicist against the Christian missionaries, but he was one of the most colorful and widely known. As a public speaker he was an acknowledged master of his audience and its prejudices. His published writings achieved a measure of popular notoriety in his time partly as they reflected his robust exposition, but also because, unlike other defenders of orthodox *dharma,* he conceded some possibilities of change and reform and challenged his modern audience to live up to what he termed the ideals of a Vedic golden age. He attempted to project onto contemporary nineteenth-century politics and statecraft a vision rooted, he claimed, in the Hindu religion. Certainly in his muscular defense of Hindu belief and his verbal assaults upon Christianity, Vishnubawa anticipated the careers of later, better known Hindu reformers and revivalists such as Dayananda Saraswati. Although given scant attention by Western historians, his place in the history of Maharashtra seems assured as the "overlooked first Hindu missionary."[18] His writings fit well into a collective consideration of vernacular religious polemicists, their messages, and their impact on religious revival in nineteenth-century Indian society.

The Career of Vishnubawa Brahmachari

Vishnu Bhikaji Gokhale was born in 1825, the tenth child of a modestly placed Konkanastha (Chitpavan) Brahman family, residing in a village, Shiraval, near Mahad in the Thana (now Kolaba) district. His education appears to have consisted only of a few years in a village school along with some study of the Veda in preparation for his sacred thread ceremony.[19] Owing to a reduction of the family fortunes, young Vishnu took up service as an assistant in a grain merchant's shop at Mahad and at the age of fourteen found a vacancy as a candidate-volunteer in the customs office at Sangamseshvar Bandar, leading in a few months to appointment with pay at Thana in the Customs Department. Thus young Vishnu seemed safely on the path of the *laukika* (secular) brahman, secure in "service." Yet this bureaucrat-in-becoming seems to have spent his own time engaged in religious exercises and disciplines, memorizing *stotras* and mingling with *sādhus.* His customs service postings were at several places in the Thana area—Vasai, Bhiwandi, and Kalyan—each of which was also in close proximity to Bombay. While Vishnu Gokhale could hardly be counted a member of the urban cosmopolitan elite of Bombay, neither was he a hopeless rustic, totally out of touch with news of events in the city.[20]

It was while posted at Urun, a small port on the harbor opposite Bombay, that Vishnu Gokhale sensed that other work awaited him. As he was drowsily emerging from sleep one morning, he heard what he took to be a divine voice calling: "*Are,* Vishnu. If you live in the company of beasts, are you therefore one? Take a decision—who am I? Abandon service, go into the wilderness lost in philosophic meditation."[21] Inspired, Vishnu resigned his appointment, retained but a loin cloth and a staff, and commenced several years of penance and meditation at the sacred hill of Saptashringiri near Nasik.[22]

There, he later said, he had further visions giving him a mandate to propagate *dharma* throughout the land. In 1852 or 1853, he moved first to Nasik and then on to Pandharpur. He stayed on at this great pilgrimage center for three years during which time he learned traditions of the *vārkarī panth,* studying Eknath's *Bhāvārtharāmāyanā.* Subsequently the young ascetic, now known as Brahmachari Bawa or Vishnubawa Brahmachari, published his own book, *Bhāvārthasindhu* (Sea of Devotion), which gave emphasis to *dynan* or "special knowledge." *Dynan,* he explained, would be found only in Vedic religion and realized through devotion (*bhakti*) as expressed by the saint-poets of Maharashtra. Apparently, he also heard Christian missionaries at Pandharpur criticizing Hinduism and resolved that he would answer them. This resolve was furthered by the patronage of a government Educational Department inspector, Mahadevshastri Kolhatkar, and some other gentlemen who enabled Vishnubawa to visit a number of important places in Western Maharashtra—Sangli, Miraj, Kolhapur, Wai, Satara, Pune, and Ahmednagar. Thereafter, in September 1856, Vishnubawa Brahmachari went to Bombay to step upon a wider stage.[23] Having forsworn marriage, abandoned worldly employment, and absorbed the available teachings of regional and Sanskritic religious knowledge, Vishnubawa stood poised to combat the Christian missionaries and to defend *dharma*. Yet, as we shall see, his defense by no means excluded the possibility of, even the necessity for, that Hindu society and culture could themselves be reformed.

The imperative of Vishnubawa's "mission" was colored fundamentally by the Christian challenge to Indian religions. Christians had been proselytizing in Western Maharashtra since the days of the Portuguese conquests. However, the nineteenth century saw the entry of a new element—British and American Protestant missionaries fired with a zeal for bringing India to Christ and doing it rather quickly, too. Although the East India Company attempted to restrict their activity, as early as 1812 a few American missionaries had reached Bombay. Relying upon the sympathy of the Governor, Sir Evan Nepean, they ultimately established residence in the city. Initially utilizing the Serampore Press Marathi grammar, dictionary, and New Testament, these missionaries commenced a vigorous campaign of street preaching near Hindu temples in Bombay.[24]

In these public discourses, the missionaries not only propounded Christian doctrine, they also sought to exploit seeming inaccuracies or inconsistencies in Hindu texts. When the American Congregationalist Gordon Hall discovered that a Bombay Brahman astrologer confessed that his texts did not tell him whether the earth was a sphere or a plane, the missionary was jubilant. It would "ultimately be highly serviceable in pulling down the fabric of Hindu superstition that their religious books, held equally sacred, are directly at issue on several points in geography and astronomy."[25] Hall also found a target in the Hindus' concept of God—"some dark, indescribable and unintelligible notion of a supreme, invincible abstract existence or being who is no more than a negation of all qualities." This was, he observed, yet another example of how Hinduism "presents a shapeless mass of cruelties."[26] Hall's innocence of Hinduism may account for his judgments, and his unmistakably hostile tone probably did little to attract the many Indian converts he so ardently sought.

The halting pace of evangelism may also be explained by the small numbers of mission workers. In 1825, there were six missionaries (four Scots, two Americans) in Bombay aiming to convert twelve million Marathi speakers. The following decade brought changes. The 1832 East India Company charter revision legally opened India to foreign missions, which led in turn to a steady growth in numbers of mission stations and staff.

A second change was episodic, not systemic. In 1829, Dr. John Wilson arrived in Bombay. This Scottish missionary brought, along with his evangelical ambitions, a strong intellectual grounding in Indology which allowed him to analyze Hindu or Zoroastrian texts. He sought to find new points of contact and confrontation.[27] Building upon his growing command of Marathi and Sanskrit, Wilson attempted to draw Indians into public religious discourse. He foresaw that debates would allow him to question the foundations of his opponent's religion, while setting forth Christian doctrine. Some inconclusive attempts at such discussion had occurred in Pune in 1829.[28]

In May 1830, public debates were inaugurated at Bombay by Wilson and an Indian convert with one *pandit,* Lakshman Shastri. Among members of the audience, the discourses' finer philosophical subtleties might count for less than a clever turn of phrase, yet the nature of the meetings opened the issues to an unbounded public. Wilson's biographer records that the outcome of the debates was highly gratifying to the missionaries, for: "the benefit of the discussion was not confined to the crowds who heard it. Two editions of the report in Marathi were speedily exhausted; all Hindu Bombay talked of it; it stirred up inquiry as nothing else could have done."[29] In the following year another *pandit* Morobhat Dandekar debated Wilson for six successive evenings. Dandekar subsequently published a tract setting forth his views, *Shrī Hindudharmāsthāpana* (Foundations of Hindu Religion) which in turn called forth rebuttals published by Wilson.

Wilson also commenced in 1831 his first tour into the interior of Maharashtra, going even beyond British territory into the Marathawada region of the Nizam's state. Wilson toured sacred places and engaged in public lectures and personal dialogues. By the 1840s, it was becoming common to see Western missionaries visiting the holy towns of the Deccan, including Nasik and Pandharpur, where it seems young Vishnubawa first heard them.

It is likely that news of the *Khristi lok's* missions were already known to Vishnu. In his postings within the Thana custom circle, he remained in proximity to Bombay, and it is probable, though not provable, that he would have known of the great controversies which had erupted in the city in 1843 when, for the first time, a mission-school-educated Brahman, Narayan Sheshadri, requested baptism. Hindu opinion, whether conservative or liberal, expressed alarm; the subsequent complications of negating a proposed conversion of Narayan's underage brother and further controversies concerning his readmission to Hindu society filled the press with anxious considerations of Christian intentions and of the need to defend *dharma.*[30] While some "liberals" like Bal Shastri Jambhekar concentrated upon the readmission issue, Wilson's old "conservative" adversary, Morobhat Dandekar entered the fray with a new broadside against Christianity, *Upadesha Chāndrika* (Moonlight of Admonition), which a missionary journalist in *Dnyāno-*

daya asserted even went so far as to use arguments of the "books of infidels like Voltaire and Tom Paine."[31] Thenceforth there were many who would speak or print against the missionaries, such as the later *Vichār Lahari* (Wave of Deliberation) of Pune.[32]

Thus anti-Christian and pro-Hindu sentiments were by no means unknown in the Maharashtra of the youthful Vishnu Bhikaji Gokhale, nor were the missionary challenges. Hindus were beginning to utilize the same technologies employed by their Christian antagonists. The missionary J. Murray Mitchell recalled that at mid-century Christian tract distribution had to be reinvigorated since: "The Hindus by this time, had begun to lithograph large editions of their religious works. These were usually embellished with pictures of gods and temples and commanded a very large sale. Until of late these books had been only in manuscript and were comparatively little known. Was the press to be turned into an auxiliary of Heathenism?"[33] Furthermore, the utility of debates and public meetings had opened a new era in the region's patterns of religious discourse. As noted above, debates and polemics had been the special preserve of those with the qualifying Brahmanic status and education. Now, particularly as the oral debates were recorded and printed, and as additional polemics were published, literacy rather than caste status became the key to participation. The audience was changed. In place of the quorum of learned *pandits* there was now public opinion.

The questioning of Hindu traditions by the Christians also unsettled Hindu society by an echoing indigenous criticism of orthodoxy. Mahatma Jotirao Phule's significant critique of Brahmanic values and pretensions—the charter of the non-Brahman (*bahujān samāj*) movement in Maharashtra—clearly drew strength and inspiration from these challenges. At the time, however, most of the audience of missionary polemic responded more impulsively. Missionaries found that attempts to make public sermons were often greeted by heckling, verbal abuse, and, on occasion, violence.[34]

In this context of over a quarter of a century of Christian-Hindu disputation and polemic, and with the intensification of missionary endeavors provoking greater apprehension and hostility among Hindus, Vishnubawa Brahmachari was not the first Maharashtrian Hindu to enter the lists against Hinduism's critics. Rather he was the first to launch a widely recognized defense of Hindu *dharma,* using an effective style reinforced by an aggressive counterattack against Christian doctrines. Even his missionary opponents had to concede that he possessed "an agreeable manner, remarkable fluency and ease, a fine command of the Marathi language, [and] an air of sincerity and piety."[35]

The exact circumstances of his 1856 visit to Bombay have not been discovered in the historical record. It would seem that Vishnubawa's tour of Western Deccan towns and/or the publication of his *Bhāvārthasindhu* brought his name to the attention of some leading Bombay Hindus. It appears that most of Vishnubawa's early supporters were drawn from the ranks of the Pathare Prabhu and Gaud Saraswat Brahman communities—two groups that had enjoyed considerable secular success and status in Bombay since the eighteenth century but whose ritual position within the regional *varna* hierarchy was inferior to that of Maharashtra Brahmans of the Deccan. Thus the administrative union linking Bombay to the Deccan, brought about in 1818 after the overthrow of Peshwa Baji Rao II, increased contacts of the coastal elites with the brahman-dominated Deccan society. Prabhus and Saraswats were more likely to be made conscious of their less-favored status in the eyes of Deccani Brahmans. This ambivalence of status may have served as a stimulus to a collective enthusiasm among the Bombay members of these coastal castes for supporting the Hindu revival.[36]

In any event, Vishnubawa Brahmachari commenced lectures at the Prabhu Seminary—the school sponsored by the Pathare Prabhu caste at Thakurdvar, Bombay—in September 1856. These meetings in defense of Hindu *dharma* were "densely thronged," according to missionary sources who noted with surprise that the large turnout was "not as one might suppose by old Hindus, but by the more enlightened and awakened classes of the community."[37] Vishnubawa decried the fact that because Hindus were ignorant of their own religion, they consequently could not defend it against missionary critiques. He pointed out the usefulness of analogies to defend Hindu traditions and usages. For example, to answer Christian criticism of "idolatry," one might invoke the use of pictures: "as images of absent friends serve to aid our recollection of them, so the idols tend to keep alive in the mind the recollection of the gods." He also whipped up enthusiasm for speaking out against the Christians by pointing out the limits of supposed European superiority. The whites had much useful knowledge, no doubt, but their superiority to Hindus in worldly matters was consistent with their inferiority in matters of the spirit.[38]

The conception of God quickly emerged as an issue. A missionary in the audience said that if Hinduism were of divine origin, it would show the impress of God and godlike character. Vishnubawa retorted that neither beauty nor ugliness could be attributed to God—such terms were suitable only for finite things. Here began a theme of mutual incomprehension that would appear throughout later debates—the highest Hindu conception of divinity—the cosmic spirit without qualities (*nirguna*), seemed fair game for missionary attack, while Vishnubawa regarded the Christian descriptions of divine attributes in physical terms a proof of inferiority. Also, the Christian tactic of pointing out inconsistencies or inaccuracies in Hindu texts as a means of invalidating the entire tradition stimulated first a response that such inconsistencies reflected changes in the world since the ancient times when the texts were compiled. Later it would be more practicable for defenders of Hinduism to counterattack by seeking out inconsistencies in Christian texts.[39]

Although Vishnubawa had obtained his hosts' permission for the missionaries to be present at his lectures, there was sentiment among the sponsors to exclude untouchables, (ex-Mahar Christian converts) from the proceedings. This led George Bowen and other evangelists to decline further attendance, and it was given out by some as proof that the missionaries had been unable to meet Vishnubawa's arguments, but through the medium of *Dnyānodaya* the Christians urged that the Bawa meet them in the open, where caste could not serve as a bar.[40] The lectures proceeded without them, yet further criticisms arose from some Bombay Hindus who took exception to Vishnubawa's freewheeling expositions of Vedic religion. Bhau Mahajan, editor of *Prabhākar,* a reformist newspaper which had earlier published Lokahitavadi's "Shatapatren," launched a new paper, *Dhūmaketu* (Comet) in which Bawa was denounced as a "hypocrite and infidel." Other Hindus were perplexed by Vishnubawa's suggestion that family deities (*kuladevatā*) be abandoned in a quest for a purer and higher Vedic religion.[41]

A new organization led by some Gaud Saraswat Brahmans, the Suddhurm Bodhuck Subha (Society for Instruction in Good Religion), sponsored further talks in a new venue after it became clear that Vishnubawa was no longer welcome at the Prabhu Seminary. Admission to the talks was now by ticket only—there was a definite intent to control the size and, perhaps, the composition of the audience.[42] The editor of the Christian *Dnyānodaya* proposed that the two sides meet openly in a public debate, time and place to be chosen by the Hindus, but within a strictly defined framework of debating rules, specifying only one spokesman on each side.[43] An agreement was reached whereby Vishnubawa Brahmachari would hold forth on successive Thursday evenings at the Back Bay seashore. It is possible that tensions had developed between Vishnubawa and his erstwhile supporters, encouraging him to accept such an arrangement; reports from that period indicate that he was being excluded from the "houses of the gentlemen who at first favored him."[44] Whatever the reason, the debates were now literally out in the open. The concept of open discourse did not, however, appeal to all Hindus. At about the same time advertisements appeared for lectures by persons other than Vishnubawa in defense of Hinduism. The notices made it clear that these other lecturers were addressing meetings that were open only on a basis of high caste status.[45]

A fairly complete record of Vishnubawa's confrontation with the missionaries exists, since George Bowen published reports each week in the *Bombay Guardian* covering the series from January 15 until May 28, 1857. Although Vishnubawa claimed to have defeated the Christians, they in turn felt sufficiently vindicated to publish the debates in book form, first in English and later in Marathi.[46] Because of the authorship of the reports, the Christian viewpoint always had the last word, yet Vishnubawa only once complained concerning certain details of one weekly report. Otherwise he appears to have accepted the gist of the proceedings.[47]

In the new venue, Vishnubawa Brahmachari chose to shift the focus of his eloquence. In the hall he had defended Hinduism as he saw it; on the beach he would attack Christianity and do so basically through the same techniques that Christians had used against Hinduism—examining religious texts for contradictions or evidence of a less than ideal divine nature. At about five o'clock each Thursday evening the Bawa would arrive at the Back Bay shore and place copies of the Marathi Old and New Testaments and some manuscript notes on a table that had been set up for him.[48] It became clear that he had a remarkable grasp of the word, if not the spirit, of the Bible and used this knowledge to raise a series of criticisms of the character of Jesus, Mary, Joseph, the apostles, and most other biblical characters.[49] Taking up Isaiah's prophecy that "a virgin shall conceive," he questioned the meaning of the term *virgin* for nearly two hours. According to Bowen "he did nothing but harp upon this word in a way that may have been very agreeable to men of impure minds."[50] George Bowen thought that he recognized in the Bawa's discourse evidence of knowledge of the agnostic writings of Thomas Paine and others; he commented ruefully on the fact that it was "European infidels who have taught the Hindoos to utter such things."[51]

Vishnubawa often pointed to extracts from both Old and New Testaments which seemed to contradict missionary claims for the divine character of God. If, in Genesis, God made man in his own image, or if the spirit of God moved upon the face of the waters, this surely was a contradiction to the proposition that the Christian God was immaterial (*nirankār*). The missionary responded that man was made in God's moral image only. The Bawa replied, "that may be, but the question is whether the passage in Genesis had any such meaning. This is an interpretation that you padris put upon it in order to reconcile it with just representations of God," but the meaning was plain enough. The Bawa then moved to passages from Revelation, thereby prompting Bowen to wonder why a Hindu would object to such language when the Hindu's own texts abounded with such manifestations of God. Clearly Bowen had missed the point that such passages in Hindu texts had long been targets of Christian attack.[52]

In some instances it became clear that the basis for Vishnubawa's attacks were true misunderstandings arising from inadequate translations in the Marathi Bible. Confusions over mistranslations of the words for *miracle* and *sign* and passages relating to drunkenness and "unholy" as opposed to "unclean" flesh added an additional element of misunderstanding.[53]

On one occasion Vishnubawa quoted from Proverbs 23:20, "Be not among wine-bibbers: among riotous eaters of flesh: for the drunkard and the glutton shall come to poverty." This passage showed, he said, that it was wrong to eat flesh. The missionary retorted that the passage showed it was wrong to be gluttonous. The Bawa retorted that in Genesis 1:29 God was represented giving "every herb bearing seed" and "every tree in which is fruit—to you it shall be for meat"—surely a divine command for a meatless diet! The missionary said that he had misread Genesis and called attention to a passage concerning Noah, but Vishnubawa read the text and said that it clearly showed that God had commanded that man not eat flesh with the life thereof, which is the blood thereof shall ye not eat." The missionary response was to explain that this was merely permission to eat flesh, but only of animals that had been properly slaughtered.[54] Although by no means all Hindus were vegetarian, and certainly the major share of the audience who were Parsi had no pretensions to vegetarianism, nonetheless, this issue offered an attractive club with which to belabor the missionaries. On another occasion the issue of Christian meat eating again arose. Vishnubawa noted the commandment "Thou Shalt Not Kill" and enquired why then Christians killed animals. On being told that that commandment applied to human life only, he took up Leviticus 17:3–4, a passage relating to ritual slaughter, and suggested that it really meant that killing an ox or lamb or goat was like murder and therefore "You Christians must all then be guilty of it."[55]On at least one occasion Vishnubawa congratulated George Bowen on his good qualities, but led on to dramatically underscore his own appreciation of the public interest the debates had generated: "You do well to meet me here, and try to convince me that the Bible is true, for if I am converted a great many others will come over with me."[56] In the stratagems of public confrontation, humility had little appeal.

On broader terms of comparison of religions, Vishnubawa tended to use conventional defenses of "lower" forms of religious practice. Once, while attempting to attack the Christians as having a clear concern with the images of God as found in Genesis, Vishnubawa was drawn into discussion of the use of images and, according to the missionary's account, offered what was a conventional Hindu defense: "Idolatry may not be the highest form of worship, but it is well enough for those who are ignorant. There are three steps to the knowledge of God and idolatry is one of them. The child that begins its studies learns first its A.B.C."[57]

The Bawa's reputation as a defender of *dharma* extended beyond the seaside debates. When a twelve-year-old Brahman boy fled his family to become a Christian, his mother begged Vishnubawa to get the lad restored to his family. Vishnubawa went at the head of a large throng to the missionary-run Robert Money School, in those days adjacent to Dhobi Talao, where the boy was reported to be staying. In the confrontation which followed, the Bawa claimed that the missionary had assaulted him. Subsequently the crowd occupied the building until evicted by police. The boy was returned to his family, and Vishnubawa's reputation much enhanced. In the following Thursday's debate, a heavy police patrol was present, and the Bawa averred that he could not understand why. He claimed that "his only weapons were words and he would leave it to others to resort to more violent measures." The "saved" young Brahman appeared at a later debate at Vishnubawa's side—a sort of trophy of combat.[58]

The drawbacks of doing battle on the Christians' own theological field seems not have daunted Vishnubawa, although when additional meetings were proposed, he said that he wished to meet only once a week.[59] It should be understood that the phenomenon of a public debate had qualities of an entertainment as much as—if not more than—a serious theological discourse. Clearly many of the audience came to enjoy the Bawa's famed repartee and, as with other Indian audiences, were not above heckling their hero. One party told him that if his wisdom were weighed in the balance against that of the Christian padris, that theirs would be as an elephant and his as an ant. Vishnubawa did not disappoint. He replied, "Granted we are very insignificant and you are very great; we are but an ant and you are an elephant; but and ant can creep into the trunk of an elephant and cause his death." The audience was reported to be "much delighted."[60]

Perhaps the lack of reverence toward Vishnubawa related to the fact that often more than half the audience consisted of Parsis, for whom he had to carefully craft his propositions.[61] The crowds grew at times to more than two thousand people, and while insults were hurled at missionaries and Christian converts, the overall behavior was peaceful—reinforced no doubt by the occasional presence of Police Commissioner Charles Forjett and a few constables.[62] The surviving missionary chronicles gloss over some of Vishnubawa's witticisms and tend to smooth the rough edges of his polemic. To their regret, it seemed that he had a better sense of the audience and its expectations than did the Christian speakers. He appeared to understand the utility of creating a dramatic, theatrical appearance of having put the missionaries to ideological flight even when the debate had been less than decisive. On at least one occasion the missionaries recorded that "the Bawa kept repeating his questions, and we declined giving any answer, having already said everything that could reasonably be demanded. The audience became very noisy; the Bawa stood on the table and made a great show as though he had gained a great victory; and the people accompanied him with hurrahs."[63]

The last few debates coincided with the outbreak in North India of the mutinies and rebellions which not only shook British rule, but also specifically took on a strong anti-Christian character. No reference, however, concerning this vast upheaval is found recorded in the debates. The Thursday evening routines continued uninterrupted until May 28, when Vishnubawa announced that as the monsoon was soon to begin, the sessions would be suspended. In fact, they were never reopened. The following autumn a letter appeared in *Vartman Dīpika,* a paper published by the Bawa's supporters, wondering why the mission padris did not return to the seashore. Perhaps they had had enough? The missionaries did not return to the debates, and thus there were none.[64] It is probable that the government of Bombay, perceiving that the cataclysm in North India may have had its roots in the religious fears of Hindus and Muslims regarding Christian missionaries, sought to avoid any unnecessary provocations of religious animosities in Western India. It seemed not to matter, for Vishnubawa had now turned to a new strategy in his campaign on behalf of Hinduism.

Vishnubawa's confrontations with the missionaries on the Bombay seashore had not ended the Christian challenge. In the weekly debates he had managed to assail the missionaries' beliefs by attacking them in terms of their own doctrines. Yet Vishnubawa appears to have recognized that Hindus had to go beyond denigrating other religions, turning instead to a clear exposition of what was essential in their own system of belief. Therefore he began writing what would be truly his magnum opus, a survey of what he took to be the ultimate kernel of Hindu faith, entitled the *Light of Vedic Religion,* or *Vedoktadharmaprakāsha.*

This work opens quite simply: "*Dharma mhanje kāy?*"—"what does *dharma* mean?"[65] The full answer follows over the next 794 pages. Vishnubawa claims that he is not following in a specific *gurūparampara* (spiritual lineage), but obtained his insights in visions from the god Dattatreya, the goddess Parvati, and the medieval philosopher Shamkara. This visionary experience of the divine calls to mind the career of his Bengali near-contemporary Ramakrishna. The *Vedoktad-*

harmaprakāsha seems founded on intuition and experience rather than on systematic study. There is a defense of orthodox Hinduism bubbling through the many pages, yet there is also a sense of a need to reform through revival.

The ultimate source of authority is always the Vedas. Early in the text Vishnubawa asserts: "When you make a study of Vedic religion you find more knowledge because the Vedas *are* knowledge—nothing exists which is not contained in the Vedas."[66] The *Veda* means knowledge and as such is a part of the supreme God, and this is the knowledge which brings liberation. Philosophically the message is one of pure monism, stressing the ultimate reality of the formless *Paramātman.* Vishnubawa did not cleave arbitrarily to the *Veda* alone in delineating the ideal arrangements of his life in this world. Admitting that ultimately the world was all illusion, he nonetheless urged the need for people to fulfill the social and ritual obligations of their station in life. Brahmans should not bemoan the fact that people no longer respected them, but should earn popular respect by properly offering rituals. Everyone in society would find their lives more comfortable and fulfilling if they would become practicing vegetarians.[67] (He had harried the Christians on this matter in the debates when discussing the Old Testament sacrificial offerings and the modern Christian practice of eating meat—did not animals have souls?)

Vishnubawa defended what he regarded as the Vedic social order as an ideal system which could be followed in modern India. Not only did this mean he was propounding a positive definition of what was to be an ideal Hindu life, he was also providing an indigenous basis for reforming those aspects of Hindu society which were a source of vulnerability to Christian critics. He urged respect for Brahmans, but was prepared to criticize the pretensions of priests who did not live in *dharma*-fulfilling ways.[68] At the other end of the social scale he seemed to recognize that the institution of untouchability marked an inherent weakness in Hinduism. He questioned the degree of pollution of untouchables and argued that they were not disqualified from participation in the society of caste Hindus. Nonetheless his analysis of the matter suggested that while untouchables had a place in society, it would be within a caste identity suitable to their situation and capacities.[69] His views on caste and untouchability probably struck most hearers as conventional wisdom, not dangerously radical reformist talk. While discussing contemporary Bombay's urban problems, a self-professed follower of Vishnubawa Brahmachari pointed out that caste could serve as a basis for maintaining a city's life. Caste not only produced purity of life, obedience to parents, the rise of commerce, industry, and science, but also could promote the health and cleanliness of cities. To prove this point he offered what might be called a Vedic-social Darwinian analysis resonant with the arguments of Vishnubawa's tract:

> The filth of Bombay, the hotbed of every corruption, was owing to inducements held out to sweepers to follow other occupations than that to which they were born; having left that for others for which they were by nature unfitted, they had degenerated and were too feeble to keep the town clean.[70]

Vishnubawa's arguments on behalf of his Vedic model began in the form of persuasion but were ultimately justified on an appeal to history. Things clearly had been better in the past during a Golden Age when Vedic Indians achieved great accomplishments—not only in matters of spirit. They knew science, steam engines, airships, telescopes, and printing presses then—truly all the great material accomplishments, which in modern times the Europeans claimed as their own, originally existed in India.[71] For that matter, the existence of the Indo-European family of languages, as seen in the array of cognate words in Latin, Greek, English, and Persian, was further proof of Vedic superiority. Originally all knowledge had been in Sanskrit, which was not a mere linguistic cousin to these other tongues but, in fact, their beneficent ancestor.[72] Swami Dayananda Saraswati never said it better.

During the 1860s Vishnubawa Brahmachari stayed on in Bombay, making a few tours of Madras, Calcutta, and Benares.[73] Perhaps in response to the new British rule, or to the rapid changes in Bombay, the Bawa began to extend his prescriptions from religion into the realm of politics. He had included some ideas on political forms in his magnum opus.[74] In 1867, however, he brought forth a new work in "an essay on the right form of government which would yield the greatest happiness to the people."[75] Seeking to bring his wisdom to the attention of non-Marathi-speaking Europeans, he had an English translation published and distributed.[76]

Some analysts have characterized the essay as an exhortation to a kind of utopian socialism—a "Marathi *avatār* of *The Communist Manifesto*."[77] In one sense this seems remarkably apt. The initial theses do have a utopian socialist resonance, emphasizing that a king is the head of a family of all his people to whom he is responsible. Vishnubawa's essay included propositions that all people are one family; the entire land should be improved and cultivated, with its produce being the joint property of all; railways, factories, and telegraphs should be established; all should eat the same food—vegetarian, of course—in common dining places, and the king should arrange marriages. Here was a world in which all desires were satisfied and hence all ill will would vanish.[78]

In such a world, it might be asked, who would clean the latrines, carry palanquins, polish shoes and the like? Those who ask should know that "men are not all endowed with the same kind and extent of sense [or]...extent of taste and are consequently not habituated to the performance of the same kind of duties."[79] Hence the king should find out the natural capacity of each child and arrange a suitable education. Only those who do their work would receive food, clothing, and benefits. And while some people would have the work of cleaning latrines, their children would be "trained up in the professions for which they in turn may be found fit and when they grow up they will follow those professions accordingly."[80]

Vishnubawa did not expect that his ideal society would arise only after the introduction of specific social reforms. He did not hold out the possibility of ending the reign of caste or of requiring that there be an end to the use of images in worship. However, he insisted that these reforms would come eventually, but only after the policy of defining all people as belonging to one family had been adopted. The implications were radical, but not secular. The ultimate sanction of the new policy was to be found, not in logical reason, but in a devotional awareness of every person's duty to the supreme lord, *Parameshwara.* The political solutions were never explained, only proclaimed. Vedantic philosophy and *bhakti* devotion provided the inspiration. The model was unrealistic in appearance because Vishnubawa included political economy as part of a dependent topic, to be considered only in subordination to religious perfection. While his political essay did gain him some attention, in fact the bulk of his post-1859 writing continued to be devoted to development of religious insight.[81]

Still the utopian quality of Vishnubawa's political vision seems such an unusual product of what was believed to be a "rustic intellect," that some source might need to be posited. Although Vishnubawa himself had little knowledge of English, certainly many of his supporters had been in contact with Western education and the English-language press of Bombay. (The missionaries were particularly regretful of the degree to which the "benighted Hindus" were aware of European atheistic and deistic ideas and able to use them against the evangelical mission.)[82] Vishnubawa never indicated particular knowledge of Western sources—there is no parallel here to a radical Eurocentered social critic like Henry Derozio of Calcutta.

However, Vishnubawa Brahmachari probably was not significantly dependent upon a particular source. His great strength lay in his readiness to adapt new information into a rather inchoate mass of facts and fables, secured by an overarching belief in an idealized Vedic age and sustained by his own rhetorical powers. His monism rested less in the recaptured documents of a rediscovered classical past and more upon the evolved heritage of ethics and metaphysics perpetuated by the medieval Marathi saint-poets Dnyanadev and Eknath. The Christian missionaries regarded what they took to be his inconsistencies as proof of Hindu inferiority and accepted his polemic as an opportunity for them to put forward their own position. Probably they never worried, if they even realized, that among many Maharashtrians it was assumed that Vishnubawa had in fact triumphed and turned back the tide of conversion.

In Summary

Vishnubawa's relationship to other nineteenth-century religious revivalists and reformers has been mentioned above. Certainly his approach to religious experience and his lack of concern with conventions of caste remind one of Swami Ramakrishna Paramahamsa (1836–1886). His stress on Vedic revival and a golden age finds parallels in the teachings of Swami Dayananda Saraswati (1824–1883). It is intriguing to wonder if the young Dayananda was aware of the seaside debates at Bombay or of the *Vedoktadharmaprakāsha,* which was translated and published in Hindi about 1868.

Vishnubawa Brahmachari died in the Viththal Mandir at Bombay on Mahashivaratri, February 18, 1871.[83] It has been said by way of criticism that he never founded a *samāj,* or "association." Indeed no institution lived on after him to perpetuate his teachings. Soon after the publication of his great book, Bombay entered into a speculative cotton boom sparked by the American Civil War. Many Bombay citizens dedicated themselves to pursuit of *artha* (gain) rather than *moksha* (release). When, in 1867, a new religious movement was started in Bombay, it was the theistic Prarthana Samaj, emphasizing a comforting *bhakti* message within a form that was attractive to the emerging educated Maharashtrian middle class. Yet if Vishnubawa founded no organization, he nonetheless had a large circle of admirers: Hindus, both Gujarati and Maharashtrian, and some Parsis. Perhaps the lack of great specificity and focus in his interpretation of Hindu religious history, coupled with his idiosyncratic breadth of argument and pointed criticism of social convention, left potential followers without a vital kernel around which to build. He was not ignored. Even after his death his writings were published and republished.[84] A biographical essay was published in 1872 and awarded the Dakshina prize.[85] The eminent reformer Mahadev Govind Ranade credited Vishnubawa's *Vedoktadharmaprakāsha* as a work which stood out in the task to "represent the best portion of orthodox thought stated so as to be generally acceptable to all parties."[86] Perhaps it was so acceptable, in fact, as to provide no basis for movement forward. Vishnubawa's revivalist efforts represented an important meeting point of cultural and religious confrontation. He became a symbol of resistance to the criticism launched against Hinduism by evangelizing missionaries, and in his considerations of what *dharma* truly meant, he contributed to the objective survival of the ancestral faith. In their vigor, his polemics did defend *dharma* without foreclosing on the desirability or possibility of reform. True to his given name, he remained Vishnu—the preserver.

Bibliographic Essay

The bibliographic universe of nineteenth-century Hindu polemics in Maharashtra is not easily accessible in English language sources. In recent scholarship, the most comprehensive companion to exploring the entire range of Maharashtra's intellectual creativity is Matthew Lederle, *Philosophical Trends in Modern Maharashtra* (Bombay: 1976), which attempts to summarize and categorize all significant nineteenth and early twentieth century thinkers of the region. The only comprehensive survey of modern Marathi literature is a monumental, but idiosyncratic and outdated, compilation by Govind Chimnaji Bhate, *History of Modern Marathi Literature, 1800–1938* (Mahad, Kolaba District: Govind Chimnaji Bhate, 1939). One recent exploration of a highly significant Maharashtrian polemic—that of Jotirao Phule against the pretensions of brahmans—is Rosalind O'Hanlon, *Caste, Conflict, and Ideology: Mahatma Jotirao Phule and Low Caste Protest in Nineteenth-Century Western India* (Cambridge: 1985). Another recent examination of polemics in Maharashtra is Richard P. Tucker, "Defence of Dharma in Maharashtra, 1840–1870," in A. G. Pawar, ed., *Maratha History Seminar* (Kolhapur: 1971), pp. 375–89. Richard Fox Young, *Resistant Hinduism: Sanskrit Sources on Anti-Christian Apologetics in Early Nineteenth Century India* (Vienna: 1981) includes analysis of Sanskrit polemics generated by Maharashtrians.

Turning to the actual literary production of the period before and during Vishnubawa's career, we face two major problems. One reflects the marginality of this material, particularly that written in Indian languages, especially Marathi. In fact relatively little polemic literature written from the Hindu point of view has survived. For that matter, the Christian anti-Hindu tracts also deteriorated over years in the Indian climate. However, Christian tracts were often sent back to the West, where they occupied dusty corners of missionary society or theological seminary libraries. Thus, while full runs of important Marathi papers like Bhau Mahajan's *Prabhākar* and *Dhūmaketū* and Krishna Shastri Chiplunkar's *Vichār Laharī or the Vartaman Dīpika,* (said to be edited by disciples of Vishnubawa), have not survived, we find their contents reported in missionary papers, particularly the *Oriental Christian Spectator* and the Anglo-Marathi *Dnyānodaya.*

Publication of the Marathi literature of Hindu-Christian polemic (excluding Father Thomas Stephen's *Krista Purāna*) commenced in the aftermath of John Wilson's debates in 1829 and 1830. Morobhatt Dandekar's *Shrī Hindudharmasthāpana* Foundations of Hindu Religion (Bombay: 1831) was an account of a debate with John Wilson and a reiteration of a defense of Hinduism, described by Bal Shastri Jambhekar in *Bombay Durpun* as "the first instance of a Brahmin coming forward publicly to vindicate the Hindu Religion, and entering the field of public discussion by publishing a work in defence of it." (*Bombay Durpun,* April 13, 1832, in Ganesh Gangadhar Jambhekar, ed., *Memoirs and Writings of Acharya Bal Shastri Jambhekar (1812–1846),* vol. 3 [Poona: Ganesh Gangadhar Jambhekar, 1950] pp. 36-38). This in turn stimulated publication by John Wilson of *An Exposure of the Hindu Religion* (Bombay, 1832).

Morobhatt Dandekar made a further contribution to religious polemic in his serial publication, *Upadesha Cendrikā* (Moonlight of Admonition), which was published for one year in 1844, although the twelfth issue, labeled December 1844, actually appeared in January 1845. A principal motivation for its appearance was the controversy concerning the question of readmission to the Deshastha Brahman caste of Shripat Sheshadri, younger brother of the Christian convert Narayan Sheshadri.

In turning to the works of Vishnubawa Brahmachari, not all prove to be equally useful, although all are marked by the handicap of their comparative rarity. Vishnubawa's first book, *Bhavarthasindhu* (Bombay: 1856; another edition, Satara: 1856), does not directly engage in polemical argument, although it seems clearly intended to reaffirm Hindu values. The actual debates with George Bowen, Narayan Sheshadri, and other missionaries are reported in the pages of the *Bombay Guardian* for 1857 as well as in two missionary produced books: *Samudrakinārī Vādavivād: Brahmacārī Bava anī Khristi Upadeshaka yamadhyē Dharmavishāyī je vadavivād Mumbāīs jhālē tyānci hakīkata* (Bombay: 1872). The English version of these debates is found in George Bowen, *Discussions by the Sea-Side* (Bombay: 1857).

Vishnubawa's major work, *Srī Vedōktadharmaprakāsha* (Bombay: Sh.

1781 [A.D. 1859]) enjoyed a revival when a second edition was published (Bombay: 1882) with the addition of his other essays. Prior to his death, Vishnubawa also published a commentary on core verses culled from the *Bhagavata Purana* in *Catuhshlōki Bhagavāta yānca artha* (Bombay: 1867). Vishnubawa's next religious discourse appeared in his *Sahahsthitica Nibandha* ["Essays on Natural Condition") (Bombay: Sh. 1790 [A.D. 1868]). The preceding year saw his excursion into political theory in *Sukhadayāka Rājyaprakāranī Nibandha* (Bombay: Sh. 1789 [A.D. 1867]), for which he obtained an English language version, *An Essay in Marathi on Beneficent Government by Vishnubawa Brahmachari, translated at the desire of the author by Captain A. Phelps* (Bombay: 1869). It should be noted that Vishnubawa caused translations of several of his works into other Indian languages to be made; several essays were published in Gujarati and a Braj rendering of *Vedokta Dharma Prakash* was published in 1869. A lengthy commentary on the *Bhagavādgītā,* the *Setubandhānī Tika-Prakrta (Srīmadbhagavādgītā)* (Bombay: 1890), was left unfinished by Vishnubawa and completed by Ramachandra P. Raut.

On Vishnubawa's life and thoughts two contemporary or near-contemporary studies are available: Ramachandra Pandurang Sastri Ajrekar, *Srī Vishnubava Brahmacārī yānce caritra* (Bombay: Sh. 1794 [A.D. 1872]) and Mangesha Hari Nerurkar, *Srī Vishnubava Brahmacārīkrita Vedōkta Dharmaca Vicār vā Khristimat khandan* (Bombay: 1874 [A.D. 1872]). Regrettably, Vishnubawa's publications remain difficult to obtain, even in libraries of Maharashtra.

Two

Arumuga Navalar and the Hindu Renaissance Among the Tamils

D. Dennis Hudson

In the context of Western and Christian influence in eighteenth- and nineteenth-century India, what did Tamils say about what it meant for them to be Hindu—not in English or in French, but in Tamil? A full and satisfying answer will have to include the little known but highly influential work of one man, Arumuga Navalar of Jaffna (1822–1879). He is regarded as the "father" of modern Tamil prose and a staunch defender of Shaivism against Christian missionary attacks. Less well known are his attempts to reform Shaivism itself. This chapter will examine his career as a religious activist between the ages of nineteen and thirty-two, when he plowed the social and intellectual fields he cultivated the rest of his life.[1] Arumuga worked within the heritage of Shaiva scholars as he responded to the newer challenges of an intrusive Western Civilization.

The Religious Context of the Shaiva Literati

In the early centuries of the common era, Buddhists and Jainas provided the occasion for the Tamil Hindu literati to define their own cults and literature. Most notably they produced the Tamil poems of the *bhakti* saints, the Nayanars and Alvars. Devotees consider these poems the "Tamil Veda." By the twelfth century, Tamil Shaivas and Vaishnavas—with their literature in Tamil and Sanskrit, their monastic systems, their networks of temples and pilgrimage sites, their elaborate public and private liturgies, and their Brahman and non-Brahman leadership—had systematized the definition *Hindu* and institutionalized it as the basis for Tamil literary culture.

The Vellala and Brahman literati were mostly Shaiva members of the largest and most influential religious tradition (*samayam*) among sectarian groupings. Any religion not based on the traditions that Shiva had revealed in the Veda and the Agama, they believed, was founded on delusion. During the thirteenth through eighteenth centuries, Shaiva theologians defined the details of their religious tradition and called it *Saiva Siddhānta*, or "Shaiva Orthodoxy."

The way the Shaiva Siddhanta literati perceived themselves in relation to other traditions is instructive for our discussion. Their perception used the common Indian idea of the *mandala*, a center that expands outwards into peripheries bounded by barbaric and demonic powers.[2] At the center of the *mandala* stood Shaiva Orthodoxy. Around it four circles expand concentrically,[3] three inside the realm of *dharma* (*puram*), and a fourth outside of *dharma* (*purappuram*). This was the realm of darkness and delusion, where those sects reside that altogether reject the Veda and Agama. Shaiva theologians did not formally include the Muslims and Christians in this classification, but it was evident that they fall in the outermost circle to dwell in the wilderness with the Buddhists, Jainas, and demon worshippers. Intellectual encounter with Muslims and Christians, it seems, was a task never taken by the monastic leaders who had provided this scholastic mapping.[4] It was left to "lay" Shaivas, who encountered an increasingly aggressive Muslim and Christian presence in their everyday lives. They felt pressed to address such issues as the "monotheistic" nature of their theology, their own definition of a "heathen," and the relation of Shiva and his temple to the cults of the popular and violent deities of the villages.[5] Arumuga Navalar was the first of these Tamil laymen to undertake as his life's career the intellectual and institutional response of Shaivism to Christianity.

Hindus opposed the Christian missions from the earliest days they were established among the Tamils; literary evidence for it is indirect,[6] largely because the printing press was not available to Tamil ownership until 1835.[7] Hindus, who wrote anti-Christian literature during this period, circulated it as oral literature or in handwritten copies, few of which survive.[8] Hindu works that did appear before 1835 were printed on government or missionary presses and were written generally by Tamil scholars who worked for Europeans.[9] Once Tamil Hindus gained ownership of presses, they immediately used them for two religious purposes. One was to strengthen the realm of *dharma* (*puram*) in those places where its social basis was eroding, namely Madras and Jaffna. They transferred currently popular Hindu literature from palm leaf to printed book, sometimes adding new commentaries. The second was to attack Christian propagandists who had used the press to condemn *dharma* from a position of privilege in the European domain.[10] Arumuga Pillai became adept in this propaganda war; he was the Shaivas' most successful strategist who served them as social organizer, apologist, and reformer.

Hindu-Christian Disputes in Tamil

Arumuga Pillai, Navalar's original name, belonged to a high-status caste known as Vellalas, a class that along with Brahmans had produced most of the Tamil literati for centuries, perhaps millennia.[11] Born in 1822, he grew up in the Tamil regions of Sri Lanka where the total population was less than two hundred thousand.[12] His home was in the town of Nallur on the Jaffna peninsula, a forty by fifteen mile strip of land separated from southern India by the Palk Strait.[13] Jaffna—the name of both the principal town and the peninsula—was predominantly Shaiva with a Tamil Shaiva culture distinct from that of the Sinhalese Buddhists elsewhere on the island, but closely linked to the Shaiva culture of southern India.

Because his father was a Tamil poet, Arumuga Pillai received a solid foundation in Tamil literature at an early age. Like many high-status boys of the second generation to live under British rule, he entered a Christian mission school to study English. Arumuga was twelve when he attended this school as a day student. He did so well that he was asked to stay on at the Jaffna Wesleyan Mission School to teach English and Tamil. More importantly, the missionary principal, "the gifted and plodding" Peter Percival, asked him to serve as his own Tamil *pandit,* to assist him in writing and editing treatises and hymns and, most importantly, in translating the prayer book and Bible.[14] Arumuga Pillai worked with Percival from 1841 to 1848, eight years in his late teens and early twenties, when he wrestled seriously with the question, What does it mean to be Hindu?

At the time of Arumuga Pillai's birth, Protestants from England and America had established stations in nine villages on the Jaffna peninsula from whence they conducted vigorous campaigns to convert the Hindus and Muslims into Christians.[15] The first significant Hindu opposition to these efforts emerged in 1828 when the teachers of the American Missionary Seminary at Batticotta (Vattukkottai) began to stress the Shaiva scripture Skanda Purana (*Kanta Purāṇam*) in their school. The decision angered Jaffna Hindus, who doubted that in such a foreign setting the sacred quality of this Tamil story of Murugan, the warrior son of Shiva, would be respected or that its esoteric meanings would receive a sympathetic hearing. A missionary report of this incident[16] noted that the Christians had difficulty obtaining a copy of the text, for

> The Scanda Purana is in the hands of but few persons in the Country, excepting those immediately connected with the Hindoo Temple, as it is generally thought unsafe to have the book in the house, lest it should be in some way defiled.

Once they had received a portion of this text, the report continued, the principal Tamil instructor of the Seminary refused to teach it.

> He urged that the Scanda Purana is one of the most sacred books used in the Country—that it should be taught only in sacred places—that the Mission premises are, in the estimation of the people, very far from sacred—that it would not be possible to perform on them those ceremonies which ought ever to precede, accompany, and follow, the reading of that book—that the members of the Seminary were not fit persons to be instructed in the Purana, and finally, that he could not subject himself to the odium that would be cast upon him by the people, for thus teaching it.

The study nevertheless took place.

Christians had their portion translated from poetry into prose and trained a senior student to teach it. The classes immediately created a stir. Though they were voluntary, social pressure caused attendance to gradually dwindle until they were abandoned. From the Shaiva point of view, this act by Christian educators had pulled a text from the sacred center (*akam*) of *dharma* out into the darkness of the wilderness (*purappuram*), stripping it of its ritual context and laying it bare for profanation. Indeed this is what the educators had intended, as the end of the report said:

> Enough, however, was read to convince all who would reflect, that the book is filled with the most extravagant fictions, many of which are of an immoral tendency, (just as the Bible says,) "for the people will walk every one in the *name* of his god."

Two long anti-Christian poems appeared around this time in Jaffna. They reflected an increasingly vocal opposition. The Vellala poet, Muttukumara Kavirajar (1780–1851), wrote the "Kummi Song on Wisdom" (Jnanakkummi) and "Abolition of the Jesus Doctrine" (Yesumataparikaram). The timing of their publication suggests a connection with this opposition.[17] The "Kummi Song on Wisdom," moreover, attacked the Christian Bible and Christians just as the Christians had criticized the *Skanda Purāna* and Shaivas.[18]

Events in Jaffna had their effect in Madras. Polemical literature circulated widely, it seems, even when it was not printed. Muttukumara Kavirajar's "Kummi Song on Wisdom" received a rejoinder in Madras from a recently baptized Shaiva *sādhu*[19] whose own "Kummi Song on Wisdom" (Jnanakkummi) appeared in print in 1827. It was followed in

1840 by a *kummi* on the Hindu scriptures written by the Vellala Protestant Vedanayaka Shastriar: *Shāstirakkummi: A Satirical Poem on the Superstitions of the Hindoos.*[20] In 1840 or 1841, Hindus in Madras organized the Association for the Philosophy of the four Vedas, which resembled the Calcutta Brahmo Samaj in its worship. It was led by educated Christians who had renounced their conversions. The Samaj proceeded to defend Hinduism against Christian attacks.[21] In this charged atmosphere, a Madrassi Vellala Hindu published a condemnation of the Bible entitled *The Misunderstanding of Veda* (Vetavikarpa) and a Vellala Catholic responded with *Contempt for 'The Misunderstanding of Veda'* (Vetavikarpa tikkaram).[22]

In Jaffna, meanwhile, the Christian assault on Shaivism intensified. Just like the Shaivas' view of Christianity, Christian leaders saw Shaivism as in a dark wilderness. In 1841, two Tamil Christians at the American Mission Seminary launched a semimonthly and bilingual periodical. They devoted *The Morning Star* (Utaya Tarakai) to "Education, Science, and Literature, and to the Dissemination of Articles on Agriculture, Government and Religion, with a Brief Summary of Important News." The intentions of the editors were clear. Europeans, they observed in volume one, were politically and economically powerful and prestigious because of their secular and religious knowledge. Tamils did not have this knowledge since most of the "useful sciences and arts" were not written in Tamil. Only a few science courses were taught to "the higher classes of society and Brahmins," except for those who attended English schools. Therefore, the editors intended this periodical to fill the educational gap between ordinary Tamils and Europeans, "imitating the Europeans in the improvements they have made by such means."[23]

Because they were Protestants of the early nineteenth century, the Tamil editors were naively confident that the emerging knowledge and values of modernizing Anglo-American culture were perfectly consistent with their interpretation of the Christian Bible. They assumed that the fulfillment of human nature depended upon knowing the truths about God and the world and that assumed that all people had the innate ability to learn to read and understand those truths found in a single text, the Christian Bible. As devout Protestants, they took great efforts to translate the Bible and distribute it among the Tamils. The editors of *The Morning Star* were confident that those who read the Bible would see the truths, choose them, reject evil, and undergo an improvement in moral character. These aggressive Tamil Protestants persistently challenged Catholics, Muslims, and Shaivas to open their sacred books for public scrutiny and judgment. The fact that they did not do so could only mean that these non-Protestant religious leaders believed their own scriptures were too weak and obscure to withstand public scrutiny.[24]

This dualistic, black-and-white point of view admitted few gray areas. Shaivas, Muslims, and Catholics all lived in the darkness of falsehood. But of the three, Shaivism was the most evil system in the moral wilderness. These religious journalists stated that:

> There is nothing in the peculiar doctrines and precepts of the Siva religion that is adapted to improve a man's moral character or fit him to be useful to his fellow men.... If the world were to be converted to the Siva faith no one would expect any improvement in the morals or the happiness of men. Every one might be as great a liar and cheat—as great an adulterer—as oppressive of the poor—as covetous—as proud, as he was before—without sullying the purity of his faith.[25]

Believing that Shaivism was a creation of the Brahmans and contained nothing of value, these converts admitted of no middle ground:

> We repeat, for we wish all our readers to understand it, if the Siva religion is true, Christianity is false, and will be overthrown; for that which is of God will stand, and that which is of the devil will fall, and human effort will be unavailing to sustain the false or to destroy the true system.[26]

In this struggle between God and the devil, they intended the *Morning Star* to reveal the falsity of Shaivism.

The Tamil Hindu literati of Jaffna could not deny the power of Christian civilization as they experienced it, but they rejected the validity of the *Morning Star*'s judgment about Shaivism. In the long run, the Tamil Hindus' task would be to use the instruments of Western civilization's knowledge without undermining their own traditions in the process. Could they bring elements of the barbarian wilderness (*purappuram*) into the center (*akam*) of the *mandala* without polluting Shaivism's world view and removing its sacred power? The Christians thought not, for they believed true knowledge to be all of a piece and in harmony with the Bible. The Shaivas in Jaffna had not yet tackled the issue formally, but in 1842 they made a beginning.

In September of 1842 over two hundred Hindu men of high status gathered at the monastery (*matam*) of the Shiva temple in Jaffna to discuss plans for establishing a Veda and Agama school to teach Shaivism. Five wealthy leaders had called the meeting and spoke to this question. According to a letter to the *Morning Star* written by a Hindu sympathetic to the idea, probably Arumuga Pillai himself, the speakers declared that Christian doctrine was the creation of the missionaries and that Tamils converted because they knew little about Shaivism. The gathering expressed pity and compassion for the converted. At the third meeting it was decided to collect money to open a school to help ward off future conversions of students.[27] They agreed to purchase a printing press, if possible, in collaboration with "the white men of this place," the Eurasian burghers, and to publish tracts on the absurdities of the Christian religion, "which would effectually shut the mouths of the missionaries and stop their abuse."[28] The school opened in October. The organizers planned to send to India for a man to teach the Agamas and in the meantime appointed a former teacher from the Christian Seminary as an instructor of grammar and literature.[29] The twenty-year-old Arumuga Pillai may have reported these developments to *The Morning Star.* Subsequent events suggest that Arumuga Pillai had been part of these educational efforts all along.[30]

Arumuga Pillai's Emergence as a Shaiva Activist

In October 1842, when the Veda and Agama school opened, Arumuga Pillai had been teaching Tamil and English at the Wesleyan Mission School and working with the British missionary Percival for a year. He read the *Morning Star* and wrote to it. His first published letter appeared in September 1841, with a question about the science of the eyes and the nature of "vision."[31] But almost twelve months later, eleven days after the first meeting to discuss the idea of a Veda and Agama school, he wrote a letter to explain what the speakers at the meeting meant when they said "Christian doctrine is doctrine fabricated by the missionaries." He dated the letter October 10, 1842 and signed it anonymously as "The lover of good doctrine who is the son of a Shaiva."[32] The name suggests that his father was on his mind.[33] In the letter, Arumuga Pillai presented himself as a Shaiva who had heard the preaching of the American missionaries and had read their books. Sympathetic to their arguments,[34] he studied the Christian path. He read the Bible regularly, he said, but while doing so began to have questions about it.

The first question arose from the striking parallels he noticed between the liturgies of the temple in Jerusalem and the temples of Shiva in Sri Lanka and India. After providing many examples of ritual injunctions in the Old Testament, he asked, What are the differences between the rites and ceremonies of Shaivas and those of the Bible? Using the words of the editors' translation, modified slightly, he drew parallels between the Shaiva worship of God in the *linga,* and the Mosaic worship of God in the tabernacle and temple:

> The Israelites who were chosen by God as his own children believed that the Lord who dwelt in the ark made of wood, and who lived between the cherubims had bestowed grace upon them. The Shaivas

> believe that God dwells in the image. They [the Israelites] made a sanctuary for the worship of God. The Shaivas build temples. The Israelites worship Cherubim and bronze serpent. The Shaivas worship the images made of gold, and silver. The Israelites had shew bread and wine in their sanctuaries. The Shaivas keep fruit as prasada. The Israelites had incense. The Shaivas have it too. The Israelites burnt heifer and took its ashes for their use. The Shaivas use ashes from the dung of a heifer.[35]

Given their similarities, he next asked, Why do the missionaries mock as meaningless the Hindu distinction between the pure and the polluted and other observances? They are analogous in many ways to what the Lord commanded through Moses.

> Upon investigating these matters, the Christian missionaries do protest against the idol worship, rubbing ashes, observing the immemorial custom and usage, and other similar rites, and say that these ceremonies are not in the way to please God, and God will never command or order such kind of unmeaning ceremonies, and they are against our own understandings, and also ridiculous even to children.

But should the missionaries argue that the Mosaic rites were only symbolic and were pedagogically useful, the same may be said of the Shaiva rites:

> if you say that their [the Israelites'] rites and ceremonies are not the idol worship, but as God is an invisible Being they performed these ceremonies in order that the thoughts of God may be more indelibly impressed upon their heart...will not the Shaivas have the same reason to answer so?

Arumuga Pillai then made a personal confession, ending with a metaphor expressing his intellectual dilemma.

> When I heard the teachings by the gurus of the Christian path, my mind was very sympathetic and changed and I thought for a time that the Tamil sect might be false and the Christian true, and so I studied the Vedagama called the Bible.

But while reading the Bible he found a striking resemblance between temple worship in the Bible and temple worship in Shaivism. The similarities were so strong, he said, that he felt like the demon who came up from a well. The demon was afraid to go to the village of the tiger, so he went to the village of the jackal, only to find that the jackal's village belonged to the tiger too.

This brought him to his third question: since God in the Bible said that the rites and ceremonies of temple worship should continue forever and Christ and the early Christians followed them, how could the missionaries abandon them? The Bible makes it clear, he reminded the reader, that it is the duty of every Christian to observe those ceremonies it describes, just as did Christ for his disciples. Thus it was unreasonable for Christians to scoff at them when they were practiced by Shaivas. He concluded that the Lord of the temple in Jerusalem and Shiva in the temple icon were both able to give grace to all. And that the Shaivas' ceremonies were not ridiculous unless Christians said that God was ridiculous in setting up the temple in Jerusalem and Jesus ridiculous to worship there.

It was significant that Arumuga Pillai admitted that at one time he had been moved by the Christian teachings and had entertained the possibility that Shaivism was false and Christianity is true. Probably this occurred during his student years at the Seminary. It indicated that he was not deaf to Christian teaching, but that having opened himself to it in the way Protestants urged—by studying the Bible directly—he turned away in favor of his own heritage. His reaffirmation of his family's tradition was thus self-conscious. It was linked to a penetrating insight into the vulnerability of a Protestant system that staked everything on doctrines found in a book that had been divorced from the cultic context that produced it. Indeed, because of his own temple-centered culture, Arumuga Pillai probably thought he had a greater understanding of the liturgical context of Jesus' own life and worship than did the Protestant missionaries.

Peter Percival had provided Arumuga Pillai the occasion to analyze the Christian Bible in detail as Protestants interpreted it. Pillai's analysis, however, did not focus only on the domain of doctrine, which the Protestants cherished, but also on liturgical behavior, which Shaivas cherished and Protestants largely ignored. His was a comparative study of religions, one that led him to the conclusion that at the basis of both religions there was temple-centered worship with similar liturgical patterns. From this point of view, the Protestants were inconsistent with their own Bible when they insisted that Shaiva worship was false and only Protestant worship was true. Protestants need not give up their path and follow Shiva's, he maintained, but they did need to see that on the basis of their own scriptures they had every reason to respect the Shaiva path and to leave it alone.

Arumuga Navalar presented his interpretive stance at the beginning of a letter that expressed a Shaiva Siddhanta doctrine but in a manner that a Protestant could have affirmed as well:

> The eternally joyful and holy Supreme Being who created, protects and rules all the worlds, is gracious to this land and sends gurus from the distant land of America where a prosperous order and the Chris-

> tian path prevail, and in order to bring the people of this place to a high and full condition, he chastises them. May the Supreme Being be greatly praised for this boundless compassion.

The missionaries interpreted the "high and full condition" as conversion to Christianity and to Western civilization. Arumuga Pillai meant it differently, viewing Shiva as the one who had brought the missionaries to chastise Shiva's disciples and to awaken them to his own path, from which they had departed. The missionaries did not know it, he suggested, but Shiva was using them to punish the Shaivas and to awaken them to the truth that he had revealed in the Agamas. Christianity belonged to Shiva too, as Arumuga Pillai said in a veiled way when he referred to himself as the demon who came out of a well: Just as the royal tiger rules both his own village and that of the wild jackal, so Shiva rules both the realm of *dharma* (*puram*) and that of the barbaric Europeans (*purappuram*).

The editors of *Morning Star* knew they had a difficult task in responding to this long and carefully wrought document. It took them three issues to do so. They understood this calculated challenge, for they referred to its contents as "the pretended Resemblance between the rites and ceremonies of the Mosaic dispensation and those of the Sivas."[36] Whether they knew that the man who wrote it was in mission employ and was translating the Bible, however, is not clear.

Arumuga Pillai worked with Percival until September 1848 when, nearly twenty-six, he quit to devote himself fully to his own projects. He had studied in depth the Agamic literature forming the scriptural component of Shaiva orthodoxy, a task that required him to learn Sanskrit. He was now adept in the three literary languages of modern religious discourse in the Tamil world: Tamil, Sanskrit, and English; he would draw upon the religious literature of all three for his projects. Not surprisingly, his reputation had been growing among local Shaivas as a man who knew more about obscure Agamic literature than anyone else.[37]

It was his immersion in the Agamas, which began years earlier, that fueled his desire to turn into realities the projects that the Hindu literati had gathered to discuss in September 1842. The Veda and Agama school had not survived and a printing press was still a dream. The press required considerable funds, but teaching was cheap. In January 1846, therefore, Arumuga Pillai began night and early morning classes in the primary and secondary literature of Shaivism. His students were a few of his friends, young Vellala, Brahman, and Cettiyar men.[38] The classes were free and informal. He also persuaded two Vellalas not to take Christian baptism from Peter Percival, despite the fact that it could have cost him his job.[39] In June he crossed the Palk Strait and went with a companion to Madras to look at schools and to meet scholars, perhaps his first trip to the continent.[40] A Shaiva school was clearly on his mind.

His knowledge of the Agamas also led him into conflict with the leaders of the temple of Murugan near his home. The Kandaswami Temple in Nallur had been built about a century earlier, but not in accord with the Agamas. During its festival in the month of Ati (July–August), Arumuga Pillai took it upon himself to advise its trustees that they violated the Agamas in three ways: by the manner of the temple construction, by using a spear as the primary icon of Murugan rather than an image, and by employing Brahmans who had rejected Agamic initiations to conduct the worship. The trustees did not accept his advice, and this disagreement ultimately led to a lifelong conflict.[41] At the heart of the dispute was the authority of local custom, which the Kandaswami Temple followed, versus the authority of the Agamas: this contest pitted unwritten and immemorial practice against revealed and written scriptures.

The issue of revealed scriptural authority for the religious life had been alive in Shaiva Orthodoxy for centuries. The aggressive Bible-centered tradition of the Protestants, however, had intensified its importance in Arumuga Pillai's mind as he reconsidered the meaning of Shaivism. He seems to have decided that Shaiva practice demanded possessing a written and revealed set of scriptures that paralleled the Christian Bible in its comprehensive authority. On the one hand, Agama scriptures eliminated some elements of popular Shaiva culture, such as animal sacrifices and the worship of malevolent deities and demons, that the missionaries attacked ceaselessly and that had no scriptural basis. On the other hand, they provided a sophisticated and profound theological interpretation of temple worship and of the Puranic stories of the gods that nullified the sneers of the missionaries. Arumuga believed that the Sanskrit and Tamil scriptures of Agamic Shaivism purified popular and Puranic religion, elevated the ignorant, and inspired the literati.

Struggling against Christians and some Hindu reformers as well as orthodox priests, he made a dramatic move at the end of 1847 to spread the "Splendor of Shiva" (*Sivaprakāsam*) and disperse the "darkness" shared by Hindus and Christians. Religious tensions at this time were high. The Christian assault on Hindu culture had accelerated dramatically through the preaching of a catechist convert from Point Pedro and through missionary insistence on integrating an untouchable student into the Wesleyan Central School. Vellala and Brahman students, nearly half the student body, left the school in response and formed their own. Moreover, they persuaded the chief Tamil tutor at the Wesleyan school, a Christian, to be its headmaster.[42]

On December 31, 1847, Arumuga Pillai took the preaching methods of the Methodists into the Shaiva temple. He became a circuit preacher. Every Friday evening at the Vaidishvaran Temple in the suburb of Vannarpannai, Arumuga Pillai read sacred texts and preached. He was assisted by the Brahman Karttikeya Aiyar of Nallur (his friend and former student at the Wesleyan school) and by his students. Preaching (*prasanga*) was not new to Shaivism, but Pillai's systematic and scripturally based style was, as was the circuit of preachers he eventually developed. He intended to educate and morally reform his largely Vellala and Brahman audience. He believed that if they knew the rudiments of Agamic Shaivism and acted on them, they would strengthen *dharma* and weaken the Christians. He threatened to sue the *Morning Star* if that paper published any unauthorized report of the meetings.[43] The sermon topics were mostly ethical, liturgical, and theological and included the evils of adultery, drunkenness, the value of non-killing, the conduct of women, the worship of the *linga,* the four initiations, the importance of giving alms, of protecting cows, and the unity of God.[44]

He attacked Christians and Hindus as well, specifically the trustees and priests of the Kandaswami Temple in his home town; they accused him of slandering Murugan himself.[45] The lecture series and its circuit continued regularly for several years and produced a "Shaiva revival," for an informed piety developed and grew among many Jaffna Hindus.[46] Inevitably, such openly public work on behalf of Shaivism brought him into conflict with Peter Percival. Arumuga Pillai was no longer anonymous. When missionaries complained to Percival that his own Tamil *pandit* was successfully undermining the very reason for their being in Jaffna, Percival raised the issue with him: "I hear that you preach every Friday right in the Shiva temple. And I hear that now and then you talk as an enemy of our sect. What about it?" Arumuga Pillai's reply was simple and to the point: "Is there is anything wrong in my fulfilling my duties? If there is, please tell me." Percival said nothing. He told the other missionaries that his *pandit* was too valuable a scholar to lose.[47]

Arumuga Pillai was indeed invaluable to Percival. From the end of 1845 the missionary scholar had been devoting himself entirely to Bible translation, working six hours a day with his Tamil assistants, of whom Arumuga Pillai was the chief.[48] Even after Arumuga Pillai had launched his preaching sessions, Percival took him to Madras between March and July of 1848. Their Bible translation was being considered for publication by the Madras Auxiliary of the British and Foreign Bible Society. It was in dispute, and he needed Arumuga Pillai to help him defend the majestic literary style they had created, a style shaped by Arumuga Pillai's own immersion in Shaiva literature.[49] His break with Percival finally came, but it was not because of their disagreements. Arumuga Pillai decided to devote full time to his work for Shaivism. In August 1848, he founded a Veda and Agama school, the School of Shaiva Splendor (Saivaprakasa Vidyasala), and in September he left Percival.

Navalar Arumuga Pillai, "The Learned"

Twenty years later Arumuga Pillai briefly described the desire that had driven him during his early twenties.[50] His sole source of income at the time, he recalled, was the salary from Percival and the Wesleyan school. He had received no patrimony and nothing from his four brothers, though they had money and jobs. Nevertheless, Arumuga quit his teaching position even though Percival urged him again and again to stay at a higher salary. He knew that he could easily get a job commensurate with his abilities and live prosperously, as had many who had studied English under him. Arumuga knew that not holding a job would only bring him disrespect, but he did not wish to do so. Nor did he want to get married, for in Jaffna, he said, the bride provided the bridegroom with everything—house, lands, garden, jewels—and took in return, presumably, his independence.[51] He left his secure job and future family life, because he wanted to use his learning to make Shaivism prosper, a desire that had been with him since childhood.

Having abandoned future prosperity and the householder's life, the very basis of *dharma,* he must have appeared socially irresponsible to others in the community. Few gave him their support.[52] He began the school of Shaiva Splendor in a house opposite the Vaidishvaran Temple in Vannarpannai and after six months moved it to the temple's monastery (*matha*). Its teachers were his own students, and they received no salary except what came by way of donations. Their task was to teach the pupils not only the curriculum common to the traditional schools, but sectarian texts as well, for Arumuga Pillai sought to produce Shaivas who were grounded in their own tradition and had the ability to dispute others when necessary.

Navalar's concept of the school was something new in Tamil Shaivism; it was an adaptation of the Protestant schools he knew intimately. The traditional Tamil school primarily served the educational needs of the higher castes. It taught the values of *dharma* shared by those who lived within its cultural borders (*puram*). These values were imparted through Tamil texts like Valluvar's *Kural* and Auvaiyar's *Ātticūti,* texts that avoided divisive doctrines that split the inhabitants of the *puram* into various sects.[53]

Writing, reading, arithmetic, literature, and ethics were taught to a group of boys according to a fixed syllabus. Each pupil progressed according to his ability to imitate, memorize, and comprehend. The teacher explained the texts in vernacular Tamil, but the texts themselves were in poetry, often accompanied by prose commentaries in a style difficult to understand. Perhaps twenty boys would be taught by one man, and each pupil advanced at his own rate; success was affected by pressure from the teacher and other students, since each boy was rewarded when he began a new book or chapter of a text.[54] Compared to the method of instruction used by the British and Americans, in which all the students were instructed simultaneously in the same subject and progressed at the same rate, the Tamil system, one British scholar observed, "turns out every pupil a fair scholar, though at a great waste of labour. The class system ensures a much higher average, but permits confirmed dullards."[55]

Once an unusually motivated and talented student completed this education, he might want to pursue higher studies in Shaivism without becoming a *sādhu.* He was left to find a teacher. In some cases it might be a relative or a local resident, in others someone affiliated with a monastery, but not necessarily a *sādhu.*[56] The degree of sophistication that any student attained, therefore, depended entirely upon his individual talent, motivation, and personal circumstances. Tamils might be Shaivas by birth and yet know little about their tradition, except what they absorbed through stories, songs, festivals, and family instruction, or through whatever expositions of the epics and Puranas they gained from temple attendance. Among these aspirants, some would receive one or more initiations into the Agamic worship of Shiva from a *guru.* Such rituals included instruction in the specific doctrines of Shaiva Orthodoxy and explanation of the esoteric meanings of the rites to which they committed themselves. A very few, the motivated intellectuals who may or may not have received Agamic initiation, would study Shaiva texts in Sanskrit and Tamil and become, eventually, the local Shaiva scholars from whom others would seek out private instruction.

Arumuga Pillai believed that the traditional system would not offer the kind of education Shaivas needed in the modern world. As he had indicated in 1842, Shiva was chastising the Tamils through the missionaries in order to elevate them. Educating Shaivas was his response. To be efficient, Shaiva education had to use the classroom system of the West, and to be modern, it had to include some imported subject matter, but that meant a complete revision of teaching methods. Instead of relying on palm leaf books that students would copy out by hand and memorize at their own rate, Shaiva education needed printed books that everyone in the same class could read, memorize, and understand simultaneously. This meant that difficult poems and commentaries had to be transformed into comprehensible prose, but the prose itself had to be sufficiently elegant to convey the contents of the poems in order to improve the thinking of the students. When Navalar founded the School of Shaiva Splendor, he assumed three enormous tasks: constructing a Shaiva curriculum designed for sequential classes, creating an appropriate style of Tamil prose in which to write it, and establishing a press in Jaffna on which to print it.

In July 1849, Arumuga Pillai, together with his former student and colleague, Sadashiva Pillai, set out for Madras to purchase a printing press. The money had been donated by wealthy benefactors. On the way they visited the important Tiruvavatuturai Atinam monastery (in Tanjore District), whose leaders periodically sent specialists in the "Tamil Veda" (*Tēvāram*) to recite it publicly in the temples of Jaffna.[57] Through this channel and others, the monastic leaders (*mathādipati*) had heard of Arumuga Pillai's unusual knowledge of the Agamas and his efforts on behalf of Shaiva Orthodoxy. When he arrived, they examined his knowledge and heard him preach. Impressed by his mastery of the tradition, they conferred on him the title *nāvalar,* "the learned." Considerably enhanced in his status among Shaivas by this "honorary degree" from the scholastic heart of Orthodoxy, he has been known ever since as Arumuga Navalar, or simply as Navalar.

Arumuga Navalar: Writer, Publisher, Polemicist

While waiting for his press in Madras, Arumuga Navalar published two texts he had been editing from various copies. One was an important educational tool, the *Cūdāmani Nikantu,* a sixteenth-century lexicon of 1,197 easily remembered verses giving approximately eleven thousand words in both their verse and prose forms.[58] The other text, *Saundaryalaharī,* a poem in praise of the goddess, was important for devotion, and was published with explanatory comments (*urai*).[59] These first efforts at editing and printing Tamil works for Shaiva students and devotees reflected a talent for producing unusually reliable editions, a talent for which he was to remain famous.

Returning to Jaffna by way of the monastery at Tiruvannamalai, he set up the printing press in a building near the monastery where the school met, a building that a wealthy Cettiyar of Vannarpannai had turned over to him late in 1849.[60] He named it The Preservation of Knowledge Press (Vidya-anubalana-yantra-sala) and hired workmen to operate it who had been trained by the American mission press at Manepy.[61] In order to direct both the press and the school, he spent his nights in the monastery, which became, in effect, his residence.[62]

The new press started publishing early in 1850. It produced a list of pamphlets and books that Arumuga Navalar had been working on for years.[63] His two-volume *Lessons for Children* (Bala Patam) appeared in 1850 and 1851. They were graded readers, simple in style, similar in organization to those used in the Protestant schools.[64] A third volume appeared in 1860.[65] It consisted of thirty-nine more advanced essays in clear and dignified prose, discussing subjects such as God, Soul, The Worship of God, Crimes Against the Lord, Grace, Killing, Eating Meat, Drinking Liquor, Stealing, Adultery, Lying, Envy, Anger, and Gambling. Contrary to one missionary's judgment, these three volumes of *Lessons for Children* were not the "blending in conflict and compromise of Hinduism and Christianity,"[66] but were simply the presentation and explanation of values imparted in the traditional Tamil schools and in the teaching of Shaiva Orthodoxy. Some of those values were shared by both Shaivas and Christians.

Other texts published in 1860 included "The Prohibition of Killing" (*Kolaimaruttal*) by Shantalingaswami of Tirutturaiyur,[67] a devotional poem about Murugan with his own commentary (*urai*),[68] and a grammar.[69] Navalar wrote and published "The Rule for Darshana in the Shiva Temple" (*Sivālaya-darshana-vidhi*), a manual to teach Shaivas the ways to worship Shiva in a temple, as the Agamas prescribe it, for the four social classes (*varnas*) and the four stages of life (*āsrama*).[70] He also published small bits and pieces known collectively as "The Essence of the Shaiva Religion" (*Saiva-samaya-sāram*) for their doctrinal education.[71] His first major literary publication appeared in 1851, the 272-page prose version of Cekkilar's *Periya Purānam,* a careful retelling of the twelfth century hagiography of the Nayanars, the saints devoted to Shiva.[72] *Periya Purānam* set a new standard for prose in Tamil, a standard Navalar maintained the rest of his life.

Like "The Rule for Darshana in the Shiva Temple," his version of the *Periya Purānam* revealed to Navalar the importance of piety and how far from satisfactory it seemed to be in mid-nineteenth-century Jaffna. In "The Rule," for example, he gave the following evaluation, beginning with the traditional affirmation of how fortunate one was to be born a Shaiva:

> Human birth is rare to obtain, even more so birth in this meritorious land of Bharata (South Asia) where the Vedas and Agamas, the true books are esteemed. Birth among those who perform asceticism is even rarer. And most rare of all is birth in a lineage of Shaivas.

Then he described the indifference some Shaivas felt towards this great blessing:

> Nevertheless, many Shaivas do not value these things in the slightest. They have studied and heard about the greatness of Lord Shiva, the treasure of compassion, and about meritorious deeds (*punya*) and sins (*pāpa*) and their fruits, but they do not comprehend them. They detest sins but they do not perform meritorious deeds. They thus spend their lives in vain, turning themselves into food for burning hell.

He observed how ignorance could trap even those who make some effort to be pious: "A few, however, do try to perform a few meritorious deeds one way or another, but they have no idea at all how to perform them correctly...and so they only go on gathering more sins for themselves."[73]

By "meritorious deeds" (*punya*) he meant liturgical acts that, like those of the Vedic fire sacrifice, brought well-being when performed correctly and harm when performed incorrectly. Navalar intended the pamphlet to instruct the devotee how to behave when he or she went to see Shiva in a temple. By being so informed, he believed, the Shaiva's educated acts of worship would focus his or her mind, speech, and body on love for Shiva and would bring the devotee eternal joy.

The same concern fueled the enormous labor required to turn the lengthy *Periya Purānam* into prose. In the introduction to his prose rendering he noted that Cekkilar wrote the work in finely wrought poetry that was now useless to anyone except scholars. He intended his prose version, he said, for everyone—learned scholars, failing scholars, literate lay people, and illiterates who could listen to it being read. Although it was in prose, it was still a Shiva Purana and would confer its benefits only on those who read it or listened to it in the proper ritual context and with the appropriate attitude. First they must have received initiation from a Shaiva *ācārya* and they must have lived in purity by abstaining from meat and liquor, by applying sacred ash daily to their bodies, by using consecrated *rudrāksa* beads for reciting the five-syllable mantra, and by worshipping regularly in the temple. He then described how it should be read:

> Those who want to read aloud any books that speak of Lord Shiva's majesty should first purify their bodies and perform the required rites, and then place a throne in a pure place, set the sacred scripture on it, worship both it and the teaching priest (*ācārya*) who will explain it, sit down, and with love that softens and melts the heart begin reading. Anyone who wants to listen while it is being read should listen in the same manner. The Shiva Agamas and Shiva Puranas declare that anyone who does not recite it or listen to it in this manner will not receive the fruits that such acts produce.[74]

The analogy, of course, is to the way Protestants used the Bible in their worship services. And Navalar's motivation in this task of "translation," as in his later prose renditions of sacred texts, was analogous to the work of translation he had assisted Peter Percival with for eight years. In his case the translation was from medieval poetry to modern prose, a style he largely had to create, but to his mind the prose did not alter the sacred nature of the work.

His most dramatic use of the press, however, was the publication of anti-Christian tracts between 1852 and 1854. In 1852, Navalar, together with Ci. Vinayakamurtti Cettiyar of Nallur, printed the "Kummi Song on Wisdom" (Jnanakkummi) that Muttukumarakavirajar had composed about twenty years earlier. It immediately angered some Christians, and they wanted to get rid of the press. Christian preachers and papers—presumably the *Morning Star*—attacked the "Kummi Song on Wisdom," and one minister started vilifying Shaivism as he made his circuit. Navalar could not tolerate this, so he wrote "The Diamond Axe" (Vajra-damda) against them and published it in Vinayakamurtti Cettiyar's name.[75]

In 1853, Navalar printed Nakkirar's "Tirumurukarrupatai," adding his own commentary.[76] It was a devotional poem to Murugan that was part of the canon of Shaiva Orthodoxy. Whether this prompted the attack by Christians on Murugan that appeared in their preaching and newspapers at the time is not clear, but the missionaries aimed their verbal weapons at this portrayal of God who married one woman and seduced another who became his second wife.[77] To missionary minds, Murugan-Skanda was neither God nor a moral example for people to follow. Navalar, of course, would not abide this sneering slander at the Lord whom he believed to be Shiva himself. So that same year he published "Radiant Wisdom" (Subhra-bodha), his explanation of how the stories embody differing levels of meaning.[78] He also matched the missionaries' treatment of Puranic lore by compiling with a Brahman colleague, Ci. Centinatha Aiyar, examples of indecent language from the Bible and published it as "Disgusting Things in the Bible" (Bibiliya Kutsita).[79] Another Brahman, Nirveli Civa. Shankara Panditar from Cunnakam, aided him in these disputes. He wrote three attacks on the Christians under Navalar's direction during this period, but they were not published until about 1877.[80]

Arumuga Navalar's most effective weapon, however, appeared in 1854. It was a booklet published for the use of Shaivas in their opposition to the missionaries—a training manual of sorts—entitled "The Abolition of the Abuse of Shaivism"(Saiva-dusana-parihara), which he signed in the name of "the members of the Splendor of Shaivism Association" (Saiva-prakasa Samajiyar) rather than his own. He wanted to focus attention on the subject instead of on himself.[81] The booklet was a further development of Navalar's approach to Protestant teachings taken twelve years earlier in his letter to the *Morning Star* of October 1842.

A Wesleyan missionary, who had worked in Jaffna, described "The Abolition" thirteen years after it had appeared:

> displaying an intimate and astonishing acquaintance with the Holy Bible, (the author) labors cleverly to show that the opinions and ceremonies of Jehovah's ancient people closely resembled those of Shaivism, and were neither more nor less Divine in their origin and profitable in their entertainment and pursuit. The notion of merit held by the Hindus, their practices of penance, pilgrimage, and lingam-worship, their ablutions, invocations, and other observances and rites, are cunningly defended on the authority of our sacred writings! That a great effect was thus produced in favour of Sivaism and against Christianity cannot be denied.[82]

"The Abolition of the Abuse of Shaivism" was widely used in Sri Lanka and Madras; it was reprinted at least twice in the nineteenth century, and eight times by 1956.[83] It appears even to have influenced the formation in 1857 of a Christian sect in South India that employed Israelite and Hindu rituals and called their leader "Rabbi."[84]

In the booklet Navalar admonished Shaivas to study its contents for their own salvation—"do not leave piety off for the next birth," he urged, "for this birth as a Shaiva is the boundary of the end of all births"—and to study it to use against Christians when they abused Shaivism. His comparative discussion of the ritual practices recorded in the Bible and those prescribed by the Agamas took up most of the booklet. It was a sophisticated counter to the Protestant argument that the rituals of this "Old Dispensation" were symbols whose meaning was the crucifixion of Jesus, which, now that the crucifixion had taken place, no longer served a valid function in the "New Dispensation." What was significant for this discussion, however, was the manner in which he urged Shaivas to oppose the missionaries.

Without bothering to study Shaivism on its own terms at all, he observed, missionaries described it incorrectly and then attacked their false understanding in printed pamphlets that circulated widely.[85] The Agamas and Tamil hymns, he said, proclaim it was a great sin for Shaivas, for reasons of fear, friendship, or wealth, to sit back and accept such abuse. Shaivas did not need to fear punishment from the English government if they openly opposed missionary excesses, he noted, for even though the government was Christian, it protected all religions equally and had even threatened to expel the missionaries from the country if they continued to harass Hindu temples. Even if Shaivas did suffer because they opposed the abuse aggressively, Shiva was in charge: "He controls all events, he knows all of our deeds, and he determines what we shall experience at a given time. The purpose of this birth was to serve him and to attain *moksa,* not to gain pleasures for the body." He added,

> Have not the Shiva scriptures themselves confirmed that those who give up their bodies in order to get rid of such great sins as the abuse of Shiva are certain to attain release?[86]

Therefore, he said, fearing no one but Shiva, contemplating him alone, and relying only on his grace, "it is our duty to oppose the missionaries who abuse Shiva, to refute their vile Christian doctrine, and to endeavour to establish Shaivism, the true religion (*Sat Samaya*)."[87]

Like the Methodists, Navalar used a method based on the regeneration of the individual. First, he said, pray everyday with deep devotion for Shiva to remove the obstacles to this virtuous deed. Second, help each other out generously for the expenses of this work. Third, with this money purchase the books we print and read them carefully over and over. Fourth, explain what you read to others very clearly so they will not fall into the Christian pit. Fifth, whenever missionaries and their catechists abuse Shiva and preach Christian doctrine, "do not seek to please them in anyway, but stand up against them, refute the abuse they heap on Shaivism, oppose their doctrine, and shut their mouths." Sixth, do not allow your children to associate with those of other doctrines (*matam*) and at the right age have them initiated and properly instructed in Shaivism. And seventh, select men outstanding in their knowledge and devotion to the Guru, to the *linga,* and to the Assembly of Sadhus (*guru-linga-sanghama-bhakti*), appoint them as Shaiva propagandists, and have them conduct weekly teaching sessions for everyone in the temples, monasteries, and other pure places of the villages. In this way, he concluded, we can spread the great light of Shaivism throughout the land of the Tamils, destroy the darkness of other doctrines, and many will attain salvation (*mukti*).[88]

In 1857, "The Abolition of the Abuse of Shaivism" received a rejoinder from a Protestant Tamil, D. Carroll Vishvanatha Pillai, in his essay "The Dazzling Light" (Subhradipa).[89] This sixty-page refutation may have convinced others, but in the long run, it was not persuasive to its own author. He later repented and became a Shaiva.[90]

Arumuga Navalar had now laid out the lines of work he would continue the rest of his life: writing, publishing, preaching, teaching, and reform. As the result of his growing fame, pressures on him to marry increased. He had no intentions of marrying, yet he had no intentions of becoming a *sādhu,* for that would prohibit his active involvement in society. Late in 1854, therefore, he and his student Sadashiva Pillai closed the door to marriage by receiving the final initiation in the series of four rituals conferred by *ācāryas,* the *nirvāna dīksa.* It required daily liturgical acts that the normal pollution of the householder's life would not allow. Now the two men were officially recognized as religious celibates, *naistika brahmācārins,* each committed to the daily and private service of a *linga* appropriate to his *varna* status and to his level of knowledge.[91] Carrying his personal Shiva *linga* with him wherever he went, Arumuga Navalar was always in Shiva's temple.

The Impact of Navalar: The Later Years

Arumuga Navalar lived his most active and productive twenty-five years after his initiation as a *naistika brahmācārin.* He did not open any new fields to work; however, he vigorously weeded and harvested the ones he had already sown. A full examination of his life is yet to be done in a Western language,[92] but a sketch of some of his achievements will indicate his significance in the history of religions in South Asia.

Although Navalar began in Jaffna, he worked both sides of the Palk Strait, establishing twin centers for his reforms. To the printing press he set up in Jaffna, he added one in Madras; the School of Shaiva Splendour he established in Vannarpannai was matched by one in Chidambaram; he battled non-Agamic Brahmans in Jaffna and struggled against Dikshitars of the Nataraja Temple; a challenger to the devotees of "erroneous" Shaivism in Sri Lanka, he also opened conflict against the followers of a Siddha saint in Madras; and everywhere he disputed the claims and refuted the abuses of the Christians. His financial support in both places came from wealthy benefactors to whom he frequently made ardent appeals for money. Much to his personal distress, he was opposed not only by Christians but also by some Hindus in both places.

His literary production was amazing. Among his approximately ninety-seven Tamil publications, twenty-three were his own creations, eleven were his commentaries (*urai*), and forty were his editions of those works of grammar, literature, liturgy, and theology he thought Tamils should know.[93] With his recovery, editing, and publishing of ancient works, Navalar laid the foundations for the recovery of lost Tamil classics, a task his successors continued.[94] In his own writings he created a style that "bridged" medieval and modern prose, as Kamil Zvelebil characterized it:

> Although today we would probably describe his prose as dry, pedantic and monotonous, colourless and full of restraint, he deserves praise and gratitude for some of the great changes he introduced, and thus paved way for the writers of the "Tamil renaissance".... (In) an overall assessment of his work, one has to agree with T. P. Meenakshisun-

daran who says: "Arumugakanavalar of the nineteenth century is the father of modern literary prose—the simple, elegant but grammatically correct prose."[95]

Navalar was the first in Jaffna to establish a Hindu school adapted to the modern world that succeeded and flourished. No doubt its success was due in large measure to his skill in adapting Protestant methods of education to Shaiva institutional and curricular needs and to his ability to gain patronage for it. While the school he established in Chidambaram in 1865 has survived to this day, similar schools seem to have spread only to two nearby towns.[96] In Sri Lanka, however, the School of Shaiva Splendour became the center of eleven schools, all but one in the Jaffna region; and one was an experiment in using English as the medium of instruction.[97] Eventually more than one hundred and fifty primary and secondary schools emerged in Sri Lanka from his work.[98] Navalar, however, viewed the school in Chidambaram and that in Vannarpannai as parts of one establishment; both were administered by a single man and shared funds.[99]

The students educated by these schools were the measure of their impact. It appears that their influence was considerable. Many of Navalar's students articulated a temple-centered Shaivism in both Jaffna and Madras Presidency that, by the end of the century, stood up convincingly to the neo-Hinduisms of the Brahmo Samaj and the Theosophical Society. Navalar's temple-centered Shaivism effectively engaged the minds of young intellectuals through The Association for Shaiva Orthodoxy (Saiva Siddhanta Sabha) founded in 1886, seven years after his death. Due to Navalar's scholarship and reform, intellectuals of the early twentieth century, like the householder Tiru. Vi. Kaliyanasundaram (1883–1953), and the *sādhu* Maraimal Adigal (1876–1950), were able to develop their own independent thinking without leaving the context of the Shaiva temple and its devotional heritage.[100] Also, the prolific Tinnevelly Shaiva Siddhanta Works Publishing House that emerged in 1920 can be traced back to Navalar's vigorous literary productivity, for it took his flawless editions as its standard.[101]

In Summary

The impact Arumuga Navalar made on missionary efforts to spread Protestant Christianity among the Tamils is difficult to assess. How does one count people who might have converted if he had not existed? Judging from the literature of dispute that continued throughout the century, however, Navalar's own intellectual critiques and his organized preaching circuits were powerful weapons that Shaivas used effectively to win the loyalty of the Shaiva literati in Jaffna. As Bishop Sabhapathi Kulendram observed, when comparing the promise Christian conversions showed in Jaffna at the beginning of the century to their disappointing results, this low rate of conversion was largely due to Navalar.[102]

In the larger Madras Presidency, he could not have such a decisive impact. But his aggressive preaching of a Shaiva cultural heritage led by properly initiated Vellalas and Brahmans no doubt contributed to the growing Tamil "nationalism." This movement had a specifically Shaiva component that fostered the idea that Shaiva Siddhanta preceded all others as the original Tamil religion.[103] Navalar's insistence on the Agamas as the criteria of Shaiva worship, moreover, gave momentum to the tendency among high-status Tamils everywhere to subsume local deities under the Agamic pantheon and to abandon animal sacrifice altogether.[104]

In today's Tamil world, Arumuga Navalar's reform would be seen by many as too conservative. On the one hand, his affirmation of caste ideology is officially unacceptable to "secular nationalism," while on the other hand, his affirmation of the status of initiated Brahmans and of Sanskrit is unacceptable to "Dravidian nationalism." Nevertheless, in the middle of the nineteenth century he articulated and nurtured the belief shared by many of the literati that the meaning of being Hindu lies in Shiva's temple and in the culture it generates at the center of *dharma* (*puram*); and he did enable that belief to thrive in the twentieth century and to continue to face the "wilderness" (*purappuram*) of modernity on its peripheries. From the viewpoint of this belief, Navalar was a model of devotion like the great saints of the past; his response to Shiva's compassionate chastisement of the Tamils by the missionaries was to strengthen the temple at the center (*akam*) and to weaken the Christians on the edges. Now, many believe, he dwells with Shiva eternally, freed from these issues. Today Tamil Shaivas, however, are anything but free from them, confronted as they are by nationalisms of various sorts that Arumuga Navalar no doubt would say are the ways Shiva is now dancing his *Tripura Tandava* to bring them *moksa*.

Bibliographic Essay

Works in English about the life and thought of Arumuga Navalar are relatively thin. A small summary of his life based on a Tamil biography was written by S. Shivapadasundaram, *Arumukha Navalar* (Jaffna, 1950) and published at the press Navalar had founded. The most extensive English biography was likewise based on earlier Tamil biographies and is summary and laudatory: V. Muttucumaraswamy, *Arumuga Navalar: The Champion Reformer of the Hindus (1822–1879): A Biographical Study,* new rev. ed. (Colombo, 1965). Two studies that I have not yet seen may be more scholarly and analytical: K. Sivathamby, "Hindu Reaction to Christian Proselytism and Westernization in 19th Century Sri Lanka," *Social Science Review* (Colombo) 1 (1979): 41–75; and S. Thanajeyarajasingham, *The Educational Activities of Arumuga Navalar* (Colombo, 1974). Bishop Sabapathy Kulandran analyzes Navalar's contribution to the translation of the Christian Bible in "The Tentative Version of the Bible or 'The Navalar Version,'" *Tamil Culture* 7 (1958): 229-50.

The Tamil studies of Arumuga Navalar are rich resources for historical detail. The most traditional biography was written as a poem by a student the Tiruvavatuturai Atinam: Sivakasi Arunacala Kavirayar, *Yālpānattu Nallūr Srī la Srī Ārumukanāvalar carittiram* (The Life of the Venerable Arumuga Navalar of Nallur, Jaffna) (Madras, 1898). There is a copy in the Swaminathaiyar Library. The earliest prose biography was by a disciple: Ve. Kanakrattina Upattiyayar, *Ārumukanāvalar carittiram* (The Life of Arumuga Navalar) (Jaffna: 1882; reprint, Jaffna: 1968). A nephew of Navalar later wrote a biography with the same title: T. Kailasa Pillai, *Ārumukanāvalar Carittiram* (Madras, 1918; a slightly expanded version appeared in 1955). Perhaps the most useful biography, its appendix contains valuable primary sources in English and Tamil. At an unknown date a dramatic play depicting Arumuga Navalar's life was published: Suttananta Paratiyar, *Nāvalar Nātakam* (The Drama of Navalar) (Madras, n.d.). There is a copy in Swaminathaiyar Library. A life of Navalar addressed to students was written by Ka. Mayanti Parati, *Nāvalar perumān* (The Noble Navalar) (Madras, 1955; reprint 1962).

The single most useful tool for analyzing the data provided by the biographies is a memorial volume commemorating the centenary of his death: *Nāvalar Nūrrāntu Malar 1979,* edited by K. Kailasapati (Chunnakam, Sri Lanka, 1979). It contains thirty-four essays examining Navalar from a variety of perspectives, including a useful chronology of his life and work and bibliographies of primary and secondary sources.

A valuable collection of Arumuga Navalar's prose tracts addressed to events in Jaffna and Madras between 1853 and 1876 is T. Kailasa Pillai comp., *Srī la Srī Ārumukanāvalar Perumānin Pirapantattirattu* (The Collected Works of the Noble and Venerable Arumuga Navalar), 3d ed. 2 vol. (Madras, 1954–1955).

These and other works by Arumuga Navalar have been reprinted frequently by the press he founded in Madras, the Arumuga Navalar

Vidyanubalana Accakam (25 Tangasalai Teru, Madras 600 001). An organization that fosters his work is the Sri la Sri Arumuga Navalar Saivaprakasa Vidyasalai Arakkattali in Cidambaram (24 Malaikatti Teru, Cidambaram 608 001). Many of his publications are available in the British Library, London, and are listed in the three volumes of *A Catalogue of Tamil Books in the British Library: Department of Oriental Manuscripts and Printed Books* (1909 Supplementary Catalogue, 1931; Second Supplementary Catalogue, 1980). Many works are also available at two libraries in Madras: The Tirumaraimalai Adigal Library (Lingi Chitty Street) and the U. V. Swaminathaiyar Library (Tiruvanmiyur, Madras 41). Other archives and organizations dedicated to Navalar's memory and career exist in Jaffna, but I am not yet acquainted with them directly.

Three

Swami Dayananda Saraswati's Critique of Christianity

Kenneth W. Jones

The Punjab, after centuries of Hindu rule followed by over five hundred years of Islamic dominance and half a century of Sikh control, contained three religions. Two of these converted, Islam and Sikhism, while the third, Hinduism, had neither the concepts nor the rituals necessary for conversion. In 1849, the British annexation of Punjab introduced the aggressive conversion faith of Christianity. In time, it threatened each of the coexisting religions. Christian missionaries brought with them new forms of organization and techniques of proselytism that were adopted by the other religions with whom they came into contact. Consequently, each of these communities developed assertive forms of proselytism that included paid missionaries, numerous publications, and the use of street preaching. Proponents of different religious ideas sought to defend their beliefs and to discredit those of the opposing groups. It was a struggle of *mandan-khandan,* of disseminating one's "true" ideas and of rejecting others' "false" concepts.

Religious polemics had appeared in Punjab as early as the 1850s in printed tracts of both prose and poetry. Two forms developed, internal polemics between reformists, different sects, and orthodox members of a religious community and external polemics between defenders of their own faith and all opponents of differing religions. In the mid-1860s conflict between reformist associations patterned after Western, particularly Christian, religious organizations, became part of Punjabi life. Multi-sided struggles developed as proponents of diverse ideologies defended them from other religious groupings. *Other* meant opponent. By the last two decades of the nineteenth-century, religious controversy that originated in Punjab and the Western section of the United Provinces intensified when it spread throughout adjacent territories. Although the Christian missionaries did not create such religious conflict, they did bring new forms of organizational structure that made aggressive conversion campaigns feasible. They demonstrated the usefulness of the printing press and paid missionaries. For many representatives of the indigenous religions Christian missionaries were identified with the British-Indian government, which was perceived as aiding them. Exponents of Islam, Hinduism, and Sikhism struggled to defend their religions in general and sectarian ideologies in particular against the missionary attempts to proclaim the superiority of Christianity and against each other.

This chapter will explore the arguments of one defender of a sectarian division of Hinduism, the Arya Samaj. We will examine the logic, the critical techniques, and the style of disputation employed by Swami Dayananda Saraswati in his attempt to destroy all claims to superiority made by missionaries who proclaimed that Christianity possessed the only "truth," as revealed to Jesus Christ and substantiated by the Bible. We will see what elements of Christian doctrine he perceived as most vulnerable and what techniques he used to demolish the arguments made by Christian proponents and defenders. We will do so by allowing the Swami to speak for himself through his own writings. Although from Gujarat, it was in the Punjab that Dayananda's arguments found their greatest acceptance and so were used repeatedly. The Swami laid the foundation for the anti-Christian writings of his adherents throughout much of northern India and as far south as Madras.

Swami Dayananda Saraswati (1824–1883) was born in Tankara, a small town on the Kathiawar peninsula of Gujarat. He ran away from home in search of his release from the cycle of rebirth and in the process became a *sanyāsī,* taking the name of Dayananda Saraswati. During his travels he met Swami Virajananda, studied with him, and acquired a vision of Vedic Hinduism that rejected many of the elements of contemporary religion. His restructured Hinduism had no place for idols, Brahman priests, a host of deities, pilgrimages, a variety of socio-religious customs, and any scripture that did not agree with the Vedas. After leaving his guru, Virajananda, Swami Dayananda traveled extensively, condemning existent or "puranic" Hinduism as he sought adherents to his own reformed religion. In 1875, he wrote the *Satyārth Prakāsh,* a basic statement of beliefs, and also founded the Arya Samaj as the organizational expression of his ideas.

In 1877, Dayananda visited Punjab where he found enthusiastic acceptance of his Vedic Hinduism. Local chapters of the Arya Samaj spread rapidly throughout Punjab. Dayananda was obdurate in his condemnation of untruth, which included Christianity along with Islam, Sikhism, Buddhism, and Jainism. In chapter 13 of the *Satyārth Prakāsh* he spent seventy-seven pages discussing Christianity and its errors. He was responding, in part, to Christian missionaries who had rejected his form of Hinduism because they failed to differentiate it from contemporary Hinduism with all its errors and superstitions. They did not understand that his was the only "true" version of Hinduism, which was, as well, the only "true" religion. Thus both Dayananda and the missionaries argued from the position that their faith and only theirs was correct, and that they alone held the key to the future.

The Old Testament

Dayananda claimed to have constructed his discussion of Christianity from a single source, although he had debated and held private discussions with different Christian missionaries. "Our criticism is based exclusively on the Bible as it is accepted as the Holy Book by the Christians as well as by the Jews etc.... I have read its Sanskrita and Hindi translations, and many doubts have risen in my mind." He declared his motives to have the highest moral quality and that he did not seek to denigrate Christianity, but merely to express truth in order to separate it from error.

> My purpose is only to uphold truth and suppress untruth. I never mean to injure anybody's feelings or indulge in vain fault-finding. People will know from my writings what sort of book the Bible is and what sort of doctrines Christianity believes in.... Over and above this, religious knowledge of the public will increase and after...it will be easier for all men to accept the truth and reject the untruth.

His was, he claimed, an unbiased view recognizable to intelligent and literate people who would inevitably accept his arguments and the superiority of Vedic Hinduism.[1]

The main body of chapter 13 in the *Satyārth Prakāsh* began with a dialogue between Dayananda and an unnamed Christian, but after six pages shifted to citations from the Bible followed by his comments and interpretation. Throughout this work Dayananda combined Judaism with Christianity since they used the same religious text. The initial subject of discussion was the creation (*shrishti*) of the universe, a concept clearly foreign to Dayananda.

Concerning the ability of God to create, Dayananda asked, "Is God's power beginningless (*anādī*) or new?" His Christian answered with "Beginningless." Dayananda's response brought out a fundamental Hindu objection to this concept. "If beginningless, then the material of the universe is beginningless. How do you say, then, that existence comes out of nothing?"[2] To create something from nothing was not possible to Dayananda. The Hindu understanding of cyclical time with dissolution of the cosmos followed by a restructuring and then four ages of decline that lead to another dissolution *ad infinitum* held no place for the creation of the universe from nothing. In approaching this subject he raised one of the basic questions and themes of his critique on Christianity, namely whether or not the Bible was *ishvarkrit,* written or revealed by God:

> Comment—What do you mean by "beginning"?
>
> Christian—The first creation of the Universe.
>
> Comment—Is this creation the first? Was there no creation before it?
>
> Christian—We do not know whether it was or not.
>
> Comment—If you do not know it, then why did you have faith (in a) book which cannot remove the doubts and why do you preach to the people at large a religion which is so full of doubts? Why do you not embrace the Vedic faith which removes all sorts of doubts? When you do not know about God's creation, how do you know about God?[3]

This initial interchange demonstrates the pattern of dialogue between Dayananda and the Christian spokesman he imagined. Questions were followed by answers that "proved" his opponents' responses were self-contradictory because of either error or ignorance. This, in turn, gave him a chance to expound truth and the superiority of Vedic Hinduism. The Christian always lost these interchanges.

In another exchange Dayananda offered his own concept of God in contrast to the inferior and contradictory descriptions of the Christian God whose spirit (*ishvar kā ātma*) moved "upon the face of the waters."

> Firstly what is meant by the "spirit of God?"
>
> Christian—A conscious Being.
>
> Comment—Is he bodied or unbodied? All pervading or localized?
>
> Christian—He is corporal, intelligent, and pervading. But particularly dwells on such places as the Sanai (*Sanāī*) mountain or the fourth heaven etc.

Dayananda gave arguments to his Christian spokesmen that were easily refuted. If God were all pervading he was everywhere and could not "move upon the waters"; if incorporeal he would not be seen. Dayananda concluded that "If he is not all pervading then He can neither create the world nor maintain or dissolve it."[4] The limited nature of the Christian God, as Dayananda saw Him, proved He was not and could not be God. He was a conscious being (*chetan*) with a corporeal body (*sākār*), and thus he was neither all pervading (*viyapak*) nor all-knowing (*sarvagya*), but a localized (*ekadeshī*) being. Dayananda returned again and again to his claim that the Christian God was not the ultimate God, nor any kind of God.

The Christian God was merely "A localized substance lacking universal attributes, localized action and (a) localized nature. Such a being cannot be God." To Dayananda "God was all-pervading, infinite in attributes, actions and nature, self-existent, self-intelligent, and blissful, eternal, pure, conscious, free by nature, beginningless, and endless.... Such is the conception of God as given in the Vedas. Have faith on this. Then only will you be happy? Otherwise not."[5] The Christian God could in no way compare with the universal God of Vedic Hinduism.

Moving from the creation of the world to the coming of man, Dayananda turned to his main critical technique, the use of a literal reading of the Bible. Commenting on God's creation of man in his own image, Dayananda remarked, "If God made Adam in his own likeness, why is he not like Him in holiness, knowledge, bliss etc.? If Adam is not such, it is evident that he was not made in God's likeness. If the created Adam is in God's likeness, then God Himself is created. If so, He is non-eternal." God himself was thus a made (*banāyā*) being like man or man was not in his image (*apne svarūp me*), for man lacked divine qualities. The Old Testament's account of man's creation then was fraught with error and contradiction. If the Christian God was himself created then he was not and He could not be God who must, to Dayananda, be eternal and uncreated.

If there was substance, then there did exist a thing in addition to God. If an attribute, then no substance can be made from an attribute, for example, shape or color cannot create fire, nor taste water. If God were the material cause of the universe, then it should have been like God in attributes, functions, and nature. As it is not, it is clear that God is not the material cause of the world. A world and the universe in which it existed should have had the same attributes, the same qualities as did God, but such was not the case, therefore God had not made the world or the universe and the Christian God was not God as they claimed.

Commenting on the creation of Adam and Eve, Dayananda found the whole process strange and bewildering.

> When God made Adam from dust, why did He not make his wife from dust? If He made the woman out of a rib, why did He not make Adam of a rib? If the woman is so named because she was made out of man, why was not the man named after woman? (because man is born out of woman).

As Dayananda continued developing his arguments, he emphasized the illogicality of the Christian God's actions:

> O learned people, see what philosophy this God has. If He made the woman out of a rib taken out of the man's body, then the woman should have only one rib in her body as she is made of one rib. Was it not possible to make the woman out of the material of which the whole universe was made?[6]

The ideas and processes described in this passage made no sense to Dayananda. Consequently no answer to this question was at hand or expected. Having laid the groundwork for his critique, the Swami proceeded to demonstrate the ungodlike qualities of the Christian deity. Dayananda concluded from the Garden of Eden story that God lacked the quality of omniscience (*sarvagya*). Further evidence substantiated this, for "why did He make the wicked serpent, i.e. the Satan?... Had he not made him wicked he could not have done mischief." God could not foretell the future as He should have been able to do if he were a deity.

Dayananda also disagreed with the concept of Satan (*Shaitān*) as a fallen angel or a serpent; instead, the Biblical account "proved" he was merely human. "To tell the truth he was not (a) serpent, but man; had he not been man, he could not have spoken the language of man." After rebutting the logic of the Biblical account, Dayananda condemned the Christian God for His actions and presented his own interpretation of Satan.

> Whosoever is himself false and misguides others should be named as Satan. But here in this case the Satan proves truthful. He did not misguide the woman but told her the truth. It was God who told a lie to Adam and Eve that if they would eat the fruit they would die.[7]

The Christian deity then was a liar who lacked the crucial attributes of God, omnipotence and omniscience; thus, he was not a deity, but merely a man.

Dayananda maintained that the Christian God's lack of divine power was clearly demonstrated in his relations with Satan, a figure he created, but could not control. "So went Satan forth from the presence of the Lord and smote Job with sore boils from the sole of his foot unto his crown" (Job 2:7).

> Now look at the power of the Christian God. Satan smites His devotees. But he can neither punish Satan nor protect His devotees. Nor can any messenger of His oppose the Satan.... Moreover, this Christian God is not omniscient, otherwise why should he have Job tested by Satan?[8]

The Christian God lacked knowledge, was powerless to shape events, and was given to unwise action, when he made the monstrosity called Satan. A true and perfect God would not create the embodiment of evil and then turn him loose on the world. Dayananda noted that

> On the earth the God of the Christians does not hold even one thousandth part of the kingdom which is under the sway of the Satan and God cannot dislodge him. It shows that the God of the Christians is not even equal to those Christian governors who punish thieves and other criminals promptly.

To Dayananda the Christian God was unable to expunge evil and its embodiment, Satan.

The Swami summed up his condemnation of this false deity and those who followed him.

> Thus God is no God, nor this book God-revealed. The Vedic conception of God is of a Being who is absolutely free from sin, pain, sorrow, and affliction, who is self-existent, all intelligent and all bliss.[9]

The themes set forth so far were repeated as Dayananda drew on other Biblical tales that showed the weakness of this Christian Deity and His inability to control events. From the inexplicable concepts of Genesis, Dayananda moved on to explore the religious actions of God and the customary behavior of the ancient Israelites.

One of the most repugnant Biblical customs for Swami Dayananda and upper caste Hindus was eating meat and particularly the flesh of cows. The Bible offered many instances of this practice and of its predilection in favor of meat eaters. The Cain and Abel story was an excellent example.

> If God were not a flesh-eater, He would not have respected Abel and his offering of sheep nor disrespected Cain and his offering (of fruit), God is also instrumental in causing this discord and bringing about Abel's death.[10]

The preference for a meat offering over a vegetarian one could not have been shown by God (*ishvar kī nahīn*), but only by a man (*manushyon kī banāī*) and a barbarous one at that; a deity would have made the opposite choice.

Dayananda showed a similar reaction to the animal sacrifice offered by Noah. "And Noah builded an altar unto the Lord; and took of every clean beast, and every clean fowl, and offered burnt offerings on the altar" (Genesis 8:20). God also told the sons of Noah that animals were to be their food. "Every moving thing that liveth shall be meat for you, even as the green herb have I given you all things."

> Comment—Is not the God of Christians merciless as He gives enjoyments to one at the cost of another's life? Those parents are great sinners indeed who feed one of their children with the flesh of another. All are sons in the eye of God. If their God does not behave so, He is just like a butcher. It is He who had made man violent: Why is not [the] God of the Christians a sinner, as He is destitute of mercy?[11]

Dayananda's revulsion over examples of violence and slaughter may have gone beyond the desire to criticize Christianity and represented instead a genuine loathing for much of what to him violated Hindu values and customs. There was also the question of caste, for one who acts "like a butcher" (*kasāīvat*) may well be what he seems to be, namely an untouchable.

The Old Testament provided numerous instances of actions that were unacceptable to the Swami and to others within the Hindu community. He reacted with shock and disgust to Abraham's feast which included "butter, milk, and the calf."

> Comment—Now see, O gentlemen! How can [the] worshippers of that God, leave the flesh of cows, calves, and other animals, who Himself eats the flesh of a calf? He who has no mercy and is ever covetous to eat flesh, cannot be God, a cruel man he may be.... For these very reasons, the wise never look upon this book as God-revealed nor such [a] being as God.[12]

The Christian God then showed the qualities of a barbarian, a *jangalī wāllā,* of a cruel man (*hinsak manushya*), a killer devoid of mercy (*kuch dayā nahin*), who could never be mistaken for a deity, but should be seen as the debased leader of a violent people.

Dayananda found further evidence of this primitive behavior in Leviticus 1:5–9, "And he shall kill the bullock before the Lord: and the priests, Aaron's sons shall bring the blood, and sprinkle the blood round about the altar that is by the door of the tabernacle of the congregation.... To be a burnt sacrifice, an offering made by fire, of a sweet savour unto the Lord."

> Just look! The devotees of God slaughter an ox in His presence and He allows it. They sprinkle the blood all round and burn the flesh in fire as an offering, and God smells it. Is it not all like a butcher's house? Therefore, we say that the Bible is not a God-revealed book. Nor is he God who behaves just like a wild man.

Sacrifice for salvation, particularly the killing of cattle in a sacred place, was morally repugnant to Dayananda. Further reading of the Bible did not alter this situation.

The Swami, like most Hindus, did not practice blood sacrifices as a form of atonement, but saw them as brutal and totally unreasonable religious practices. When God instructed a priest who had sinned to repent by making a sacrifice, He demonstrated again the offensive nature of Biblical practices.

> If the priest that is anointed do sin according to the sin of the people; then let him bring for his sin, which he hath sinned, a young bullock

> without blemish unto [the] Lord for a sin offering. And he shall bring the bullock unto the...Lord; for a sin offering: and [he] shall lay his hand upon the bullock's head and kill the bullock before the Lord (Leviticus 4:3-4).[13]

These actions were disturbing enough, but the logic that accompanied them made no sense and seemed to promise a reward for blood sacrifices instead of punishment,

> Comment—Now look at the atonement for sins. First he commits a sin, then he slaughters benevolent animals like cows, etc. And God allows it. What sort of people are these Christians that they believe him to be God who does such things and expect salvation from him![14]

Christians and their God showed themselves to be a cruel people who engaged in animal sacrifice and meat eating.

The destruction of Sodom and Gomorrah demonstrated that God would kill on a mass scale against men, women, and children. The Swami reacted with disgust.

> Comment—Now see another achievement of the God of the Bible. He felt no mercy on children etc. Were they all sinners that they were killed by overthrowing the ground? This is against justice, mercy, and consideration. When God does such things, why should not His worshippers?[15]

Here he linked the violence of the Christian God, himself a meat eater (*mānsāhārī*), with that of his followers from whom one could expect little else, given their penchant for eating meat.

Events in Egypt and the means used by God to free the ancient Israelites once more revealed the true nature of Christianity. After reading this account Dayananda responded with,

> Comment—Horrible! This God of the Christians goes at midnight like a robber and mercilessly kills children, old men, and even cattle; shows no kindness; there is a great bewailing in Egypt, but his cruelty knows no abatement. Such things cannot be expected even of an ordinary man—let alone God, but there is nothing strange. Flesh eaters know no mercy. The God of the Christians is a flesh-eater. How can He be merciful to them?[16]

In this instance Dayananda drew the conclusion that "Flesh eaters (*mānsāhārī*) show no mercy." In short, Christians were brutal, and without compassion. In addition to violence Dayananda found other ideas that were, in his opinion, repugnant and immoral.

The Swami was repulsed by the concept of inherited sin and a deity who seemed to act out of spite. "For the Lord, thy God am a jealous God, visiting the iniquity of the fathers upon the children unto the third and fourth generation of them that hate me" (Exodus 20:5). He reacted to this statement:

> Comment—What justice is it to punish up to the fourth generation for the sin of their father? Does not a good father beget bad children and a bad father good? If it is then what sense is there in extending the punishment up to the fourth generation?... It is unjust to punish anybody without a fault.[17]

This form of justice ran counter to the basic Hindu concept of *karma,* with its linking of individual action and punishment or reward. Christian belief, by contrast, appeared as a form of vindictiveness rather than divine justice. According to the Swami not all Christian customs, and here he included practices of the Israelites, could be considered vile; some were simply strange or, perhaps, merely silly.

When Dayananda read a description of circumcision he responded with a degree of practicality as well as condemnation.

> Comment—Now look at the absurd order of God! If circumcision was desirable to God, he should not have made the foreskin in the very beginning. If it is made, it is for protection. Just as there is a skin over the eye called [an] eye-lid similarly is the foreskin to protect the private organ, as it is very delicate. If there were no foreskin even the biting of an ant or a slight injury would have proved very troublesome. Besides it checks the drops of urine from spoiling clothes. It is very bad to cut it off.[18]

According to Dayananda these customs again demonstrated that God lacked foresight when he created foreskins, then declared them unnecessary, and later required that they be removed.

Similarly, the Swami deemed the custom of burial undesirable. His reasons were practical and based on concern for the environment, good health, and respect for a loved one. Dayananda returned to the use of dialogue to make his points.

> Q.—Look here. It is not a good thing to burn a man whom we love. Burying is only equal to laying a man to sleep. Therefore burial is good.
>
> A.—When you love the corpse, why do you not keep it in your house? The soul whom you loved has passed away. To love the putrefying body is meaningless. If you love it why do you bury it in the ground? If you say to any man that you will bury him, will he be pleased with you? Is it a mark of love that you throw on its mouth, eyes, body, dust, stones, bricks, lime etc. put a stone on the breast. To put the corpse into a box and bury it produces a very offensive smell which makes the air impure and gives rise to diverse diseases.

Burial both showed disrespect for the dead and polluted the environment, and, in addition, it consumed much needed space:

> Secondly the burial of one dead body requires at least 6 cubits long and 4 cubits broad pieces of ground. Now calculate what a great waste of land it is to bury a hundred, a thousand, a hundred thousands or ten millions of dead bodies. You cannot use it as a farm, as a garden, or a dwelling place. A slightly less obnoxious [way] is to throw it into the water, as watery animals at once devour it. But whatever bones, or other stuff remains is sure to cause harm to the world.
>
> Next throw it into [the] jungle, as carnivorous beasts and birds at once pounce upon it and eat it up. But bones, marrow, etc. remain. They pollute the air and injure public health. Burning is the best as it reduces the body into very fine particles and spreads them in the atmosphere.[19]

He could find nothing good about burial; it had a wide number of drawbacks, while cremation was seen as morally and environmentally advantageous, the only true and proper way of disposing of the dead.

In reading the story of Noah, Dayananda saw something that was simply unreasonable. It was silly, and only ignorant people could believe such obvious nonsense.

> Comment—Can any learned man accept him as God who speaks such unreasonable and impossible things? Can a boat of these dimensions contain an elephant, a camel, she-camel and millions of creatures with their family and provisions? This proves that the book is a composition of some man and that too is not learned.[20]

Once again the Bible was shown not to be the product of divinely inspired sages or even learned men. This absurd story could not be part of "revealed truth." Moving from the Old Testament to the New did not improve the picture of Christianity, but instead added more tales of the absurd, uneducated, and savage; of miracles and superstitions.

The New Testament

With his examination of the New Testament, Dayananda shifted the focus of his criticisms from God to Jesus Christ. He sought to disprove Christ's claims of divinity and his role as the son of God. To begin with, he objected to the concept of the virgin birth.

> No educated person can believe such things. It is only the ignorant and wild savages, and not the civilized and cultured man who can admit to be true things which are opposed to valid reasoning...[and the] laws of nature.

The Swami classed this along with the miracles described in the *Purānas,* a set of Hindu religious texts that he had also faulted because they were filled with error and superstition and were devoid of religious authority. They had no logical basis either, for they were not grounded in "valid reasoning" (*pratyakshadi pramān*) or the "Laws of Nature" (*ahritikram se viruddh*).

Dayananda saw as dangerous the concept of an immaculate conception, an idea that might lead to a loss of social control over women. "If we begin to believe such things, any virgin who happens to conceive would give it out that she conceived through God and that the messenger of God has told her in [a] dream that it is so."[21] Once again only the ignorant and gullible could believe in the Christian doctrine with its God-given pregnancies.

Swami Dayananda attacked the character of Christ and used the text in Matthew 10:35 as one of his sources for his assessment: "I am come to set a man at variance against his father, and the daughter against her mother, and the daughter in law against her mother in law." For Dayananda, this showed that "Christ came to spread discord [that] we find going on everywhere in the world. How wicked it is! Strife is always the cause of unhappiness to men, and this is, it appears, the master key of all Christian dealings." With Christ's design being conflict and dissension, then, it was hardly surprising that Christians engaged in these same activities. "When Christ thought it good to set one person against another, then why not these [his followers]? To set members of a house against other members of the same house is becoming of only Jesus Christ and not of a good man."[22] For the Swami, Christ appeared as the quintessential outside agitator who came not to bring peace, but to destroy it.

Further evidence of the disruptive nature of Christ came from the story of his encounter with a fig tree, which he cursed when it proved fruitless, so that it withered away (Matthew 21:18–19). The Swami responded to this by questioning the personality of Christ and also the extent of his knowledge about the processes of nature.

> All Christian missionaries say that Jesus Christ was very calm, peacemaking, and free from anger etc. But this account shows that he was very hot tempered [and] destitute of knowledge of [the] seasons. He would behave like [a] wild savage. The tree is a lifeless object. What fault could it commit to deserve [this] curse?[23]

The ignorance and ill temper displayed by Jesus did not surprise Dayananda; after all, it fitted with his occupation and his place among an uncivilized people.

From the perspective of a Hindu *brahman,* Christ was born of an artisan family, belonged to a lower caste, and was uneducated. "Joseph was in fact a carpenter. Therefore, Jesus was also a carpenter. For some time he worked at his trade. But thereafter he aspired to be a prophet and succeeded in being God's son."[24] What, after all, could one expect of such a man? In commenting on Matthew 24:29, with its predictions of cosmic disaster, Dayananda responded,

> Bravo Honored Sir! What science told you that the stars would fall? What powers of heavens are there that will shake? Had Jesus a little education he would have known that the stars are worlds and could not fall down. It shows that Jesus was born into a carpenter's family. His familiar objects were the sawing of the wood, and peeling, cutting or joining the pieces.[25]

In this commentary Dayananda brought together several of his criticisms of Christianity. He also demonstrated his desire to discredit rather than to understand. The opening of this comment, *wah jī Isā,* had a sense of contempt that was followed by his labelling of Jesus as a *barhai,* merely a carpenter who lived in a *janglī desh,* a land of barbarians.

Among these ignorant people Christ, a *kārīgar,* an illiterate craftsman, could say the most outrageous things and be believed by his fellow men.

> All of a sudden a wave rose in his mind that he should also pose as a prophet in that uncivilized country. He began to talk like this. He said many good things, but many more bad. The savages of that country believed them. Had Europe been as enlightened in those days as it is now, his super human claims would have produced no effect. Now they are educated to a great extent, but political considerations and obstinacy do not allow them to forsake this hollow religion and incline towards the Vedic faith. It is a great defect in them.[26]

Educated Christians continued to believe in their dogmas out of "political considerations and obstinacy" (*vyavahār ke pech aur hath se*), and this kept them from admitting the superiority of Vedic Hinduism. Dayananda had, at last, found his explanation for the continued appeal of Christianity to the educated and a corresponding rejection by its followers of the superior Vedic religion.

The fact that Christ taught his disciples to pray for their daily bread showed that he and they were backward and poverty stricken. Dayananda Saraswati interpreted this as evidence of their low status: "This shows that at the time when Jesus was born, people were wild and poor, and so, was Jesus himself. This is why he prays for the daily bread and asks others to pray for the same." Yet Dayananda also criticized Christians for their riches and concern for material goods. They did not seem interested in piety and the ascetic life of a truly religious person. "Why are the Christians busy in accumulating wealth? They should not act against the teachings of Jesus Christ. They should give away in charity all their belongings and embrace poverty."[27] Dayananda was not always consistent in his arguments, for poverty and wealth both showed the inferior quality of Christians and of their prophet.

The question of wealth and Christianity arose once more when Dayananda commented on Matthew 20–24: "And again I say unto you It is easier for a camel to go through the eye of a needle, than for a rich man to enter into the kingdom of God."

> Comment—This shows that Jesus was a poor man. Rich men might not have held him in respect. It is why he wrote this.
>
> But the principle is not correct. The rich and the poor both have good men as well as bad men. Whoever does a good action get good fruit and whoever does a bad action bad.[28]

Christ's bias against the rich seemed to be a matter of spite and was, according to Dayananda, poor theology, since the quality of action—and not the pocketbook of the actor—determined its value. Here, as in many of his other criticisms, Dayananda worked on the basis of Hindu doctrine. Christianity, after all, was built on a different set of principles that shaped its theology into a form unacceptable to a learned Hindu. Nothing demonstrated this divergence better than the approach to justice as presented in the Bible compared to Hindu conceptualization of the same subject.

The Christian handling of sin and salvation had no direct counterpart in orthodox Hinduism except for the saints and deities of the *bhakti* tradition, which Dayananda rejected, as they were not part of his Vedic Hinduism. His response to Christ's statement that "I am not come to call the righteous, but sinners to repentance," illustrated Dayananda's adherence to Hindu principles.

> The forgiveness of sins is only a tempting ruse for simple folk...the sin committed by a man does not go to any other man: he himself suffers, not another. This is the law of God. If the sin of one were to go [to] another, or the judge were take it on himself, or if the doers of the sin were not to suffer in due proportion of the sin, it would make God unjust. It is righteousness itself which is helpful and not Christ or any one else.[29]

Only following one's *dharma* can lead an individual to salvation (*moksha*). The action of an intermediary figure cannot save one from sin (*pāp*) and it is absurd to presume a path to salvation that could be provided by an ignorant carpenter who had no knowledge of the Vedas.

Two incompatible theories of justice were at work here, one Christian and the other Hindu:

> Comment—Now see. The God of the Christian is obviously unjust. Justice means that the fruit of the action should exactly tally with the action in quantity as well as quality. If it is a lot more or a lot less, it [is} called injustice.[30]

In this section Dayananda still sought to discredit Christianity, but also imbedded in his discussion was adherence to his Hinduism that clashed with the Christian idea of salvation through faith. The different ideas of salvation and justice emphasized the fact that Christianity was a religion of foreigners, men from another race and civilization.

Dayananda approached two scriptural passages from the context of a colonial environment, not from a theological position, and drew conclusions that Westerners would not have expected.

> Jesus said unto them, verily I say unto you, That ye which have followed me, in this regeneration when the Son of man shall sit in the throne of his glory, ye also sit upon twelve thrones, judging the twelve tribes of Israel.

Christians were promised a permanent celestial superiority over all mankind and with this the authority to judge others as well as to award punishments to those whom they condemned. Such power amounted to cosmic imperialism.

> Comment—Now look at the secret designs of Jesus Christ: He wanted that even after his death people should not get out of his net. Even that wicked person who betrayed his master for thirty rupees will sit with him on the throne and not only will the house of Israel be judged with partiality, but all their sins will be forgiven and they will sit a judge over other houses.[31]

The idea of Christians as judges over others fitted well with the realities of the colonial world where the rulers maintained positions of power and superiority. Dayananda used the Hindi term, *sāf guna* (the white race), for *Christian.* For him these terms seemed interchangeable.

For Dayananda the lesson was clear and he was, in this case, quite specific as to his conclusion.

> It appears that is why the Christians are very partial to the Christians; if a white man kills a black man, he is for the most part declared not guilty and acquitted. The same must be the justice administered in the paradise.[32]

The religion of Jesus Christ was the white man's religion and it supported them in their position of superiority over black men, whom they suppressed and even killed (*kāle ko mār diyā*). This was the religion of barbarism, ignorance, and white colonialism.

The execution of Christ proved to Dayananda that Jesus could not have been the son of God. He was only a man who did not possess any special powers and was thus unable to protect himself from the authorities and even from his own followers.

> Comment—Now see, Jesus Christ had not even this much capacity or occult power of that he might have created [a] strong faith in his disciples; they should not have with greed betrayed their teacher even at the cost of their lives or disowned him, or told lies, or forsworn him. Besides Jesus had no miraculous powers...these Christians have set up a huge hoax, now-a-days, on the powers of Jesus Christ. Anything would have been better than such a disgraceful death i.e. fighting to death, or leaving the body by *Yogic Samadhi* or ending his life in any other way.[33]

Ignorant, weak, devoid of the ability to perform miracles, and lacking in occult powers (*kuch karāmatī nahīn*), Jesus could not save himself. As a result Christ died an ignoble death. Jesus Christ's death was evidence of weakness, not noble sacrifice, and once again demonstrated that Jesus was not the prophet, as he claimed, but just a man of no learning and great pretensions.

Dayananda could not understand why Christians depended on such a powerless figure as Jesus Christ. The Swami saw Christ as a prophet who had failed to protect himself or others and was, as well, unable to command the absolute loyalty of his own disciples.

> Comment—Now the Christians are going about preaching "come and embrace our faith, get your forgiveness and be emancipated," [it] is all absurd. Had Christ possessed the power of forgiving sins, creating faith, or purifying the impure, why did he not make the souls of his disciples sinless, faithful, and happy?

The lack of faith among Christ's disciples also meant that the New Testament was written by men of questionable religious and moral character.

> When the disciples of Jesus Christ were devoid of even a grain of faith and it is they who wrote the book, wherein lies the validity of the book? To pin their faith to the writings of the faithless, impure, and irreligious persons is not proper for those men, who seek their happiness.

This state of affairs was validated through the scriptural statements. The Bible itself gave evidence of the minuscule amount of faith possessed by Christ's disciples, since they measured their belief in "mustard seeds."

> If anybody claim that he has full or partial faith ask him to remove the mountain from the path. If the mountain is removed, then also there is not full faith: it is just equal to a grain of mustard seed. And if it is

> not removed, then the conclusion is that there is not a jot of faith, devotion, or religiosity in them.[34]

This demonstrates the literalism that Dayananda used in reading and interpreting the Bible.

The teachings of Christ were those of an illiterate man who taught other men more ignorant than himself. In Dayananda's judgement Christians needed to be immature, and the New Testament seemed to support this.

> Verily, I say unto you, except ye be converted and become as little children, ye shall not enter into the kingdom of heaven (Matthew 18:3). To ask men "to become like little children" shows that Christ's sayings are unscientific and his desire that people should accept his word like children without examining it blind-folded. Many Christians behave like children, otherwise how could they believe in such unreasonable things?[35]

Again and again, Dayananda assumed that educated, intelligent, and civilized men must see the truth and accept Vedic Hinduism. Conversely, only the uneducated, illiterate, and stupid would remain disciples of Christ and adhere to his absurd teachings. His vision was a mirror image of the missionaries who "knew" that, once educated, an intelligent "native" must inevitably come to Christ and convert to the one true faith.

Perhaps the most shocking and disturbing passage within the Bible was the description of the Last Supper (Matthew 26:26–28):

> No civilized man will do such things except an uneducated and wild savage—to tell his disciples that their bread is his body and their drink his blood. And this thing the Christians of these days call [the] "Lord's supper" i.e. on whatever they eat and drink, they impose the idealism that it is the flesh and blood of Jesus Christ. How awful! How can those men leave others alone, who could not spare the flesh and blood of even their own preceptors from conceiving it as their food and drink?[36]

To Dayananda the Last Supper, a *prabhubhojan,* the ritual eating of one's master, was morally repugnant and set an unfortunate precedent. Disciples do not eat their *gurus,* a form of action that was totally unacceptable to the Swami and proved beyond doubt that this religion was savage and beyond all understanding. Further evidence, however, was given in the final book of the New Testament.

No other section of the Bible supplied such a collection of bizarre and illogical passages as the writings of Saint John, especially when taken literally. An excellent example was found in the description of heaven with its thrones, beasts, and other magical details that seemed ridiculous to Dayananda.

> Comment—Now see. The Christian paradise is like a town, and their God is lamp-like fire. It is absurd for God to wear [a] gold crown etc. or for beasts to have eyes in front and behind. Who will believe such things?[37]

When St. John provided a more realistic description with measured walls, gates, streets, and buildings, all decorated with a wealth of jewels, Dayananda raised questions of population control.

> Comment—Hear the description of the heaven of the Christians! When so many Christians die and new ones are born, how will the town of the said dimensions accommodate all of them? There will be only immigration, but no emigration.[38]

The dimensions did not give enough space for all the souls who would arrive and the picture of this city of gold was neither rational nor believable.

Along with the strange and bizarre, there were questions of race raised in heaven, questions that stemmed from the fact that God had a face.

> Comment—Look at the residence of the Christians in heaven. Will God and Christ remain sitting on the throne forever? And will their servants constantly stand looking at their faces? Now pray tell us what kind of face your God has? White like European? Or black like African negroes? Or like that of men of other countries?... He who has a face can never be God, omniscient and the Lord of all.[39]

The Christian heaven then was concrete in its size, gates, streets, and thrones, with a God who had a body and face. It also was a place with strange sights, such as animals with eyes in both the front and the rear of their head.

The most disgusting and ludicrous of all of heaven's characteristics had to do with its army of two hundred thousand horses described in Revelation 9:16. Dayananda responded to this with,

> Comment—Where would so many horses stay in heaven? Where would they graze? Where would they dwell and where would they throw out their dung? How awful would be the bad smell of the dung! We all Aryas have washed our hands of such a heaven, such a God, and such a religion.[40]

The Christian heaven then was a crowded city complete with horses (*gore*), their dung (*līd*), and the resulting stench (*durganh*), a place that no right thinking man would wish to visit, let alone live in for eternity.

The strange and bizarre events pictured here gave the Swami numerous examples of unbelievable and unacceptable tales. He had already rejected similar stories within Puranic Hinduism, claiming that they were false and erroneous accretions to the true Vedic religion. Now he attacked the same elements that he found in Christianity. The difference between his discussion of Hinduism and of Christianity was that the latter had no viable core of truth, as did Hinduism.

The heavenly marriage of Christ raised serious questions to a celibate religious leader, for whom the very idea was repulsive. Because Hindu holymen remain celibate so must a prophet who claimed divine status as the son of God. "For the marriage of the Lamb is come, and the wife hath made herself ready" (Revelation 19:7). To Dayananda the concept of a married holyman had numerous difficulties. "Let us ask who were his father-in-law, mother-in-law, brother-in-law, etc.? How many children had he?" There was, as well, physical degeneration as a result of marriage. "The loss of the vital fluid must have led to the deterioration of strength, intellect, prowess, life etc., and by this time Christ must have given up his body."[41] Relatives, children, and the loss of semen (*vīrya*) were the very pleasures that a Hindu, who had chosen religion, abandoned in order to seek his release from rebirth. The idea that all this was taking place in heaven and by the supposed son of God clearly showed Christ could not be a dedicated religious leader, since he could not even remain celibate.

In Conclusion

Dayananda shared with his missionary opponents a normative approach to their religions, and the yardstick by which he measured all faiths was his Vedic or Aryan Hinduism. The Swami also had the social and cultural values of a Hindu brahman. With this as his starting base, he judged Christianity with the desire to discredit it. Dayananda had no wish to discover good qualities in Christianity or Christ, nor did he want to discuss points of mutual concern or elements of similarity. He did not seek equivalence, but began with the assumption that he alone had the true religion for Hindus and for the world.

In his reading of the Old Testament, Dayananda found much to "prove" the validity of his basic suppositions and to provide evidence to support his aims. For the Swami sought to demonstrate that the Bible was not a text revealed by God, as were the Vedas. It was not *ishvarkrit,* but made by man and it reflected less than divine attitudes. He also wished to establish beyond question that the Christian God was not God, but merely a man. Dayananda's attempt at divine character assassination had a great deal of evidence to support it. The Bible seemed to be filled with tales that illustrated crude and savage behavior, all attributed to the Christian God, who was neither omniscient nor omnipotent. He had not the powers or attributes of a deity and so must, by logic, be a man—in this case, a barbaric one. His followers fit the same mold. They did despicable things and could be classed only as wild men (*jangalī log*), people lacking all elements of civilization.

As Dayananda moved on to discuss the New Testament, the major goals of his arguments were the denial of Christ's divinity, as the son of God, and his role as savior of mankind. He spent less time on the validity of the Gospels, since they were openly understood by Christians and non-Christians as being written by men. In addition, Dayananda saw these authors as uneducated, ignorant, and lacking in faith. The Gospels could not be considered revealed literature, but like the Puranic texts were illegitimate, absurd, and full of silly tales. Ridicule became the mainstay of his textual criticisms when he dealt with the Revelation of Saint John, where he always discovered ample material to support his opinions. Reading Revelation literally produced a host of four-eyed beasts and horses in heaven. With such evidence he could feel confident that he had destroyed any claim to religious superiority on the part of the Christians and had instead showed that Christianity could hardly be classed as a religion.

There was in Dayananda's criticisms a stream of anti-British and anti-white comments. Many of his readers understood that meat eaters killed non-whites. Only occasionally did Dayananda make this position explicit, but it was implicit in several of the Biblical stories that he examined. For instance, in his critique of the Old Testament, he sympathized with the Egyptians and not the ancient Israelites when God slaughtered the sons of that land. In attacking the divinity of Christ, the Swami cited a wide range of evidence: the virgin birth, Christ's occupation as a carpenter, his purpose of sowing discord on earth, his anger with the fig tree, his lack of divine power when threatened with death, and finally the revolting events of the Last Supper. Besides condemning the Christian God and Christ as the savior of the world, Dayananda also denigrated the followers of Christianity throughout his commentary. He classed them as either illiterate and ignorant people who believed even the most absurd tales or as educated men, like the British, who held to this religion out of "political considerations and obstinacy."

Dayananda drew different conclusions from the Biblical stories than those taught in the Christian world. He read the Bible from a literalist position. It meant exactly what it said. Two factors contributed to this approach. First, Dayananda had no cultural heritage that could provide him with the ability to see analogies within the Bible or to reinterpret its statements in terms of an inner meaning. Second, he had no motivation, no purpose to attempt to understand the Bible, but sought only to reject it. His was a literalist reading possible only for someone outside of Western Civilization. Thus, for the Swami, reading the Bible did not confirm the validity of Christianity; rather it gave him all he needed to destroy its claims as a religion. This was, for Dayananda, an act of *khandan,* of rejecting falsehood and *mandan,* proclaiming truth.

Bibliographic Essay

The basic textual source for this article was the popular English translation by Ganga Prasad Upadhyaya, *The Light of Truth.* (Allahabad: 1956). The English translation by Durga Prasad, *An English Translation of the Satyārth Prakāsh* (Delhi: 1970) provided a comparable text. Durga Prasad wrote in somewhat more elegant English, but does not appear to be any more accurate in its rendition of the Hindi than the translation of Ganga Prasad. Both tend to be rather idiomatic, in that the authors occasionally translated according to their own prejudices and interests. Neither was a scholarly translation. In the early 1880s Shri Paramahansa Vrajat Acharya and Shri Maddayananda Saraswati prepared Swami Dayananda's text for publication. It was reprinted as the *Satyārth Prakāsh* (Ajmer: vikrami samvat 1937 on the cover, 1948 on the title page). Today this is the standard Hindi version of the *Satyārth Prakāsh,* and is accredited to Swami Dayananda. During the 1950s, another edition was issued, without changes in the text but in a smaller and less expensive format. (Ajmer: vikrami samvat 2015) (A.D. 1957–58).

Perhaps the Arya polemicists who drew most upon and then elaborated Dayananda's criticisms of Christianity, was Pandit Lekh Ram. In his tract *Sabūt-ī-Tanāsukh*(Proofs of Rebirth), Lekh Ram both attacked Christian rejection of rebirth and discovered "proofs" for this in the Bible. It was, however in *Krishchan Mat Darpan* (Mirror of the Christian Religion) in which Lekh Ram developed his most extensive statement against the validity of this religion; he did so by extending Dayananda's own arguments. In the first chapter, entitled "Not the Son of God, but rather the son of Joseph the carpenter," using humor, common sense, and a sharp tongue, Lekh Ram attempted to destroy any Christian claims to Christ being divine or born of a virgin. The pandit then went on to charge Christianity with being sinful, unable to provide salvation for its followers, merciless and tyrannical and claimed it possessed numerous other failings. He also questioned the manner in which

Christianity had spread throughout the world. Christianity gained its adherents through the power of Europeans, as he further delineated in his Urdu tract *Religious Deception of the Padri's White Complexion.* The only sources of these writings of Pandit Lekh Ram that I located was the *Kullīyāt Ārya Musāfir,* (The Collected Works of Pandit Lekh Ram) (Lahore: 1897) in Urdu. Shri Pandit Jagat Kumar Ji and Shri Pandit Shanti Prakash Ji translated into Hindi the first third of the *Kullīyāt* (Jullundur: 1964). The entire volume was to be translated, but, I believe, the project was never completed.

The monthly Urdu journal *Ārya Musāfir,* (Jullundur City: 1898–1902) followed closely the writings of Lekh Ram and the original criticisms of Swami Dayananda. Anti-Christian writings appeared frequently over the years, some in a series of articles and others in a single issue. One of the first was a series entitled "The Christ of Nazareth." It ran from October 1898 through August 1899. Other anti-Christian writings included: "Peculiar Sects Among the Christians," January 1900; "The Establishment of Truth and Falsehood," February and March 1900; "Who Wrote the Bible?" a series that appeared in October 1899 and May, June, and July 1900; "Falsification of the Contents of the Bible," May, June, and July 1900; "The Truth about the Word and Its Usage in the Bible," August 1900; "The Truth about the Word 'Prophet' used in the Bible," August 1900.

Tracts that followed the logic of Dayananda's and Lekh Ram's writing appeared during the last two decades of the nineteenth century. Harnam Singh, in his *Anjīl Khuda kā Photo,* (A Picture of the God of the Bible) (N.p: 1891), focused on verses of the Old Testament to criticize Christianity. Kanshi Ram took up Dayananda's arguments on the nature of the Bible in *Bible Kalām Ilahī Nahīn* (The Bible Is Not a Revealed Book) (Jullundur: 1900). Durga Prasad, in his tract *Satyāsatya Vivek* (Distinction between Truth and Untruth) (Lahore: 1889), turned to the arguments used by Dayananda in his debate with the Reverend Mr. Scott. Bhajan Lal also adopted the vehicle of debate, this time a dialogue that he constructed between an Arya Samajist and a Christian in *'Aina-ī-Hidāyat* (Mirror of Guidance) (Ludhiana: 1888).

Through the first half of the twentieth century and particularly after independence, criticism of Christianity tended to focus on the activities of Christian missionaries. At times the national and state governments appeared as allies in this contest. An example of this situation occurred with the publication in the *Veda Prakāsh,* a monthly journal of the Arya Samaj, of *Īsāī Mishanrī Gatividhi Niyogī Junch Samiti, Madhya Pradesh kī Sarkārī Riport,* a Hindi translation of Madhya Pradesh Government's *Report of the Niyogi Investigating Committee on the Activities of Christian Missionaries* (Delhi: Govindaram Hasanand, March 1957).

After independence Christian missionaries were often viewed as a political as well as a religious threat, in short, a foreign menace. This approach was taken by Shri Om Prakash Ji in his *Bhārat Men Shayankar īsāī Shadyantra* (The Fearful Christian Conspiracy in India) (Delhi: n.d.). Internal evidence indicates that this tract appeared after 1958. A similar discussion of Christian missionaries, entitled "The Stinking Bouquet of Christianity," was presented in the April 1963 issue of *Paropkārī,* the journal of the Paropkarini Sabha, (Ajmer).

Anti-Christian writings continued to appear. One of the writers who most consistently produced such tracts was Ganga Prasad Upadhyaya. He wrote "The Arya Samaj and Christianity" (Allahabad: 1965). It was a revised version of the second edition that appeared in 1941 and was also published by the Arya Samaj of Allahabad. Both of these were small tracts of fifteen pages. A much longer edition by Ganga Prasad Upadhyaya appeared in 1941 as part of the Religious Renaissance Series, number 7, under the title *Christianity in India* (Allahabad: 1956), 162. Ganga Prasad followed the main arguments of Dayananda beginning with a rejection of the virgin birth to arguments against the validity of the crucifixion and resurrection. Pandit K. Jnani in *Hinduism vs. Christianity or Christian Teachings Scrutinized Through Hindu Eyes,*(Madras: n.d.) also turned to Dayananda's anti-Christian arguments for his own writings.

The large number of anti-Christian polemics by Arya Samajists have depended in the past and still do on chapter 13 of the *Satyārth Prakāsh.* Although new topics are exploited, such as the missionary presence in India and its foreign support, the members of the Arya Samaj still prize and utilize the writings of their Swami Dayananda with its extensive critique of Christianity. In this one source there is a rich and varied set of comments that provide an impressive condemnation of the white man's religion. No one has replaced Dayananda's critique of Christianity with a more extensive and effective statement and it is unlikely that any one will do so. Unless someone does, chapter 13 of the *Satyārth Prakāsh* will continue to be the definitive source for criticism of Christianity for members of the Arya Samaj.

Section Two

Muslim-Christian Polemics

Four

Muslim-Christian Confrontation: Dr. Wazir Khan in Nineteenth-century Agra

Avril A. Powell

Encounters between Indian Muslims and Protestant missionaries in the years following British expansion into the old Mughal heartlands of North India established a mode of interaction and conflict which re-erupted at intervals during the rest of the nineteenth century. A Muslim medical doctor who found himself, somewhat accidentally, enmeshed in this conflict played a significant part in setting the terms of much subsequent religious polemic not only in this region, but also in the rest of the Muslim world.

Dr. Muhammad Wazir Khan was a Sunni Muslim of Afghan lineage and Sufi inclinations who joined the East India Company's medical service in the North-Western Provinces after training at the Calcutta Medical College. His posting to Agra in the early 1850s brought him face-to-face with a group of evangelical Protestant missionaries whose particular target was the local Muslim *'ulamā.* One of the missionaries, Carl Pfander, who was already experienced in "Muslim controversy" in the Caucasus, was circulating Persian and Urdu editions of a book, the *Mīzān al-Haqq,* an evangelical exposition of Christianity which also criticized Islam and the prophet Muhammad.[1] Wazir Khan, together with some of the local *'ulamā,* decided that the moment had come to challenge this type of Christian evangelism. From 1852 until 1855 he participated in debates, assisted in the publication of books in defense of Islam, and entered into a lengthy and acrimonious correspondence with Carl Pfander. These Agra controversies stopped, seemingly abruptly, in 1855. Wazir Khan, however, came to public attention again two years later when he was a key figure in the Agra rising of July 1857. After active participation in the fighting in both Delhi and Oudh, he did *hijrat* to Mecca, never to return to India in spite of British attempts to extradite him.[2]

Although many details about his early life and his stance within Sunni Islam remain shadowy, the sources available from the 1850s suggest that Wazir Khan's hostility both to the Christian religion and to Company rule did result in his exchanging the pen for the musket in 1857 in true *mujāhid* style. This has been claimed for some other North Indian Muslims, but only in the case of Wazir Khan has it so far been substantiated that sustained anti-Christian activity was followed by disillusion and, in 1857, the seizing of the main chance.

The purpose of this article is to focus only on Wazir Khan's participation in the Muslim counterattack on Christianity in order to assess his longterm influence on patterns of polemical interchange both in northwestern India and in the wider Muslim world. For he was responsible, in conjunction with Maulana Rahmat Allah Kairanawi (later known in the Middle East as 'Dihlavi'), for introducing a new method of argument into the age-old conventions of Christian-Muslim polemics.[3] This was to argue that the Bible had been "corrupted" and using evidence not from the Qur'an, as earlier polemicists had done, but from Western critical sources, including authors avowedly Christian, as well as those who were skeptical or outright "unbelieving." The timing of this counterattack was significant, for evangelical missionaries of Pfander's background were either unfamiliar with, or extremely hostile to, the researches of the Biblical critics. By using their findings to undermine from within, the Muslims were able to declare an easy, if temporary, victory. Missionary accounts referred to Wazir Khan's discovery of the Achilles heel of the Christian claims.[4] Although the next generation of missionaries managed to redirect their preaching, the question of textual corruption continued to be the main issue in Christian-Muslim polemics in the Middle East, as well as in India, long after the Agra phase was over. While Rahmat Allah's role in *fann-i-munāzara* (the skills of religious debate) has been well documented, Doctor Wazir Khan's initiative has so far not received critical attention.

An alliance of this kind (for a polemical purpose) between a Bengal-trained medical doctor and a local *'ālim* was somewhat unusual, for although *munāzara* (disputation) was a sporadic occurrence among Indian Muslims, the participants were usually *'ulamā*. But several sources make it clear that *'ulamā* of a traditional background deliberately sought out Wazir Khan's assistance because of his fluency in English at a time when this was still unusual, even among Muslim officers in British service in the North-Western Provinces.[5] During debates he used his understanding of English to intercept private exchanges between the missionaries, who assumed that none of the Muslims could understand them. He was the first Muslim, not only in this part of India, but probably also in other parts of the Muslim world, to possess the linguistic skills, as well as the inclination, to challenge Christianity not only by analyzing the Bible, but also by assessing critical literature written in European languages. An important factor here was his medical training in Calcutta in the early 1840s, which, after his transfer to the North-Western Provinces, put him in the position of adviser on European matters to those Muslims in his circle who had a more traditional Islamic education.

But why was he prepared to put himself forward in this unlikely role as public polemicist? At one level his repeated professions of reluctance were merely intended to emphasize that the missionaries were the instigators, an important debate tactic for putting the opponent in the wrong. Yet his show of studied reluctance was rather more than a conventional formality, for at the time of the Agra debates he was heavily occupied at the new Thomason Hospital with a rural vaccination scheme for which he was largely responsible and for which he won the praise of his British superiors.[6] Just at this point Pfander's long campaign of preaching against Islam came to a climax with a conversion scare in Delhi, which at last alerted the *'ulamā* to the dangers of his activities. Rahmat Allah, of nearby Kairana, was a well-respected *'ālim* with an unparalleled knowledge of the Arabic, Persian, and Urdu translations of the Bible, but it was Wazir Khan alone who could provide the "external" evidence of Biblical corruption on which the Muslim attack was to rest. Although the records of these encounters suggest that Wazir Khan always remembered his place as the assistant, or "second" to his *'ālim* friend, it was his timely interventions at certain key stages that resulted in the advantage passing to the Muslims. He was a natural debater, quick to marshal his points with devastating effectiveness and to find the issues which could divide his opponents. Missionary descriptions of that period call him "a very stout and bigoted Mahomedan" and "a shallow but imposing man." Although conventional in their dismissal of an opponent's character and learning, these comments contained a hint of the extent to which they were actually unnerved by Wazir Khan.[7] Pfander professed to discount his arguments but recognized that a reappraisal for his own claims about the Biblical text were now inevitable. Rahmat Allah later complained to Pfander that the missionaries deliberately tried to exclude Wazir Khan from speaking because they had noticed, and now feared, his prowess in the debate arena.[8]

Public disputation proved to be an excellent medium for the Muslim leaders' single-minded purpose of restoring the confidence of the local Muslim community after years of persistent missionary pressure. Public exposure of admissions of textual changes was simple to understand and seemingly irrefutable: a sure crowd rouser in an unashamedly controversial situation. No time was to be wasted on seeking or evaluating either equivalence or difference on doctrinal questions. For the target audience was primarily Muslim, not missionary, and although Hindus and Sikhs also attended in considerable numbers, Wazir Khan was addressing, in his own phrase, all Muslims, both "high and low," who might have heard Pfander's bazaar preaching, or have read the *Mīzān al-Haqq*.[9]

He did not, however, really come into his own until, as a follow-up to the debates, he engaged in a separate correspondence with Pfander. These letters might be considered as the third and final stage in a consciously contrived sequence of encounters, which occurred between January and September of 1854. In the first stage, Rahmat Allah and Wazir Khan visited the home of one of the missionaries to engage him in conversation of a kind which would allow assessment of weaknesses in the Christian claims and of possible divisions between the missionaries.[10] This successful private dispute paved the way for the second stage: a formally organized public debate, accounts of which were published in newspapers and tracts.[11] This proved to be the climax of the Muslim counterattack and the beginning of Maulana Rahmat Allah's reputation as the defender of Islam. Although Wazir Khan's interventions were crucial in both of these stages, especially in the preparation of the agenda and the provision of the external evidence for the charge of *tahrīf* (corruption), his natural deference to the *maulānā* obscured his own considerable contribution. Also, the presence of a number of highly placed British government officials made expedient a facade of polite subservience, even when the most destructive points were being made. In the third and final stage—exchange of letters—Wazir Khan felt able to abandon constraints of both kinds, even though the correspondence was subsequently published by both participants. Therefore these letters, more than any other source, allow a closer examination of an otherwise rather shadowy figure.[12] Even then he continued to play out the role expected of a religious polemicist. Certain characteristics of the debate techniques remained, but the letter as a medium of communication allowed him to experiment with some new tactics and also to provide a fuller exposition of his new evidence for the "corruption" charge.

Wazir Khan certainly now felt free to abandon all his earlier restraint in using ridicule, sarcasm, and insinuations of a personal nature in order to cast a very unflattering light on Pfander's character and motives. His most persistent taunt was to suggest that the missionaries were motivated by financial considerations in coming out to India in the first place as well as in their plans to convert Muslims. In reply to Pfander's insinuation that he relied on the views of European rationalists was because he too was really *dahrī* (atheistical), the doctor implied that Pfander had abandoned Lutheranism for Anglicanism for mercenary motives connected with his second marriage to an English woman.[13] Such taunts were always part of the battery of polemicists of various religious persuasions and were to be expressed in language which became more and more offensive as the century progressed.

Ridicule of the opponent's linguistic abilities had rather more serious implications. It was certainly one of the conventions of missionary *munāzara* to attack linguistic shortcomings, and it is no surprise that it happened in this encounter, even though both Wazir Khan and his opponent, Pfander, were exceptionally gifted linguists. Wazir Khan seldom criticized Pfander's Urdu—the medium of communication between them—but reserved his scorn for his alleged mispronunciation of Qur'anic Arabic.[14] Pfander, in turn, paid somewhat backhanded compliments to Wazir Khan's fluency in English but argued that he was totally unfit to judge the "corruption" of the Biblical manuscripts without knowing Hebrew, Greek, and Latin.[15] Accusations of this kind were designed to raise the accuser and, correspondingly, lower the accused in the eyes of the target audience.

A more significant area of misunderstanding between them arose, not from these alleged shortcomings in the mastery the classical languages, but from their differing and largely unacknowledged perceptions of key Christian and Islamic terms when translated into Urdu. Both were aware that they attached different and incompatible meanings to the key term *tahrīf*.[16] After long argument about it, their mutual refusal to give an inch of ground resulted in an impasse, which in the end caused an abrupt end to their correspondence. Yet neither of them seemed to recognize, or chose not to, that the meaning of other key terms, such as *ilhām* (inspiration), *injīl* (gospel), and *hawārī* (apostle) had not been established between them. In order to examine in more detail the consequences of both the acknowledged and the unacknowledged areas of misunderstanding, the two principal but interrelated themes of attack will be isolated, focusing first, on *tahrīf* and second, on *ilhām*.

The *tahrīf* charge had always been part of traditional Muslim riposte to Christianity. Hitherto it had been subordinate to other themes (notably, comparison of miracles and the assertion of the irrationality of the Trinity) and had anyway been based on Qur'anic evidence. The new elements in Wazir Khan's assertion were the emphasis on questions of textual integrity and the weight he attached to evidence from more than thirty published works of criticism and commentary by European (and some American) scholars. His sources ranged from seventeenth- and eighteenth-century rationalists

(Spinoza, Paine, and Voltaire)[17] to Biblical commentaries by orthodox Anglican clergymen (the works of Henry and Scott, D'Oyly and Mant, and, most heavily used, the four volume commentary of T. H. Horne, first published in 1818).[18] He had quickly realized that great harm could be done to the missionary cause by showing that believing Christian clergymen had themselves pointed out examples of textual corruption. Although Pfander might brush aside the statements of the Deists, skeptics, and avowed unbelievers as inimical to all revealed religions, he was hard put to explain the mildly critical views of Anglican clergymen such as Thomas Scott and T. H. Horne. The latter, for example, accepted not only that there were accidental errors in the Biblical manuscripts, but that "willful corruption" by "believing Christians" had also occurred.[19]

Wazir Khan was the first Muslim scholar to use publications of this kind and to make them available to the *'ulamā,* through whose Urdu tracts they were later transmitted to a wider circle of critics of Christianity. He gained access to such literature by an easier route than some writers have suggested. For although some Urdu works state that he visited London to pursue his medical studies and there collected a library of theological literature, there seems to be no firm evidence for such a journey.[20] Also, although he had certainly studied in Calcutta, his own writings show no awareness of the religious controversies between Hindus and Christians which had been a characteristic of the "Bengal Renaissance" era. Pfander may, however, have been correct in thinking that Wazir Khan's strong interest in Western rationalist thinking was a product of his Calcutta years.[21] Yet his intensive reading on Christianity seems to have taken place only after his arrival in Agra in 1851: nearly all the works of criticism, history, and general knowledge which he cited were available in the libraries of the Agra and Delhi Anglo-Oriental Colleges, many of them, ironically, the gifts of his own evangelical opponents.[22]

Evidence from these European sources was used for the single purpose of proving that the charge of *tahrīf-i-lafzī* (textual corruption) was justified, by showing that "believing" as well as "unbelieving" scholars had already admitted the charge. It is difficult to assess from the debate records alone whether or not Wazir Khan distorted his sources to extract the necessary evidence. Still his letters to Pfander over a four-month period offer, through the process of assertion, denial and reassertion, a more satisfactory basis for judging his scholarly qualities. He was indeed very well read, but not as well read as he initially claimed. Pfander forced him, in the end, to admit that he had not actually read all the works of the thirty or so European authors he had quoted. This was second hand reading: he had in many cases imbibed their views and quoted their evidence from only a small handful of commentaries and histories, but he did not admit this until pressed.[23] Furthermore, most of them he had read in English. Again, when challenged, he argued that there was no need for him to know German, although the German contribution to Biblical criticism had been the most significant, because the key works were by then available in translation.[24] This was certainly true of one of his main sources, D. F. Strauss's *Life of Jesus,* which Wazir Khan consulted in George Eliot's three-volume translation of 1846.[25] The extent of his knowledge of Greek, Hebrew, and Latin, supposedly learned during a visit to London, is less clear-cut. It assumed importance during discussion of the dates of the various Biblical codices, Pfander asserting that until Wazir Khan had learned Greek and studied the manuscripts for himself, he must accept his own dating. Wazir Khan replied facetiously, but somewhat enigmatically, by asserting that his mastery of these three languages was better than Pfander's of Arabic and that perhaps it was the *rūh al-qadas* (Holy Spirit) who had misinformed Pfander.[26] A fair assessment would seem to be that he was dependent on his access to English translations of most of his sources, but that for the past two or three years (since he first became enmeshed in missionary polemic in Agra) he had been teaching himself Greek, and possibly the other languages too.

As his linguistic skills were clearly somewhat less developed than has been claimed for him, consideration of his methods take into account only those English sources he is indisputably known to have read, either in the original or in translation. On many occasions he practiced selective quotation, extracting only those sentences from the commentaries which supported his own criticism. On the dispute about whether Matthew's gospel was originally written in Hebrew or in Greek, Wazir Khan cited T. H. Horne as an authority for the former view. But Horne had, in fact, supported the case for two original gospels, both written by Matthew, one in Hebrew and one in Greek. He had put forward the names and arguments of scholars who supported other views the better to assess the evidence for each view.[27] Pfander not unnaturally felt that Wazir Khan was distorting Horne's position by quoting only part of the discussion. This was indeed so, in a purely scholarly sense. However, in an ongoing polemical struggle where the doctor's sole object was to show that Biblical critics, many of them believing Christians, were in disagreement about the authority of certain Biblical passages, his method was certainly effective for the end he wanted to achieve. Pfander might be held equally open to criticism for propagating a dogmatic, fundamentalist view of the Bible which had long been unacceptable to many Protestant scholars. Whether Wazir Khan would have stood by his assertions in a nonpolemical situation is impossible to judge from the records available. It seems likely that his stance was already preconditioned by an Islamic assumption which was proffered in both debates, as well as in the letters, that a single example of *tahrīf-i-lafzī* (textual corruption), even if affecting only a single verse or a single word, was sufficient to condemn a whole book or document.[28] Using this rigid criterion the Bible could only be condemned.

Pfander tried to challenge this assumption by distinguishing between *sahw-i-kātibon* (clerical errors)—which he reluctantly agreed had occurred—and the *tahrīf-i-lafzī* that the Muslims claimed existed. This distinction was totally rejected by Wazir Khan; he refused to accept Pfander's limitation of the term *tahrīf* to only such alterations of the text which might substantially affect any essential Christian doctrine or teaching. In Pfander's view, of course, no such changes had actually occurred.[29] In the doctor's view, however, his own case was won as soon as Pfander could be persuaded to admit a textual error or doubt of any kind, no matter how minor in doctrinal implications. This the missionary had done on a number of occasions, both in the public debate and in subsequent tracts and letters.[30] On these four or five admissions Wazir Khan based his "victory." For him the citing of statements by the Biblical critics on up to 30,000 "various readings" had been a means to the end of persuading his immediate adversary, Pfander, to admit only a handful of such errors. Within the framework of his own assumptions, Wazir Khan's charge of "corruption" seemed fully justified.

From a Christian point of view, however, he had proved nothing detrimental to the essentials of the Christian faith. If it was a resounding polemical victory in Muslim eyes, it had not even touched on any of the doctrinal differences which separate Islam and Christianity. Only a few years later the Biblical exegesis of Sayyid Ahmad Khan would draw on the same European sources to focus on *tahrīf-i-ma'anawī* (corruption of meaning) instead of *tahrīf-i-lafzī*.[31] This interpretation would provide a way out of the impasse for any Muslim disposed to seek compromise rather than conflict with Christianity. But from 1854 onwards most Muslim polemicists chose to follow Wazir Khan in demanding that *munāzara* "rules" should prohibit any argument or evidence taken from the Bible itself because it was a corrupt text. Wazir Khan's method of arguing on *tahrīf,* if responsible for a much-needed victory in Agra in 1854, had the longer term effect of stultifying all discussion between Muslims and Christians for the next few decades.

Underlying both Muslim and Christian attitudes to the Biblical text was the question of "inspiration," about which Wazir Khan and Pfander argued at length without ever acknowledging that they were at cross-purposes. At least partly responsible for this was their failure to explore how they were using and understanding the Urdu words *ilhām* (inspiration) and *wahī* (revelation). This was belatedly acknowledged by Wazir Khan only when he (or his editor) added a postscript to the published version of the letters, saying,

> Be it known that the word *ilhām* has been used in several places in this correspondence—its meaning is the *wahī* which was granted to the *paighambaron* (prophets/messengers); not that *ilhām* which was also given to *sulahā* (pious men).[32]

Understanding *inspiration* to mean, in this context, transmission from God to a prophet of a revealed text, Wazir Khan had repeatedly attacked the extant versions of the Bible for containing not only "uninspired" passages, but even whole books which, according to his definition, were not divine revelations.[33] The timing of the controversies once again allowed him to capitalize on current dissensions among Biblical critics, divisions which were, to some extent, also reflected among his missionary opponents. Pfander held to the traditional Christian belief in the "plenary inspiration" of the Scriptures and was therefore prepared to defend the inspiration of the given authors of each book of the extant Bible. The apocryphal books, on the other hand, he considered had rightly been rejected, because their authors, and hence their contents, were "uninspired." At this point Wazir Khan made use of his encyclopedic knowledge of the decisions of the Church councils, the early heresies, and differences between the Catholic and the Protestant canon to highlight the difficulties inherent in the plenary view.[34] By this date many Biblical critics, and even some of the Agra missionaries, had, as a result of textual examination and comparison, conceded that human intermediaries, even if they were prophets, did not always speak and act under full inspiration. They found it possible to distinguish therefore, even within the extant Bible, between passages which were written under inspiration and others which were not inspired, even if attributed to the same authors. Pfander's inability to admit the possibility of the inclusion of uninspired material within the Bible was partly responsible for his unyielding position on *tahrīf,* and in this area, too, Wazir Khan easily invoked the Protestant biblical critics against him.

Their arguments on inspiration centered on the *Injīl* (gospel) as the vehicle of God's revelation to Christians. It is clear from the correspondence that Wazir Khan understood the *Injīl* to be those words which had been revealed to Christ, but which had not been recorded or had since been lost. When Pfander reminded Wazir Khan that the Qur'an urged the *ahl-i-kitāb* (people of the book) to adhere to the *Injīl,* he gave the usual Muslim reply, that the extant, but corrupt, versions of the Bible did not contain the original *Injīl.*[35] Pfander's ultimatum, constantly repeated demand was to see a Biblical manuscript dating from the time of the Prophet Muhammad which could be shown to be different from the extant Bibles. But at the root of their counterclaims was a failure to agree on the meaning of *Injīl.* The term was used loosely, as it had been in earlier Muslim-Christian encounters, its meaning being variously understood as those words actually spoken by Christ, one or all of the Synoptic gospels, the entire New Testament, and on occasion, even the whole Bible. Imprecision of this kind compounded their confusion over inspiration, and Pfander's demand to compare the seventh-century *Injīl* with any extant New Testament was constantly refused by Wazir Khan on the grounds that none of the surviving New Testament codices dated from earlier than the ninth or tenth centuries.[36]

Another point of confusion concerned the terms used in Urdu for *prophet,* in the sense of "transmitter of revelation." *Paighambar, rasūl,* and *hawārī* were all used at various points in the discussion. As Pfander believed that the compilers of all the New Testament books, not only those attributed with the authorship of the Synoptic gospels, were inspired, he had used the term *hawārī* for all of them. Wazir Khan, on the other hand, denied the inspiration of much of the New Testament, mainly on the grounds that its compilers were ordinary men, not prophets. He, like many Muslim polemicists before him, reserved a particular hostility for the idea that Saint Paul, an upstart and sinner, who converted to Christianity only after Christ's death, and was not therefore among the original twelve apostles, should be considered a *hawārī,* and his epistles raised to the status of *wahī.* In his view the gospel writers and Saint Paul were *hawārī* in the Islamic sense of companions and *hadīs* writers, rather than prophets, and their records carried no special authority.[37]

Many of the characteristics already noted in Wazir Khan's method of attack on the textual integrity and the inspiration of the New Testament were highlighted in his onslaught on the Gospel of Matthew, for his argument here owed its entire formulation to European Biblical criticism. After the public debate in April 1854, the missionaries reported that Wazir Khan had placed on the table before him the three volumes of D. F. Strauss's "infidel" work, the *Life of Jesus.* Strauss's name did not feature directly in the ensuing debate, but shortly afterwards, when Pfander sent some books to the doctor, inviting him to translate them into Urdu (one of them was Aloys Sprenger's *Life of Muhammad*), he replied that he would prefer to translate, instead, Strauss's *Life of Jesus.*[38] In a subsequent letter he listed seven objections Strauss had made to the genealogy of Christ as it was recorded in the first chapter of the Gospel of Matthew, demanding that Pfander should answer them.[39] At first Pfander refused, objecting that Strauss was a *mulhid* (unbeliever) whose views were irrelevant to the discussion.[40] When pressed further, Pfander gave answers which failed to satisfy Wazir Khan, and the Matthew question remained a source of contention between them until their correspondence was finally broken off.[41]

The incident provides a number of insights into the nature of this phase of polemical interchange. First, it focused attention, in a most dramatic manner, on the new weapon which was now in the Muslims' possession. For Strauss's book had been responsible for a degree of bitter controversy within the Protestant world, which was to be surpassed only by the publication of *On the Origin of Species*. At this date (1854) Strauss still claimed to be a Christian but had remonstrated unsuccessfully against his dismissal from the theology faculty of Tübingen University. The notoriety which was attached to his name by those who had merely heard of his views, even if they had not actually read his book, served the doctor well, for his adoption of Strauss immediately made him a talking point among the European community in Agra: he was distinguished at the debate as "the Muslim who had read Strauss."[42]

Whereas his reliance on other Biblical critics, such as T. H. Horne, has been characterized as, on the whole, selective quotation to suit his own ends, his use of Strauss was both more idiosyncratic and more difficult to interpret. For it seems that either he missed the main point of the book, or else he deliberately chose to ignore it: Strauss's revolutionary contribution was to argue that the events of Christ's life, though unsupportable historically in a literal sense, were nevertheless amenable to a mythological interpretation. Wazir Khan completely ignored this central theme, and his letters to Pfander contain no reference at all to myth. Concerned only to make use of Strauss's arguments to bolster his own skepticism about the integrity of the extant New Testament, he ignored altogether the author's own resolution of the impasse.[43]

This explanation seems plausible, for the myth theory, if scandalous in Europe, would certainly be even more uncongenial and puzzling to a Muslim reader as an explanation of a revealed religion. But why did he confine his attention to only one subsection of one early chapter, when subsequent chapters provided examples which would be equally convenient for his own argument on *tahrīf* and *ilhām*? It is tempting to say that he never actually proceeded further in his detailed reading of Strauss than the first chapter of the first Gospel. This was sufficient to provide him with an attack on the genealogy of Christ that accorded well with his own methods of historical analysis. For Strauss's seven objections centered on inconsistencies in Matthew's statement of Christ's *nasabnāma* (genealogical descent), which were found to be incompatible with various tables in the Old Testament books.[44] In the eyes of a Muslim scholar, a faulty genealogy was in itself incontrovertible evidence of textual corruption, of the lack of inspiration of its alleged author, Matthew. In fact, it implied a slur on the prophet Christ, begotten of such forefathers. When he could no longer avoid a reply, Pfander attempted to reconcile the alleged inconsistencies by arguing that Matthew had deliberately abbreviated the Old Testament tables and by explaining other inconsistencies through semantic differences between Hebrew and Urdu.[45] Wazir Khan persisted, however, in arguing that the Straussian objections were valid.[46] The dispute never moved beyond these few verses: it seems that Wazir Khan, having won what he saw as a significant victory on this narrow front, found neither time nor inclination to pursue Strauss any further through the Gospels.

Their correspondence ended suddenly in mid-August 1854 after mutual accusations of giving irrelevant answers and using offensive language. The former reflected the impasse which had been reached on the definition and significance of *tahrīf,* the latter was a usual feature of *munāzara* situations which gave Indians a rare opportunity to ridicule and satirize the European sahibs. The jibes which struck deepest were insinuations that Wazir Khan, like his mentor, Strauss, was a *dahrī* (atheist), to which the doctor replied by implying that Pfander had mercenary motives for abandoning Lutheranism for Anglicanism and for marrying a second English wife. In mid-August each sent back the other's final letter unopened.[47] Although both threatened to prepare and publish further rejoinders, there was to be no opportunity for any further direct encounter. Soon after the debate, Pfander's mission decided to transfer him to Peshawar. His loud protests were ignored, and the missionaries who remained in Agra did not share his enthusiasm for controversial methods of evangelism. Even had he remained, it is unlikely that Wazir Khan would have resumed contact. Although superficially he seemed jubilant, letters to his medical superiors indicate that he was at this time actually very dejected. On the grounds of ill health he made repeated, but unsuccessful, attempts to be transferred away from Agra.[48] He did complete one tract, which was published as an appendix to his correspondence with Pfander, but after that he left it to other Muslims in the locality to publish the spate of tracts, *fatāwā,* and newspaper articles, which emerging out of the debate, would consolidate the "victory" achieved by his new methods of argument.

The significance of Wazir Khan's activities in Agra (apart from their connection with the ensuing revolt) lies in his influence on subsequent polemical interchanges both in northwestern India and in the wider Muslim world. Although the Agra debate was not the first of its kind to be held between Muslims and Christians, it was the first to receive widespread publicity: the "great debate" of 1854 became an important reference point when, later in the nineteenth century, Muslim polemicists resumed the counterattack. For although polemical interchange virtually ceased following the 1857 uprisings, by the late 1860s challenges to *munāzara* resumed with much greater frequency than before. By the mid-1800s, debates between spokesmen of various traditions became a commonplace occurrence in many small towns and villages of the North-Western Provinces and the Punjab.[49]

The rules of debate procedure put forward by Rahmat Allah and Wazir Khan established conventions concerning issuing of invitations, drawing up of the agenda, forms of address, and use of evidence. Most significantly, Wazir Khan's main line of argument, together with some of his evidence, were drawn on not only by Muslim polemicists of the next generation, but also by spokesmen of other persuasions, notably the Hindu Arya Samaj, to discountenance the missionary cause.[50] A direct link between these two eras of encounter was provided by Maulavi 'Imad al-din, who, at Wazir Khan's request, had preached against Christianity in the Royal Mosque in Agra in the early 1850s.[51] After conversion to Christianity in the 1860s 'Imad al-din was ordained and subsequently took up the leadership of Christian evangelism of Muslims in the Punjab and the North-Western Provinces. His "inside" knowledge of Wazir Khan's arguments made him well placed to commence a scholarly rebuttal and also to apply the same kind of charges to the Qur'an.[52] A second convert from Islam, Safdar 'Ali, had also been present at the 1854 debate. He too used the inside knowledge he had gained in the opponent's camp to reformulate the missionary claims in the 1870s.[53]

These Christian restatements made little impact on the rest of the *'ulamā,* who continued to affirm that the *tahrīf* issue was central to their objections to Christianity. As a result the age-old polemical issues, such as the divinity of Christ and the Trinity doctrine, comparison of the characters and deeds of Christ and Muhammad, and comparison of prophecies and miracles, were neglected in order to concentrate more and more narrowly on textual issues. This narrowing of the scope of controversy continued until a new generation of Protestant missionaries, who had begun to come to terms with Biblical criticism, succeeded around the turn of the century in accommodating the corruption question to other and more doctrinal questions.

By this time Wazir Khan's researches had been carried to the Middle East by his debating partner, Rahmat Allah, who fled to Mecca after the 1857 risings. Wazir Khan had also gone to Arabia but it seems that he never again participated actively in polemical discussions. It was Rahmat Allah alone who incorporated their earlier joint endeavors on the *tahrīf* question into a new Arabic work in refutation of Christianity, the *Izhār al-Haqq.*[54] It has remained the classic work in this field and was translated into several other languages in the late nineteenth century.[55] It has recently been republished in Cairo to combat the effects of a new dissemination of Pfander's *Mīzān al-Haqq* in various parts of the Muslim world.[56] Its author, Rahmat Allah, certainly won renown as the archetypal master of Muslim-Christian *munāzara,* but the part played by his medical doctor friend, Wazir Khan, in the early stages of the counterattack, has not hitherto been examined. It was he who first drew attention to the Achilles heel of the missionary claims (the corruption of the Biblical text), who backed up the *maulānā* in public debate, and then consolidated the advantage through his long correspondence with Pfander during the summer of 1854.

Bibliographic Essay

Both parties to the Muslim-Christian controversies published extensively. The evolution of Protestant missionary efforts to draw Muslim attention can be studied, for the pre-1857 period, through the correspondence of C. G. Pfander with his home missions. He wrote in German to the Basel Evangelical Mission and in English to the Church Missionary Society. The letters are extant, but many of them were published in full, or in part, in the journals of the two societies (the *Evangelische Heidenbote,* the *Missions Magazin,* and the *Church Missionary Intelligencer*). Among Pfander's published works are the following editions of the Persian and Urdu translations of his three main evangelical tracts on Islam and Christianity. They show the modification of his arguments under pressure from the *'ulamā: Mīzān al-Haqq* (German MS, 1929; Persian, Schusha, 1835, Calcutta, 1839, 1849; Urdu, Mirzapur, 1843, Agra, 1850); *Miftāh al-Asrār* (Persian, Calcutta, 1839, Agra, 1850, London, 1861; Urdu, Agra, 1850); *Tarīq al-Hayāt* (Persian, Calcutta, 1840, Agra, 1847, London, 1861, Ludhiana, 1875; Urdu, Agra, 1853, Ludhiana, 1867).

Most of the Muslim replies to these and to other missionary publications of this period can be tracked down in various libraries in India and Pakistan, notably the following works of Maulana Rahmat Allah Kairanawi: *Azālat al-Auhām* (Persian, Delhi, A.H. 1269 [A.D. 1852–53]); *Azālat al-Shakūk,* (2 vols., Urdu, Delhi, A.H. 1269, [A.D. 1852–53]); *I'jāz-i-'Īswī* (Urdu, Agra, A.H. 1271, [A.D. 1854–55]); *Asahh al-ahādīs fī ibtāl al-Taslīs,* (2d. ed. Urdu, Delhi, 1875). Several accounts were published, in both Persian and Urdu, of the "great debate" held in Agra in 1854.

They include the following: Sayyid 'Abd-Allah Akbarabadi, ed., *Pahlā hissa mubāhasa-i-mazhabī kā* (Urdu, Agra, A.H. 1270, [A.D. 1854]; Persian, Agra, A.H. 1271, [A.D. 1854–55]); *Murāsalat-i-Mazhabī: Dusrā hissa-mubāhasa-i-mazhabī kā* (Agra, A.H. 1271, [A.D. 1854–55]); Wazir al Din, *Al-bahs al-sharīf fi asbāt al-naskh wal tahrīf* (Persian, Delhi, A.H. 1270, [A.D. 1854]).

The completeness of the record, on both sides, allows a degree of objectivity which is sometimes difficult to achieve in studies of polemical interchange. However, in focusing, in this particular paper, on the brief interchange between Dr. Muhammad Wazir Khan and the Reverend C. G. Pfander, the available sources proved to be rather less well balanced. In this instance the record of interchange was much more complete on the Muslim side than on the Christian, for almost as soon as the exchange of letters was finished, it was decided to include a complete copy in the *Murāsalat-i-Mazhabī* (Agra, A.H. 1271, [A.D. 1854–55]). Pfander's eleven letters as well as Wazir Khan's fourteen appear in full in this work, although some important enclosures (e.g., lists of books consulted) which had been referred to in the letters, were not published. The letters were followed by a long "rejoinder," written by Wazir Khan as further comment on one of Pfander's letters. This has provided the main basis for my assessment of his understanding of Christianity. The letters themselves constitute a detailed, and perhaps unrivalled, source for following the dynamic of Muslim-Christian interchange at this early stage of encounter in nineteenth-century India. The copy of the *Murāsalat-i-Mazhabī* that I used belongs to the Maulana Azad Library at Aligarh Muslim University.

The missionaries, on the other hand, appear to have paid very little attention to the Pfander-Wazir Khan correspondence. Indeed, whereas they recorded, and then published, detailed accounts of the initial contacts in Agra, the climax of the controversies in 1854 received only cursory mention in their journals. Pfander himself was content to select and abridge from the voluminous notes and letters at his command and published only a short book in Urdu, the *Ikhtitām dīnī mubāgasa kā* (Agra, 1855). Together with some of his letters to Maulana Rahmat Allah, the *Ikhtitām* contained Pfander's own tenth letter to Dr. Wazir Khan, selected in order to reinforce a particular polemical point, and leaving him open to the Muslim charge of publishing only what was convenient to his cause. However, this single, but very long letter, is identical to the letter in the *Murāsalat* version (except for some clearly indicated "additional comments") and its existence makes it possible to presume that the rest of the letters in the *Murāsalat,* which cannot be checked in the same way, were probably equally carefully and fairly transcribed from the originals.

Thus it has been possible to treat Wazir Khan's fourteen published letters to Pfander, together with his eighty-four-page "rejoinder," as an authenticated source for assessing the first Muslim refutation of Christianity which was based on Christian rather than Islamic sources. It has so far not proved possible, because of source limitations, to place Wazir Khan's anti-Christian polemics in a broader religious and political context. Although his career in the medical service of the East India Company can be traced using Company records, from his student days until 1858, very little is known about his family or his earlier education. His movements in 1857–58, for which there is evidence in both British and Muslim sources that he was an active "rebel," can be placed in the wider context of Muslim participation in the risings, but the trail is lost again after his flight from India in 1858. So far, stray references to the resumption of his medical career in Arabia and to his relations with other Indian Muslims who had settled in Mecca, are insufficient to allow any meaningful examination of the last years of his life.

Other, and wider, aspects of this phase of Muslim-Christian polemic have been examined in the following: A. A. Powell, "Maulana Rahmat Allah Kairanawi and Muslim-Christian controversy in mid-nineteenth century India," *Journal of the Royal Asiatic Society,* no. 1 (1976): 42–63; A. A. Powell, "Muslim Reaction to Missionary Activity in Agra," in C. H. Philips and M. D. Wainwright, eds., *Indian Society and the Beginning of Modernization, c. 1830–1850* (London, 1976), 146–57; *Muslim and Missionaries in Pre-Mutiny India* (Curzon Press, 1988), revised version of "Contact and Controversy between Islam and Christianity in northern India, 1833–1857." (Ph.D. diss., School of Oriental and African Studies, London University, 1983.)

Five

Muslim-Christian Polemics and Religious Reform in Nineteenth-century Bengal: Munshi Meheru'llah of Jessore

Rafiuddin Ahmed

Conflict and Competition

Nineteenth-century Bengal witnessed an increasing concern with religion, among both Muslims and Hindus. This was partly a response to Western colonialism and partly due to a gradual decline in the older order following the disintegration of the Mughal Empire. The Muslim reaction was markedly more intense and bitter than that of the Hindus for a variety of reasons, and it manifested itself principally through a number of purificatory reform movements. This was further compounded by Christian missionaries who, in the second half of the century, became increasingly eager to preach to Muslims. The tension generated in Muslim society found expression through sectarian debates (*bahās*) between rival sects and groups, polemical writings, and, finally, intercommunal disputations with the Christian missionaries. Muslim sectarian literature of the period was written in the mixed language known as Musalmani Bengali, which had Bengali as a basis with the intermixture of Arabic, Persian, and Urdu idioms and expressions; these writings were basically concerned with Islamic theological questions. But as the proselytization efforts of the Christian missionaries intensified, leading to a gradual decline in sectarian tension, the tone and character of the literature also showed signs of change. Muslims shifted away from sectarian issues to debates aimed at countering the anti-Islamic propaganda of the missionaries. This led to the publication of a stream of fresh polemical works designed to destroy the effectiveness of Christian arguments and to assert Muslim superiority.

This chapter assesses the nature and extent of Muslim reaction to

Christian missionary activities in Bengal during the second half of the nineteenth century, and focuses attention on the specific issues and questions that Muslim-Christian polemics addressed. How did the Muslim reformers counter the criticism of Islam and the person of the Prophet Muhammad? How did they launch their own campaign of religious reform to turn the ordinary Muslims away from the Christian missionaries? What exactly was their message to the unlettered Muslim villagers, who knew very little about their own faith and could perhaps, by effective propaganda, be persuaded to change their religion? Lastly, we will direct our attention to the activities of a little studied Muslim preacher from Jessore in East Bengal, Munshi Muhammad Meheru'llah (1861–1907) who, for nearly a quarter of a century, played an important role in countering the challenge of the Christian missionaries and organized a powerful campaign to check the growth of Christianity in rural Bengal.

Muslim-Christian Conflict in Colonial Bengal

Bengali Muslim society was in a state of religious ferment, induced largely by purificatory movements. Two of the movements were particularly notable in this regard, namely, the Tariqah-i-Muhammadiya and the Fara'idi. Each had its own program of religious reform and political reorganization that created great controversy in Bengali Muslim society. At the same time, they alienated the British government and the Hindu *zamīndārs* and *jotedārs,* as well as the larger section of the Hanafi *'ulamā* and the aristocratic Muslims. The latter were generally known by the generic term *sābiqī,* literally the "traditionalists." Their conflict with the fundamentalists took a serious turn when the latter openly attacked some of the traditionalists' cherished religious institutions, such as *pīrism* and *mīlad mahfil. Mīlad mahfil* usually referred to a ceremonial gathering by Muslims on the birthday of the Prophet of Islam and came to be regarded as an essential feature of Sunni Islam in South Asia. The term *pīrism* had a more pervasive connotation and meaning that was associated with mystics and saints, either living or dead. The living *pīrs* considered themselves heirs to the mystic saints and were regarded as spiritual elites by ordinary Sunni Muslims. Their claims to religious authority as intermediaries between God and man were based on traditions, and they wielded great influence in the Muslim society. The reformist criticism of *pīrs* caused great excitement in rural Bengal in the nineteenth century and led to numerous publications of intracommunal polemical works in Musalmani Bengali. Contemporary Bengali literature demonstrates the intensity of this sectarian tension and points to the nature of debates between these groups.[1]

Although the militant leadership of the fundamentalist movements was effectively suppressed by the British by the 1860s, this did not put an immediate stop to the sectarian controversies. The issues that were particularly responsible for creating bitterness between the reformists and the traditionalists and within the ranks of each group were the two questions of *mazhab* (School of Islamic Law) and *dār-al-harb* (Zone of War). Whether *mazhab* was an essential feature of Sunni Islam and whether India under the rule of the British could be described as *dār-al-harb* were questions that agitated the minds of many. A period of debate was inaugurated in Bengal that was supported by a stream of sectarian writings. Even Maulana Keramat 'Ali (1800–74), who took a leading role in the propagation of the Tariqah-i-Muhammadiya doctrine, could not stay aloof from controversy; he seceded from the main movement over differences on the question of *dār-al-harb*.[2] Later Keramat 'Ali repudiated the reformist position regarding India being *dār-al-harb* under British rule and castigated them for their extremism on other issues. Debates on doctrinal issues touched almost everyone in Muslim society, and ultimately many became involved in these controversies. Munshi Meheru'llah was a product of this generation and could not escape involvement in these debates.

Most importantly, the active participants in the anti-Christian discourse were mostly members of the traditionalist Hanafi school. The reformist position on this issue remained obscure. Although they did oppose the traditonalists yet in the latter's fight against the missionaries, their presence was hardly noticeable. Partly this may be explained by the fact that the areas where the Christian missionaries were most active were far removed from where the reformists lived and worked. While the former mostly concentrated their activities in the border districts of West Bengal,[3] the latter were most active in southeastern Bengal and parts of West Bengal.

The reformists had two reasons for limiting their participation in the intercommunal debates with the Christians. First, they were more concerned with their own purificatory programs among the rural Muslims. Second, it was prudent to maintain a low profile during this period, one of repression by the British government following the 1857 Indian Mutiny—in which they were known to have taken an active part.[4] What is surprising, however, is that the reformist literature of the period did not even mention the Muslim-Christian debates. In any case, the initial response to Christian missionary activities in Bengal came principally from educated urban Muslims living in Calcutta and not from the *'ulamā*. They were outraged by the nature of Christian missionary propaganda against Islam; to them it was part of an overall

Christian strategy to undermine Islam. Their fears were compounded by some unfriendly English biographies of the Prophet Muhammad.[5]

Syed Ameer 'Ali (1849–1928) was one of the first among the few Western educated Muslims to react against Christian writings on Islam. Born in a Shi'ah family in Hughli in West Bengal, Ameer 'Ali was influenced by Maulana Keramat 'Ali. Educated in England, Ameer 'Ali composed works entirely in English to convince the West of the greatness and glories of Islam. Because he sought to establish the superiority of Islam over Christianity, he did not involve himself extensively with polemical writings against the Christian West. Thus, writing about the glories of Islam in Spain, he stated that were it not for Christianity

> Spain, at one time the favoured haunt of learning and the arts would not have become the intellectual desert it now is, bereft of the glories of centuries. Who has not mourned over the fate of that noble race, exiled by the mad bigotry of a Christian sovereign from the country of its adoption, which it had made famous among nations. Christianity drove the descendants of these Muslim Andalusians into the desert...and made the land a synonym for intellectual and moral desolation.[6]

But Ameer 'Ali had a basic cultural problem in communicating with the Bengali-speaking Muslims. He was a member of the traditional upper class (*ashraf*) Muslim society that regarded itself heir to the Imperial Mughal culture and looked upon itself as a foreign presence in India. Despite his great erudition and learning, he had a very poor understanding of the people of Bengal, among whom he was born and lived a considerable part of his life. Most Bengali Muslims were plebeians (known to the upper classes as the *atrap*, or the lowly born); they were separated from the *ashraf* by wide social and cultural barriers, one of the most important of which was language. Thus Ameer 'Ali's writings did not make the desired impact on the Muslim Bengalis of his time. His influence, however, was keenly felt by some English educated Muslims who were inspired by his references to the past glories of Islam.

Ameer 'Ali encouraged the *ashraf* to take a firm stand against Christian missionary propaganda and induced them to publish books in Bengali showing the greatness of Islam.[7] He thought this particularly important in view of the aggressive proselytizing activities of the missionaries in rural Bengal and the reported conversion of a number of Muslims. Thus Muslim periodicals increasingly began to take an interest in religious activities, urging Muslim preachers to fight against Christian propaganda. Those associated with the Calcutta periodical, *Sudhākar*, which published known Muslim writers like Shaikh 'Abdur Rahim (1859–1931), Muhammad Reazuddin Ahmad (1862–1933), and

Pandit Reazuddin Ahmad Mashadi (1859–1919), took measures to raise funds and organize Muslim preachers to counter the proselytizing activities of the missionaries.[8] In Calcutta, during 1890, they formed an association for this purpose known as the Islamic Mission Society and invited the educated urban Muslims as well as the *'ulamā* to cooperate. It was the first in a series of such attempts involving the *'ulamā* and the professional classes in a struggle to preserve the honor of Islam and to check the growth of Christianity.

It is doubtful, however, that the general response of educated Muslims was favorable to this program. The ultimate responsibility for confronting the Christian missionaries had to be shouldered by ordinary preachers whose dedication to the cause of Islam remained unquestioned. In a letter to the *Sudhākar* in 1889, Munshi Meheru'llah bitterly criticized the educated Muslims for their failure to respond to Christian propaganda. He wrote that it "was useless to hold sham religious meetings [to protest against Christian propaganda]. Men who whilst professing the faith of Islam can put up with the denigration of the Prophet are not worthy of the name of Musalman."[9]

Although there is no direct evidence of large scale conversions, we do come across the names of a number of prominent Muslims in the list of Christian converts and would be converts. Reverend John Tackle claimed in 1914 that "quite a large number gathered into the Bengal Christian Church from Islam. In nearly every district, there are to be found Moslem converts, and in most mission stations there are evangelists, catechists, teachers, colporteurs, or other workers who have discarded Mohammad and consecrated their lives to the services of our Saviour. In one district, *Nadia, there is a Christian community, at least five thousand of whom are either converts or descendants of converts from the Mohammedan faith.*"[10]

Although the presence of five thousand Muslim Christians in a single district sounds significant enough to arouse consternation among the Islamic community, the fact is that this was the result of years of hard work and certainly not the pattern everywhere. The number should not be considered too high for a community that claimed over twenty million adherents in 1901. Christian missionaries, working among the Bengali Muslims, acknowledged the slow rate of progress in conversion and the difficulties encountered by Christian preachers in a typical Muslim society.[11] The census reports and the district gazetteers of Bengal clearly suggest that in 1891 the majority of the Christian population in Bengal, which totalled 81,843 and included more than 26,000 European Christians, came from the depressed communities, such as the *namasūdras,* the *chandālas,* and the non-Hindu tribal groups. There were few conversions among the higher caste Hindus.[12] What, then, were the reasons for

Muslim alarm? A single important factor, perhaps common to all religions, was a sense of pride of the *'ulamā* in the superiority and the ultimate truth of the Islamic creed. Even a stray case of conversion could and did hurt community pride. When one Reverend Munro of Nadia reportedly converted a few Hindus and a Muslim youth to Christianity sometime in the 1880s, reaction was sharp and almost instantaneous, uniting Muslims and Hindus against the Christian missionary.[13]

The Muslim clergy, as well as members of the upper class, were always suspicious of such Christian activities as their humanitarian and educational programs. All these were considered part of a grand program of evangelization of the local population.[14] The extent of missionary involvement, particularly in health and educational matters, was so enormous that educated opinion in the country could hardly ignore the long-term consequences of the existence of Christian institutions.[15] This made them apprehensive, and ultimately they opposed even the humanitarian activities of these institutions. This apprehension was greatly responsible in deterring many well-to-do Muslims from sending their children to English schools, let alone to church-managed institutions.

What hurt the sentiment of the Muslims most was the nature of Christian missionary condemnation of Islam. In their attacks on some of the most fundamental aspects of Islam, such as the prophethood of Muhammad or the divine origin of the Qur'an, the missionaries aroused bitter reaction. Decrying such an attitude, Meheru'llah wrote:

> They preach that other than the Bible there is no revealed book in the world. They also suggest that none other than Jesus is sinless in this world; that only Lord Jesus is sinless and innocent.... The Christians are never shy of vilifying the thousands of saintly people of the world [who do not subscribe to Christianity].[18]

Christians chose their targets with a purpose. During the first half of the century, in the initial phase of their proselytizing, the missionaries experienced problems in convincing Muslims about the truth of the Gospel and became well aware of the Muslims' particular objections to Christian doctrines. These included arguments regarding the Christian concept of Trinity and the authenticity of the Bible. It was, however, the difficulty of the divinity of Jesus Christ that provided the greatest problem. As a Christian missionary later pointed out:

> What is the greatest stumbling block to a Moslem in the Christian faith? Is it not the very person of Jesus Christ, our Lord? Who was He? What significance shall we attach to him?[17]

Muslim reservations about Christian doctrines touched the basic foundation of that faith and could not be "fully replied to, without entering upon the entire range of evidences of Christianity before an audience wholly incapable of appreciating the critical arguments on which the genuineness of the books of the New Testament is based."[18] The Christian strategy in the later period was thus directed towards destroying the effectiveness of the Muslim position by condemning its very basis. They sought to achieve their purpose by twofold methods: first, by making a direct attack on the principal points of Muslim beliefs—notably the prophethood of Muhammad—and then, by asserting the divinity of Jesus Christ and the superiority of the Bible over the Qur'an by citing verses from the Islamic scriptures.

To gain the first objective, they often took recourse to the wildest criticism of the personal life of the Prophet. As Reverend Rouse wrote:

> Muhammad robbed the caravans of merchants, put men to death and kept many wives.... His wife 'Ayisha used to say that Muhammad was specially fond of women, sweet odours, and food. Is it right to give one's mind to worldly pleasures of this sort?[19]

In almost all Christian works of the period, this was the familiar pattern of attack. Muhammad was depicted as a sensual, worldly person, possessed of "several evil qualities." His marriage to Zainab, the divorced wife of his adopted son, Zaid, was often cited as an example of his sensuality. The purpose was to demonstrate to the ordinary Muslims that a person of such character could not have been a prophet.

In contrast, the sinlessness and divinity of Jesus Christ were constantly emphasized in all such writings. He was represented as the most beloved of God, the son of God, intercessor at doomsday, and the performer of miracles. Christ's purity was stressed to prove to a Muslim audience His greatness as compared to the Prophet Muhammad:

> Jesus Christ was never under the power of passion. He never looked upon any woman with an evil eye.... Jesus Christ had only good qualities and the Injil [the Gospel] contains nothing but truth. Therefore, brethren, cease to trust in Muhammad and the Quran, receive the Injil and exercise faith in Jesus Christ.[20]

The divine origin of the Qur'an was equally the target of attack:

> All acknowledge that the Taura't, Zabur and Injil [Torah, Psalms, and Gospels] are the word of God. It is clear therefore that the Quran which gives teaching contrary to the word of God, can not be itself the word of God.[21]

Many missionaries argued that the Prophet used the Qur'an merely to justify his actions, including his marriages; others mostly concentrated on questions of its authenticity and divine origin.

There were missionaries who argued more subtly by citing references from the Islamic scriptures. Thus the Qur'an was often quoted by those asserting the superiority of Jesus Christ to Prophet Muhammad and ultimately of Christianity to Islam. One of them wrote:

> Like any other human being Muhammad died of illness; but Jesus Christ sacrificed himself [on the Cross] for the salvation of the humanity. And while Muhammad still remains buried in his grave...the messiah Jesus rose from his grave on the third day, and, then, ascended to heaven after forty days. He will reappear again on the day of Judgement to preside over the final trial.[22]

Obviously these arguments were not intended for the consumption of the educated Muslim or the *'ulamā;* the ordinary person was the primary focus of this propaganda. As the latter knew little about his own religion, the Christian missionaries thought that any reference to the Qur'an in support of Jesus and Christianity would help influence him. To make the appeal more comprehensible to Muslims, the missionaries increasingly wrote in Musalmani Bengali, because of its popularity with rural Muslims. In fact, they borrowed idioms and expressions from similar works by the *mullāhs.* In order to better understand the Christian tracts of this genre, it is essential that we examine the character of the Muslim tracts whose popularity and appeal inspired the missionaries to produce similar tracts.

Generally referred to as Musalmani or Islami *pūthīs,* the origins of this literature may be traced to the labor in the mid-sixteenth century of the moderate *'ulamā* in Bengal. These were primarily didactic compositions, produced by men who lived closer to the ordinary people, often the rural *mullāh* and *pīr.* Their basic aim was the religious education of rural Muslims, who were ignorant of the traditional Islamic languages, Arabic, Persian, and Urdu. In doing this they deviated from orthodox practice by including Bengali, a language they associated with non-Muslims. Gradually this endeavor created a new type of Bengali poetry that drew heavily upon Islamic terms. By the middle of the nineteenth century, Musalmani *pūthīs* became the most powerful medium of communication between the Muslim clergy and the laity. The preachers of the reformist movements, in their drive to reach the unlettered masses, relied heavily on this literature and, in turn, encouraged the traditionalists to do so. Eventually it developed its own style, idiom, and mode of expression, different from the chaste Bengali of the towns.[23] The *pūthīs'* enormous appeal to the Muslim villagers made it necessary for the missionaries to take up this medium in order to convey the message of Christ. Reverend John Tackle later acknowledged that the missionaries produced and distributed free of charge "hundreds of thousands of tracts in Musalmani Bengali."[24] There was a basic difference in style, however, between the sets of literature produced by these two religions. While the *pūthīs* of the *mullāhs* were invariably composed in verse, the Christian tracts were written in prose, although the language used was Musalmani Bengali.

The Christian Bengali tracts that are known to us rarely discussed serious theological questions. On the contrary, they are mostly polemical in nature; their primary purpose was to destroy the image of Islam held by ordinary Muslims and then attract the readers to Christianity by emphasizing its superiority. These tracts were written in a popular style. It is difficult to assess the extent of popularity that they achieved in rural Bengal. What is known, however, is the reaction they caused among the more enlightened members of the Muslim community, particularly a section of the *'ulamā*. In 1839, an earlier reaction to Christian propaganda against Islam was demonstrated when a number of Reverend Pfander's disparaging religious tracts were circulated in Bengal. Rev. C. G. Pfander (1803–65) was one of the most aggressive evangelists who ever came to the sub-continent. He was attached to the Church Missionary Society at Agra and caused considerable controversy in northern India by his combative methods of propaganda. Some of his works, however, were distributed among Bengali Muslims, including: *Mīzān u'l-Haq* (The Scale of Truth), *Tariq u'l-Hāyāt* (The Way of Life), *Miftāh u'l-Israr* (The Key of Secrets), and *Thamārati Shajār u'l-Hāyāt* (The Fruit of the Tree of Life). They represented some of the earliest attacks on Islam by the Christian missionaries. Written in Persian, they reportedly "greatly excited" the Muslims "all over Bengal" and aroused the *'ulamā*, who were the target of these works. In return, the *'ulamā* prepared "tracts and books in opposition to Christianity" and sent "emissaries in every direction" to organize protests.[25]

It does not seem, however, that educated Muslims were the principal focus of Christian missionary activities at that stage. An 1842 conference of Christian missionaries in Calcutta acknowledged the "unwillingness" of learned Muslims to "listen to the preaching of the Gospel" and decided to concentrate their efforts elsewhere, primarily among the depressed communities.[26] After the Mutiny of 1857, when they renewed their efforts to convert Muslims—publishing religious tracts, addressing open gatherings, and encountering Muslim preachers in *bahās* meetings—educated Muslim reaction was quick and sharp. In effect, the Muslim preachers adopted the missionaries' own strategies and arguments to counter Christian propaganda. Thus, just as the missionaries had made the Prophet of Islam and the Qur'an their primary targets of criticism, the Muslim preachers singled out Jesus Christ and the Bible as the focal points of their attack.

Unlike the Christian missionaries, they had a severe problem in so doing. For Jesus was also one of the most important prophets of Islam.

Similarly, the Bible had a special place in Islamic belief, because none of the four revealed books, namely, the Torah, the Zabur, the Injil, and, finally, the Qur'an, could be denied. The Christian missionaries, on the contrary, felt no such scruple either for Prophet Muhammad or the Qur'an, and thus could freely indulge in open criticism. For the Muslim preachers the choices were complex: the status of Jesus and the Bible were well defined in the Qur'an and thus could not be made objects of contempt, and yet it was essential for them to repudiate the Christian concept of Christ's divinity and assert the superiority of Islam. Muslims had always paid respect to Jesus the prophet, his virgin mother, Mary, and the Gospels, but were aghast to see their prophet and the Qur'an distorted in Christian publications. Even during the period of the worst controversy with the Christian missionaries, their theological position did not change, although they found it difficult sometimes to restrict their polemics to a mere stricture of the Christian doctrines and spare criticism of Jesus Christ.

It was, however, the question of the father and son relationship between God and Jesus, the cardinal Christian belief, that they found wholly unacceptable. The Muslim position in this regard was explicitly based on pronouncements in the Qur'an that stated categorically that Jesus was no more than a prophet. In Chapter XIX, verse 88, it thus reads: "They say; [God] Most Gracious has begotten a son! Indeed, you have put forth a thing most monstrous." The birth of Jesus in the womb of a virgin mother is explained as a miracle—rather an expression of God's will and power:

> It is not befitting to [the majesty of God] that He should beget a son. Glory be to Him! When He determines a matter, He only says to it, "Be" and it is. (Chapter XIX, verse 35.)

In order to remove any misunderstanding in this regard, the Qur'an repeatedly describes Jesus as *Isā Ibnē Marium* (Jesus, son of Mary) and records him as saying, "I am indeed a servant of God; He hath given me revelation and made me a prophet" (Chapter XIX, verse 30).

The Muslim position on the relationship between God and Jesus was known only to those who were well versed in the Islamic scriptures. Ordinary Muslims, who were the objects of Christian propaganda, had little understanding of these delicate questions; perhaps they could be swayed by Christian arguments in favor of Christ because they were evidently derived from Islamic scriptures. The Christian missionaries could use advantageously certain verses from the Qur'an to substantiate their own position and repudiate Muslim claims. The author of the polemical work, *Hazrat Isā Masihēr Ilahiyāt O Insaniyāter Dalīl* (Evidence on the Divinity and Prophethood of Messiah Christ), devoted this book to the question of Christ's divinity and supported his arguments with Islamic theology. He concluded that Jesus was accorded a position superior to the Prophet Muhammad.[27]

Christian missionaries thus found the Qur'an an effective source of material that could support their position regarding the status of Jesus; the Muslim preachers found no such Biblical evidence in favor of their Prophet for the simple reason that Christianity predated Islam. Although the Bible was occasionally cited in Muslim writings, such as predicting the advent of Prophet Muhammad, but these references were often too distant and had merely an academic value compared to what was said about Jesus in the Qur'an. Therefore, Muslim preachers had to concentrate on demolishing the basis of Christianity by a direct attack on the concept of Christ's divinity. Their first task was to question the authenticity of the Bible. Once this could be achieved, they would have little trouble in questioning the very basis of Christianity. Thus dozens of polemical works were produced challenging the authenticity of the existing Bible. These were written both in Musalmani Bengali and modern Bengali prose; they used many of the same idioms and expressions that were being used by Christian advocates. While the missionaries continued to cite the Qur'an and Islamic theology, the Muslim preachers increasingly took recourse to the Bible to disprove Christian contentions. In consequence, an era of intense intercommunal religious debate—through literature, newspapers, *bahās,* and open-air meetings known as *waz mahfils* (propagatory meetings)— was inaugurated between the preachers of the two communities.[28]

The Career of Munshi Meheru'llah

Meheru'llah was born in the district of Jessore, then a part of the Presidency division. He had little opportunity of receiving a formal religious or secular education. His background was of genteel poverty. His biographical works indicate that his father, Munshi Waresuddin Ahmed, did not own any sizable amount of land and apparently depended mostly on his functions as a rural *mullāh* for his earnings. When he died he left no money or property for the upkeep of his family. Meheru'llah was barely nine or ten at that time and had to seek a livelihood when, under ordinary circumstances, he should have been studying at a *madrassah* or in a school. Although he could not attend school for any length of time, he mastered enough Arabic, Persian, and Urdu to undertake the work of a Muslim preacher and came to be recognized as an *'alim.*[29] He received immense moral support from his mother, who encouraged him to seek an Islamic education. He studied under Maulawi Mohammad Isma'il of Jessore, who maintained a private *madrassah* in the suburb of that town. Maulawi Isma'il initiated Meheru'llah to the world of Islamic learning, gave him basic training in the Islamic languages, and urged him to pursue further studies.[30] It was not, however, the Islamic scriptures alone that received Meheru'llah's attention. His writings on Christianity displayed a knowledge of the Bible, which he quoted profusely. This was no mean achievement for a man who received little formal education in a theological seminary. Bengali was Meheru'llah's mother tongue, and he never expressed reservations about its status as a Muslim language, as did many of his contemporaries.[31] In fact, he published all his works in Bengali, most of them in modern prose, and addressed his religious gatherings in that language, lending it respectability in the world of Bengali Muslims. He also learned a little English and Sanskrit in later life.

Meheru'llah began his career as a tailor in Jessore town sometime in the 1870s. But soon he found himself deeply committed to religious preaching, which, in time, became his dominating passion. Meheru'llah's life as a preacher started as a protest against missionary activities in his area. He confessed that at one point he was greatly influenced by them and had almost accepted Christianity but that later, after reading a number of treatises by Muslim theologians, he changed his mind—not his faith. Meheru'llah specifically mentions two such works that helped him: *Kshrīstān Dharmēr Vrastatā* (The Fallacy of Christian Religion) by Hafez Neamatu'llah, and *Injīl-i-Hazrat Muhammadēr Khabar Achē* (There is News of Prophet Muhammad in the Bible) by a former Christian missionary, Mohammad Ehsanu'llah. (These are typical polemical books that deal with a variety of issues relating to Christianity and Islam from the Muslim point of view.)[32] Thereafter, Meheru'llah decided to join a group of preachers and protesters who were actively engaged in organizing a counterpropaganda campaign against the missionaries. This group included men from different backgrounds and professions: newspaper editors, school teachers, and *mullāhs* from rural areas, as well as members of the *'ulamā*.

The concern felt by Munshi Meheru'llah about Christian proselytizing in Bengal was shared by many others of his time. This was a significant development in Bengali Islam, which was then sharply divided over sectarian issues. Technically Meheru'llah himself was a party to the sectarian controversies as a leading member of the Hanafi school who was known to have taken part in at least two *bahās* with the reformists.[33] Yet he never formally delineated his theological position on the questions that had agitated Bengali Muslims since the 1840s and 1850s; he made all possible efforts to remain above sectarian debates. His principal concern was the missionaries, and he considered his struggle with them more important than unnecessary sectarian conflict.

When Munshi Meheru'llah joined the anti-Christian debate in the eighties, he shared the concern felt by many of his coreligionists about the nature of Christian propaganda. Ultimately, no one played a more prominent and persistent role in the movement than Munshi Meheru'llah, and no one else contributed as profusely to Muslim polemical literature of the period. His life epitomized the dual needs of the time: first, to curb the influence of the Christian exponents on ordinary Muslims and, second, to reform and Islamize Muslim society from within so that it was strong enough to face challenges from without. His first tract, the *Kshrīstīya Dharmer Asāratā* (Hollowness of the Teachings of Christianity), published in 1886, was clearly inspired by what he termed as the Christian intolerance of Islam. "In the present-day world," he wrote, "there is a tendency amongst the preachers of different religions...to boast about the greatness of their respective faith. But none else can stoop so low and show such contempt for others' religions than the preachers of Christian doctrines."[34] As a devout Muslim, Meheru'llah made it his first priority to argue against the Christian concept of the divinity of Christ and to dispute Christian claims that the Bible was *the only* Book of God. He analyzed portions of the Bible, trying to provide examples of inaccuracies and inconsistencies, thereby suggesting that the original Bible, as revealed to Jesus, no longer existed.

In general, Meheru'llah's arguments reaffirmed the position held by Muslims on the spurious character of the present Bible, an accusation of which the Christian missionaries were not unaware. An earlier publication (1871) had stated:

> O Muslim friends! Many amongst those who believe in the religion of Muhammad suggest that the Christians have made many changes in the Bible. [But] there is evidence to show that the Jews and the Christians did not make any change in their holy Books [whatsoever], not even a dot.[35]

Reverend William Goldsack, writing a few years later, went further to challenge the Muslim contention in this regard by suggesting that such accusations were mere ploys on the part of the Muslim theologians to hide the changes and distortions that they themselves had made in the contents of the Qur'an. In his view, it was the Qur'an—and not the New Testament—that bore evidence of change and inaccuracy.[36]

Meheru'llah was undoubtedly reacting to such arguments in the Christian publications that denigrated the character of the Prophet of Islam and questioned the authenticity of the Qur'an. He was, however, careful not to direct his attack against "Jesus, the prophet" and made it clear that "the Christ of the Bible" was not the same person as "the Jesus, son of Mary," who, in his opinion, was a later innovation and possessing the vices of an ordinary person. As a strict monotheist, he found the concept of the Trinity incomprehensible and repugnant to logic and reason:

> If the father God and the son Jesus be one and the same, then, when Jesus was crucified by the sinners and he suffered untold agonies for three days, did God also die [on the Cross] and suffer similar pain during those days? If that be so, who was in charge of the earth and the heaven at that time?[37]

Meheru'llah was aggressive in making his points and had no hesitation in describing "the God of the Bible" as "a liar." His emphasis was, of course, on the spurious character of the Bible, which, he argued, could not be relied upon for a correct picture of God or the real Jesus. He repeatedly stressed the Muslim position regarding Jesus as being only a prophet secondary to Muhammad and lamented that the Christians had denigrated even the Creator Himself by associating a human being, Jesus, with His person. "Truly speaking," he declared, "Jesus is not God, he is a slave of God, and only a religious preacher. That is the truth."[38]

Meheru'llah further elaborated the point in a later edition of *Raddē Kshrīstān O Dalilol Islām* (Refutation of Christianity and Evidence on Islam) (1895). Here he refrained from making any disparaging remarks against the Bible, because he was using it to help make his point. "The Bible," he wrote, "points to the fact that Jesus spoke to God as father out of genuine affection, and he [Jesus] referred to all others as his brothers." Meheru'llah specifically referred to the New Testament, wherein Jesus is quoted as saying "go to my brethren, and say unto them, I ascend unto my Father, and your Father; and to my God, and your God" (John 20:17), to further substantiate his contention that Jesus was no more than a spiritual son of God.[39]

Evidently, Munshi Meheru'llah was addressing a largely Muslim audience—people who could have been influenced by Christian propaganda—to make the suggestion that there was no reason for anyone other than a biological father to be called a father. He argued that even if someone lovingly addressed a person as "father" for any special reason, it did not give that "son" the right to inherit; their relationship would continue to remain unreal. The question of the divinity of Christ so greatly agitated Meheru'llah that he devoted considerable time and attention to its discussion. In 1891, he encountered a number of missionaries in Pirojpur (district of Backergunj) and as a result published a series of articles in the Bengali periodical *Islām Prachārak.*

He constantly hammered on the issue, emphasizing the Muslim point of view.

It was his unflinching faith in monotheism that led Meheru'llah to take an uncompromising stand on the question of the divinity of Christ. He blamed the Christians, not Jesus Christ, for making claims contrary to the original formulation in the Bible by interpolating material into it, thereby distorting its meaning. In his opinion, the extensive alterations of the Bible were responsible for the fact that it now took two distinct and different forms: one for Catholics and another for Protestants. Christianity, in any case, had lost its relevance to mankind with the advent of Islam and thus the Bible stood abrogated.[40] Although Meheru'llah never questioned the position of Jesus as one of the great prophets of God, his desire to assert the superiority of Prophet Muhammad and the Qur'an sometimes made it difficult for him to restrain from making Jesus an object of criticism. "The missionaries," he wrote, "describe Jesus as the divine protector of peace of the world! Readers, he is that Jesus whose advent caused the death of thousands of innocent children in Jerusalem.... If he is the protector of peace to the Christians, we have of course to congratulate him!"[41]

With Meheru'llah, the questions of Christ's divinity and the authenticity of the Bible continued to be the principal concern in his writings as well as in debates with missionaries. His sensitivity to Christian criticism became obvious when, in 1892, Reverend John Zamiruddin (1870–1937), also known as Shaikh Muhammad Zamiruddin, published a pointed attack on the Qur'an. John Zamiruddin was one of those who had turned to Christianity in the 1880s, raising Muslim fears of large scale conversions. Born of Muslim parents, he was attracted to Christianity at an early age and was baptized in the year 1887. He received religious training in missionary schools at Krisnanagar and Calcutta, finally graduating in Christian theology from St Paul's Divinity College in Allahabad. He proved effective as a preacher among the Muslims and so was posted in Nadia, where he won the acclaim of the Church by converting a number of Muslims and Hindus. Recalling his own success, Zamiruddin later stated that his writings against Islam had created great impact among Muslims and helped him win many Muslim converts.[42] His attacks on Islam could be quite damaging in the eyes of many Muslims, because of his background and sound knowledge of Islamic theology. To make matters worse (for the Muslims), he quoted profusely from the Qur'an and the *hadīth* to substantiate his points. It was not, however, until he made the Qur'an a target of attack that the Muslim religious leaders reacted, and, not surprisingly, the first response came from Munshi Meheru'llah.

There was, however, nothing new in John Zamiruddin's arguments against the Qur'an; he relied heavily on the Reverend Pfander's *Mīzān u'l-Haq,* the Rev. Aminuddin's *Tāli-i-Muhammadī,* and partly on Reverend Jacob Kanti Nath's *Eslām Darshān.* Many others joined the attack in the same period in their effort to establish the superiority of the Bible, but no one before Zamiruddin had made such a pointed attack on the Qur'an on the basis of evidence from the *hadīth* and other sources of Islamic theology. Munshi Meheru'llah's prompt reply was characteristically sharp. The debate that ensued created a stir in Muslim society, raising new issues and bringing into clear focus the nature of Muslim-Christian controversy in Bengal.

In the offensive article, "Asal Kor'an Kothaye" (Where is the genuine Kor'an?), published in June 1892 by the Calcutta Christian journal, the *Kshrīstīya Bāndhab Patrikā,* Zamiruddin acknowledged the divine origin of the Qur'an, but argued that it had lost its originality and authenticity by later interpolations of material and the sectarian controversies between Shi'ahs and Sunnis. He contented that 'Usman, the third caliph of Islam, purposely destroyed certain chapters of the Qur'an that eulogized 'Ali, who was the fourth caliph of Islam, and the son-in-law of the Prophet of Islam. Zamiruddin referred to the alleged differences in the contents of the Qur'an of the Shi'ahs and the Sunnis; he cited a specific example of a chapter, Suratu'n Nuraīn, which, he said, formed part of the Shi'ah Qur'an, but was absent from the Qur'an available to Sunnis. Later researchers, as well as Shi'ah sources, revealed the spurious character of the chapter, invented by a fanatical Shi'ah, with no basis in the authentic traditions.[43]

In his reply to Zamiruddin, Meheru'llah was extremely critical and described him as a "misguided wretch." In two separate articles, published in the weekly *Sudhākar,* entitled "Kshristani Dhoka Bhanjan" (The Exposition of the Fraud of the Christians), Meheru'llah charged that Zamiruddin had distorted the meanings of *hadīth* only to please his European patrons. He challenged Zamiruddin to substantiate his contention that the Shi'ahs and Sunnis had different versions of the Qur'an and offered to disprove it. Meheru'llah dealt with the specific points raised by Zamiruddin, analyzed his arguments with evidence from the *hadīth,* and concluded that the Qur'an had remained unchanged all through the period of its existence. His defense of the Qur'an extended further to a refutation of the genuineness of the Bible and to an assertion of the authenticity of the Qur'an. "If for some reason," he wrote, "all the written documents, and stone inscriptions etc. of the world were to vanish, no religious scripture [other than the Qur'an] would remain intact. It is only the Qur'an which would survive in all its beauty."[44] Meheru'llah thus presented himself as a zealous Muslim preacher, deeply committed to the defense of his faith and willing to challenge the Christians directly. "Christian friends!" he wrote, "swear by your religion and say if the Bible will survive a similar test?" Zamiruddin did not reply; he soon renounced Christianity and returned to Islam to serve as a lifelong companion to the Munshi and wrote profusely against very *pādrīs* (missionaries) to whose ranks he once belonged.

While polemical writings formed the core of Muslim propaganda against the Christian missionaries in Bengal, the two sides occasionally met in open public encounters or *bahās*. Public debates were not new nor were they uncommon in the Bengali Muslim society; but intercommunal disputations were rare occurrences that served little useful purpose.[45] On the contrary, these meetings could be potentially explosive, leading at times to communal tension and violence. During this period the missionaries were particularly reluctant to debate their opponents in predominantly Muslim areas, although a number of such encounters did take place.

At the beginning of his career as a preacher, Munshi Meheru'llah had occasion to meet his Christian opponents in a number of *bahās*. This is how he was first initiated into the program of Islamic reform. The details of these encounters are not often mentioned in his biographical works, making it difficult for us to assess their nature and content. Those mentioned include an 1891 debate at Pirojpur, in the district of Backergunj, which was attended by "hundreds" of enthusiastic Muslims of the locality. The *bahās* lasted three days, as leaders of the two communities raised various issues, often provoking each other to react sharply. The questions that featured prominently in the debate were the genuineness of the revelation to Prophet Muhammad (queried by the Christians) and the divinity of Jesus Christ (questioned by Munshi Meheru'llah). The missionaries allegedly failed to satisfy the predominantly Muslim audience with their replies on the question of the divinity of Christ, and the missionaries left the meeting quickly.[46]

In 1897, Munshi Meheru'llah was invited by the Muslims of Ranaghat in West Bengal to dispute religious issues with the missionary Reverend Munro. There were allegations that Munro had converted the local Hindus and Muslims to Christianity by offering humanitarian services to the poor. This included services in a charitable dispensary and a small hospital where free medicine and treatment were dispensed. Munro allegedly published a number of religious tracts aimed specifically at the Muslims, who were despised by the local *'ulamā*. But the immediate cause prompting local Muslims to organize a debate was the conversion of a Hindu and a Muslim youth to Christianity. The debate, however, did not take place. The reason is not known, but Muslim sources suggest that Munro refused to take part in the *bahās* at the very last moment without explaining why. There is no independent account of this event to verify exactly what happened. There was great tension in the locality on this occasion, and the venue of the *bahās* filled with thousands of zealous Muslims eager to witness the "victory" of their religious leaders. Even the Hindus reportedly converged on the scene in large numbers, where they hoped to see the humiliation of the *pādrī* who had converted some of their coreligionists.

An interesting dimension was added to the pattern of Muslim-Christian religious confrontations when Munshi Meheru'llah and a Christian missionary from Noakhali debated in writing. The dates of this written encounter are not known, nor do we know why they did not meet in open debate. The contents of this written debate, however, form an integral part of the polemical literature of the period and were published in 1897 under the title *Jawābunnāsarā* (Replies to Christians). The questions addressed concerned basic issues of Christianity and Islam, such as the relative greatness of the Prophet Muhammad and Jesus and the authenticity of the Bible and the Qur'an. Altogether, thirty-three questions were enumerated by the missionaries, and Meheru'llah took pains to reply to these in great detail. He relied heavily on the Bible for his arguments and frequently quoted it to substantiate his points. The usual emotion shown in his other works is absent here, and he made no attempt to denigrate the Bible or Jesus Christ; he showed extraordinary restraint in view of the prevailing tensions between the two religions.[47] Although this was not strictly a *bahās,* it assumed such a character when the questions and answers were widely circulated in the Noakhali area by members of the local *'ulamā.* In certain respects, this written debate served a more useful purpose than the ordinary *bahās* meetings, because it addressed more substantive issues than is possible in a *bahās.*

Munshi Meheru'llah did not debate only with the missionaries on doctrinal matters. There were two intracommunal *bahās* between the *'ulamā* of the reformist Muhammadiya movement and the traditionalist Sunni Muslims; Munshi Meheru'llah attended on behalf of Sunnis. One such meeting took place in Keshabpur in 1899. The reformists were represented by three of their leading *'ulamā:* Maulawi Rahim Baksh, Maulawi Hafez 'Abdullah, and Maulawi Abbas 'Ali. After a heated discussion on the question of *mazhab* (schools of Islamic law, namely, Hanafi, Hanbali, Shafie, and Maleki), on which the two sides held widely differing views, the debate ended without reaching a decision. Although Meheru'llah was present as a representative of a particular school, he did not favor such sectarian debates at a time when, in his view, the integrity of Islam was threatened by external enemies. Therefore, he appealed to the parties to forget their mutual differences and forge greater unity for the sake of Islam.[48] Describing Meheru'llah's role at a similar *bahās* in Bogra, the local magistrate wrote: "The feeling of the two sections [the Hanafi Sunnis and the reformists] had...grown so bitter that they both applied to me for protection. The Munshi, however, delivered excellent lectures on the necessity for reform of the Musalman community and gave offence to none. Now and then, he threw a word at the Hindus telling them that the Muhammadan religion does not inculcate the duty of making war for the spread of religion or of killing the kaffir if he would not accept 'the true faith.'"[49] Indeed, this correctly reflects the mind of the Munshi; he was willing and ready to defend his own religion at any cost, but would not involve himself in unnecessary sectarian conflicts that little served the interests of his people or his faith.

Religious debates, whether intercommunal or intracommunal, proved increasingly sensitive and were gradually abandoned. The public attending a debate was often excited and sometimes armed; the presence of the police or of the magistrate, which was quite common at such gatherings, did little to help create a congenial atmosphere for a meaningful presentation of religious issues. As suggested, Meheru'llah himself did not rely much on these public gatherings to propagate Islamic ideals, or even to counteract the activities of the missionaries. These forums, however, served some useful purpose in influencing popular opinion by disgracing the missionaries in public. Victory was almost inevitable in a situation where the audience was composed largely of Muslims. Such meetings could also be used as occasional demonstrations of strength by the dominant group to reassure public confidence, especially when their opponents were believed to enjoy the support of the British Raj. The reason that particularly induced the Muslim *'ulamā* to participate in intercommunal *bahās* was to project an image of their own abilities to destroy the effectiveness of their opponents. In this strategy, the Muslim preachers were undoubtedly successful.

For the ordinary public, these occasions had another and different dimension—that of providing fun and entertainment in an otherwise monotonous rural life. The manner in which the debates were often conducted, including the questions asked and discussed, made it obvious that the combatants (specially the dominant group) played to the gallery more than answered serious theological questions. Challengers were increasingly averse to participate in a *bahās* because the outcome was often predetermined in an inter-communal debate. A preacher like Meheru'llah could, with his oratorial skill, easily sway public opinion in his favor, no matter what was discussed. While giving an account of the encounters between Munshi Meheru'llah and the Christian missionaries, Muhammad 'Abu Talib, a recent biographer of the Munshi, confirmed this view of the nature of intercommunal debates. Although the basic issues of contention between the two sides continued to be the question of the relative greatness of Muhammad and Jesus and the authenticity of the Bible and Qur'an, the discussions centered round other popular themes. Thus on one occasion a Christian missionary asked Munshi Meheru'llah to explain the logic of calling Muhammad the greater of the prophets when the latter was not even chosen by God to ascend to heaven, whereas Jesus Christ's ascension to heaven is accepted even by Muslims. The Munshi replied that God raised Jesus to heaven because of his insignificance compared to Muhammad; a lighter substance readily jumped into the sky, while Jesus, a heavy thing, would have remained on the ground [had he not been raised up by God]. The Christian missionaries were equally adept in taking recourse to similar popular arguments in debates that hardly touched fundamental theological questions.[50]

Meheru'llah thought that imparting basic religious training to Muslims was the most effective means of counteracting Christian propaganda. He had before him examples of men like Shaikh Zamiruddin who, he felt, had renounced Islam due to a lack of proper understanding of the faith. Mere propaganda against the missionaries was thus not enough to protect the integrity of Islam; the important thing was to strengthen the religious foundation of the community, and awaken in the community a consciousness of Islamic identity. Thus Meheru'llah embarked upon a dual program of actively teaching among the Muslims of rural Bengal and of writing anti-Christian polemics. He addressed religious gatherings or *waz mahfils* in distant places, and wrote manuals of religious instruction.

Unlike the contentious *bahās,* the *waz mahfils* (propagatory meetings) were peaceful assemblages designed to educate the masses in the basic tenets of Islam. Meheru'llah used these effectively to counter Christian propaganda as well as to instill a sense of confidence among his coreligionists. His biographical works contain references to a number of such *mahfils,* which he addressed; they attracted people from all levels of the society, including members of the Hindu community. In one instance, Meheru'llah turned a proposed *bahās* with the Reverend Mr. Munro into a *waz mahfil* when the latter failed to arrive. On another occasion, a planned *bahās* between the Sunni *'ulamā* and the reformists was transformed into a joint *waz* by the preachers of the two groups at Meheru'llah's initiative. At these gatherings the topics were not limited to religious issues: intercommunal problems—even political questions—formed part of the preachers' sermons. In a meeting in Rangpur in 1898, Meheru'llah dwelt at length on the question of cow protection, which had been bedeviling communal relations between the Hindus and Muslims for some time, and he reportedly impressed the Hindu *pandits* with his arguments.[51]

Meheru'llah was largely responsible for popularizing the *waz mahfīl* as an effective medium of communication with the masses. His charisma and oratory impressed the ordinary people. Educated urban Muslims were equally swayed by his sermons and attended these meetings in large numbers. Senior Muslim officials often took pride in chairing meetings addressed by the Munshi; and there is at least one instance of a *mahfīl* in Noakhali town when the English district magistrate presided over it. One of Munshi Meheru'llah's unknown admirers stated that the Munshi created such a momentum in the religious life of Bengali Muslims through his *waz mahfīls* that people of all classes and opinions felt impelled to attend his meetings. Referring to the 1898 *mahfīls* in Noakhali, he wrote:

> The first *waz* was held at the Jubilee School premises making everyone happy. The second *waz* was held in the Town Hall...attracting judges, collectors, magistrates, *munshīs, maulvīs,* and *'ulamā* of all persuasions. Well known Hindus (of the locality) and a number of Christians also attended.[52]

Increasingly, preachers and politicians recognized the importance of *mahfīl* in reaching the people and took recourse to this unique medium of communication. Rev. William Hart, who worked in Bengal during this period as a missionary, mentioned that even the missionaries tried this medium to propagate the gospel of Christ among the local people, though with limited success. He wrote that the Muslim preacher was often a "strikingly patriarchal figure" attracting "a much larger congregation than the Christian evangelist in another part of the same square."[53]

Of equal importance was Munshi Meheru'llah's efforts to communicate with rural literates through religious tracts. The first example of his effort in this direction was the *Meher ul-Islām,* published in 1895. Written in Musalmani Bengali, the book gives details about the basic religious beliefs and observances of Islam, for example, faith, prayer, fasting, and ablution. Meheru'llah's aim in writing the book was simple: to try to impart a basic understanding of Islam to the untutored Muslims. He referred to the activities of the Christian missionaries and explained that religious education was necessary to counteract Christian propaganda. For the same reason, he also established a religious seminary, known as Madrassah-i-Karamatia, to train younger people to continue the work that he initiated.

Meheru'llah's reformatory measures were, however, not confined to educating the ordinary person; these were equally directed toward the conservative upper class Muslims and also Hindus. His treatise on widow marriage, *Vidhabā Ganjanā O Vishād Bhandār* (The Persecution of the Widows and the Depository of Sorrow), was highly critical of both these classes for their social conservatism and attitude towards widow marriage. By quoting profusely from Manu, the ancient Hindu law giver, he sought to show that remarriage of widows was permitted in Hindu law. He, however, emphasized that it was not the Hindus alone who maltreated their widows. Even in many Muslim households[54] "countless young widows are leading an unbearable life."[55] Shaikh Zamiruddin recorded that the publicity received by the book created a great impact in society and resulted in the remarriage of a number of Muslim women from conservative families.[56]

In effect, Munshi Meheru'llah's total efforts were directed toward a single objective: the glorification of Islam. He believed in the ultimate truth of the Islamic creed and was convinced that it was only through a proper appreciation of those principles that it could meet its external enemies—in particular, the Christian missionaries. He not only sought to counteract Christian influences on Muslims, but thought it equally important to reform the Muslim society from within. In this effort, he found willing allies in the ranks of Maulana Keramat 'Ali's disciples, notably his son Maulana Hafez Ahmad and Pir Shah 'Abu Bakar of Furfura. Meheru'llah also worked closely with the *Sudhākar* group in Calcutta. Those involved with this group were among the pioneers in organizing a countercampaign against the proselytizing activities of the Christians. They published a number of valuable works in Bengali, collected funds to support rural preachers, and held protest meetings. One of their first publications was *Ēslām Tattva* (The Substance of the Religion of Islam), a Bengali translation of a Persian work by the great proponent of pan-Islam, Jamaluddin al-Afghani (d.1897). This was followed by other works in Bengali written to impart useful information on Islam, particularly to the educated Muslim youth. It was, however, the weekly *Sudhākar*, after which the group was named, that played the most important role in rousing Muslim resentment against Christian missionary activities. It printed stories about conversions and the nature of Christian propaganda side by side with attempts to project the image of Islam by referring to its greatness, its principles, and its glories. To the *Sudhākar*, Munshi Meheru'llah was a valuable partner and collaborator; and this partnership continued uninterrupted until his death in 1907.

What made the role of Munshi Meheru'llah particularly significant in the rural-urban dichotomy in Muslim Bengali society was his close contact both with the educated in the towns and cities and the masses in the countryside. He was an equally familiar presence in rural *bahās, waz mahfils*, and at meetings of Muslim educational committees and conferences held in towns to promote Muslim education. He acted as an effective link between the urban Muslims and their rural coreligionists. Although he was not educated in a traditional religious *madrassah* and technically was not a member of the elite *'ulamā*, his position as an *'alīm*, a learned Islamic scholar, was never in dispute. The *'ulamā* never expressed any reservations about his qualifications and, on the contrary, joined him on many occasions in *bahās* and *waz* meetings. It is, however, not clear why he was always addressed as a *Mūnshī*, a term reserved for the lesser clergy, and not a *maulānā*. Even his most dedicated admirers never preferred a higher appellation for the man who was almost a legend in his own lifetime.

In Summary

Our discussion leads us to several important conclusions. It is worth remembering, however, that Muslim response to Christian polemics during the period was part of a more general reaction to the impact of Western colonialism. The earlier manifestations of Islam's challenge to Western domination and Western ideas was through reform movements seeking to organize the Muslims on the basis of a definite ideology. Those who did not agree with the reformists in their views and program, either opposed them or kept aloof but did not generally collaborate with the rulers. After the suppression of the Mutiny in 1858, the situation changed, and Muslim opinion became divided in its attitude towards the colonial rulers. In general, the *'ulamā* maintained a distance from the Raj and continued with their work of Islamic reform. Christian missionary campaigns among the Muslims in the later nineteenth century only helped to reinforce their suspicions about the real motives of the Christian rulers, and made them particularly sensitive to the question of Muslim identity. Defenders of Islam responded to the proselytizing activities of the missionaries in two ways: first, they met the missionaries face to face to arrest their growing influence among certain diverse classes of Muslims, and second, they asserted Islam's superiority to Christianity. The challenge to the proselytizing activities came immediately through the efforts of itinerant preachers and a section of the educated urban youth who organized Muslim protests against the missionaries and tried to impart useful information on Islam to the average Muslim.

Christian polemics against Islam were similarly countered by a direct attack on Christianity itself, particularly the concept of the Trinity and the authenticity of the Bible. In this, they were only following their Christian counterparts, who earlier had initiated a campaign aimed at destroying the effectiveness of Islam by denigrating the character of the Prophet of Islam and questioning the authenticity of the Qur'an. The Muslim polemical writings that followed were duplicated in every detail. Although a thin line of distinction was sought to be drawn between "Jesus, the Prophet," and "Jesus the Lord," often it was quickly forgotten. One must remember that polemical writing had only one objective in view. At that stage each side sought only to challenge the validity of each other's arguments, defend its own respective positions, and, in the case of the Muslims, mobilize the people under their own banner.

Munshi Meheru'llah occupied a central position among the Muslims of Bengal involved in anti-Christian crusade in the nineteenth century. He had an unflinching faith in the superiority of Islam and thought it his duty to protect it against Christian attacks. To this end, he endeavored to rid the Muslim society of conservatism, sectarianism, and non-Islamic pitfalls, somewhat like his great North Indian contemporary Sir Sayyid Ahmad Khan (1817–98), although the two men worked in totally different contexts and situations. Meheru'llah preferred to stay within the bounds of orthodox Islam that Sir Sayyid transgressed by an excessive admiration of Western ideals and values. Munshi Meheru'llah was virtually unconcerned and unimpressed by them. His principal concern became the defense of Islam, and he remained committed to this task while he contributed significantly to the polemical literature intended to defend his own faith. Although his language and style of writing did not quite remain confined within the bounds of decorum, his contributions to Bengali Islam cannot be ignored. He was an extraordinary man in many ways and did more to counteract the influence of Christianity than any other single individual. Although he lacked clarity of views on many subjects, this mattered little in a social context where groups made little effort to understand each other.

At the social level, Muslim-Christian polemics in Bengal had the undoubted effect of creating new tensions and diffusing old ones. While the debate between the preachers of the two religions turned acrimonious, with serious theological issues receding into the background, it also contributed to a gradual lessening in sectarian tension within the Muslim community. As the *'ulamā,* belonging to differing schools, became more and more involved with their Christian opponents, the intensity of sectarian issues lost momentum, although it was not resolved. In the districts where the Christian exponents were particularly active, such as Jessore, Khulna, Faridpur, Pabna, Backergunj,

Burdwan, Maldah, and Murshidabad, there was an appreciable decline in sectarian tension. This was in marked contrast with the situation in the 1840s through 1870s, when intracommunal quarrels in the Muslim society threatened the integrity of the community. Muslim-Christian polemics in Bengal thus added a new dimension to the social situation and provided the *'ulamā* with a common cause. It also induced a large number of educated urban Muslims join hands with the traditional *'ulamā* in defense of their faith, and ultimately to become involved in a program of reform and Islamization.

Bibliographic Essay

The primary sources used in this chapter consist mainly of what have come to be known as the Musalmani-Bengali vernacular tracts, both polemical and liturgical, which also include Christian missionary tracts produced in the same local tradition. Although this formed a significant part of a rich heritage in Bengali literature, the apathy of the educated elite towards it—their urge to identify themselves closely with the modern Bengali prose created in the colonial tradition and the debate whether to regard these tracts as part of their heritage—has left this material virtually untouched and unutilized for historical research. This is specially true of the Muslim-Christian polemical writings in Bengal, thus creating a void in our understanding of the historical significance of these nineteenth-century intercommunal religious debates.

A pioneering work, partly addressing this issue, is Anisuzzaman's monumental work in Bengali, *Muslim Mānos O Bānglā Sāhitya* (Dhaka, 1964). While analyzing the character of the Musalmani-Bengali vernacular tracts, the author raises pertinent questions on the nature of popular response of Bengali Muslims to colonial rule and offers appreciable insights into the dynamics of social and political change. Others, whose contributions either preceded or followed his, for example, M. A. Hai and S. A. Ahsan, *Bānglā Sāhityēr Itivrītta* (Dhaka, 1956), A. R. Mallick, *British Policy and the Muslims of Bengal, 1757–1856* (Dhaka, 1966), Sufia Ahmed, *The Muslim Community in Bengal 1884–1912* (Dhaka, 1974), often failed to appreciate the merit of popular response to colonial rule and could only give a circumscribed account of the developments. A. F. S. Ahmed's *Social Ideas and Social Change in Bengal, 1818–1835* (Leiden, 1964), and M. Mohar Ali's *The Bengali Reaction to Christian Missionary Activities, 1833-1857* (Chittagong, 1965) are useful in assessing the initial response of the mainly Hindu elite, but they only give a partial view of a very complex situation and can be used primarily for background study.

For an understanding of the developments in the Muslim society of Bengal at the popular level, Muinud-Din Ahmed Khan's *History of the Farā'idī Movement in Bengal, 1818–1906* (Karachi, 1965) is extremely useful. Equally important is his study, *A Bibliographical Introduction to Modern Islamic Developments in India and Pakistan, 1700–1955, Appendix to the Journal of the Asiatic Society of Pakistan* (Dhaka, 1959). Wilfred Cantwell Smith's *Modern Islam in India* (London, 1946) remains a classic example of a pioneering effort in assessing the Muslim position under British rule in an all-India context. M. T. Titus's *Indian Islam* (London, 1930) provides useful background information. Among later publications, Aziz Ahmad's *Studies in Islamic Culture in the Indian Environment* (Oxford, 1969), and Peter Hardy's *The Muslims of British India* (Cambridge, 1972) are significant contributions and worth examining.

There is, however, an apparent lack of interest among these authors in studying the mind of the *mofussil* Muslims, those who lived in rural or semi-urban areas. One of my earlier works, *The Bengal Muslims 1871–1906: A Quest for Identity* (New Delhi, 1981, 2nd edition, 1988), was in part an attempt to examine the developments in the rural Muslim society of Bengal in the nineteenth century; but intercommunal religious polemics did not feature prominently in my discussions. Barbara Daly Metcalf's *Islamic Revival in British India, Deoband 1860–1900* (Princeton, 1982), covers significantly new ground in this regard, although in the North Indian context, and provides interesting details about the nature of Muslim-Christian religious debates in nineteenth-century India (especially in chapter 5). Annemarie Schimmel's *Islam in the Indian Sub-continent* (Cologne: Leiden, 1980) makes an equally useful survey (in chapter 6) of the pattern of Muslim intellectual response to Christian writings on Islam.

However, the basic material that needs to be examined in any study of the Muslim-Christian religious polemics is the vernacular literature. It is amazing to find dozens of these tracts in the Bengali holdings of the British Library in London, the National Library of Calcutta, and in the different collections in Bangladesh. The richness of this material and its importance in understanding the tension in the rural and semi-urban Bengali Muslim society in the nineteenth century is beyond question. Although the literature lacks sophistication and discipline, it does give an unadulterated view of the developments. Yet no one seems to have ever taken note of these valuable historical sources.

To understand the nature of Christian missionary polemics against Islam in Bengal, one must specifically refer to the vernacular tracts that they produced in Musalmani Bengali. The most representative works of this genre are: *Muhammadī Dharmer Vīsayē Kathabārtā* (1870), *Allahtālār Nabi Haibēr Dalīl* (1871), *Hazrat Isā Masihēr Ilāyāt O Insaneyāter Dalīl* (1876), *Isā Masihēr Pesh-khabarī* (1877), *Islāmē Kor'an* (1906), and the English version of a vernacular tract, *Tracts for Muhammadans,* edited by Rev. G. H. Rouse (1913), the original of which I could not trace. These were all published in the nineteenth century as part of an overall Christian missionary campaign in Bengal to win converts from among the ordinary Muslims.

Munshi Meheru'llah's writings epitomize the typical reaction of the *mofussil 'ulamā* to missionary attacks on Islam. His polemical works thus constitute the basic material for understanding the Bengali Muslim point of view. The *Kshrīstīya Dharmer Asāratā* (1886), *Raddē Kshrīstān O Dalīlol Islām* (1895), and *Jawābunnāsarā* (1897) are important in this genre. His works on social reform and religious education include *Meherūl Islām* (1890) and *Vidhabā Ganjanā O Vishād Bhandār* (1897).

Participating in the debate were the Christian missionary journals and the Muslim press. *The Calcutta Christian Observer* and later *The Moslem World* generally outlined the missionary position and are immensely informative. The educated Muslim opinion was similarly represented by the *Sudhākar* (later renamed the *Mihīr O Sudhākar*) and the *Islām Prachārak,* both published from Calcutta. Munshi Meheru'llah's articles in both the journals are particularly important. Anisuzzaman's bibliographical study on the Bengali Muslim press, *Muslīm Bānglār Sāmayīk Patra* (Dhaka, 1969), is helpful in locating the right material in these journals.

The three early biographical works on Munshi Meheru'llah, namely *Meher Charīt* (1909) by Shaikh Muhammad Zamiruddin, *Meheru'llāhr Jivanī* (1914) by Muhammad Asiruddin Pradhan, and *Karmavīr Mūnshī Meheru'llāh* (1934) by Shaikh Habibur Rahman, are highly informative. Shaikh Muhammad Zamiruddin, who worked in close concert with Munshi Meheru'llah in his later life, also contributed profusely to the stream of Muslim-Christian polemical writings in the early twentieth century. These have not been covered in the present study and may be fruitfully used in any further examination on the subject.

While the literary sources provide indispensable information on the nature and contents of the religious controversy between the Christian missionaries and the Bengali Muslims, the Bengal volumes of the Census Reports of India for 1881, 1891, 1901, and the relevant volumes of the Bengal District Gazetteers are more than useful in analyzing and quantifying the developments during the period. One may also refer to the Annual Reports of the Bengal Administration for specific information.

However, in a bibliographical note one can merely hint at the rich variety of material that exists. Any exhaustive study on the subject would require a deeper understanding of the dynamics of rural Bengali Muslim society and social change in colonial India to a much wider degree than is the scope of the present study.

Note on transliteration of Muslim names in Bengal: Most Muslim names mentioned in this paper are typical Indianized Arabic names, for example, Meheru'llah (for Mihir 'Allah), Zamiruddin (for Zamir al-Din), etc. I have preferred to retain the Indianized names without going for the orthography of Arabic spelling.

SECTION THREE

Hindu-Muslim Struggles Over Language

Six

Images of Virtue and Vice: The Hindi-Urdu Controversy in Two Nineteenth-century Hindi Plays

Christopher R. King

The Historical Context

In the November 1902 issue of *Saraswati*, the leading journal of the Hindi literary world for many years, appeared a drawing of two women. On the left stood a Muslim prostitute, decked out in all the finery of her profession. On the right, facing the other, sat a Hindu matron, modestly clothed in an ordinary *sārī*. The caption "Hindi-Urdu" and the verses below clearly showed that on the left stood Urdu personified, and on the right sat Hindi.[1] This picture illustrated one of the main themes of several decades of controversy between Hindi and Urdu speakers as expressed by the supporters of Hindi—that Urdu, and the Urdu script[2] promoted fraud, deceit, and other vices, while Hindi and the Nagari script[3] enhanced truth, honesty, and similar virtues.

In this chapter we will explore one side of the Hindi-Urdu controversy through a comparison of two polemical Hindi plays, both written during the late nineteenth century. To understand them more deeply, we must also place them in the context of the linguistic, political, and social conflict from which these works arose. After an introduction, which provides an historical setting, the reader will find a complete translation of the shorter of the two plays, followed by a systematic comparison of both works.

The Hindi-Urdu Controversy

From one point of view, the origin of the Hindi-Urdu controversy of nineteenth and twentieth century North India might be traced back to the medieval Muslim invasions of India and the resulting Indo-Persian linguistic synthesis which came to be known as Urdu. In a recent book an Indian scholar posits another possible origin. He argues that the excessive Persianization of Hindi/Hindavi, formerly the common literary medium of Hindus and Muslims alike, led to a dramatic linguistic and literary split.[4] Yet another explanation could be sought in the language policies of the East India Company, which in 1837 replaced Persian as the official language of much of India with English and various vernaculars. In North India this meant that a highly Persianized Urdu written in the Urdu script replaced Persian written in the Persian script, a minimal change. All three historical events point to one indubitable fact: Urdu grew out of and symbolized a joint Indo-Persian culture. When that culture came under increasing attack in nineteenth century North India, Urdu could hardly escape.

The more immediate origins of the controversy, which began in North India in the 1860s, lay partly in contradictory language policies. On the one hand, the government encouraged the growth of primary and secondary schools using two mediums of education, Hindi and Urdu. On the other hand, it discouraged the use of either Hindi or the Nagari script for official purposes. As a "vernacular elite" (those Indians educated chiefly in Hindi or Urdu and looking to government service for their livelihoods) began to develop with the spread of government schools, a clash of interests proved inevitable, a clash which took an increasingly communal form.[5]

One of the first major expressions of this conflict appeared in a memorandum written in 1868 by Babu Shiva Prasad of Banares, a prominent advocate of the Nagari script.[6] Prasad opened his statement with an emphatic declaration of the antiquity of Hindi, went on to accuse the former Muslim rulers of North India of forcing Hindus to learn Persian, and then castigated British language policy, "which thrusts a Semitic element into the bosoms of Hindus and alienates them from their Aryan speech."[7] Moreover, he continued, this policy "is now trying to turn all the Hindus into semi-Muhammadans and destroy our Hindu nationality."[8] Prasad concluded with a plea for the government to drive the Persian script from the courts and put Hindi in its place.

In the next three decades, the Hindi-Urdu controversy in the North-Western Provinces and Oudh flared up and died down several times. While vernacular newspapers provided the major forum, the opposing sides quickly seized other opportunities. For example, the Hunter Commission (known thus after its chairman, Sir William Hunter) was appointed by the Government of India in 1882 to review the progress of education in India, and it had no mandate to investigate or decide on the respective merits of Hindi, Urdu, or other vernaculars as mediums of education and government business. Nevertheless, in the North-Western Provinces and Oudh, Hindi, and Urdu advocates used the Commission to promote their respective causes.[9]

A major portion of the debate focused on the question of the proper language and script for government courts and offices. Hindi supporters argued that: the great majority of the population used Hindi; the introduction of the Nagari script into government courts and offices would give them considerable impetus to the spread of education by enhancing their prospects for government service and that experienced Nagari writers could write as fast as their Urdu counterparts. Further proponents of Hindi argued that the Urdu script had a foreign origin that made court documents illegible, encouraged forgery, and fostered the use of difficult Arabic and Persian words. The protagonists of Urdu maintained that: even the inhabitants of remote villages spoke Urdu fluently; the official script and language had no relation to the spread of education; and Nagari writers could not write as fast as Urdu writers. The Urdu language had originated in India even though its script may have come from outside. They maintained that any script could lend itself to forgery, that dialects of Hindi lacked standardization, and that Hindi had an impoverished vocabulary, especially for scientific and technical terms.[10]

In the North-Western Provinces and Oudh, however, the Hindi-Urdu controversy reached new heights when the government issued a proclamation in April 1900 ostensibly granting equal status to both the Nagari and Urdu scripts. A deluge of shocked and amazed protests arose from Urdu supporters who quickly rallied to hold massive protest meetings. Simultaneously, the joyful approval of Hindi supporters flooded the vernacular press. So intense did feelings become, that the language figures for the 1901 census were vitiated. Yet when all the tumult had died down, the April resolution amounted to little more than a symbolic victory for the proponents of Hindi, for the government had ordered only the *permissive* use of the Nagari script, not the *exclusive* use. In actual practice, Urdu remained dominant in most, if not all, districts of the North-Western Provinces and Oudh until independence in 1947.

Behind these political events lay a long history of social developments dating back to the early nineteenth century. A comprehensive description of these lies outside the scope of this chapter. We can, however, summarize the principal facts by presenting the status of Hindi and the Nagari script in the North-Western Provinces and Oudh during the last decades of the nineteenth century. Hindi's subordinate position in government courts and offices contrasted with Urdu, which was well entrenched in the higher reaches of administration. Hindi predominated on the lower levels of education, as compared with Urdu's superior status on the higher levels. Hindi was associated with Sanskrit learning and past resistance to Muslim rule. The Brahmans, Rajputs, and Baniyas held an inferior position in government service and opposed Urdu, upheld by Muslims and those Hindu castes, chiefly Kayasths, with a vested interest in Indo-Persian culture and a well-protected position in government service. Hindi whose stronghold lay in the eastern part of the province, where the Hindu merchant tradition was more powerful, contrasted with Urdu whose strength lay in Oudh and the western part of the province where the Indo-Persian service tradition was more dominant. Hindi, with centers of publication in the eastern districts, increasingly outpaced Urdu, with its centers of printing in Oudh and the western districts. Finally, Hindi and Urdu were studied almost entirely by high-caste Hindus and Muslims, with the great bulk of the illiterate population speaking regional or local dialects.

In sum, then, we might embody all the foregoing in a series of dynamic equations. At the beginning of the nineteenth century Indo-Persian culture dominated in North India, and the equation, Urdu equaled Hindus plus Muslims, was widely accepted. At this time Hindi, in the sense of a highly Sanskritized variety of the regional dialect Khari Boli hardly existed, though there was a potential for its creation. By the 1860s, however, this equation began to be challenged by the Hindu castes mentioned above, and two newer equations emerged, namely, Urdu equaled Muslim and Hindi equaled Hindu. Both the older and the newer equations continued to exist side by side during the lengthy Hindi-Urdu controversy, with the newer equations eventually triumphing almost completely with the independence of India.

More than any other factor, the ineradicable differences between the Urdu and Nagari scripts made the Hindi-Urdu controversy an intractable one. While the grammars of Hindi and Urdu were almost identical, and while their vocabularies on the everyday level of discourse overlapped considerably, the two scripts focused and heightened the differences between the Hindu and Indo-Persian cultures. Like different channels from two cultural reservoirs, they allowed the influence of Sanskrit, and Arabic and Persian, to pour separately into Hindi and Urdu, bypassing the existing linguistic mixture found in everyday speech. This artificial irrigation created highly Sanskritized Hindi and highly Persianized Urdu, almost mutually unintelligible, served to distinguish the rival Hindu and Indo-Persian cultures from each other. We will find the uncompromising Hindu view on these languages embodied in the two plays under review.

Pandit Gauri Datta's Play

The first of our plays, dating from sometime between 1883 and 1900,[11] consists of dialogues in Khari Boli verse interspersed with narrative sections in Khari Boli prose. While the author has included some Sanskrit words, he has also introduced numerous words of Persian or Arabic origins, especially in the dialogues spoken by the partisans of Urdu. The entire action of the play, written in the folk theatre tradition of *swāng,*[12] takes place in a courtroom over which a Hindu judge, Maharajah Righteous-Rule, presides. In an inversion of the actual power structure of society at the time typical of the *swāng,* the judge brings the case to a close with a decision, based on sacred Hindu law, in favor of Nagari.[13]

The author, Pandit Gauri Datta, had an unusual career. A Saraswat Brahman, he earned his living by teaching until the age of forty, when he renounced his career, made over all his property to the cause of Nagari, and became a *sanyāsī,* spending the rest of his life in this cause. Wherever a fair or festival took place in the area around Meerut, there he would be found with a crowd of boys behind him, speaking on the virtues of Nagari. He helped to found several Nagari schools, authored school books as well as a dictionary and this play, published a monthly Hindi newspaper, the *Devanagari Gazette,* and became the president of the Devanagari Pracharini Sabha (Society for the Promotion of Devanagari) of Meerut.[14] Where other Hindus used the greeting "Jaya Ram" (victory to Rama), he used the greeting "Jaya Nagari ki" (victory to Nagari).[15]

The Translation

A Mime of Hindi and Urdu[16]
namely
A Play of Hindi and Urdu[17]

Pandit Gauri Datta, the President of the Devanagari Pracharini Sabha, Meerut, has written this in such a way that whether it is shown as a mime or as a play, it will turn out very well in either case. Those who have staged it as a mime and as a play have been very pleased with it. Wherever it may be presented as a mime or as a play, send a letter to us and we will publish it in our Sabha paper. You will be pleased, and you will make those who promote Nagari in this country happy when they hear the news.

Meerut

1) The well-known Pandit Hardev Sahay, editor
2) Vidyadarpan Press Manager Munshi Kalyanray, printer
Government Schoolmaster Pandit Ramnath, publisher

Appear, Shri Ganesh, I bow to thee

In this country of Aryas when this country's kings ruled, there was the light of truth, there was the beneficent influence of good deeds, there were not even names for secrecy; fraud, ingratitude, deception, bribery, and other evil deeds, the king and his subjects were happy, and the sounds of joy were heard.

The reason for this is that Queen Devanagari held sway over all works of wisdom and virtues: letters and papers, account books and bonds, notes and official documents, and all the business of the country was carried on through Queen Devanagari. What is to come cannot be forestalled. To the misfortune of the country, because of evil deeds its rule was turned topsy-turvy, the monarchs of the west [Muslim rulers] became this country's monarchs and along with them came a certain Begam Persian. In the kingdoms of the rajahs the rights that had been Queen Devanagari's became those of Begam Persian. After a little while Begam Persian bore a daughter who was named Urdu. With the establishment of English rule the position of Begam Persian was taken by Begam Urdu. Justice demanded that Queen Devanagari should receive this position; for this reason from this very time the quarrel of Begam Urdu and Queen Devanagari began. This quarrel grew and grew to such an extent that it was necessary to go to Government. Many among the people were advocates of Queen Devanagari; some backed the cause of Begam Urdu. But Doctor Hunter Sahab made a bad decision.[18] Things were to remain as they had been. Then Queen Devanagari went to the abode of Maharajah Righteous-Rule [*dharmrāj*] and lodged a complaint against Begam Urdu, and from there [Maharajah Righteous-Rule's abode] a completely favorable decision came about.

Doha[19]

Keeping his attention on God[20] above alway,
May Gauri tell of Urdu and Nagari in a play.

Chauvola

Gauri wrote a mime, and Gauri told a tale.
He thought much, knew much, wrote with great travail.
Happiness and peace to him who gives this play,
To him who sings and plays it, happiness alway.[21]

The Beginning of the Mime or Play

Maharani Devanagari chose Babu Moral-Law [*karmma*] Singh for her lawyer and wrote the power-of-representation document thus:

Doha

For my lawyer here Karmma Singh I claim.
Arya [Hindu] land's my place, Nagari's my name.

Chauvola

I have given my power to Karmma Singh, pleader.
Whatever he does, in that he's my leader.
Whatever he says, that I have said,
And whatever he pleads, that I have plead.

Babu Moral-Law Singh, lawyer, wrote a petition on behalf of Empress Devanagari and presented it in the court of Maharajah Righteous-Rule. Chitraguptaji,[22] the chief writer of Maharajah Righteous-Rule, read it aloud as follows:

Doha

Urdu has taken that which belonged to me.
Now let it be restored to me, wretched Nagari.

Doha

Where now Urdu rules was all mine, this land.
I beg now for a piece no larger than your hand.

Chauvola

Oh Maharajah Righteous-Rule, officer and judge,
Such a heavy chain's on me that I cannot budge.
Offices and state business—for these I won renown;
Urdu now has taken these and turned them upside down.

Maharajah Righteous-Rule ordered that a copy of the petition and a summons be sent to Begam Urdu.

Doha

Urdu defendant, Nagari plaintiff; to such a state have
matters come.
Send out the summons and sift through the case, in my
very own court in my kingdom.

Chauvola

Write out an order and sent it to Urdu to come and
present herself here.
Tell her to search out and bring all her witnesses;
they may appear without fear.
When she is present, I'll give out an order to let all
the business begin.
Whoever deserves it will surely receive all the business
of state, she can win.

When this summons reached Begam Urdu, she made Mirza Tricky [*fitarat*] 'Ali Khan Sahab her lawyer. His power-of-representation document was written in this manner:

Doha

Tricky Ali, very smart, he is my lawyer, see?
Pleasant in his chit-chat and devoted to his duty.

Chauvola

Tricky Ali has agreed me to represent;
No matter what he says or does, I know I'll not repent.
Whatever he may say here in front of all of you,
As far as I'm concerned you may consider it as true.

Mirza Tricky 'Ali Khan Sahab wrote a defendant's statement on behalf of Begam Urdu and presented it in the court of Maharajah Righteous-Rule. The most excellent Chief Reader Chitraguptaji read it aloud in this manner:

Doha

My mother Persian, intelligent and clever;
All the emperors here trusted her forever.

Doha

Maharajah Ranjit Singh whose name was many splendored,
Caused the workings of his state to be in Persian rendered.

Chauvola

From the time that the English became India's kings
Urdu has gotten their trust in all things.
Urdu's profession, so pleasingly, refined;
Urdu's held sway here, time out of mind.

When the plaintiff, the accused, the lawyers of both, and the witnesses of both gathered in the court, then Maharajah Righteous-Rule ordered that the testimony of the complainant Maharani Devanagari should be presented. Maharani Devanagari gave her testimony thus:

Doha

Nagari's my name and wisdom, virtue are my work.
Consider this to be the truth: from these I'll never shirk.

Athvola

This is my work: I'll teach that which is right,
I'll speak only truth, run from lies in a fright.

Continue your business and have a good time;
Learn your work, acquire riches, be wise in your prime.
No falsehoods or fraud will dare come close to me;
The sound of my name will make weep bribery.
My word will be valued as true as can be;
All men will be good and will learn Nagari.

When Maharani Devanagari's testimony had finished, Maharajah Righteous-Rule ordered that now Maharani Devanagari's witnesses testimony be taken. First of all, Maharani Heavenly-Dame [*vidyādharī*] was called and testified as follows before Maharajah Righteous-Rule:

Doha

All who live between the Ganges and the Jumna know
That truth for me is duty, and lies I overthrow.

Chauvola

Nagari is the model of knowledge and virtue;
She will shed the light of truth on me and on you too.
Everyone here knows that this land belongs to her;
Everyone agrees she's good and wise—except a cur.

Then Maharani Abode-of-Truth [*satya dhāmā*] was called and her testimony before Maharajah Righteous-Rule was given thus:

Doha

The officers all present here certainly must know
To speak the truth of sages is my duty here below.

Chauvola

Hear, great king and judge, our Nagari's a true lady;[23]
Use *her* for all your business, and there'll be nothing shady.
Here's where Nagari dwells, here her own dear country;
Here our queen was born, in sacred holy Kashi.[24]

Then Maharjah Light-of-Knowledge [*jyān prakāsh*] was called and standing before Maharajah Righteous-Rule gave his testimony as follows:

Doha

Nagari is most wise and her wisdom knows no bounds;
Nagari is a servant who faithfully makes her rounds.

Chauvola

Our Nagari, fount of wisdom, the ruler of this place.
All who sit here have agreed she's wise and full of grace.

This country here which Urdu seized belongs to Nagari;
This vile intruder Urdu's brought our queen great misery.

Then Maharajah Righteous-Rule ordered that Sir Maharajah Merciful [*shrī mahārāj dayāvant dayārām*] be called and his testimony taken. Sir Maharajah gave his testimony before Maharajah Righteous-Rule in this way:

Doha

Mercy, basis of religion; Nagari, wise, not naughty.
Nagari, who shines out truth; Nagari not haughty.

Chauvola

Since my birth, I must declare, I've always truly known
That Nagari is a lady true,[25] that Nagari is my own.
This country here belongs to her; hear this well, great king:
Nagari has helped so many, helped in everything.

When the witnesses of Maharani Devanagari, the plaintiff, had finished their testimony, Maharajah Righteous-Rule commanded that now the testimony of Begam Urdu, the defendant, be taken. Begam Urdu stood before Maharajah Righteous-Rule and presented her testimony as follows:

Doha

Persian is my mother, Urdu is my name.
Here my birth took place, and here I will remain.

Athvola

This is my work: passion I'll teach,
Tasks of your household we'll leave in the breach.
We'll be lovers and rakes, living for pleasure,
Consorting with prostitutes, squandering our treasure.
Give heed you officials, batten on graft,
Deceiving and thieving till riches you've quaffed.
Lie to your betters and flatter each other,
Write down one thing, and read out another!

When the testimony of the defendant, Begam Urdu, had finished, Maharajah Righteous-Rule ordered that her witnesses should give their testimony.

First of all, Begam Urdu's witness Begam Wanton-Pleasure [*ishrat*] was called before Maharajah Righteous-Rule and gave her testimony in this way:

Doha

All have love for Urdu, ask anyone you want.
No one cares for Nagari, Nagari old and gaunt.

Chauvola

Urdu's friends before us; all are dandies, fops;
Nagari's friends, alas, all illclad and just slobs.
See how nicely Urdu performs her pleasant task;
Plunged in wanton pleasure, she gives you all you ask!

Then Begam Lady Twenty-Nine Delights [*bi vahar unnisa*] was summoned to give witness for Begam Urdu and coming before Maharajah Righteous-Rule she gave testimony thus:

Doha

When Lady Urdu came to us, this desert became a garden;
She brought flowers, spring, and blossom—think of this and
pardon.

Chauvola

Listen, O great king: now there's dance and merriment,
Night and day instruments play, all to passion bent.
Such a sale of wine and flesh goes on and on these days;
Come down to the market, have good food, good girls,
good plays.

Then Nawab Passion-Addict [*ishak bāz*] Khan was called as a witness for Begam Urdu and, appearing before Maharajah Righteous-Rule spoke thusly:

Doha

Brahmans, Kshatriyas, Vaishyas, all dwellers in this land,
Had no fun in knowledge, virtue, charity—how bland!

Chauvola

The instruments of passion in towns where'er you look;
Urdu's caught the kings here with her baited hook.
Let's all enjoy pleasure, and revel in luxury.
Burn up these tired old virtues—come have fun with me!

Then Begam Urdu's witness Emperor Ease-Lover [*bādshāh arām shāh*] was called and, going before Maharajah Righteous-Rule, gave the following evidence:

Doha

Were there such pleasures before? Did we so enjoy spring?
Did we ever have time before for such a magnificent fling?

Chauvola

To what delusions and snares Urdu leads!
All leave their studies, their worship, their beads.
Nothing but merriment, dancing, and fun,
While disciples their *gurus* abandon and shun.

When Begam Urdu's witnesses had all finished their testimonies, Babu Moral-Law Singh, Maharani Devanagari's lawyer, said to Maharajah Righteous-Rule, "My client wants to say something in person." The order was given for her to speak, and Maharani Devanagari, weeping and sobbing bitterly, related her misery and affliction in such distress and in such an agitated tone that Maharajah Righteous-Rule's heart was filled with tears and all the spectators began to weep.

Ragani

A great disaster's fallen on me; from you, oh Urdu, this contumely!
You've taken my kingdom forcibly; now look at you giving me mockery.
You've taken my wealth, you've taken my riches; now you sit so proudly and scornfully.
A great disaster's fallen on me; from you, oh Urdu, this contumely!
I ruled in the gates of palaces, all the kings of that time found me lovely.
Demanding my exile this usurper Urdu, banished lovely me most speedily.
A great disaster's fallen on me; from you, oh Urdu, this contumely!
See my home now, see my condition now; this from Urdu's enmity.
Now we'll see how she wriggles out of this, how she tries to explain her trickery.
A great disaster's fallen on me; from you, oh Urdu, this contumely!
At the door of the great king Righteous-Rule, from Nagari comes this plea:
Oh let my kingdom be returned to me; I throw myself on your mercy.
A great disaster's fallen on me; from you, oh Urdu, this contumely!

Maharani Devanagari's lawyer Babu Moral-Law Singh made a request of Maharajah Righteous-Rule thusly: "I wish to make an appeal on behalf of my client." The order was given for him to speak. He said:

Bhairavi

All the people will be happy!
When Nagari receives her kingdom back, every house will fill
with glee.
Righteous-Rule will do her justice; he supports her graciously.
All the people will be happy!
Men and women, all will dance and leap and clap most joyfully.
They will sing such pretty songs, and speak to all so pleasingly.
All the people will be happy!
With drum, guitar, and tinkling cymbals, clapping hands they'll
sing so sweetly.
If Lady Nagari should sing, oh ho! what clapping there would be!
All the people will be happy!
The age of falsehood[26] will become the age of truth[27] for all to see.
Fraud and guile will disappear, falsehood too will vanish quickly.
All the people will be happy!
All will eat and feed the Brahmans, good works will increase by three.
All the boys and girls in school will study Nagari.
All the people will be happy!
Quarrels and hatred soon will end, all will clever come to be.
Friends will come from enemies, all will live in amity.
All the people will be happy!
Knowledge will be shared by all, there will be no enmity.
Wisdom will belong to all, error soon will cease to be.
All the people will be happy!

Then Begam Urdu's lawyer Mirza Tricky 'Ali Khan Sahab made a request of Maharajah Righteous-Rule thusly: "I too wish to make an appeal on behalf of my client." The order to speak was given. He said:

Doha

Name and place in Nagari?[28] Can't read, will lead astray.
Banish Urdu? Harmful! Restore her place today.

Chauvola

All the English lords who came to rule us here,
Recognized our Urdu as queen for many a year.
For offices and courts, Nagari will not do;
Were she to do our work here, all would go askew.

When the plaintiff, the defendant, the lawyers, and everyone else had spoken (when the debate had finished), Maharajah Righteous-Rule, taking paper and pen, made his decision and read it aloud thusly—decision:

Doha

Now I'll write the verdict, I'll do the work of state.
Today this case will end as sacred Hindu laws dictate.

Athvola

This is Nagari's country, and Nagari is its queen.
Both parties spoke as one on this, clearly is this seen.
All spoke of many injuries received from Urdu's hand;
All spoke of Nagari's virtues, Nagari great and grand.
If Urdu should confess, then see, she'd weave a spell
She would destroy the truth, and further falsehoods tell.
Nagari's good friends, we've seen them here today;
All, concerning Urdu, had nothing good to say.

Maharajah Righteous-Rule, having written his decision thus, at the end wrote this final order and read it aloud:

Doha

Now we've looked at every side, we hand down this decree:
It's the means to right all wrongs in this our fair country.

Chauvola

All of Urdu's faults have here today been shown,
So we cast her out of here, let her be alone.
Nagari had no faults, yet Nagari suffered wrongs.
Now my decree the law will be: this land to her belongs.
Here ends the play or mime of Lady Devanagari.

Munshi Sohan Prasad's Play

The second of our two plays, *Hindī aur Urdū kī Larāī* (A Fight between Hindi and Urdu) dates from 1886. The author, Munshi Sohan Prasad, taught school in Gorakhpur district in the northeastern region of the North-Western Provinces and Oudh. The first edition of his play, which is written in Avadhi verse with a sprinkling of Khari Boli, appeared in pamphlet form during the first half of 1885. It aroused a considerable controversy between Hindus and Muslims in several of the eastern districts. Prasad's alleged disrespect towards the second caliph, Umar, in this edition led to a criminal prosecution against him by several Muslims of Gorakhpur. Muslim opponents and Hindu friends of Prasad both raised subscriptions for legal expenses, but the two sides eventually reached an amicable settlement when Prasad agreed to burn the whole first edition and to strike out the objectionable verses in the forthcoming second edition.[29]

Prasad's play, which ran to a little over four hundred couplets, consisted mainly of a dialogue between Hindi and Urdu, personified as two women. English (also personified as a woman) listens to both sides of the quarrel and adjudicates. The comments of the author, which provide the opening and closing of the play as well as a brief interlude in the middle, take up most of the remainder of this work. Only a few minor lines are left for Muslims, Urdu-loving Hindus, and Hindi-loving Hindus. Unlike Datta's play, in which no direct confrontation between the two protagonists occurred, short heated exchanges between Hindi and Urdu take up the first two-thirds of Prasad's work, giving each play a different "rhythm." Datta carries us quickly to the more controlled atmosphere of the court of Maharajah Righteous-Rule, while Prasad waits until the last third of his play to have English step in as a supposedly neutral arbitrator.

The greater intensity of pace in Prasad fits well with a greater intensity of language. As the play progresses, Hindi and Urdu hurl more and more insults at each other. Some of these insults take the relatively mild form of unflattering comparisons. Thus Hindi tells Urdu:

> The lion can't live with the dog, nor can he live with the jackal.[30]
> If I were to live with you, people would scornfully cackle.[31]

Other insults express extreme hostility and physical violence in graphic terms. Thus Hindi says to Urdu:

> Now if you keep talking I'll cut you in two.
> I'd spit in your face if Aryas [Hindus] ruled you.[32]

Still other stanzas describe the extreme emotions of both characters when reacting to each other's taunts and jibes.

The play reminds one of nothing so much as a long exchange of *gālī* (insults) very similar to Prakash Tandon's description of quarrels between village women in the Punjab:

> Minutest details from the past were brought out and painted in word pictures of the most damaging colours, with ogress, eater of her dead children, eater of husbands, immodest, burnt, drowned, all generously used as adjectives.[33] Sometimes in the heat of the fray, a casual thrust might draw blood from a spot unknown and unsuspected by the person dealing the innocuous blow. The victim would burst into a long wail and sob bitterly.... The neighbours would rush to the side of the defeated in genuine solace, while the victor was left shamefaced with a hollow victory, protesting that she did not realise.[34]

The vitriol Prasad's two protagonists express towards each other, however, surpasses anything Tandon describes, and the eventual victor, Hindi, is triumphant rather than shamefaced, while the loser, Urdu, wins no sympathy from any except her own partisan supporters. The charm and light-heartedness which prevail in Datta's work are lacking in Prasad's play, which possesses a heavy, didactic, humorless flavor. Despite these contrasts in tone, the two plays have much in common; let us turn to a systematic comparison of their similarities and differences.

The Two Plays Compared

Similarities

Neither play leaves us in any doubt that the author intended his work to be polemical. Hindi or Nagari[35] emerges victorious whether the judge is Hindu or English. The speeches given to Hindi/Nagari and her supporters outnumber those of Urdu and her supporters by roughly two to one. Moreover, the speeches of Urdu and her friends do her more harm than good. In Prasad's play, for example, Urdu several times boasts of her ability to change the shape of words and taunts Hindi with her dullness in sticking to one meaning per word. For example:

> Not even two words out of one from you; you haven't a drop of cunning.
> Thousands in seconds from me before all; my performance is nothing but stunning![36]

In Datta's play, what Urdu considers her strengths count only as vices in the eyes of the lovers of virtuous Queen Nagari. Prasad takes this one step further when he has Urdu protest her innocence publicly:

> Listen to my words, Hindi, please to lend an ear;
> You blame me without reason, you only want to jeer.[37]

but later confess her guilt to herself:

> Muslims, Hindus, and English, if they learn the truth about me,
> All will rally to Hindi, and defeated I will be.[38]

Clearly both authors stack the odds against Urdu in terms of virtue versus vice.

While Datta does not explicitly say that Urdu is a prostitute, her testimony and that of her witnesses certainly imply that. Prasad goes further and puts a direct accusation into Hindi's mouth:

> Leave your husband for another, and you become a whore.
> Virtuous women ne'er behave thus. Listen you whore and more![39]

Whores like you wander here and there, bringing men under their thrall.
When they live with you then they lose their duty, their religion, their all.[40]

The theme of Urdu's corrupting versus Hindi's ennobling influence runs through both plays. The same theme appears in other contemporary sources. For example, Bharatendu Harishchandra, a major figure in the nineteenth century Hindi literary world and a leading citizen of Banaras, gave the following testimony before the Hunter Commission[41] in 1882:

> There is a secret motive which induces the worshippers of Urdu to devote themselves to its cause. It is the language of dancing-girls and prostitutes. The depraved sons of wealthy Hindus and youths of substance and loose character, when in the society of harlots, concubines, and pimps, speak Urdu, as it is the language of their mistresses and beloved ones.[42]

Clearly the vices of Urdu portrayed in the two plays come from widely held assumptions about the moral contexts in which the language was used.

Each play looked back to a golden age before the damaging influence of Urdu and Muslims, a time when Hindu kings ruled India and Nagari/Hindi[43] held sway in courts and offices. For each author this period, like the *Rāmarājya* (the righteous rule of Rama) of Hindu mythology, saw virtue reign supreme. Truth, goodness, justice, devotion, honesty—all these and other virtues characterized this marvelous age. Poets garnered fabulous rewards in those days, Hindi tells Urdu in Prasad's play; she even mentions that the Mughal Emperor Akbar rewarded the Hindi poet Bihari Das with an immense sum for writing a single volume.[44]

Apparently, a shared—although never explicitly stated—assumption of both authors was that part of Hindi/Nagari's virtue stemmed from her indigenous origins, which fit her to the country and the people in a way no outsider could ever hope to match. Similarly, both shared the view that Urdu's origins made her the tool of alien interests, fit only to corrupt or destroy the values of indigenous culture. Prasad repeatedly put the contemptuous Sanskrit word *mlecch,* with its strong connotations of foreign, barbarous, sinful, uncultured, and impure, into the mouth of Hindi in reference to Muslims and Urdu.

In Datta's play, Muslim rule initiated an age of oppression, of free reign for all of Urdu's nefarious tricks.[45] Similarly, Prasad has Hindi express the evils of Muslim rule and the harm wrought by Urdu.

Many Turkish[46] emperors oppressed the suffering folk.
Alexander [*sic*], Aurangzeb, Ala-ud-Din; their yoke.[47]
The people of this country are wretched from your hate.
When you stand before your Maker, dread will be your fate.[48]

Urdu's central fault, which dwarfs all the others, lay in her vaunted ability to manufacture several words out of one, and Hindi recites eight stanzas of the misreadings of various words by Urdu to prove her point to English. With some pride, Urdu compares herself to a fashion-crazy woman who changes makeup and clothes from one moment to the next.[49] Hindi condemns her for behaving like a corrupt and unchaste woman.[50]

How then did Muslim rule and Urdu succeed in fastening themselves on India? Datta only mentions "evil deeds" in passing, while Prasad labels Hindu disunity as the cause that allowed this catastrophe. Only through Hindu unity could India cleanse herself of the impurity and corruption brought through Muslim rule. And only through Hindu unity would Hindi once again assume her rightful place.

In both works, the restoration of Nagari and Hindi to their rightful places would mean the return of the golden age, the regaining of all the previous virtues. In this estimate of the situation, both plays echo another passage in the memorandum of Shiva Prasad previously mentioned: "Cursed be the day which saw the Muhammadans cross the Indus; all the evils which we find amongst us we are indebted to our 'beloved brethren' the Muhammadans." In short, only the entire elimination of Urdu's position would suffice. Neither of the plays offers a hint of compromise: no middle ground existed between virtue and vice, just as no compromise script[51] existed between Nagari and Urdu. No joint Hindu-Muslim cultural tradition could or should exist.

Given the irreconcilable differences between Hindu and Muslim, Hindi and Urdu, which our two authors insisted on despite the obvious existence of many Hindus with a foot in each camp, both Datta and Prasad turned to a third party to resolve the conflict. Although supposedly neutral, this third party in both cases favored Hindi/Nagari from the beginning and ultimately decided in her favor. This wishful thinking reflected the exact opposite of the power situations of that time. Hindu rulers could not make Hindi/Nagari the official vernacular of British India, and the Government of the North-Western Provinces and Oudh had no desire to bestow the sole proprietorship of courts and offices on Hindi/Nagari, despite official encouragement of the development of a large class of Hindus educated chiefly in Hindi. As these plays suggest, only the restoration of Hindu rule could bring about the complete ascendance of Hindi, and this had to wait until 1947.

Differences

While both authors use the device of an outside arbiter, the characters of the two judges are quite different. Maharajah Righteous-Rule decides on the basis of Hindu sacred law, looking backwards to the golden age. English, on the other hand, claims a decision on the basis of rationality:

> English thinks repeatedly, from many viewpoints, widely.
> Between these two here—Hindi, Urdu—a monstrous gap I see.
> Then calling both of them to her, she spoke to them quite frankly:
> I'll speak the truth, sans taking sides, and for my truth you'll thank me.
> I'll tell of you what's good and bad, so please do not get irked.
> I've searched my heart and taken thought, no effort have I shirked.[52]

Yet this supposed rationality masks a strong bias against Urdu. From the very beginning of the process of questioning, English makes plain where her sympathies lie: all but one of her questions to various witnesses elicit Urdu's faults, not her virtues. In the artificial world of polemical literature, rationality and logic serve to destroy the enemy.

While Datta has Maharajah Righteous-Rule decide for Queen Nagari, Prasad, speaking as author, addresses a long plea to contemporary Hindu monarchs who neglect their royal duties:

> This is Hindi, this her country, once they reigned supreme.
> Wealth and wisdom, mighty kingdoms—now it's but a dream.
> And now our kings without a care waste money on loose women.
> Nor do they think that Hindi weeps, nor cows to death are driven.[53]

These rulers cheerfully gave to churches and to town funds, but bestowed not a penny for the progress of their country. The great rulers of the past always thought for Brahmans, cows, and the poor, but those of the present sit inactive and show no pity. If ten or twenty kings became united, they could protect Hindi, cows, and country.

Prasad's tirade against contemporary Hindu rulers suggests that they, like numbers of other Hindus (especially Kayasths) had only lukewarm feelings towards Hindi/Nagari. Indeed, this forms one of the major themes of the play, which the author emphasizes by giving a few lines to an Urdu-loving Hindu to explain the attractions of Urdu:

> In his mind he thinks like this: Now nothing but lies from me.
> If I don't speak up for Urdu now, I'll lose my job speedily.[54]

When English commands this Hindu and a Muslim to swear oaths on their sacred books, however, they feel compelled to tell the truth:

> With Urdu you change but a dot and everything's turned 'round, alas!
> With Hindi, however, each word reflects back its shape like a glass.[55]

In short, Prasad suggested that Hindus like the Kayasths found themselves compelled to support Urdu for economic reasons, against their own better judgement, since the offices used Urdu as the official vernacular. Several times Urdu taunted Hindi on her most vulnerable point, namely, if she possessed such virtues, why did *she* not control the offices and courts? Hindi could only answer that the *mlecch* had not recognized her worth when they conquered India, and put the work of the government into Urdu's hands.

Another central theme of the poem is that Muslims and Hindus had mutually corrupted each other. When Urdu chides Hindi with the unorthodox behavior of Hindus—such as keeping the Ramazan fast, worshipping Muslim saints, and visiting Muslim holy places—Hindi responds that such Hindus are a curse who spoil earth and heaven. When Hindi chides Urdu with the unorthodox practices of Muslims—such as Muslim wives putting vermillion on their heads, using hemp drugs, playing instruments for weddings, and failing to arrange for the marriage of widows—Urdu responds that Muslims have forgotten their customs because of the company of Hindus.[56] Both agree that:

> He who clings to race and faith, he's a son for bliss.
> He who leaves his race and faith, he's a son like piss![57]

In short, Hindi and Urdu firmly rejected the possibility of any kind of joint culture. They saw any adoption of the other religion's practices as a betrayal of one's own identity. To Hindi, Muslims as Muslims, Muslims who became like Hindus, and Hindus who became like Muslims, were all equally reprehensible; Urdu's sentiments were similar.

Near the end of his work, Prasad adds two themes not included by Datta, namely, the protection of cows and the abolition of child marriage. These and the promotion of Hindi[58] all appear in one stanza uttered by English in anger at the Hindus who have accompanied Hindi:

> You do not think of Hindi, or cows, or brides, I fear
> Nor yet of faith and duty—how unconscious you appear![59]

English is angry because Hindi has been explaining why Hindus do nothing:

> Hindus know full well the awful death of cattle.
> With hearts like stone, however, they stay at home and prattle.
> They can't unite to speak to government with just one voice.
> They only sit at home, quiet, without a noise.
> Instead of this, they worship *tāziyā,* grave, and *pīr.*
> They quite ignore their own religion and their duties here.[60]

In short, Hindus had been corrupted and diverted from their religious duties towards cows, child brides, and Hindi by the Muslim influence.

Perhaps the most important theme of all appears in insults exchanged between the two protagonists early on in their quarrel. I refer to the Hindu concept of purity and pollution. Hindi says to Urdu:

> I cannot come too close to you, too near to you I mean.
> For you are Muslim, I am Indian, and will not be unclean.[61]

Similarly, Urdu said to Hindi:

> You too are like a *bhishtī* [low-caste water carrier] dear, your nature is impure.
> Not Hindus nor the Muslims like you, don't be such a boor.[62]

Each rejects the other as defiling, no middle ground lay between them, just as no middle ground existed between *shuddh* (pure) Hindi and *sāf* (pure) Urdu. Carried to extremes, the two are mutually unintelligible. In the same way, the language of these two polemical plays admitted no compromise, no joint culture.

Conclusion

These two plays form part of a more general context of social and political problems expressed in polemical (and in other) literature. For example, in its April 1889 issue, the *Devanagari Gazette* of Meerut reported that Hindi advocates had performed four dramas during a recent fair. In one of these, the plot turned around a Sub-Inspector of Police mistaking the word *kishtī* (boat) for *kasbī* (prostitute) because of the ambiguity of the Urdu script, and the resulting confusion in the personal affairs of his superior, the District Superintendent of Police.[63] In 1890 a high court lawyer in Allahabad published a more even-handed play in which a personified Hindi and Urdu opposed each other in a court of law, whose one Hindu and two Muslim judges decide to gradually introduce Hindi as an official vernacular.[64] Themes of virtuous and oppressed Hindus, and vicious and tyrannical Muslims, appeared in two or three of the plays of Bharatendu Harishchandra, written in the 1870s and 1880s.[65] In all probability many more such polemical works from the same period—in both Hindi and Urdu—remain to be discovered.

Our two plays partially reflect another and still larger social and political context—the vernacular press. In plays and press alike we find the same accusations of Urdu's ambiguity and illegibility, similar fears of the study of Urdu turning Hindus from their religion, the same castigations of Urdu's foreign origins. They also contain the same assumptions of Urdu being Muslim and Hindi being Hindu, the same claims of economic prosperity for Hindus following on the heels of the introduction of Hindi, and the same surmises of economic necessity driving Hindus to learn Urdu. Nevertheless, the overlap was not complete, partly due to the difference in medium. The press laid more stress on the technical qualities of scripts and language, the educational benefits of the introduction of Hindi/Nagari, and the political justice of catering to the majority of the population. These plays, expressed the emotional aspects of the situation, emphasized the moral contrasts between a virtuous Hindi and a vicious Urdu. Being works of fiction, the plays could portray an inversion of the actual power structure.

This situation, as we have seen, gave the pride of place to Urdu over Hindi. School language enrollment statistics, examination statistics, and a provincial government survey of the language abilities of employees in courts and offices all showed the dominance of Urdu in the higher reaches of education and employment. These sources also showed the disproportionate representation of Muslims and Kayasths in government service. As the twin equations Hindi equalled Hindu and Hindu equalled Hindi gained more support, Kayasths found themselves in an increasingly difficult position. Their economic interests in government service and strong cultural attachment to Urdu language and literature lay in one direction, and their wish to retain a Hindu identity in the other. As a result, Kayasths displayed a consistently ambivalent attitude towards Hindi/Nagari: on the one hand willing to make nominal gestures of support, but on the other unwilling to donate any significant amounts of time or money.[66]

Datta's use of a Hindu king as judge, and Prasad's appeals to and denunciations of contemporary Hindu rulers, suggest yet another context to which the plays relate. Hindu monarchs could not only enhance the prestige of causes to which they leant their support but also provided substantial funding.[67] Monarchs also had limited power to act within their own territories, to invert within their own realms the power structure obtained in British India: in several cases, Hindu rulers replaced Urdu with Hindi as the official language of their states.[68]

The uncompromising nature of polemical literature lends itself to exactly such issues of communal identity in which no middle existed. No intermediate script could be devised between Nagari and Urdu, no one could be part Hindu and part Muslim, and no cow could be partly killed. In the either/or thinking that characterized both authors, one side won and the other lost. In their imaginary worlds, Urdu started as the winner and Hindi the loser but finished in the opposite positions. In the real world the positions of the two rivals reversed themselves six decades later when India became independent.

To study the imaginary worlds of authors such as Datta and Prasad allows us to learn about the "agenda" of those who expressed themselves in Indian languages,which was not necessarily the same as those who expressed themselves in English. Thus we can make a cogent argument for the necessity of combining both vernacular and English sources in a complementary relationship to adequately understand some of the complexities of India's linguistic, social, and political history.

The study of this polemical literature also helps us to feel the emotional intensity lying behind popular movements. In the case of the Hindi-Urdu controversy, this intensity partially accounts for the prolonged and bitter struggle for dominance between the two mediums first on the provincial and then on the national level. Finally, this study of literature enables us to grasp another perspective on controversial issues in Indian history. For as one scholar of communication has pointed out: "It is perhaps the most basic law of human behavior that people act or react on the basis of the way in which they *perceive* the external world."[69] Whether or not Hindi and Urdu deserved their images of virtue and vice respectively, many supporters of Hindi perceived them thus and banished Begam Urdu.

Bibliographic Essay

The two chief sources for this article, the plays of Pandit Gauri Datta and Munshi Sohan Prasad, have already been thoroughly discussed. We have seen something of the qualities of the language in which they were written, the biases of their authors, and the nature and structure of their contents. Nevertheless, there remain a few points worth making about date of publication, and methods and difficulties of translation.

We know the exact dates of the two editions of Prasad's work, but can only estimate the date of Datta's. Since *Nāgarī aur Urdū kā Swāng* refers to the Hunter Commission of 1882, but does not refer to the

1900 proclamation by the government of the North-Western Provinces and Oudh, we can safely assume that the work must have appeared some time between these two dates.

Both plays (as well as a third mentioned in the conclusion) were found in the library of the Nagari Pracharini Sabha of Banares, not as the result of a systematic search, but rather through serendipity. Since this library had no photocopying facilities, the entire texts were typed on a Hindi typewriter for later translation, a procedure which may have led to a few minor inaccuracies.

The translations themselves presented various difficulties. The language of *Hindī aur Urdū kī Larāī,* mainly Avadhi, has significant differences from standard Khari Boli Hindi. This made necessary the employment of a translator whose English version was then considerably polished. The language of *Nāgarī aur Urdū kā Swāng,* Khari Boli Hindi, proved relatively easy to translate without help. The verse portions of each play posed the usual problem of trying to render both meaning and form (meter and rhyme) without too much distortion. My solution was to largely ignore meter and to favor rhyme (even if this meant adding words not in the original) but not at the expense of meaning.

Among the most useful materials available in the Nagari Pracharini Sabha (NPS) library are the various records and publications of the Sabha itself, which give a unique picture of the development of the Hindi movement in the North-Western Provinces and Oudh. The founding of the Sabha in 1893 means that the bulk of its history lies outside the period of our two plays. Nevertheless some of the organization's early documents corroborate evidence from other sources of the nature of the Hindi-Urdu controversy. For example, the early membership lists of the Sabha show a social background corresponding almost exactly to that of students choosing Hindi in indigenous schools nearly fifty years earlier.

Another important document also turned up in the library of the NPS, namely Shiva Prasad's *Memorandum: Court Characters, in the Upper Provinces of India.* Prasad, at the time an Inspector of the Department of Public Instruction of the North-Western Provinces, went on to become an important figure in the public affairs of the province. His *Memorandum,* printed in Banares in August 1868, and labelled "For Private Circulation," has significance not only as one of the first major pro-Hindi statements but also as an example of the confused thinking typical of the whole Hindi-Urdu controversy. Seven months earlier, Prasad had written another memorandum in his capacity as Inspector, in which he maintained that only one vernacular existed, Urdu, and that Hindi was "the creation only of our school Pundits." Nevertheless, he firmly supported the use of the Nagari script in education despite the resulting tendency to introduce difficult Sanskrit words into school books. Although he inveighed against the use of such words "never spoken or heard of by the people," he himself later approved a popular Hindi school book full of pedantic Sanskrit terms.

Such confusion of thought also characterizes several important official sources, most notably a series of documents in the *Proceedings of the Government of the North-Western Provinces and Oudh in the General Administration Department* for October 1900. These reflect the deliberations of several levels of government that resulted in the proclamation granting supposedly equal status to the Nagari and Urdu scripts in the North-Western Provinces and Oudh. For example, in a series of three letters spread over ten months, the government of the North-Western Provinces and Oudh expanded the area in which the majority of the people speak "Hindi" from the three eastern most divisions of the province (Gorakhpur, Banares, and Allahabad) to all eight divisions. A more fundamental level of confusion appears in documents from the governments of the North-Western Provinces and Oudh and the rest of British India, whose writers thoroughly confused language and script, referring to Hindi as both "language" and "character." (In fairness, I should also add that other documents in this series show an admirable clarity of thought).

Other relevant official documents of the period have varying strengths and weaknesses. The different education reports offer many kinds of valuable information over more than a century: statistics on the numbers of students studying languages at different levels, requirements for teachers of vernacular languages, educational experiments such as the introduction of the Kaithi script for several years into government schools in Oudh, the earlier memorandum of Shiva Prasad, and much else of value. Their greatest shortcoming lies in their lack of consistency: different officials stress different aspects of education, statistical summaries change formats and add or drop items, and the depth of reporting varies considerably.

The Education Commission reports, both provincial and national, provide many important insights into the thinking of some of the most prominent Hindi and Urdu supporters. In the North-Western Provinces and Oudh, for example, Sir Sayyid Ahmad Khan testified on behalf of Urdu, while Raja Shiva Prasad and Bharatendu Harishchandra spoke for Hindi. In addition, the reports added depth to various aspects of government language policy, such as the introduction of the Kaithi script into Bihar. The chief drawback of these sources is their onetime occurrence; no subsequent education commission evoked similar controversy over the issue of language.

Among the most valuable sources for any researcher into nineteenth century Indian history are the Government of India's *Selections from the Vernacular Newspapers Published in the Panjab, North-Western Provinces and Oudh* (Allahabad: 1989–99). These weekly translations or summaries of various items from Hindi, Urdu, and other vernacular newspapers, which began in 1868, present a wide spectrum of Indian opinion on a variety of issues. Unfortunately, the nature of their content varies considerably from one official translator to the next, and continuity suffers. Nevertheless, for my purposes they give a wealth of detail about the Hindi-Urdu controversy and occasional invaluable insights into small events such as the controversy surrounding the publication of Munshi Prasad's play or the decisions of Hindu rulers to make Nagari the official script in their realms.

Finally, an important source, as yet relatively untapped, is the quarterly *Statement of Particulars Regarding Books and Periodicals,* which began in 1868 for the North-Western Provinces and Oudh and in 1868 or later for other provinces. Although suffering from several imperfections, particularly in the earliest years (such as lack of consistency in the coverage of certain more ephemeral publications), this source provides by far the most complete and detailed information available on the publishing history of India. Relative consistency from year to year means that long-term comparisons can be reliably made. The information given for each publication usually includes: the place and name of the publisher, the place and name of the printer if different from the publisher, the title of the book, the name of the author, the language of the book, and the number of copies printed. Such detail allows one to trace, for example, the contrasting fates of different languages or language combinations in terms of total numbers of publications, which in turn reflects shifting language attitudes and priorities.

PART TWO

Internal Polemics: Religious and Social Reform

Seven

Viresalingam and the Ideology of Social Change in Andhra

John Leonard and Karen Leonard*

We argue here that religious polemic sanctioning social change became part of regional ideology in coastal Andhra during the early twentieth century. The Telugu language and communication through the vernacular were powerful shapers of that message. In Andhra, Indian nationalism had an anti-priest, anti-orthodox, anti-ritual, and anti-authoritarian stance which was unusual. Nationalist ideology was modelled on Bengal's Brahmo Samaj in its commitment to religious and social reform and its neutrality to Christianity. One powerful personality, Viresalingam (1848–1919), shaped much of the thought and social reform activity of coastal Andhra as well as that region's cultural identity. Speakers of Telugu and Tamil, almost equal in number, were combined under British rule in the Madras Presidency, and both cultures flourished in the capital city of Madras. However, because of Viresalingam's work, the area's two vernacular cultures proved quite distinct.

The emphasis on regional cultural traditions, characteristic of nationalism in coastal Andhra, ultimately proved to be more significant on an all-India level than the stress on Sanskritic cultural traditions, which was part of social reform and then nationalism in Madras. The demands for recognition of Andhra's identity irritated the leaders of the Indian National Congress from 1913 to 1920 and the leaders of the Indian Union from 1946 to 1952, confronting the national leadership with what it considered to be a threat to the national integrity of India. The leaders eventually gave way in both cases and accepted the Andhra

*When John died in 1985, an outline for this article was on his desk. I have relied heavily on his two unpublished manuscripts to complete it. I am indebted to Professors G. N. Reddy and K. V. Narayana Rao of Sri Venkateshwara University [the former was John's Telugu professor] and Professor Charlotte Furth of the University of Southern California and Professor Montgomery Furth of The University of California, Los Angeles, for their helpful readings of the manuscript.

demands: in 1920, for the local Congress organizations based on linguistic boundaries and, in 1952, for the creation of an Andhra state. These concessions signified the recognition of a political pluralism which has since become accepted and extended throughout India.

The Coastal Andhra Region

The cultural center of coastal Andhra was the city of Rajahmundry located in the Northern Circars[1] that stretches along the Bay of Bengal to the northeast of Madras. This area formed by the deltas of the Krishna and Godavari rivers was the traditional center of Telugu culture. Rajahmundry was a religious center, the most auspicious one on the Godavari River. Traditionally, every Hindu pilgrim from coastal Andhra to Banares had to stop on his return trip at Rajahmundry. The Brahmans in the town were noted for their "great sense of devotion to sacrifices and rituals,"[2] and an important element of regional Hinduism in the Circars was the Sankaracharya, or religious authority, one of several spiritual heirs of Sankara, founder of the Smarta Brahman sect. The Sankaracharyas were influential public figures respected by most Hindus, although their legal jurisdiction was limited to Smartas. Coastal Andhra Smartas owed allegiance to the Sankaracharya whose *math* (center of learning and preaching) was at Virupaksha. He occasionally came on tour to Rajahmundry, which was famed for its learned as well as its religious Brahmans. Since the eleventh century, Rajahmundry had been the center of the Telugu literary world.[3]

In 1769, the British assumed direct administration of the Northern Circars. They made Rajahmundry the headquarters of Godavari District; although the Collector shifted to Kakinada in 1859, other government institutions were not transferred.[4] In 1875, Rajahmundry had a District and Session Judge's Court, a Sub-Collector's office and a Tahsildar's office, a Provincial School and a Telegraph Office, the Superintendent of Police's office and two (central and district) jails.[5] Government service became a major source of employment. Several *zamīndārs* abandoned their family estates to live in the town. Missionaries and local Hindu merchants began schools. Rajahmundry retained its reputation as a sacred center, and Brahmans continued to perform rituals and sacrifices, but the character of the town was irrevocably altered, not only by the addition of new institutions but by social and cultural changes which flowed from Madras, capital of the Presidency. Madras was a city of 406,000 in 1881, while Rajahmundry's population was 25,000.[6]

In Madras Presidency, as elsewhere in India, the educational system constructed by the British had a certain complementarity with the indigenous system of education, especially at the lower levels. The government's first actions were concentrated at the collegiate level, and after their unquestioned success, provincial and then lower schools were added. Education up to the second form, or through the fourth class, was in the regional languages, and neighborhood schools performed this function. Christian missionaries established alternative schools, and these were more widespread, if less coordinated. In many towns, the missionary system was the only one, and Hindu parents sent their children despite fears of conversion, because of the incentives to acquire education. To provide what the government would not, and to avoid Christian religious instruction, Indians began to establish private schools in the various district towns. Most of these schools began as acts of charity by individuals, but then upper caste, Western-educated urban Hindus formed committees and established Hindu secondary schools.

The chief beneficiaries of English education throughout Madras Presidency were Brahmans, traditionally the literate group. By 1891, for every non-Brahman who knew English there were eight Brahmans who did, although Brahmans composed only 3 percent of the population.[7] The first institutions of higher education were in Madras, so Tamil Brahmans dominated the Civil Service. Telugu Brahmans played a subsidiary role in the public life of most of the Madras Presidency,[8] and until 1877 their closest college was in Madras. College classes for the first two years of the college curriculum began in Rajahmundry's Provincial School only in 1873, and in 1877 the Provincial School became the Rajahmundry Government High School and College. This was the only school in the Telugu-speaking area to offer a baccalaureate program, beginning some three decades after Madras. The Rajahmundry College did not entirely replace the Madras colleges for the northern districts, but by 1880–81 over thirteen times as many Godavari District students obtained a collegiate education in Rajahmundry as were enrolled in Madras colleges.[9]

Christianity was represented in Rajahmundry by the time Viresalingam was growing up, although less so than in other areas of South India. Government schools and private schools set up by Indians, many of them government approved and subsidized, dominated Western education in Rajahmundry. In 1881, mission education accounted for only 7 percent of the boys and 12 percent of the girls in Rajahmundry schools.[10] The only missionaries in Rajahmundry were the American Lutherans, most of whose activities were conducted outside the town. Lutheran missionaries had started several schools in Rajahmundry, including a girls' school, which catered chiefly to Christian converts from the Mala, or untouchable, caste. The mission suffered from manpower and financial limitations and concentrated on evangelism, not education.[11] Some of the missionaries who served in Rajahmundry were allies of Viresalingam and some were rivals, but they played relatively minor roles in social reform and politics. They did not set the context or shape the ideology of social and political reform in important ways in coastal Andhra.

The introduction of the printing press and the consequent modification of the South Indian scripts in the early nineteenth century radically altered the conditions of creation, transmission, and distribution of literature. This technological innovation was for a long time limited to Madras, which in 1875 had forty-eight presses and produced 616 books in English and the South Indian regional languages. Coastal Andhra in 1875 had only about eight presses and produced 31 books, and most of the presses in coastal Andhra were owned and operated by the British administration, European merchants, or missionaries. Godavari District had three presses but published only 2 books or pamphlets in 1875.[12] This imbalance was evident also in books printed in the regional languages: in 1876 Tamil books outnumbered Telugu books 2.5 to 1.[13]

Viresalingam and His Work

The social reform movement and the rise of regional consciousness in coastal Andhra began with the activities of Kandukuri Viresalingam, and his character was indelibly stamped upon it. The reforms which he initiated were continued by his followers, and his ideas were adopted by the next generation. His central place in the formation of Andhra's modern identity was recognized by those who followed:[14]

> Mr. Viresalingam conveyed to his generation in a multitude of forms the consciousness of the power of these changing causes [from] contact with Western culture and Christianity. We are led to conclude that, if he was not the original centre and first cause of them all, he had, however, laid the foundation for many of them in a sound and secure manner. He was, as it were, the initial principle of change throughout the whole course of the Telugu advance in recent times.

Viresalingam, the central figure in Andhra social reform and nationalism, was a Telugu Niyogi, or secular, Brahman whose family had migrated from Kandukur in the Nellore District to the Godavari delta area. Born in 1848, he grew up in one of only two double-storied houses in the old section of Rajahmundry. This large house indicated the high status of Viresalingam's grandfather. *Dīwān* to a local *zamīndār,* his position had enabled him to support many relatives, donate land to learned scholars, and celebrate marriages with great pomp. Viresalingam's grandfather had spent rather than saved his money, however, and since Viresalingam's father and uncle had not obtained the same high position,[15] the house symbolized to the young Viresalingam the contrast between past and present achievements.

This sense of current decline was further enhanced by domestic troubles.[16] His father had died when Viresalingam was four, and his uncle was the sole support of the joint family. Viresalingam's mother and his uncle's wife quarreled constantly, making a strong impression on Viresalingam that was reflected in his writing on the beneficial effects of education on women.[17] Viresalingam was married at thirteen to a ten-year-old girl from a nearby village; he later educated her and drew her into his social reform activities. Continued quarrelling in the home led the uncle to partition the joint family, leaving a fifteen-year-old Viresalingam with his bride and widowed mother in the spacious Rajahmundry house.

Viresalingam's memories of his early religious training were not very strong. Aside from his initiation as a Brahman at age six, he recalled only the ardor of his religious devotion[18] that persisted throughout his life, despite changes in his specific beliefs. His early education was typical of boys heading for government employment. He learned the rudiments of Telugu and even memorized some Sanskrit verses in *pyal,* or neighborhood schools. He learned to read and write classical Telugu and at age ten was apprenticed to a relative who worked as a clerk in a government office.[19] Before he went to the office he was tutored in Sanskrit, and at night his uncle instructed in him in English and arithmetic. Viresalingam persuaded his mother to let him resume studying full time, and at eleven or twelve he entered the government school at Rajahmundry. His proficiency in Telugu won prizes that paid the school tuition.[20] Marked by his classmates as a scholar, he composed poems of exceptional virtuosity in 1868–69, one of which became a text for the Bachelor of Arts examination in Telugu. He also tutored the English principal of his school in Telugu and contributed articles to the Telugu journal that the principal established.[21] Viresalingam completed his schooling in 1870.[22]

Education in a Western-style school changed Viresalingam's ideas, those on religion first of all. Keshav Chandra Sen, the Bengali religious reformer and Brahmo Samaj leader, visited Madras in 1864. Three years later Viresalingam's curiosity led him to read Sen's speeches. That same year, a new secondary school teacher, Atmuri Lakshminarasimham, encouraged students to meet and discuss Brahmo Samaj doctrines opposing caste and idolatry and advocating education, particularly for women. The group of five or six met either at the teacher's home or at Viresalingam's,[23] and Viresalingam's earliest writings show the influence of Brahmo Samaj tenets.[24]

After his schooling, Viresalingam took teaching jobs, qualified for various government posts,[25] and, finally, chose a publishing career. Viresalingam began a monthly journal, *Vivēka Vardhani,* in 1874.[26] Depending upon the press for a living was precarious, but the government adopted several of his Telugu books as school texts, which earned him substantial sums. The independent life of a publisher and author attracted him.[27] But pressure from his family, friends, and relatives to take a regular job coincided with an offer from the Rajahmundry Provincial School, which he joined in 1876 as an assistant teacher of Telugu. He remained there for the next twenty-one years.[28] Viresalingam's autobiography gave his motives for returning to teaching: he wanted a job which would be independent and not compromise his strict moral values. Thus he ceased looking for government or legal positions, both of which required actions that he considered repugnant and demeaning.[29]

Viresalingam's search for an independent profession rested upon his stubbornness and his inability to compromise in personal relations, which offended many and drove away all but the most devoted of his friends. He recalled an incident as he walked with a group of friends:

> While I was the only one who favored the river path, the others preferred the market road. They all set off down that road, looking back to see if I would follow them. Then I started along the river bank and reached home. The same thing happened the next day. We disagreed about which way to go, and so I began to take the river path. Then they followed me, saying that whatever I think I follow it adamantly without caring for what others say.[30]

Viresalingam's aggressive, independent ways had certain advantages, evident in his initial reform efforts in Rajahmundry, but those same ways repeatedly deprived him of close allies and drove him from Rajahmundry to Madras and then back again at the end of his life.[31] Yet the impact of his activities and his ideas spread beyond Rajahmundry and decisively shaped the development of Telugu culture.

Viresalingam's initial impact on regional and Hindu self-consciousness among Telugu intellectuals came through journalism. His venture with *Vivēka Vardhani* in 1874 was a continuation of the tradition of mixing literature, items of public interest, essays on religion, and social comment, but he also reported on the news. *Vivēka Vardhani*'s English section had a variety of editors and reported news prominently, while much of the commentary was in the Telugu section that Viresalingam edited. He consistently criticized the government and he made his journal the leading advocate of social reform in coastal Andhra. He did so partly by attacking the policies of the leading Telugu scholar at Presidency College, Madras, Kokkonda Venkataratnam, and indulging in polemics with him on nearly every conceivable topic. These were polemics by scholars and for scholars, written in classical Telugu.[32]

Viresalingam's early literary works conformed to scholarly traditions and were lauded for their virtuosity. He wrote poetry, and he specialized in *achcha* Telugu, or non-Sanskritic Telugu. This was a technical feat, since it restricted the writer's choice of vocabulary and made adhering to the rules for composition more difficult. In 1875, he received a silver trophy at a meeting of Telugu scholars in Madras for his literary achievements. Thus he came to know the elite among Telugu scholars, those who published books, held important positions, and presented their views to the government.[33] At twenty-seven Viresalingam was honored by this group for excelling at the traditional tasks of Telugu scholars: making translations and writing grammars. Through his journal, however, he would realize his true literary potential and be feted for quite different achievements: innovative literary forms and, through them, the expression of new social and religious reform ideas.

Religious reform via the Brahmo Samaj had made an impression on the young Viresalingam. The Brahmo movement was making an impact in Madras and coastal Andhra, although the nature of that impact differed substantially in the two places. The non-Brahman character of the Brahmo Samaj in Madras was established early. Although a Telugu Brahman revived and led the group from 1878, its reputation as a center of anti-Brahman feeling grew.[34]The South India Brahmo Samaj leadership and membership had little in common with the majority of the educated elite in Madras, the Tamil Brahmans, and the movement all but disappeared from Tamil Nadu's intellectual history.[35]

In the Telugu-speaking region, however, Brahmo Samaj ideas became part of Telugu literary and political culture. In Rajahmundry, Viresalingam and a few friends met together sporadically for prayer meetings based on the model of the Brahmo Samaj of Calcutta, and in 1878 they formed the Rajahmundry Prarthana Samaj. This society was at first secret, and members sang hymns and heard lectures in Viresalingam's home. After a year, apprehensions eased. The association moved to the Maharajah of Vizianagaram's Girls' School and invited the public to join.[36] Of the eight active members, five were Niyogi Brahmans, two were Vaidiki Brahmans, and one was a non-Brahman Telaga. By occupation, five were teachers, one was a lawyer, and one a government clerk.[37] Since most of the reformers were teachers, they could recruit students and keep the association going. This was the first religious reform organization in coastal Andhra that lasted for any length of time, and it served as a base from which other associations were formed.

The 1870s in coastal Andhra saw little evidence of debate over social conditions and little social reform activity. Machilipatnam, the district headquarters of Krishna District, had an outstanding journal, *Purushārtha Pradāyini,* but no social reform activities; in 1879 local leaders were still trying to begin an association and reading room.[38] In Kakinada, the Cocanada Literary Association was founded in 1878 and was politically oriented from its beginnings, but the Kakinada journal was not effectively tied to the association and did not campaign for the issues it discussed.[39] Elsewhere in coastal Andhra there were sporadic meetings of students and local Brahman officials to debate changing specific customs but these discussions did not produce tangible results.[40] Even in Rajahmundry, early reform activities produced few results, but journalistic activity, public meetings, organized voluntary associations, and some leaders among the educated elite forged the conditions in which a social reform campaign could be waged.

Through his journal *Vivēka Vardhani,* Viresalingam was developing an ideology of social reform and actively seeking an issue for a reform campaign. In the journal, he introduced himself to the public with a poem:[41]

> I am a Brahman who learned a foreign language and passed an examination in that language.
> I have an interest in the Telugu language, and I want to aid the development of the country.
> I have some talent for writing poetry.
> I write particularly about moral questions which are universal, in an easy style, without using difficult compounds, so that everyone may understand.
> I also use foreign words.

In the first line, Viresalingam identified himself as a member of the educated elite, while in the third he implied that he was a scholar in Telugu. Then he went on to state his concern for writing prose, and writing it so that people could understand it—he wanted to write in spoken, not classical, Telugu. He linked the development of Telugu with that of the country. Elsewhere, he stated that his journal had two aims: the improvement of the Telugu language and the improvement of the country.[42]

Viresalingam wanted to develop Telugu not only by modifying the language but also by using it to reform society. Language reform was to be carried out by simplifying Telugu to increase peoples' comprehension of it. He conceived of language as a means to combat the evil conditions in society and to propagate the moral standards essential for the country's progress. These journalistic goals represented a conscious break with tradition in Telugu usage.

The documentation of his intellectual odyssey is somewhat limited, but Viresalingam distinguished three periods when discussing the evolution of his journal, *Vivēka Vardhani.*[43] The first two periods fell before the first widow marriage he performed in December 1881, and the last followed that crucial event. The first period was brief, from 1874 to 1876. He wrote about social conditions that affronted him—the corruption of officials, the role of prostitutes in public life, the degraded position of women, and the widespread ignorance of the masses. If there was a focus to his writings then, it was on the problem of cultural contact between India and the West and the reasons for the decline of ancient Indian civilization. Viresalingam idealized the past and contrasted it with the current degraded state of society. He was especially concerned with the role of the Brahmans, keepers of the texts and traditions.

Viresalingam's explanation for the decline of ancient India became more complex with time and touched directly on the Brahmans as preservers of India's civilizational values. How he explained this decline varied with the opposition that faced Viresalingam at any one time in his career. At first, he blamed the Muslims for the destruction of ancient India's greatness: they had shattered political unity and subjugated Indians. Loss of political independence removed morality from law and order; suspicion and mutual distrust became endemic. Brahmans were humiliated and had to take up professions like low-level civil service jobs, and some were even reduced to begging. The prevailing fact in political life was oppression, and the dominant emotion in social life was fear: Indian civilization had lost its confidence and power.[44] This attribution of the decline to external forces came as Viresalingam was just beginning to write about social reform and was still committed to the role of a scholar and teacher. Opposition to his ideas was slight and came chiefly from scholars; he had undertaken no significant reform activities.

Then came a transitional period. Scholars sharpened their attacks after Viresalingam defied orthodox burial customs and began to criticize Brahmans, and a perceptible shift occurred in his account of the decline of ancient India. Increasingly Viresalingam blamed scholars for the deterioration of knowledge and standards of morality.[45] However, this internal factor, evident in his speeches and lectures during 1875–76, still played only a subordinate role in Viresalingam's thinking.

As Viresalingam attacked current practices and beliefs, he began to attribute malpractices to scholars, pseudoscholars, or teachers, basing his argument on the place of knowledge in a country's civilization. At first arguing that Muslim rule had forced Brahmans to abandon their honorable professions of preserving knowledge and had encouraged various corruptions,[46] Viresalingam began to trace the deterioration of knowledge to two new causes: one was the preference of scholars for revelation, rather than observation and inference, as a source of knowledge; the other was the scholars' concern for form rather than meaning, for Sanskrit and poetry rather than for the regional languages and prose.[47] He traced these two causes to ancient Indian civilization prior to the coming of the Muslims and saw them as precluding the rise of a scientific tradition in India. They were also the principal evils of the present day that needed to be rectified. Thus he focused on internal causes for India's decline—on scholars and their faults.[48]

During these years Viresalingam used his journal to experiment with new literary forms, farcical one-act plays about social conditions, and stories illustrating moral principles specifically for women. These innovative forms set his journal off from its competitors and were significant in the development of Telugu literature. Their content was as notable as their form. Many of his one-act plays satirized Brahmans, highlighting the evils and absurdities of contemporary society. He developed social stereotypes of "the orthodox." Viresalingam used his farces to pillory his enemies; since his attempts at disguising the personalities he portrayed were ineffective, a target of his writing could easily find himself with a new nickname, that of a character in one of Viresalingam's plays. These farces were the first instance in modern times when the Telugu spoken dialect was employed for dramatic purposes. Viresalingam used the spoken dialect for *all* his characters, Brahmans and untouchables alike (the conventions in Sanskrit drama allowed only a few low-born characters to use spoken dialects).[49]

As Viresalingam was increasingly criticized by his fellow scholars during 1875–76, his responses in his journal pointed to ancient scholars seduced by the lure of power and wealth, confused by the urge to acquire prestige, and misled into fabricating stories that the mass of illiterates believed. He began to question the later accretions to Hindu traditions, such as the *itihāsa* and the *purānās;* to note the purity of thought in *Srti* and the Vedas, including the Upanishads; and to claim inclusion of gross superstitions in *Smrti,* the *dharmasāstras,* the *itihāsa,* and the *purānas.* Since *Smrti* was often used to confute him, it was natural that he should try to discredit it. He argued that contemporary Indians were merely continuing the prostitution of education and the adoption of debased jobs initiated by the ancient Indian scholars. Contemporary scholars seldom studied the Vedas or even the *dharmasāstras,* so spurious customs based on later texts had crept in and lowered the standards of scholarship and morality.[50]

Viresalingam based his ideas about progress on the cyclical ages of Hindu cosmology, postulating that since the literal descriptions of the darkest of the four ages fit the present, contemporary society was in the last age and anything that succeeded it was bound to be better. Rejecting the inevitability of the destruction of the world, he argued that steady improvement would culminate in a future golden age, thus assimilating the Western idea of progress to traditional Hindu beliefs and making it part of his conception of societal development.[51] To justify cultural borrowing from the West, he argued that the West had first borrowed from India—mathematics, via Greece— and thus India was responsible for achievements derived from mathematics.[52] Furthermore, mutual cultural borrowing involved no subordination of one civilization to another. The leading ideas in Viresalingam's program of regeneration were in fact indigenous scholarly ones: the ameliorative power of knowledge and the intrinsic strength of a unified people. He believed that education would instill morality in the leaders of society and create a climate of opinion favorable to reform. This education would be both moral and practical, since knowledge concerning the sciences and humanities had to be tempered with a knowledge of moral principles.[53]

Education was one remedy for India, and unity—of race, religion, and caste—was the other. In his speeches and writings, Viresalingam appealed to his audience to promote unity, not just at the philosophical level of Vedantic speculation, but at a social level. He advocated the formation of debating clubs, caste organizations, trade unions, almost any kind of organization which would bind men together. These associations would be like building blocks, in themselves small and useless, but together indispensable.[54] These essentially scholarly ideas reflected his initial activities, rectifying abuses that afflicted Brahmans and combating specific corrupt practices of officials in Rajahmundry.

Viresalingam's first reform effects had been personal and idiosyncratic. He refused to call in Brahmans for rites connected with the removal of a beehive from a roof beam in his house, although it was customary to employ them to do so;[55] and he joined Basavarazu Gavarrazu, a friend, in defying Brahman burial customs when Gavarrazu's son died. The two of them buried the corpse themselves, hoping to encourage secular Brahmans to participate in funeral processions and discourage ideas about pollution.[56] He wrote against Brahman marriage customs such as bride-price, child marriage of girls, and marriages restricted by sect and kinship,[57] but he found it difficult to promote changes in these even among his friends. Girls' education was a popular reform—Viresalingam had founded a girls' school in 1874 when teaching in a nearby small town and, in 1881, he began another in Rajahmundry. Finally, in 1874, Viresalingam turned his attention to the controversial issue of widow marriage.

The Widow Marriage Campaign

That Telugu-speaking reformers took the lead on the widow marriage issue in the Presidency seems indisputable. In Madras, the Hindu Widow Re-Marriage Association had been formed in 1874 but served only briefly as a forum for voicing the arguments for widow marriage before it languished. Its leaders were Brahmans but not Tamil Brahmans, and it used English, not a regional language, for its meetings. The Tamil Brahman establishment was more concerned in the 1870s with educational policy, questions of management (by government or private institutions), and the role of Indian languages (including Sanskrit). The fear that Western education would lead to secularism was strong. After Viresalingam formed the Rajahmundry Widow Marriage Association in 1879, the Madras Hindu Widow Re-Marriage Association became active again. The Rajahmundry and Madras reformers cooperated in limited ways over the next two decades.[58]

When Viresalingam began to plan a widow marriage campaign in the Telugu-speaking Circars, he spent over a year meeting with various people and scholars to discuss the question of widow marriages.[59] Because of the scholars' reluctance to agree with his textual interpretations, Viresalingam became convinced of their unwillingness to cope with change, and he began to attack them as agents and even the sources of religious authority. In the spring of 1881, he challenged his religious superior, the Sankaracharya from Virupaksha, when he came to Rajahmundry. In his journal Viresalingam attacked the Sankaracharya, claiming that he was coercing donations from people by threatening excommunication. He also denigrated the Sankaracharya's personal disciple and presumptive heir. At a March meeting, Viresalingam presented a petition signed by thirty Niyogi Brahmans asking for the Sankaracharya's approval of widow marriages. Viresalingam spoke in favor of widow marriages and another *pandit* spoke for the opposition. Later in the meeting the audience was informed that the Sankaracharya would sanction widow marriage only if the majority of caste Hindus in Rajahmundry approved. This meant, of course, that local custom would prevail; it cut off the debate and silenced Viresalingam. Since the Sankaracharya left the meeting without commenting on the validity of Viresalingam's interpretation, Viresalingam believed he was still free to persuade other Hindus of the correctness of his argument.[60]

This confrontation was the first of several clashes between Viresalingam and the Sankaracharya. Viresalingam continued to criticize or subvert religious authority in pursuit of his reform goals. Viresalingam was a Smarta and under the Sankaracharya's religious authority, but Brahmans from different sects joined in the appeal for approval of widow marriages. Thus the confrontation illustrated the more general religious role of the Sankaracharya and also the interest in the widow marriage issue; it cut across sectarian boundaries and united reformers of different sectarian backgrounds.

Formed in 1879, the Rajahmundry Widow Marriage Association[61] held its first widow marriage in 1881, when a secret executive committee and, in effect, a new association were formed. The Prarthana Samaj had been dominated by teachers; in this new association, there were as many officials as teachers on the executive committee.[62] Many members were students from the Rajahmundry Government College. The teachers recruited students directly from their classes for social reform activities and also served as role models for their students, who were in many cases living away from home for the first time. Viresalingam in particular was admired, since he was recognized as the foremost Telugu scholar of his age, and students remembered that he advocated social reform in his classes. He concentrated especially on exposing and ridiculing the ideas and practices of orthodox Hindus, creating in the classroom the same social stereotypes that he wrote about in his journal.[63] As the widow marriage campaign aroused controversy, students formed bodyguards for Viresalingam and other leaders in danger of physical attack from their orthodox opponents.[64] After the first marriage in 1881, students went out to villages, found widows and arranged to bring them to Rajahmundry; some became bridegrooms themselves despite threats and beatings from their parents.[65] The intense excitement and enthusiasm of the 1881–84 widow marriage campaign, when ten marriages of widows were celebrated, deeply marked the young men who participated.[66] Some thirty more widow marriages had been celebrated in Andhra by 1919, making this the most intensive campaign in all of India.

From the time of Viresalingam's first speech on widow marriage in 1879 it took almost two years to find a widow who would remarry and a bridegroom for her. In December 1881, the first widow marriage was performed. It took the help of British officials to conduct it: to secure the bridegroom's leave from his job, depute a police detachment of Muslims and Christians from Madras, and threaten to arrest orthodox Hindu leaders if there were overt disturbances.[67] The orthodox had persuaded Brahman cooks, water carriers, and priests not to carry out their customary duties, but the reformers countered the threatened boycott by paying more for all the services.[68] Four days after the highly publicized wedding, another widow was brought by her mother to Rajahmundry and married; this event was even grander, since many British officials joined the procession and many more people came to watch it.[69]

Both the reformers and their opponents organized themselves for these controversial events. The Widow Marriage Association left the publicity to Viresalingam, whose journal made him the most effective spokesman, but the other leaders secured support from officials in the district towns. In Kakinada, Godavari District headquarters, a local merchant, Paida Ramakrishnayya, offered to donate thousands of rupees once the marriages began, and he kept his promise.[70] The opponents organized too. Before the first widow marriage, the orthodox opposition was led by Vaidiki or priestly Brahman scholars;[71] then an association against widow marriages was formed in Rajahmundry led by Western-educated men, indicating a shift in the leadership of the orthodox opposition. Although scholars still had an important place, Western-educated men holding government positions became the leaders. Similarly, their tactics shifted. Until this time, orthodox opponents would enforce traditional sanctions, withdraw essential domestic and religious services, and refuse to contract marriage relationships or fulfill kinship obligations. But now they asked the Sankaracharya to make the reformers outcastes. When the Sankaracharya complied, it was the Municipal Council President of Rajahmundry who convened a meeting to announce the expulsion of the reformers from their castes.[72] Some thirty people who attended the wedding meals were expelled, their readmission to caste dependent upon formal, public acknowledgement of the Sankaracharya's authority and a ceremony of penance.[73] Among the reformers outcasted by the Sankaracharya were non-Smartas, indicating his more general authority among Hindus.

This counterattack was very effective, and only Viresalingam and one friend, Basavarazu Gavarrazu, ultimately resisted submission to the Sankaracharya. Viresalingam had his own well; he and his wife had no children, and, as a Telugu Brahman *pandit,* he performed the marriages himself. The worst blow to the reformers was the loss of their chief patron, the Kakinada merchant, who performed penance and swore not to give any more money to the reformers.[74] Viresalingam was bitter about the failure of the educated elite to support the reform campaign and withstand social pressure. From this experience, he concluded that education had to be extended to women and the masses; once educated, they would not be intimidated by those opposed to social change. Enthusiasm for reform in Rajahmundry declined noticeably, and it was harder to find brides and bridegrooms. Violence used by both sides during the months after the first two widow marriages—college students fought with the young disciples of priests—resulted in the filing of lawsuits by both sides, although only the priests' disciples were convicted.[75]

Another lawsuit filed as a consquence of the first widow marriages was far more significant. One of the non-Smartas outcasted by the Sankaracharya, Atmuri Lakshminarasimham, filed a court case against him. The initial decision, against the reformers, was appealed to the Madras High Court in August 1882, and this caused misgivings among orthodox and reformers alike. (The two most prominent social reformers in Madras denied any association with the appeal.)[76] Viresalingam's closest follower, Basavarazu Gavarrazu, filed the appeal, and its outcome was surprising. The Madras High Court upheld the lower court decision with respect to Sankaracharya's ecclesiastical powers—he could expell people from caste—but decided *against* Sankaracharya because of the way he had notified reformers of his action. He had sent them postcards through the mail, and this violated the laws against defamation! They fined him Rs. 200.[77]

The real question here was whether or not the government had the legal power to pass judgement on a duly constituted source of Hindu religious authority. Advocates of reform in Rajahmundry supported the initial court case, although some were ambivalent about it, and they did not oppose the appeal. They were disappointed in the decision, fearing it would diminish support for social reform.[78] In Madras, the response was different. Just as they had opposed the appeal itself, without exception the Madras social reformers condemned the court's decision to fine Sankaracharya.[79] In Rajahmundry, widow marriages continued—four took place between the time of the appeal and the High Court decision seven months later, and four more took place before internal dissension led to the decline of the movement in 1884. By the time of the High Court decision, the reformers no longer needed police protection.[80]

These ten widow marriages had an impact far beyond their numbers. Most of the child widows were from the Brahman castes,[81] but the Rajahmundry widow marriages included two Komati (merchant) couples. There were more secular Brahmans than priestly ones among the eight Brahman couples, but every Brahman sect and branch was represented in these couples, and the tenth marriage was an inter-sect Brahman marriage. The Rajahmundry Widow Marriage Association sponsored all ten marriages and all save one were held in Rajahmundry; that one was held by Rajahmundry reformers in Madras.[82] This small group displayed remarkable diversity and involved a wide range of the educated elite and their families in controversy over the reform.

After 1884 serious dissension among the reformers caused the movement to lose momentum, although thirty more widow marriages were performed before Viresalingam's death in 1919. What is significant here is that the dissension no longer concerned whether or not widow marriages were religiously sanctioned or were a useful reform. The dissension was over how to support the married couples (many bridegrooms lost their jobs and the Widow Marriage Association provided them housing, allowances, and sometimes employment),[83] and, after 1886, over the provisions of the will of Paida Ramakrishnayya. He had honored his pledge to the Sankaracharya not to give money directly to the Rajahmundry reformers, but he had channeled money to them through the social reform leaders in Madras, and upon his death he left a trust fund containing Rs. 10,000 for the widow marriage movement. This was to be administered by Atmuri Lakshminarasimham, the teacher who had first propounded Brahmo Samaj doctrines to Viresalingam. He was now a judicial official and the filer of the court case against Sankaracharya. Viresalingam's unfortunate tendency to alienate his closest allies inspired him to attack Lakshminarasimham in a farce just at this time, so that disagreements among the reformers and bridegrooms produced factions within the association. Lakshminarasimham refused to use the trust fund for new couples, preferring to keep it for those already married.[84] There had already been rivalry among the leaders—before 1881, three of them, including Viresalingam and Lakshminarasimham, had founded competing girls' schools in Rajahmundry—but it did not interfere with the widow marriage campaign until the mid-1880s.

The widow marriage campaign in Andhra showed the impact of direct, positive action; its symbolic achievements were many. The direct challenge to religious authority, in this case that of the Sankaracharya, appealed to college students and helped keep Hindu revivalism out of the social reform movement in coastal Andhra. An antipathy to religious authority appeared in later reform movements initiated by Viresalingam's students.[85] The widow marriage movement had offered direct, positive action with tremendous potential for dramatization, maximum publicity, and controversy.

Despite the setback to the widow marriage campaign, reform activities proceeded. The dissension and the loss of old members through death (especially Basavarazu Gavarrazu in 1888) and dispute coincided with the initial experiments by the British in local government and with the emergence of nationalism throughout India. Thus the energies of the educated elite were drawn into new fields. There was, however, continuity in some areas. Religious reform remained an attractive alternative and was less threatening to orthodox Hindus; girls' education proceeded to grow and Telugu literary activities featured both innovations and controversy.

The vital relationships between social reform, religious reform, and literary activity were recognized by contemporary social reformers.

Attacks on orthodox customs and views were conducted through the widow marriage campaign, religious reform associations, and literary activity. The widow marriage campaign gave an impetus to innovations in Telugu literature; it continued under Viresalingam's leadership. In 1883, he began *Satī Hita Bōdhini,* a journal written for women, and he used this genre to inculcate his ideas on social reform. This type of writing was developed by his former pupils to become almost a separate field of Telugu prose.[86]

Literature as a means of reform became a cultural tradition in coastal Andhra, and literary activity became a suitable alternative field of endeavor for many social reformers. Telugu journalism was also pressed into the service of social reformers. Most significant, journal debate during the 1880s in coastal Andhra was carried on in Telugu and not in English—there was no English language newspaper for coastal Andhra until 1921, when the Congress leader T. Prakasam published one from Madras.[87] *The Hindu,* published in English from Madras from 1878, reported little on coastal Andhra, and this neglect was, in a sense, fortunate for Telugu journalism, for the important issues of the day were discussed and analyzed only through the Telugu journals. This strengthened Telugu journalism and forced the educated elite to use Telugu and solve the problems inherent in transforming the regional language. The negative aspects of this situation were that people in other parts of India were unaware of what was happening in coastal Andhra and that parochialism was encouraged among Telugu-speaking people. But by the 1890s, educated men and women in Andhra were committed to the use of Telugu as a serious medium of expression in journalism and literature, and they were engaged in transforming the regional language and its culture.[88]

Social reform proved to be the chief determinant of the direction of cultural change in the Telugu language and literature. The modification of the Telugu script for printing, the initial efforts at prose composition, and the introduction of new literary forms had occurred by the mid-nineteenth century, developed by Telugu scholars who tried to control the changes. The transition to a new phase of culture occurred in the late 1870s, when Viresalingam began employing innovative literary forms in his social reform publicity. The cultural change wrought by the social reform campaign also led to a shift in the men and institutions associated with the development of Telugu literature.

Scholars in Telugu began to be superseded by the educated elite as effective communicators, and consequently the structure of the Telugu literary culture was altered. The main motivation for this modernization of Telugu was the hope that it would bridge the gulf which the educated elite felt between themselves and those who did not know

English. Viresalingam's concern with the masses developed after his disillusionment with the educated elite—he emphasized the moral benefits of education for women and the masses so that they would not hold back the educated elite and could themselves participate directly in reform efforts.[89] This modernization was also an attempt to bridge the gulf between urban and rural people, and, to some extent, between Brahman and non-Brahman.

If social reform activity accelerated cultural change, it also accelerated the process of political development in the area. Because social reform was the first organized activity initiated by the educated elite in coastal Andhra, it had a significance which transcended its success or failure in the performance of widow marriages. The educated elite started journals, organized associations, recruited supporters, and planned campaigns around the idea of social innovation. The leaders of social reform recruited members and attracted sympathizers. Reform activity was an experience for students and others that accustomed them to nontraditional groups and activities. Social reform was also an arena of political activity. The centrality of the Rajahmundry Government College in the educational life of the Circars and the central position of Viresalingam in both social reform and literary activities gave a strong initial base for the widow marriage campaign and heightened its impact. But Viresalingam's stubbornness and controversial personal relations ensured that other reformers split off from him and built associations and institutions of their own. Thus reform efforts did not proceed under the direction of just one man, but through the rivalry of several major figures and the allegiance to them of many others. These shifting alignments broadened the arena for reform ideas and activities. Viresalingam's associations and institutions may have depended upon personal and financial support which sometimes proved elusive, but his ideas decisively shaped social and political concepts in coastal Andhra.

Viresalingam's Thought

Viresalingam's responses to the questions posed by Westernization changed over the years. Before 1876, he had conceived of the problems largely as arising from a confrontation between India and the West. Attributing the rise of the West chiefly to unity and a scientific tradition he harnessed these achievements to his conception of progress for India. In that period Viresalingam had been unsure about which cultural tradition or group he should favor to bring about the changes he desired in society. The second period, from 1876 to 1881, when he was actively engaged in the widow marriage campaign, was a transitional one for him in which he worked out tentative answers to these questions. From 1881 to 1888, when the first two marriages had been successfully performed, Viresalingam fully developed the ideas that he had begun to formulate during the transitional period, a period that coincided with the decline of the social reform movement and an increase of political activity at the local and national levels. Viresalingam's solutions were his ultimate intellectual response to problems that he had encountered in the early 1870s. His followers adopted many of his ideas, but faced with different tasks, they used his thought to meet the situations facing them in the late 1880s.

Viresalingam's social reform experience during the transitional period decisively shaped his intellectual development. His initiation of the widow marriage campaign in 1879 shifted his attention from assessing the reasons for India's decline to determining practical means of achieving its regeneration. Viresalingam's concerns about India's relationship to the West receded in importance as he was confronted with the immediate problems posed by Indian society. His narrowed view relegated the West to a category of "other countries"[90] where the issues of child marriage, bride price, and prohibition of widow marriage did not exist. Viresalingam invoked "other countries" in his arguments only to show that the situation in India was not a universal one. While stating that the elimination of undesirable social conditions was a universal goal, he was reluctant to point to the West as the specific model for India's future. He did not mind taking Western knowledge of natural science as a model for India, because he argued that Western science had originated with ideas borrowed from India.[91] It would have been difficult, however, for him to apply this same argument of cultural borrowing in the areas of social structure and social relationships. Hence he tried not to associate desirable social conditions explicitly with contemporary Western society. The development of universal goals absorbed his attention from 1880 onwards.[92]

Viresalingam's understanding of progress recurred throughout his writings in the phrase "the development of the country."[93] He used the word *development* to designate those activities that used rational means to improve Indian social conditions and, in the process, freed individuals from the control of traditional authorities to allow the realization of individual potential. By *country* he meant a local area, for he spoke of the many countries within the Madras Presidency. He did not intend it to stand for a nation or a geopolitical unit, either; he related progress to the improvement of social conditions and social classes. His "country" is best understood as synonymous with *society*.

Believing that education was the key development activity, Viresalingam expanded his ideas about who should be educated, though he did not change his ideas about its content. His view of education was a very broad and complex one, for he approached it from a metaphysical point of view and linked it implicitly with his ideas on religion. Thus he equated education with the particular knowledge that allowed one to perceive truths about the nature of the world. The existence of divinity was one such truth.[94] This knowledge was to be derived from observation and critical reflection; Viresalingam applied these criteria to his proofs of the existence of divinity as well as to more mundane matters.[95] He placed a new emphasis on science, especially Western science based on an empirical tradition of observation and experimentation, which he grasped as being similar to his own ideas about knowledge. In the 1880s, he began to translate scientific treatises on subjects like biology, physics, and astronomy into Telugu. He valued science because it was a systematic method of investigating phenomena that gave a consistent, "true" picture of the nature of the world, unlike the accounts of creation that he read in the Hindu epic literature.[96] Science was a tool with which Viresalingam could expose superstition and ridicule the basis of existing customs. He hoped to use scientific explanations to refute the arguments of traditional scholars and win the allegiance of the educated elite for social reform.

Morality was the second major element in Viresalingam's ideas on education. He believed that science and morality were different aspects of the truth—each represented a way of perceiving divinity and each confirmed the existence and benevolence of divinity.[97] Viresalingam deprecated the contemporary equation of Western education with material advantages, because he connected education with religious training. It was chiefly the moral benefits of education that he wanted to confer on women and the masses.[98] He advocated moral teaching of a nondenominational nature that would stress the truths common to all religions: the existence of God, God's benevolence and kindness, and the individual's need to adopt appropriate moral behavior, based on reason, in order to please God.[99]

At first Viresalingam believed the purpose of education was to create an elite group—emancipated from the inhibiting bonds of custom and tradition—to lead society to a higher level through social reform. This was his view before he tried to gain the support of the educated elite for the widow marriage campaign in 1881.[100] When he first encouraged the education of women, he was concerned only with upper-caste women, particularly those related to members of the educated elite. When this elite failed to support the widow marriage campaign and other reforms, Viresalingam understood that education for an elite group was not sufficient, because pressure from the rest of society could intimidate the few educated men and prevent them from achieving reforms. Therefore, he considered the extension of educational opportunities to the lowest levels of society as a step necessary to emancipating the educated elite.[101] He had already advocated teaching science (hygiene) and morality to high-caste women; these were now to be taught in a simplified form to the masses.[102]

With the inclusion of the masses in Viresalingam's educational goals, his concept of the elite changed, although his belief in its potential to improve the country was always a consistent strand in his thought. Even before 1876, he had praised the educated, but his essays on their role in society had conveyed a quality of ambivalence, since at that time the educated elite in coastal Andhra was small in numbers and still adhered to the lifestyle of the political elite. In that early period, Viresalingam had looked to the traditional scholars as possible promoters of change, but, from 1879 to 1881, his belief in that group's capacity to accomplish this work waned rapidly, and he turned to the educated elite as more appropriate agents of change. His hopes for support from the educated reached a high point in October 1881, when he declared that only Western-educated men should continue to write books in the regional language, since the works of traditional scholars were of no benefit to society.[103] When many of them refused to participate in social reform activities, and some even showed a reluctance to promote education, Viresalingam began to be disillusioned with them.[104] By 1884, his disenchantment was complete, but Viresalingam still believed that if change was to come it must be led by the educated, and he continually urged their commitment to social reform while he criticized them for adopting political reform exclusively.[105]

Viresalingam now envisaged a new mission for the Western-educated elite: constrained from participation in active social reform, they were to be the main instruments in the implementation of universal education. In an essay written in June 1883, he listed the tasks for the educated elite. Only one, the abolition of child marriage, was concerned with social reform; the other tasks focused on the development of education and its consequences for society.[106] After Viresalingam's redefinition of "progress" to include the improvement of the social conditions of the masses, he began to argue for universal education.[107] He argued, as he had before, that scientific and moral training should be adapted especially for women's education and would prepare them to accept changes in society.[108] Viresalingam went on to argue that the effect of education on the masses would be the same: it would drive out superstition, inculcate morality, and provide a receptive climate for social reforms. He did not expect all people to become educated, but he hoped a majority would eventually take advantage of educational opportunities and move from ignorance and poverty to a middle rank in society, a social stratum then rather sparsely occupied by the educated elite.[109] In his view, the masses occupied the lowest level of society, not for economic reasons, but because of their lack of education.

Viresalingam set several tasks for Western-educated men. He anticipated that women and the masses would not take advantage of education initially unless they were under some social pressure to do so. Therefore, the first task for educated men was to send their daughters to school and educate their wives. Next, these literate men must work to dispel the current belief that the *dharmasāstras* prohibited the education of Sudras. When this was accomplished, Viresalingam wanted members of the elite to enter the villages and persuade rural people to become educated. Finally, his program for the elite included the writing of Telugu books on science and morality for the masses. The educated elite was still to be the active agent of change in society, though Viresalingam expected help from the government in providing educational facilities.[110]

Viresalingam had called on the government school system to implement his ideas,[111] but his expectations of government assistance were actually not very great. He had difficulty obtaining approval for his girls' school, and he knew that the municipalities and the Department of Public Instruction in Madras were reluctant to expand government-managed educational facilities. Furthermore, while science classes were relatively easy to introduce or strengthen in the government schools, morality instruction (in the form of nondenominational religious doctrines) was not so easily inserted into the curriculum. Viresalingam wrote repeatedly in his journal, *Vivēka Vardhani,* on this theme of introducing moral training into the school curriculum, but the opposition was great, so he considered other ways to inculcate morality in students. In his assessment, the most effective alternative was to utilize Telugu literature.[112]

Viresalingam's identification of the regional language with a Telugu culture was shared but slightly by different segments of the population in 1882. By 1884, his belief in universal education and a Telugu medium of instruction implied linking together the different levels of culture among Telugu-speaking people. This new and broader goal became included in the meaning of his phrase "the development of the country."[113] Thus Viresalingam's concept of Telugu as a tool in the service of the educated elite had changed drastically; he now saw it as a vehicle for the transformation of the masses. The interaction between his views on reform and his ideas concerning the people who should benefit from reform eventually led him to consider changes in the Telugu language and literature that he had not anticipated in 1874, innovations that led to the fuller development of the new cultural tradition of literature as a means of reform and eventually to a new and broader culture itself.

From 1880 to 1888 there was a clear progression in Viresalingam's thinking about Indian society. Viresalingam's earlier use of metaphor, though frequent, lacked a consistent pattern. When he discussed the masses his metaphors invariably represented them as being at a low level of development—such as a child.[114] Then, with the introduction of local self-government in 1884 and the organization of the Indian National Congress in 1885, Viresalingam's images of them emphasized their "youth." He envisioned society as an organism and saw its parts in anthropomorphic terms. He did not revert to the hierarchical ranking of *varnas* or castes and their approximation to parts of the body, an image featured in the Rig Veda, for he focused on the activities of society. He made his ideas explicit in the following way: social and political reform were both growths of society and, since society was organic in nature, the two had to develop evenly. Coordinated growth was healthy, while uneven growth was a sign of disease. He stated that, in political terms, Indian society was progressing from childhood to adolescence. The government of India was the mother who would grant measures of independence as soon as the adolescent proved capable of exercising it. Viresalingam disavowed his earlier reliance on the educated elite by concluding that one segment of society should not be allowed to forge ahead of other segments, such as women or the masses.[115] This even development of all sections of society was another way in which Viresalingam expressed his idea that the unity of society was essential for progress.

Viresalingam's concept of society as an organic entity initially led him to distrust political reformers. He never quite lost this feeling, even though he came to laud the founding of the Indian National Congress. Local politicians attempted to argue that social reform was not a necessary accompaniment to progress and that contemporary customs were either admirable or impossible to change; Viresalingam reacted sharply to such assertions. He consistently criticized local political reformers for deserting social issues; yet, on another level, he praised the Indian National Congress for its work in promoting the unity of India.[116]

Ultimately, Viresalingam's thinking about the development of Indian society stemmed from two problems. The first was India's low position vis-à-vis the West; this led him to consider largely abstract ways to elevate a country's status. The second problem was the failure of the Western-educated elite to actively support social reform—social pressures exerted by the rest of Indian society meant that educated men were actually being used to enforce conformity to existing social practices. Thus leadership at an elite level obviously was not sufficient to change society; followers also had to be receptive to change, for all levels of the population had to progress together. Viresalingam's recognition of the power of uneducated people to subvert the implementation of socially desirable goals made him realize the magnitude of their power and the need to harness it for progress. This led him to campaign for mass education and the broadening need of the regional language and its literature. He began to equate the development of Telugu culture with the progress of the masses. Earlier he had identified the development of Telugu with progress of the country and its status; by this time he was concerned about the status of the masses as well as that of the country.[117] Viresalingam never made the final, direct equation—the identification of the people with the country—because he still believed in the leadership of an elite, the inherent inertia of the masses, and the wisdom of the British administration in India.[118] Yet his intellectual development, in retrospect, represents a far-reaching attempt to build nationalist consciousness on a cultural base.

One can trace in Viresalingam's intellectual odyssey the interaction of his perceptions and actual social reform experiences through time. Viresalingam began his intellectual inquiry into the origins of the decay of Indian society when he was a young teacher in a village school. His early concern for education made him stress teaching as the key to change, although he was uncertain about exactly what to change at that time. His position as a Telugu scholar inclined him toward that language as the medium of cultural change, and his position as a member of the educated elite and as a Brahman stressed the role of an elite in guiding the country's destiny. But his experience in the widow marriage campaign modified these early ideas and led him to consider mass education as a necessary prerequisite for the inauguration of social reform. Mass education could be conducted only through Telugu, and this made him consider the further expansion of Telugu as the opener for a cultural change much greater than the one he had conceived originally. Beginning as an imitator of the traditional Telugu scholars, he ended his career as a great popularizer and prophet of cultural change for the masses.[119]

Conclusion

The relationship of social reform, literary, and political activity to regional identity forged by Viresalingam decisively shaped the character of the Indian nationalist movement there and contrasted with the lack of such a relationship in Madras. From 1879 to 1913, the educated elite established organizations at three levels—local, district, and regional—and social and religious reform associations stemming from Rajahmundry and Viresalingam's widow marriage campaign were fundamental to development of these groups all over coastal Andhra. Subsequent stages of political development focused on the creation of political contacts and consciousness at the district and regional levels. In 1892, the first conference at the district level was held in Krishna District,[120] and a few delegates came from other districts too.[121] Within three years leaders initiated meetings in other districts, and social conferences were held in conjunction with these district meetings.[122] In 1905, conferences drew attendees from all of coastal Andhra.[123] Some of these gatherings were explicitly political in nature and some, like the Andhra Theistic Conference, were not. From these supra-local conferences came the impetus to inaugurate a political movement in order to secure the recognition of Andhra's separate identity.[124]

The continuing relevance of key social reform ideas to political activity in coastal Andhra, both on the regional level and eventually in the nationalist movement, was unusual, for social reform ideas became increasingly irrelevant in shaping the development of nationalism in other regions of India. But the nationalists in coastal Andhra retained the idea of attaining social modernity, social progress, with its emphasis on the educated elite as the catalyst and the Telugu language and cultural traditions as the means. Modernity was now conceived of as a series of regional political communities within the Indian nation, where law and an Indian government would be the instruments creating new social conditions. Viresalingam's rooting of the idea of progress in the regional culture and his sustained attack on Sanskritic traditions destroyed the intellectual basis for any type of Sanskritic revivalism in Andhra. Viresalingam's first attacks were on the priestly Brahmans, and then he included traditional scholars. For many years his newspaper, the leading one in Andhra, villified priests, scholars, and aspects of ancient Aryan civilization. Thus succeeding generations grew up with a declining status of priests and traditional scholars; consequently, they accepted the futility of using Sanskritic traditions to build a modern identity.

In Madras, Christians and non-Brahmans attacked Brahmans; in coastal Andhra, Western-educated Brahmans, led by Viresalingam, attacked "the orthodox." Discrediting the image of the orthodox Brahman was central to the evolving ideology of social change and national progress. The "new Brahman" conscience in Andhra questioned traditional religious authority as the social reformers sought to transform their regional culture through the modification of Telugu, the expansion of education, and social and religious reform activities. Despite his history of alienating even allies in the implementation of his ideas, Viresalingam was an ideological thinker and polemicist whose ideas decisively shaped the regional culture and nationalist ideology in Andhra. He criticized the existing structure of social and political authority and provided a vision of indigenously generated social change and national progress. He reconceived of both individuals and their collective identity in coastal Andhra, insisting that educated men confront the failure of priestly Brahmans and scholars to uphold Indian society, that they commit themselves to new goals and form new associations, that they assume responsibilities for the condition of women and the masses in Andhra society. Later leaders went far beyond Viresalingam in questioning British political authority in India. Nonetheless, his emphasis on regional cultural traditions had far-reaching political implications, and his widow marriage campaign gave future leaders a direct and overwhelmingly political experience in bringing about social change.

Bibliographic Essay

The reconstruction of the social reform movement in coastal Andhra during the period 1874–91 required a synthesis of two very different types of sources: biographies and autobiographies in Telugu, and English-language newspapers. Neither type of source was sufficient by itself because events in Andhra had few connections with events of an all-India importance. Not until 1907, when Bepin Chandra Pal toured South India protesting the partition of Bengal, did Andhras participate noticeably in events whose significance transcended the regional boundaries. This isolation meant that the history of coastal Andhra during this period of social reform was not fully understood in Madras. The English-language newspapers in Madras mentioned some of the highlights of the social reform movement and thus provided a rough chronology of events in the region, a chronology which could then be linked with major events in Madras and the rest of India. Yet this chronology was at best only an outline.

For a full understanding of social reform and its significance in Andhra, the Telugu sources were crucial. Most valuable were Kandukuri Viresalingam's autobiography and collected works. For the period preceding the widow marriage campaign his autobiography was indispensable. Newspaper reports were very brief at that time, and it would be virtually impossible to describe that early social reform activity without Viresalingam's account. Once the widow marriage campaign began, the two main sources were Viresalingam's 1885 report to the Association, "Rajahmendravara Stri Punar Vivaha Caritramu," which he included in his collected works, and an English account by Viresalingam's ex-student, D. V. Prakasa Row. Reminiscences of Viresalingam's students and followers, especially those of Rayasam Venkata Sivudu, Valluri Suryanarayana Rau, and Cilakamarti Lakshminarasimham, filled out the narrative. The opposition to social reform had to be glimpsed mainly through the eyes of the reformers themselves, for the only biography of an opposition leader, that of Vedamu Venkataraya Sastri, mentions a few relevant facts only briefly and omits any discussion of other opposition leaders or connections with them. The decline of the social reform movement in Rajahmundry coincided with the school careers of three future prominent Andhra political leaders, K. Venkatappayya, T. Prakasam, and A. Kaleswara Rao, and their autobiographies furnished revealing accounts of the social reformers' participation in reform activities.

During the decades of the 1870s and 1880s the English-language newspapers relied on correspondents in coastal Andhra for news of that region. The correspondents for the British-owned newspapers were probably Europeans, since most of their news concerned the activities of British officials and missionaries. Even Indian-owned newspapers like *The Hindu* did not pay much attention to events in coastal Andhra, for reports from there were irregular and brief even at the best of times.

Other types of sources, such as records of the Madras government or missionary reports, were of little use for this topic. The general policy of the Government of India was to refrain from undertaking social reform, and, except in individual instances, the Government of Madras did nothing to encourage social reform. This lack of interest was evident in those few cases (such as the circulation of Mr. Malabari's Notes) when the government was compelled to act. Also, British administration at the local level did not pay much attention to the social reformers or include information about them in the reports to higher levels of government, since the social reformers' actions did not impinge directly upon the administration.

The lack of missionary reports for this period was disappointing. Neither the missionary college at Rajahmundry nor its affiliate in Guntur had preserved records from the nineteenth century. The most valuable missionary sources for this study were the journals published in North America. Missionary records usually dealt with the business of managing the mission, whereas the letters of some missionaries to journals provided a few insights into social reform and Viresalingam's life.

Even the archives of the Lutheran Theological Seminary in Philadelphia has preserved only statements regarding itineraries and traveling expenses of missionaries and disputes within the mission. The Lutheran Theological Seminary at Gettysburg has an extensive collection of records and manuscripts for the Lutheran mission in Guntur. The journals of women missionaries were valuable for descriptions of social reform activities and missionary attitudes towards these. The Canadian Baptists had their Telugu Mission headquarters in Kakinada; archives are in McMaster University, Hamilton, Ontario. Although none of their records or journals illuminates any of Viresalingam's actions, there are a few letters in the *Canadian Missionary Link* dealing with Paida Ramakrishnayya. Another journal, *Among the Telugus,* first appeared in 1900 and is valuable for material on social conditions in Kakinada.

Sectarian histories of missionary activity in coastal Andhra, moreover, are uniform in their concentration on those activities which contributed to the growth of Christianity. Although the missionaries in coastal Andhra were pioneers in promoting education, and, interestingly enough, admired and utilized Viresalingam's writings on monotheism and the restrictive aspects of the caste system, they wrote little about Indian society except as it affected their work.

The diaries of Viresalingam, 1897–1916, are in the possession of Y. Venkat Rao, Rajahmundry, who picked them up one day when he noticed a pile of waste paper outside the Viresalingam Theistic High School. There were probably earlier diaries, but even so, their value is limited. Viresalingam recorded the events he considered important but did not comment on them. Most entries deal with the prices of food in the local market and would be valuable for an economic historian. Other financial entries were of value in tracing his supporters for his various projects.

Eight

Sayyid Mumtaz 'Ali and *Tahzīb un-Niswān:* Women's Rights in Islam and Women's Journalism in Urdu

Gail Minault

Historians have often explained religious and social reform in India in the nineteenth century as the result of the Western impact upon the minds of men. Others have recognized that this was entirely too simple an explanation for the intellectual and social changes that took place in India and other places that fell under foreign colonial rule. The equation of Westernization and modernization has given way to a search for the indigenous sources of social change. Recognizing the modernity of tradition is one thing; however, understanding the intellectual processes that produced indigenously generated change is another. With that purpose, we seek to analyze the thought and activities of individuals who were both religious reformers and vernacular[1] publicists. Each of these vernacular-using reformers was involved in religious controversy: with Christian missionaries, with members of other Indian religions, with members of their own faith, or all of the above. Each derived his arguments from within his own tradition, though none was reluctant to use organizational forms and printing technology derived from the West. When such a reformer did adopt an idea, he did so through a process of translation, borrowing what was congruent with his own cultural assumptions and transforming it into his own terms. In analyzing the origins and style of the arguments used by these reformers, we seek a greater understanding of the relationship between religious revival and social innovation in nineteenth-century India, the complex alchemy of change from within as well as impact from without.

Sayyid Mumtaz 'Ali: Early Life and Intellectual Background[2]

Sayyid Mumtaz 'Ali (1860–1935) is an excellent example of a vernacular-using reformer. His education included training in the Islamic classical languages and English, but he thought and wrote in Urdu, developing a clear and persuasive style. He was involved in religious debate early in life and later published polemical works of religious controversy; however, Mumtaz 'Ali was best known for his pioneering role in Urdu journalism for women. In 1898, he founded the weekly newspaper *Tahzīb un-Niswān* (roughly translated: The Women's Reformer) in Lahore in 1898 together with his second wife, Muhammadi Begam. *Tahzīb un-Niswān* was not the first Urdu periodical for women, but it was the first to survive,[3] and it changed the lives of thousands of *purdah*-observing women over the years by giving them a window on the world beyond the narrow walls of their *zanānas*.[4] *Tahzīb* contained new ideas on housekeeping and childrearing, featured and encouraged creative writing by women, discussed women's legal rights in Islam and the necessity for the mothers of the next generation to be educated, and invited letters from its readers to the editor, Muhammadi Begam, who as a woman understood their problems. *Tahzīb un-Niswān* was an important element in the broader movement for women's education among Indian Muslims in the late nineteenth and early twentieth centuries. Mumtaz 'Ali, as its founder and manager, would thus appear to be a typical Westernizing reformer, perhaps with an advanced education in English and only a rudimentary knowledge of Islamic doctrine.

Such, however, was very far from the case, for Mumtaz 'Ali had a thorough vernacular education and training in the classical Islamic curriculum. Further, his family was closely associated with the reformist intellectual tradition of Shah Waliu'llah of Delhi. His father, Sayyid Zulfiqar 'Ali, came from a landed family in Saharanpur District, north of Delhi. The family burial ground is in the small town of Deoband, the location of the principal Islamic *madrassah* (theological school) of northern India, founded in 1867.[5] Sayyid Zulfiqar 'Ali had studied in Delhi in the years before the 1857 revolt with Maulana Mamluk 'Ali Nanautawi, a leading disciple of Shah Waliu'llah's successors. One of his fellow students was Zulfiqar 'Ali from Deoband, who became one of the founders of the Deoband *madrassah* and father of Mahmud ul-Hasan Deobandi, later known to his religious followers as the Shaikh ul-Hind. Sayyid Mumtaz 'Ali and Mahmud ul-Hasan were also friends and contemporaries who studied together at Deoband under Mamluk 'Ali's successors, Maulanas Muhammad Yaqub and Muhammad Qasim Nanautawi. Mumtaz 'Ali did not complete his education at Deoband, but retained his connection to the tradition of Islamic reform institutionalized at the Deoband *madrassah.* It was a connection both intellectual and familial. Mumtaz 'Ali was not related by blood to the leaders of the Deoband school, but he shared the "familial" link of *ustād-shagird* (teacher-disciple) relations through at least two generations.

Mumtaz 'Ali's education began at an Arabic *maktab* in Deoband and continued in the Punjab, where his father was in government service. As they transferred from place to place, his education in the Qur'an, Arabic grammar, Persian literature, *fiqh* (Islamic jurisprudence), and *mantīq* (logic) proceeded until, at the age of thirteen, he returned to study at Deoband, where he studied the Islamic sciences, with an emphasis on the Qur'an and *hadīth* (the prophetic tradition), at the *madrassah.* He attended the Deoband school for only a year or two before rejoining his father in the Punjab. He was then tutored in English at home, passed his middle exams within two years, and in 1876 joined Lahore Government High School. In 1884, in spite of the fact that he was a bright student, Mumtaz 'Ali failed his Bachelor's examinations; he never repeated the attempt. The reasons for his failure are not altogether clear, but seem to be connected to his religious preoccupations during this period.

Lahore in the 1870s and 1880s was a hotbed of religious controversy. Christian missionaries and Muslim divines debated openly in the bazaars of the old city before huge crowds. Mumtaz 'Ali and his school friends not only enjoyed the spectacle, but also were caught up in discussing religious issues. In addition, the Arya Samaj emerged in this period, with its aggressive proselytizing style, and made religious disputation a three-way contest. *Munāzara,* religious debate, was obviously the most exciting game in town.[6] Mumtaz 'Ali, feeling that the local Muslim spokesmen had not adequately answered the Christian missionaries' debating points, devoured works of *munāzara* by the leading Muslim divines, including Maulana Rahmatullah Kairanwi[7] and Maulana Sayyid Abul Mansur Dehlawi.[8] Furthermore, he tried to familiarize himself with the tenets of Christianity in order to formulate better arguments to refute the missionaries, but this led his classmates to worry that he might become a Christian. Sometime in the late 1870s, in conversation with one of his teachers, Babu Chandranath Mitter, Mumtaz 'Ali expressed his dissatisfaction with Muslim debating abilities.[9] Mitter introduced him to some of the writings of Sir Sayyid Ahmad Khan, the founder of Aligarh College, and urged him to write to Sir Sayyid about his religious doubts and concerns.

Sir Sayyid, given his duties at Aligarh and as a member of the Viceroy's Council in Calcutta, was an extremely busy man, but he was touched by the young man's sensitivity and intelligence. He invited Mumtaz 'Ali to visit him in Calcutta in December 1879. Mumtaz 'Ali stayed in Calcutta for about a month, meeting Sir Sayyid frequently. They discussed religious ideas, especially in the context of Sir Sayyid's ongoing commentary on the Qur'an. Mumtaz 'Ali found his doubts answered and his faith in Islam reconfirmed.[10] He also gained new confidence in his own ability to debate religious questions. Even after failing his Bachelor of Arts examinations and taking a job as a translator in the Lahore High Court, Mumtaz 'Ali continued his disputational activities. He published a pamphlet refuting the Ahl-i-Hadith leader, Maulana Muhammad Husain Batalwi's attacks on Sir Sayyid. It is significant that about this same time, his contemporary at Deoband, Mahmud ul-Hasan, was also involved in a published debate with Batalwi over the interpretation of Islamic law, with the Deobandi employing a combination of Hanafi jurisprudence, the Qur'an, and *hadīth,* while the Ahl-i-Hadith spokesman relied almost exclusively on a literal reading of prophetic tradition.[11] Mumtaz 'Ali, in his later work on women's rights in Islamic law utilized a variety of sources for legal interpretation such as those used by the Deobandis. Nevertheless, like Sir Sayyid, he felt free to criticize *hadīth* when it was self-contradictory, or when it conflicted with the Qur'an.[12]

Mumtaz 'Ali's relationship with the Aligarh leader lasted until the end of Sir Sayyid's life. From time to time, he visited Aligarh to ask Sir Sayyid's advice, though Mumtaz 'Ali did not always take it. On one occasion, he showed Sir Sayyid the manuscript of his work in defense of women's rights in Islamic law, *Huqūq un-Niswān.* As he began to read it, Sir Sayyid looked shocked. He then turned to the second page and his face turned red. As he read the third, his hands started to tremble. Finally, he tore up the manuscript and threw it into the wastepaper basket. Fortunately, at that moment a servant arrived to announce lunch, and as Sir Sayyid left his office, Mumtaz 'Ali snatched his mutilated manuscript from the trash. He waited until after Sir Sayyid's death in 1898, however, to publish *Huqūq un-Niswān.*[13]

On another occasion, Mumtaz 'Ali wrote to Sir Sayyid asking his advice concerning a name for his proposed journal for women. Early in 1898, he sent Sir Sayyid a list of possible names, asking for his preference. Sir Sayyid replied grumpily, noting that Mumtaz 'Ali had not asked his advice on whether to start the journal or not, but he offered his views anyway. Sir Sayyid warned Mumtaz 'Ali that if he started a publication for women, he would only earn public condemnation and would ultimately fail. On the other hand, Sir Sayyid said that if he persisted in this folly, he should name it *Tahzīb un-Niswān,* in direct reference to his own social reform journal, *Tahzīb ul-Akhlāq.* Finally, it seemed, Sir Sayyid admired Mumtaz 'Ali's courage, if not his chosen cause. A few weeks after receiving the old man's letter, news reached Mumtaz 'Ali of Sir Sayyid's death. He started publishing *Tahzīb un-Niswān* three months later.[14]

Mumtaz 'Ali thus balanced the intellectual heritage of Deoband and an acquaintance with the leader of Aligarh. Both Deoband and Aligarh had their intellectual roots in the Waliu'llahi reform movement of Delhi. Religious disputation (*munāzara*) with representatives of other religions, both in print and on the public platform, became a Deobandi specialty.[15] The leaders of both Deoband and Aligarh were involved in another form of religious debate as well: with members of their own faith. Sir Sayyid's modernist commentary on the Qur'an did not ultimately carry his community. The Deobandi techniques of religious reform were, however, effective in bringing about a greater awareness of Muslim identity and a more general application of Islamic tenets to everyday life.[16] In their desire to improve the knowledge of Islamic law in the Muslim community in general, and to promote the observance of the injunctions of Islam in the personal lives of Muslims, the Deoband *'ulamā* founded a department of Islamic legal rulings, which issued *fatāwa*[17] in response to queries from Muslims all over India. In addition, the Deobandis wanted to combat the observance of traditional customs that they felt were un-Islamic. For that reason, they showed some interest in the education of women, at least to the extent of improving their knowledge of Islam, since women were the prime practitioners of a host of rituals that the reformers abominated.[18] Mumtaz 'Ali combined all these influences in his career of religious and social reform. While a young man in Lahore he was motivated by his experience of religious disputation. He derived many of his techniques and arguments from the example of his Deobandi mentors, but Sir Sayyid's avuncular interest gave him the courage of his convictions.

Mumtaz 'Ali's *Huqūq un-Niswān,* which so irritated Sir Sayyid, showed the influence of *munāzara* in its style, and in content it was a logical extension of a number of concerns of the Deoband *'ulamā.* His treatment of women's rights in Islam and concern for women's education, however, are considerably more advanced in spirit than either his Deobandi mentors or Sir Sayyid.[19] The question thus arises how Mumtaz 'Ali became interested in the status of women in Muslim law and society and made this his special cause. His intellectual background raised certain issues and gave him a method of expressing his views, but personal factors doubtless played a role in the development of his attitudes toward women's rights.

First of all, Mumtaz 'Ali's contact with Christian missionaries in debate raised issues of cultural pride and defense. The missionaries criticized Islam (and other Indian religions) for the low status they gave to women and blamed these religions for the lack of education among Indian women. Mumtaz ʻAli knew that the position of women in Islamic law was theoretically much higher than their current status was in fact. The cause of this discrepancy between the legal position of Muslim women and the actual facts of their lives in India, he felt, must be adherence to false customs. Answering the missionaries with theoretical arguments, therefore, was not enough. Changing Muslim practice had to be the highest priority. Women's adherence to custom had to be combatted, but so too—and especially—did the views of men who felt that keeping women in ignorance was part of their religion. To attain these aims, he wrote *Huqūq un-Niswān.*

Other reasons for Mumtaz ʻAli's concern about women's status were more personal. He testified that, as he was growing up, he felt special sympathy for his sisters. He lost his mother at thirteen, and his elder sisters may have played an important role in his upbringing, though this is conjectural. Although an educated man himself, he apparently chose as his wife a woman who was uneducated, a point deduced from the fact that he tried to teach her to read and write.[20] She bore him two children, Wahida and Sayyid Hamid ʻAli, and died in 1895. At thirty-five, Mumtaz ʻAli found himself a widower with two small children to raise. His personal loss may have helped focus his considerable controversialist skills on the question of male-female relations in Muslim society and led him to write, or at least to complete, *Huqūq un-Niswān.* Sir Sayyid's rough treatment of the manuscript may have convinced him that he would have to publish it himself. The chronology of this period is uncertain, but sometime before his wife's death, he left his government job to devote himself to writing and publishing. Then, perhaps during his bereavement, he became the proprietor of the Rifah-i-Am, a press in Lahore, and started a publishing firm, Dar ul-Isha'iat-i-Punjab.

Mumtaz ʻAli's bereavement and his fledgling publication projects intensified his sense of the importance of women, not only as nurturers of the young, but also as companions to their husbands. This domestic ideal, including the desire for companionship in marriage, was not usually found among Indian Muslims of that day. Domesticity was, however, a Victorian ideal that Mumtaz ʻAli had acquired either through personal contacts or through reading.[21] Most probably, he had come into contact with Victorian views of womanhood in translated books, through reading Urdu works that reflected "the angel in the house" in the mirror of North Indian Muslim culture. Mumtaz ʻAli had read the novels of Deputy Nazir Ahmad and admired them.[22] Nazir Ahmad's didactic novel, *Mirāt ul-'Arūs,* first published in 1869, provided the model for the ideal Muslim woman. Its heroine, Asghari, is a paragon: she was educated, a capable manager, a companion to her husband and a goad to his career, but she never violated social norms. She observed strict *purdah* and always gave her elders and in-laws their due respect.[23] Mumtaz 'Ali needed an Asghari. The woman he found, Muhammadi Begam (1878?–1908) was perhaps as close to that ideal as real life could afford him.

Muhammadi Begam was the daughter of Maulwi Ahmad Shafi who, like Mumtaz 'Ali's father, was an official in the Punjab government service. The families of Sayyid Zulfiqar 'Ali and Ahmad Shafi were acquainted, and they may have been related. The unpublished biography of Muhammadi Begam mentions that when she was tiny, she used to visit "Judge Sahib" Zulfiqar 'Ali's house to see his daughters, who were on sisterly terms with her mother.[24] It is clear that the women of the two families were close, if not directly related. When Muhammadi was three, her mother died, and thereafter she visited Judge Sahib's house more frequently. Her father later remarried a woman who was apparently her mother's sister, and who came from Deoband.

Muhammadi, like many girls with numerous brothers, grew up preferring boys' games to playing with dolls. She also studied with her brothers, memorizing the Qur'an and learning to read Urdu. When her sister married in 1886 and moved away, Muhammadi learned to write letters in order to remain in touch. She became a good seamstress, making and embroidering clothes for her younger brothers and her sister's children. When Muhammadi was thirteen, her stepmother spent considerable time in Deoband for a family wedding, and so she kept house, cooked, did the household accounts, and wrote daily to her sister and stepmother. Even as a teenager, therefore, Muhammadi Begam became used to managing a large household and caring for the younger children. Also during this period, she read Urdu newspapers and books and started studying English grammar. Her education, conducted at home, was somewhat haphazard and was related mainly to practical matters. Yet, she mastered academic subjects relatively easily when she found it necessary.[25]

Mumtaz 'Ali was interested in marrying a woman with some education to be a mother to his children and a companion for himself, but, above all, a partner in his publishing projects. He thus turned to the family of Maulwi Ahmad Shafi and to their remaining unmarried daughter, still quite young but already accomplished. He and Muhammadi Begam were married in November 1897, when he was thirty-seven and she was about nineteen. When Muhammadi came to Lahore, she took over responsibility for his household[26] and for his children, who apparently adored her.[27] In addition, she continued her studies: Mumtaz 'Ali taught her Arabic and Persian; an English woman came to teach her English; a Hindu woman, Hindi; and a neighborhood boy, math. As if this were not enough, she enthusiastically supported her husband's plans to start an Urdu newspaper for women.[28] Together, they began publishing *Tahzīb un-Niswān* in July 1898. Mumtaz 'Ali's treatise on women's rights in Islamic law, *Huqūq un-Niswān,* was published in the same year.

Huqūq un-Niswān: Women's Rights in Islam

Huqūq un-Niswān thus emerged from Mumtaz 'Ali's training in Islamic law, experience of religious debate, sense of cultural pride when faced with an external challenge, acute awareness of the need for internal reform, personal anguish of bereavement, and desire for an educated wife. His treatment of women's rights in Islam was not only surprising for its time, but seems enlightened even by today's standards. At the outset, Mumtaz 'Ali stated that people will probably attack him for blindly following the English,[29] but that is not the case. Anyone who knew the *sharī'at* and who followed the example of the Prophet and his family must be prepared to reject ignorant customs. He thus placed himself firmly within the framework of Deobandi reform, seeking to revalidate Islamic law and the prophetic example in Muslim daily life, and to eradicate customary accretions that were superstitious, wasteful of human potential and resources, or otherwise ill informed and un-Islamic. Deoband sought to equip the modern Muslim with a reformulation of the fundamentals of his faith,[30] Mumtaz 'Ali wished to equip Muslim women with a reaffirmation of their equality with men as human souls and with a reformulation of the fundamentals of their rights in Islamic law. Without such a reformulation, Mumtaz 'Ali feared for the health of the Muslim family and the Muslim community as a whole. He stated that keeping women in ignorance and isolation was not a requirement of Islam, and to say that it was betrayed a lack of understanding of religion as well as a fundamental mistrust of women, which was destructive of family life, of human love, and of all that the Prophet stood for in a dynamic, just, human society.[31]

In a brief presentation, one can only give the main lines of Mumtaz 'Ali's argument in *Huqūq un-Niswān,* characterize his style and comment upon the significance of the work for Islamic reform. Reading through the work, one is impressed by its careful organization, its logical step-by-step argument, and its rationality in dealing with a subject that was close to people's intimate lives and emotions. In style, it was like a debate, setting out the various arguments that his opponents might use, and knocking them down one by one. Its language was simple and straightforward. In all his works, Mumtaz 'Ali took care to write clearly and to define words, especially those from Arabic, that might offer difficulty to his readers. Throughout this work, he quoted copiously from the Qur'an and *hadīth* to support his arguments, but he was always careful to translate and interpret these passages as he went along. He had two primary reasons for writing: first, to convince men that women should be recognized as equal human beings and given their rights; second, to communicate with women, who might not know any of the abstruse terminology.[32]

Huqūq un-Niswān was divided into five parts: (1) the various reasons why people say that men are superior to women, (2) women's education, (3) *purdah,* (4) marriage customs, and (5) relations between husband and wife. The first section, an examination of the reasons why men were considered superior to women, was quite a *tour de force.* It involved Qur'anic and *hadīth* commentary, discussion of points of Islamic law, and basic psychological assumptions. It was rigorous, logical, and convincing. Of course, whether Mumtaz 'Ali persuaded his opponents that women are not inherently inferior to men was open to question, since, as he admited, the opposing arguments were falsely considered an intrinsic part of religion and hence were hard to shake by rational argument. Nevertheless, Mumtaz 'Ali would have been a formidable opponent in debate.

He began his discussion by pointing out that although men and women had different physiques and thus fulfilled different biological functions, they were nevertheless both human beings, and hence equal in God's sight. All arguments for male superiority derived either from this biological difference, or else from ignorance of the true message of Islam. He listed the arguments for keeping half the human race in bondage as follows: (1) God gave men greater physical strength, thus in matters where strength was important, including the capacity to rule, men were superior; (2) men's intellectual powers were also superior to those of women; (3) men were superior in religious matters, for God had sent only male prophets, not prophetesses; (4) verses of the Qur'an were frequently cited in support of male domination over women; (5) God first created man and then created woman to serve him; (6) in the Qur'an, it states that the testimony of two women was equal to that of one man, and in the inheritance of property, a daughter's share was only half that of a son, hence women were inferior in these respects; (7) men may have as many as four wives at once, thus clearly, God gave men more powers; (8) even in the afterlife, women had an inferior position, for God granted that men will be kept company by beautiful women (*houris*), but women were to be chaste in paradise.

Mumtaz 'Ali then considered each of these arguments in turn, in order to determine whether they were based on reason and thus truthful, or whether they were irrational and thus falsehood. First, no one can deny that men have greater physical strength, but one must also realize that this did not automatically give men the right to dominate women. Men could cut down trees or cut people's throats; they were naturally suited to jobs that require strength. But did the ability to do such things bestow on men greater nobility or true superiority as compared to women? A donkey could carry more on its back than a man, but did that mean donkeys were superior to men? As for who had the right to rule, physical strength was not the only capacity that counted. Perhaps, in the dark ages, it was correct to say that "might makes right." But with the advance of civilization and the founding of kingdoms with laws and other institutions of government, it was more important for the ruler to have understanding and compassion in order to enjoy the confidence of the ruled. Hence the right to rule belonged not to the strong, but to the wise. Further, when women have been called upon to rule, as in the case of the current Queen-Empress, Victoria, they have ruled with great skill, wisdom, and justice.

The second argument, that of greater intellectual capacity, was also without basis. "Man," in the sense of "human," was higher in intellectual capacity than other animals, but men and women were of the same species and thus must be compared to other animals as one. There was no necessary connection between greater physical strength and greater rationality or intellectual power. Any differentiation between the brain powers of the two genders must be something that society has attributed to them, not that God had granted. Indeed, if the intelligence of women were less than that of men, the human race would rapidly become stupid, for intelligence would be transmitted in lesser degree to each succeeding generation.

As for the religious reason, that there had never been a woman prophet, Mumtaz 'Ali dismissed it by saying that the extant names of the prophets in the scriptures were all men, but there were thousands of prophets whose names had not survived, and who was to say that there were no prophetesses among them? On the more serious question of the greater spiritual strength of men, he pointed out that one cannot compare all men to all women in spiritual matters. Just as some men are more spiritual than most women, so too were some women more spiritual than most men. He gave as examples Hazrat Amina and Hazrat Fatima, the mother and daughter of the Prophet Muhammad, and Rab'ia of Basra, the mystic poet.

The main reason to put men in authority over women, however, was contained in these frequently cited verses of the Qur'an:

> Men are the managers of the affairs of women for that God has preferred in bounty one of them over another, and for that they have expended of their property. Righteous women are therefore obedient.[33]

Mumtaz 'Ali disagreed with the usual male supremacist interpretation of these verses. Analyzing the original Arabic, he states that it was by no means clear who had different qualities from whom. It may have meant that some human beings have higher qualities (bounty) than others, but not necessarily men over women. Probably sensing that this was not a very strong argument, Mumtaz 'Ali then presented the view that this verse dealt with areas where men did have greater authority (business and property management), but did not mention areas where women were more competent (responsibility for children, servants, the household). Hence, one could not generalize from this verse that women should be subordinate to men in all things.

The argument that Adam was created first and Eve second and that this proved his superiority was unworthy of serious consideration, said Mumtaz 'Ali. One could as easily argue that God did not want women to be alone, so for her protection and happiness, He created man first. In the matter of court witnesses, where two women's testimony was equal to that of one man, Mumtaz 'Ali pointed out that this verse in the Qur'an referred specifically to business matters, in which women may have less experience. But their lack of experience was a product of social conditions, not an inherent defect. In testimony over marriage, divorce, adultery—matters where women were just as experienced as men—the Qur'an made no distinction. Mumtaz 'Ali went on to cite *hadīth* in support of his argument that there were cases in which one woman's testimony could be decisive. For example: in the case where a woman served as wet nurse to a boy and girl who later married, only she would be in a position to confirm that the marriage was incestuous in Islamic law. Hence, to say that a woman's testimony was unequal to that of a man was a misreading of Islamic law and deprives half of humankind of legal rights.

In matters of inheritance, it was true that a daughter inherited only half the share that a son received. But one could argue that a daughter may take a dowry from her paternal home at the time of marriage, and, in addition, she was entitled to *mahr* (dower) from her husband, so an unequal portion in inheritance was only just to her male siblings. This provision, however, in no way implied unequal rights to property, and it certainly should not be used to argue that the daughter was inferior to the son.

Mumtaz 'Ali also subjected the polygamy argument, that a man may take four wives at once, to intense scrutiny. He argued that the Arabic text permits four wives, but, once again, it was not clear whether it means one at a time, or as many as four simultaneously. He tended to favor the first interpretation, that a man, if widowed or divorced, may remarry up to four times. On the other hand, Mumtaz 'Ali also argued that if a man wished to remarry while still married to his first wife, he must seek her permission. He cited *hadīth* to support this contention, which seemed to go against his first interpretation given above. He also noted that various schools of Islamic law permitted stipulations in marriage contracts forbidding polygamous remarriage, or making divorce automatic in the event of a husband's remarrying. This ruling confirmed the necessity for the husband to obtain his wife's permission before remarriage. Mumtaz 'Ali's position on the polygamy issue, while somewhat inconsistent, nevertheless made a point concerning male and female status: men could not simply do as they pleased without consulting the women involved, and hence women were not mere chattels, but full partners in a contractual agreement, marriage. Thus, the polygamy argument was no proof of male superiority.

Finally, concerning the *houris* of paradise, Mumtaz 'Ali argued that, although in the Qur'anic verse all the pronouns that referred to "the believer" were masculine, stating that "he" will find a spouse in heaven, the true meaning of the verse is that when "one" goes to paradise, he/she will find his/her spouse there. If this grammatical analysis had not convinced the reader, Mumtaz 'Ali went on to point out that, in any case, believers who enter paradise will have changed their essence, and to the soul, all distinctions of gender were meaningless.

Having disposed of these arguments, Mumtaz 'Ali maintained that the intellectual superiority of men had in no way been proven, and in fact, experience showed that girls, if given the chance, were often quicker and more diligent students than boys. He noted that some boys went to school and derived very little benefit from it, whereas their sisters, without any formal education, might learn to read and write through perseverance. As for moral strength, he maintained that here, too, women had the edge. He gave as an example the plight of widows in India. In spite of the fact that the Qur'an granted widows the right to remarry, Muslims as well as Hindus considered this a great scandal. On the other hand, widowers readily remarried. Women therefore were expected to show greater self-sacrifice in this matter, as in so many others. Was that not evidence of their greater moral fiber?

This analysis of the first section of *Huqūq un-Niswān* gives some indication of Mumtaz 'Ali's method. He combined Qur'anic and *hadīth* commentary with logical argumentation and a certain amount of sociological acumen, the whole conveyed in a straightforward Urdu style. His position was clearly reformist, even revolutionary, in the context of his times. He showed that the distinctions made between men and women that were justified on religious grounds were, in fact, the products of social custom. If these distinctions were subjected to the cold scrutiny of reason, well bolstered by a knowledge of the religious sciences, the fallacy and injustice of male supremacy became clear.

Mumtaz 'Ali continued in this vein through the succeeding sections of the work. It is not possible to summarize the entire work here;[34] it is sufficient to note that, however revolutionary *Huqūq un-Niswān* was, it had little effect. Part of the reason for that was simply its controversialist format. Religious debate between religions, or even between sects of a given religion, may have excited public interest, especially when the arguments were brief and formulaic and convinced the members of a particular faith that their beliefs were the best. A long, carefully reasoned work such as this, one that asked every Muslim to reexamine his basic beliefs and to change his intimate behavior, was a different matter. *Huqūq un-Niswān* may have caused a few ripples when it was published, but they quickly dispersed. Its original printing of 1,000 copies was never repeated. It was undoubtedly too far in advance of its times. Given the current debate over Muslim personal law reform, however, it should now be reprinted.

Tahzīb un-Niswān: Women's Journalism in Urdu

If *Huqūq un-Niswān* had few repercussions, *Tahzīb un-Niswān* had a rather different fate. When Mumtaz 'Ali and Muhammadi Begam began publishing *Tahzīb,* they mailed it out gratis to names on the civil list, hoping to enlist subscriptions. Their prospective subscribers responded by returning the paper to sender, with obscenities scrawled on the label. Somebody plastered a poster on the outer gateway of Mumtaz 'Ali's house, accusing him of promoting prostitution. It was hardly an auspicious beginning to a publishing venture. After three or four months, the journal had only 60 or 70 subscribers. But the couple persisted, and gradually the number of subscribers increased. After four years, *Tahzīb* had some 300 to 400 subscribers. The weekly started out with eight pages, then grew to ten, and finally to sixteen pages. Both Mumtaz 'Ali and Muhammadi Begam wrote for it, and they solicited articles from friends, relatives, and literary acquaintances. Mumtaz 'Ali emphasized that Muhammadi Begam was the editor; he was only the financial manager. She exercised full editorial control over the choice of articles and subjects covered. By emphasizing that a woman was in charge, he hoped to encourage women to contribute. It worked. Over the years, the proportion of articles and letters written by women increased to a majority.[35]

Muhammadi Begam worked very hard to make the weekly a success. She rose early to pray, to take care of the children, the food, and the house. She worked late into the night to bring out the journal, personally writing a great deal of the material, editing, and answering letters, often not getting to sleep until after 1:00 A.M. It was no surprise that their first child, a daughter, was stillborn. Mumtaz 'Ali and Muhammadi Begam later became the parents of a son, Sayyid Imtiyaz 'Ali, born in October 1900. Muhammadi Begam was thus wife, mother, companion in life's work, and was educated and an accomplished homemaker. She proved that it was possible for a woman to "have it all," even in Indian Muslim middle-class society at the turn of the century. But as her sisters elsewhere have more recently discovered, "having it all" could be hard work. Her health was seriously affected. Unlike Asghari, her fictional counterpart, Muhammadi Begam was mortal. Mumtaz 'Ali became a widower for the second time in November 1908.[36]

Before her death, however, Muhammadi Begam helped to make Urdu journalism for women not only acceptable, but successful. She wrote voluminously: journal articles, novels, books of etiquette, housekeeping manuals, and cookbooks. Her novels included *Safiya Bēgam,* a didactic tale about the evils of marrying off a daughter without her consent, and *Sharīf Bēṭī,* a story about a woman starting school at home, patterned, in part, after Nazir Ahmad's *Mirat ul-'Arus.*[37] *Khānadārī* was a manual of modern housekeeping, covering such topics as household cleanliness, the proper purchasing and preparation of food, the need to keep drinking water pure, the use of ice, the rules of nutrition and child care, the care of clothing and bedding, hospitality to guests, the preparation of *pān,* among other subjects.[38] *Ādāb-i-Mulāqāt* was an etiquette book dealing with social gatherings, how to offer hospitality at such "modern" functions as tea parties, and what to do when visiting. This was especially useful information for *purdah*-observing women who were just beginning to socialize with women beyond their immediate family circle and who were unsure of how to behave.[39]

The content of Muhammadi Begam's writings reflected the content of *Tahzīb un-Niswān* during its first ten years under her editorship. The bulk of the articles in *Tahzīb* were aimed at the *purdah*-observing woman at home, focusing on her need for broadened horizons through the medium of this publication and the communication with the outside world it provided. Articles discussed education, housekeeping, and child care, gave recipes, advice to the daughter-in-law on how to get along with her mother-in-law, and tips on etiquette. A constant theme was the reform and simplification of custom, the need to eliminate wasteful expenditure on rituals and ornaments.[40] Mumtaz 'Ali's ideas in favor of women's education and women's rights in Islamic law also appeared in *Tahzīb* and achieved much greater circulation through that medium than they ever did in *Huqūq un-Niswān.*[41]

Tahzīb classified itself as a newspaper, so it also carried numerous short articles and news items, notices of women's meetings and of fund raising drives for schools, summaries of speeches to reform organizations, as well as poetry and creative writing. Longer pieces were serialized over several issues. The weekly format made possible a great deal of give-and-take between the journal and its readers, and among the readers. An article appeared, and a week or two later, a reply. Or several replies surfaced over the next weeks, offering a variety of views, often in vehement disagreement with the editorial. The style was straightforward and conversational, aimed at the reading level of women educated at home. One especially popular section was "Mahfil-i-Tahzib," which included letters to the editor and replies, but also letters from readers addressed to other readers—*tahzībī bahin,* the sisterly network of *Tahzīb*'s subscribers—asking for advice on everything from education and child rearing to gardening tips and how to remove difficult stains. *Tahzīb* thus struck a balance between popular format and reformist substance. It maintained a simplicity and clarity of style with a content both practical and high minded. Muhammadi Begam set the tone and secured the collaboration of other well-known or fledgling women writers of the time: Zohra and Atiya Fyzee of Bombay,[42] Bint Nazar al-Baqar of Sialkot,[43] Khujista Akhtar Banu Suhrawardy of Calcutta,[44] and the Begam of Bhopal. Atiya Fyzee sent back accounts of her travels in Europe, and they were published in weekly installments. Nazar al-Baqar wrote short stories and essays and also was active in fund raising for girls' schools. She later became the editor of *Phūl* (Flower), a newspaper for children that Mumtaz 'Ali started about 1910 as a companion to *Tahzīb.* Mumtaz 'Ali's publishing firm also produced didactic social novels, educational texts, and useful works of advice by a number of early women writers of Urdu, thereby encouraging women's creativity in longer format.[45]

Tahzīb overcame initial opposition and succeeded because it met a felt social need. Mumtaz 'Ali was not the only educated Indian Muslim male of his time who desired a more enlightened home life, nor was Muhammadi Begam the only literate Muslim woman of her time who lacked a source of news and an outlet for self-expression. Mumtaz 'Ali articulated his religious anguish and psychological strain in a controversialist work, *Huqūq un-Niswān,* that made little impression, perhaps because it was too cerebral. But his long-term solution to his individual domestic and professional needs struck a more responsive chord. His partnership with Muhammadi Begam also resulted in a publication that was considerably less controversial. Women writing for other women were somehow less threatening to the men who had to sanction the subscriptions. *Tahzīb un-Niswān,* in the long run, was undoubtedly more productive of social change than *Huqūq un-Niswān,* for instead of urging men to change their beliefs, it encouraged women to alter their lifestyles.

That *Tahzīb un-Niswān* survived Muhammadi Begam's death was a tribute to the magnitude of her accomplishment. Mumtaz 'Ali's daughter, Wahida, became the editor until her marriage in 1913,[46] and then his daughter-in-law, Asaf Jahan,[47] edited it. Later, his son by Muhammadi Begam, Sayyid Imtiyaz 'Ali "Taj" and his wife, Hijjab (Isma'il),[48] carried on the family enterprise.

The later volumes of *Tahzīb* reflected women's advancing level of education and a variety of activities outside their homes. The style, still clear, became somewhat more complex as the vocabulary increased. Notices of meetings grew in number; speeches by women to women's organizations were reported. Groups of women in provincial towns, following the earlier efforts of their sisters in the cities, organized to raise funds for new girls' schools. Articles discussed the necessity of English education for women, and the journal printed the names of women passing their Bachelors, Masters, and medical degrees with warm congratulations and exhortations to other readers to do likewise. Articles begin to appear on the current political scene, the events of World War I, noncooperation, *swadēshī,* and the controversy between the Muslims and the government over the founding of Aligarh Muslim University. Women started collecting funds for political purposes: the Khilafat movement and Turkish relief. *Tahzībī* sisters wrote travel accounts of sightseeing in India, in Europe (Rome, Paris, and London without a veil), and of the *hajj* pilgrimage. Literary criticism appeared. And a greater number of younger women contributors began to take issue with the strictures of *purdah,* with polygamy, and with unilateral divorce.[49]

The latter were issues first raised by Mumtaz 'Ali in *Huqūq un-Niswān,* now adopted by the readers of *Tahzīb* as their own. Mumtaz 'Ali had also advocated a reform of Muslim divorce law, anticipating by some forty years the Dissolution of Muslim Marriages Act of 1939.[50] The readers of *Tahzīb,* through their membership in women's organizations, were active in urging its enactment, which was a major breakthrough in Muslim women's legal rights. Mumtaz 'Ali, unfortunately, did not live to see that realization of a cause he had long championed. He died in Lahore in June 1935 while working on a multivolume dictionary of the Qur'an, *Tafsīl ul-Bayān.* He was buried in Deoband with his ancestors. One may view this as a symbolic return to his roots in the soil of religious controversy and reform.

Conclusion

Mumtaz 'Ali's polemical writings were initially inspired by debates with Christian missionaries and Arya Samaj reformers in the Lahore of his youth. Cultural pride and defense were very much a part of his motivation in taking up religious debate. But as he matured and gradually focused on the status of women as his prime issue, Mumtaz 'Ali increasingly addressed himself to members of his own faith. In so doing, he used Islamic sources and forms of argument to challenge established notions about women which, he maintained, were based on social customs that went against the true spirit of the Islamic message. His openly reformist work, *Huqūq un-Niswān,* was not well received, but instead of causing a stir when it was published, it was largely ignored—surely the worst thing that could happen to a message designed to change society. He was not discouraged, however, but persevered in advancing his ideas through the medium of journalism.

Mumtaz 'Ali's career, his partnership with his wife, their efforts to broaden the horizons of Muslim women through their periodical and ultimately to bring about some reform in women's status have not received their due in historical accounts. The reasons for this have to do both with their means of expression and their chosen audience. Mumtaz 'Ali and Muhammadi Begam were vernacular reformers who wrote in Urdu and based their arguments for change on Islamic traditions of controversy and internal reform. Mumtaz 'Ali brought together a number of intellectual antecedents that included the Deoband school with its emphasis on studies of the Qur'an and *hadīth,* Sir Sayyid Ahmad Khan's religious reformism, and the heated debates among spokesmen for different religions that he had witnessed while a student. He was also exposed to some English education and adopted the periodical press as his medium of communication, but his inspiration, the sources of his ideas, and his chosen language of expression were all from within his own culture.

Muhammadi Begam observed *purdah* all her life, was educated at home, fulfilled her family roles, and was in every way a respectable middle-class Muslim woman. This husband and wife team chose to reform the Muslim home from within by addressing women, a task that was neither easy nor publicly rewarding in their day. And yet the journal they founded, which survived them, spread ideas in favor of women's education, social change, and legal reform, and made a lasting impact upon the lives of educated Urdu-speaking Muslims for several generations. The study of such vernacular reformers provides a deeper understanding of processes of change in traditional societies and avoids the Westernization-modernization equation that has proven too simple an explanation for a complex phenomenon.

Bibliographic Essay

The life and work of Sayyid Mumtaz 'Ali of Lahore was one example of the concern with the status of women among Indian Muslims in the late nineteenth and early twentieth centuries. Women became the focus of a host of writings by men, and later by women, dealing with the education needed for social and religious reform and to combat Muslim backwardness. Many of these writings issued from adherents of the Aligarh movement, but others were written by *'ulamā*. Muslim thinkers were coming to terms with the new realities of political power in India and the social and cultural challenges of that situation, but they did so in terms of their own traditions of religious controversy.

Motivation behind this concern for women's status was varied. Cultural defense was a primary reaction to the religious representatives of the West, the missionaries. Early Muslim religious polemicists answered Christian arguments by concentrating on theological issues, attacking the doctrine of the Trinity as being counter to monotheism and charging that Christian scriptures had been altered and corrupted. Summaries of these early polemics appear in Avril Powell, "Maulana Rahmat Allah Kairanwi and Muslim-Christian Controversy in India in the mid-19th Century," *Journal of the Royal Asiatic Society* (1976): 42–63; and in Barbara Metcalf, *Islamic Revival in British India: Deoband, 1860–1900* (Princeton: 1982), especially chapter 5. Other useful sources for this period include Christian W. Troll, *Sayyid Ahmad Khan: A Reinterpretation of Muslim Theology* (Delhi: Vikas, 1978); Sir William Muir, *The Mohammedan Controversy* (1897; reprint, Allahabad: 1979); and Imdad Sabri, *Asār-i-Rahmat* (Delhi: 1967).

When controversy with the missionaries advanced beyond basic theological questions to social ethics, Muslims had to respond to Christian attacks on *purdah,* polygamy, and the ease of divorce in Islam. Cultural defense remained a motive in this later confrontation, coupled with pride in Muslim family life and a desire to develop a more individualistic basis for adherence to the tenets of Islam. Deoband and Aligarh both advanced ethical arguments defending the *sharī'at* as a guarantor of women's rights and attacking Christian hypocrisy. Barbara Metcalf's *Islamic Revival in British India* provides a summary of Deoband's role in legal commentary. Other secondary sources include Aziz Ahmad, *Islamic Modernism in India and Pakistan, 1857–1964* (London: 1967); and Sheila McDonough, *Muslim Ethics and Modernity* (Waterloo, Ontario: 1984). Primary sources include Sir Sayyid Ahmad Khan's articles on women in M. Ismail Panipati, ed., *Maqalāt-i-Sir Sayyid,* vol. 5 (Lahore: 1961) 186–208; and Mumtaz 'Ali, *Huqūq un-Niswān* (Lahore: 1898). Muslim ethical response also included apologetic ones, exemplified by Maulwi Chiragh 'Ali, *Proposed Political, Constitutional, and Legal Reforms in the Ottoman Empire and Other Mohammedan States* (Bombay: 1883); and Sayyid Amir 'Ali, *The Spirit of Islam* (1922; reprint, London: 1965). Both devoted chapters to the status of women in Islam, emphasizing the historical development of views on women's status within Muslim and Christian religious traditions and the importance of the Prophet's message for women in that context.

The Deobandi best known for his writing on women was Maulana Ashraf 'Ali Thanawi, whose *Bihishtī Zēwar* became the standard guidebook to religious and home life for generations of Muslim brides. Thanawi's work was an integral part of the Deoband school's drive to abolish non-Islamic customs in the home, as a part of their general program of Islamization in the personal lives of Muslims. It is perennially in print in Urdu, and a partial English translation is Rahm 'Ali al-Hashmi, *Bihishtī Zēwar: The Requisites of Islam* (Delhi: 1975). Barbara Metcalf is at work on a fuller translation; see her articles: "Islam and Custom in Nineteenth-Century India," *Contributions to Asian Studies,* 17: 62–78; "The Making of a Muslim Lady: Maulana Thanawi's *Bihishtī Zēwar,*" in M. Israel and N. K. Wagle, eds., *Islamic Society and Culture* (Delhi: 1983) 17–38; "Islamic Reform and Islamic Women: Maulana Thanawi's Jewelry of Paradise," in Barbara Daly Metcalf, ed., *Moral Conduct and Authority* (Berkeley and Los Angeles: 1984).

Another study of customs prevalent among women, written as part of the movement of reform, but also with an ethnographer's eye to preserving a record of such customs is Sayyid Ahmad Dehlawi, *Rusum-i-Delhi* (reprint, Rampur: 1965). Sayyid Ahmad Dehlawi also wrote a number of other works for women, including the didactic tale against wasting time, *Rāhat Zamānī kī Mazedār Kāhānī* (Delhi: 1910), and a guide to letter-writing style, *Inshā-i-Hādī un-Nissa mā Tahrīr un-Nissa* (Delhi: 1910). Sayyid Ahmad also started a newspaper for women which did not survive; he is best known as a lexicographer.

Writers who sought to defend Muslim culture through revitalizing family life by means of women's education include Maulwi Nazir Ahmad, whose novels *Mir'āt ul-'Arus* (1869) and *Banāt un-Na'ash*(1872) became the prototypes for a host of didactic social novels in Urdu. *Mir'āt ul-'Arus* is continuously in print and was translated into English as *The Bride's Mirror* by G. E. Ward (London: 1903). Another writer of the same generation, Altaf Husain Hali, wrote *Majālis un-Nissa* (1874), a dialogue in story form advocating women's education. *Majālis* was reprinted in 1971 by Maktaba-i-Jamia (New Delhi) with an introduction by Saleha Abid Husain. I have translated it into English, together with "Chup ki Dad," one of Hali's poems about women. They have been published as *Voices of Silence* (Delhi: 1986). *Majālis* was adopted as a textbook in vernacular girls' schools for several generations following its original publication and served as a prototype for numerous other edifying works for the education of women. These include *Tahzīb un-Niswān wa Tarbīyat un-Niswān* by Shah Jahan Begam of Bhopal (reprint, Lahore: n.d.); *Kitab-i-Niswān* by Pir Enayatuddin Ahmad (Amroha: 1914); *Baqh-i-Niswān* by S. Abdur Rashid Khan (Hyderabad: n.d.), and many more.

Didactic Urdu novels, written with an eye to reforming Muslim family life and improving women's status, were written by Nazir Ahmad's son, Bashiruddin Ahmad, and his nephew, Rashidul Khairi. Bashiruddin's novels include *Iqbāl Dulhan* (Delhi: 1914), *Husn-i-Ma'āshirat* (Delhi: 1914), and *Islāh-i-Ma-īshat* (Agra: 1917). The prolific production of Rashidul Khairi, who also founded the women's literary magazine *Ismat* in Delhi in 1908, included the tragic trilogy *Subh-i-Zindaqī, Shab-i-Zindaqī,* and *Shām-i-Zindaqī,* constantly reprinted by Ismat Book Depot in Delhi, and after 1947, in Karachi. Mumtaz 'Ali's wife, Muhammadi Begam, wrote several Urdu novels, as did Nazar Sajjad Hyder (mother of the contemporary Urdu novelist, Qurratulain Hyder). These latter were entitled *Akhtarunnissa Bēgam, Āh-i-Mazlumān* (1918), *Harmān Nasīb* (1920), and *Jan Baz* (1935). These are only a few of the many early Urdu novels, of varying literary value, but important as sources of social history. A good survey of these often obscure works is contained in Shaista Akhtar Banu Suhrawardy (Begam Ikramullah), *A Critical Survey of the Development of the Urdu Novel and Short Story* (London: 1945).

Many graduates of Aligarh and other Western-style educational institutions were concerned to find educated wives for themselves and for future generations of the emerging Muslim middle class. This group is exemplified by Shaikh Abdullah, the founder of Aligarh Girls' School in 1906 and a tireless propagandist for women's education in his capacity as Secretary of the women's education section of the Muhammadan Educational Conference. The proceedings of this conference and other Muslim social reform organizations, such as the Anjuman-i-Himayat-i-Islam of Lahore and the Anjuman-i-Islam of Bombay, contain debates about women's education and information about the founding of schools. The records of the Muhammadan Educational Conference are available at Aligarh University; the journal of the Anjuman-i-Himayat-i-Islam is in the Research Society of Pakistan in Lahore. A history of the Anjuman was published in Lahore on its fiftieth anniversary in 1938. A useful short history of the Anjuman-i-Islam of Bombay is S. Shahabuddin Desnawi, "Anjuman-i-Islām—Ek Tahrīk," *Ājkal* (October 1981):15–22, 45.

The most effective medium of communication of new ideas to Muslim women, however, was the Urdu periodical press. Further, these

Urdu journals for women, of which *Tahzīb un-Niswān* is a prime example, constitute one of the most useful sources for the social history of Indian Muslims during this period. These journals contain articles by both men and women debating the pros and cons of social and religious reform, various types of education for girls, and the abandonment of useless customs. Periodicals also provided women with useful information to improve their homemaking and childrearing skills, and offered women a forum for the public expression of their own views. In addition to *Tahzīb* (founded 1898), *Khātūn* established by Shaikh Abdullah in 1904 and *Ismat* founded by Rashidul Khairi in 1908 were the major journals reflecting the spread of women's education and women's increasing self-expression. But there were many others as well: *Mu'allim-i-Niswān,* founded by Muhibb-i-Husain in Hyderabad in the 1890s; *Pardanashīn* of Agra; *Zillus-Sultān* of Bhopal, mouthpiece of the Begam of Bhopal; *Sharīf Bībī, Zēbunnissa,* and *Nūr Jāhān* of Lahore; *An-Nissa, Khādima,* and *Safīna-i-Niswān* of Hyderabad; *Khatūn-i-Mashriq, Niswānī Dunya, Anīs-i-Niswān, Avāz-i-Niswān,* and *Sadā-i-Niswān,* all of Delhi; *Sahēlī* of Amritsar; and *Hayyā, Zīyā,* and *Harīm* of Lucknow.

The bibliography on "the woman question" among Muslims, broadly considered, is thus voluminous, and includes polemical pamphlets, studies of custom, works of educational value and advice for women, didactic novels, the proceedings of reform organizations, and journals for women, not to mention biographies, autobiographies, and collections of letters. The primary sources, almost without exception, are in Urdu, though some translations and secondary sources have appeared in recent years. I have found these sources by searching libraries with Urdu holdings in India and Pakistan and by searching out families associated with the founding of schools and journals for women. The most complete files of *Tahzīb un-Niswān* and *Khātun* are at Aligarh Muslim University library. *Ismat* can be found at the Ismat Daftar in Karachi and at the Urdu Research Centre in Hyderabad. Occasionally, as with the manuscript biography of Muhammadi Begam (see note 2), private family papers yield a treasure. I have also found pamphlets, educational works, obscure novels, and journals by haunting second hand booksellers in the Urdu bazaars of the subcontinent. To describe all the treasures unearthed, and characters encountered, in the quest for the invisible women of Indo-Muslim history would take far too long. Suffice it to say that women and the family were central to men's preoccupations as they faced the multiple challenges of the encounter with the West and sought to defend and revitalize their culture from within.

Nine

Vernacular Publishing and Sikh Public Life in the Punjab, 1880–1910

N. G. Barrier

The evolution of a modern communication system has helped shape the issues and the strategies of those involved in South Asian religious, social, and political life. No matter what class or intellectual persuasion they represented, the new regional elites were both the product of an emerging print culture and the first South Asians to explore its possibilities for their own ends. The traditional means of transmitting message and influence through personal or institutionalized relationships remained, but the rapid spread of educational opportunities, the printing industry, and the railroads, telegraph, and the postal service offered an assortment of opportunities for those who could put them to use. Indians learned quickly from foreigners such as missionaries and publicists who facilitated the transfer of new technology and, with it, powerful means of transmitting information and broadening influence. By the end of the century, there were over fifteen hundred newspapers and innumerable presses and tract societies spread across the subcontinent. Journalism was not only a new and potentially rewarding occupation, but also an integral part of the dynamic ideological debates and institution building occurring in each region.[1]

Although earlier studies on movements and events have tended to emphasize English-language sources, clearly the bulk of printed communication was in regional languages. In 1905, for example, less than 20 percent of the newspapers and journals were in English and they circulated among a small part of the literate population. This was not surprising, because most Indians who could read and write communicated primarily in vernacular languages. A burst of creativity and new uses of the written tradition also could be found in regional literatures.[2]

While the last kingdom of the subcontinent to be conquered by the British, the Punjab quickly followed in the footsteps of the provinces where earlier experiments in education and publishing had become routinized. As in other areas, the resulting network of presses, journals, and tract societies mirrored parochial concerns and were written largely in the vernacular. Of the approximately 260 newspapers and journals in Punjab in 1905, 12 were in English, 18 in two or more languages, 17 in Punjabi (Gurmukhi script), 15 in Hindi, and the remainder in Urdu. Most dealt with particular issues or reflected the editorial perspective of publishers and/or sponsors. A similar pattern was reflected in the tracts and books circulating in the Punjab.[3]

Vernacular publishing was especially important for the formulation and transmission of the vision of Sikhism associated with the Singh Sabhas. This essay explores the spread of a new and broad-based communication system among Sikhs. Since more abundant research is available on Sikh and other Punjab newspapers, particular attention will be paid to the tract literature.[4] After describing the issues confronting Sikhs in the decades after annexation and the ideological and organization world in which they lived, brief comments will be made on the implications of a widening and more systematic information network for those involved in the revitalization of Sikhism. Another section deals with the lives and role of specific authors and literary specialists in propagating views—often opposing—of history, social practice, and religious orthodoxy. Unlike the tracts and books written by other Punjabis, and the polemical literature discussed by contributors to this volume, the Sikh publications focused primarily on internal issues, and they did not register particular concern with missionaries or even fears about other competing religions. The notable exception was the ongoing struggle with Arya Samaj propagandists. A concluding section evaluates the use of tract and polemical documents in understanding not only one phase in the evolution of modern Sikhism, but also the ways in which symbols and polemics continue to affect the Sikh world today.

Singh Sabhas and the Evolving Sikh Tradition

Between the period of the Gurus and the nineteenth century, the Sikhs of the Punjab experienced social, religious, and political changes that are only beginning to be understood. Few documents were left of a dynamic phase in which new forms of social and political organization, the *misāls,* became dominant; only a handful of Sikhs recorded the events and attempted to grapple with their significance. That literature, and the customs prevalent in the Punjab during the reign of Ranjit Singh, suggests a wide variation in worship, social values, and popular culture among those who called themselves Sikhs.

Sikhs worshipped frequently at the shrines of local *pīrs* and lived in a world of omens and superstitions. Rituals and the major events of the year, such as fairs and festivals, often indicated Hindu influence. Specific rules of conduct were not generally recognized, although there were growing attempts to write down *rahītnāmās,* manuals of social and ritual practice, that could be used as a guide to proper action. Sikh social life tended to center on the *birāderī* (the patrilineal descent group generally living in close proximity). Caste with a defined sense of impurity and pollution affected marriage and political networks. *Varna* and rites of passage, with strong Brahmanic influence, were evident in daily life. Traditional religious leaders such as *bhāīs* and *gyānīs,* learned men, were revered, as were the descendants of the Gurus. Also important were the various Sikh ascetic orders such as the Udasis and Nirmalas, whose control over local shrines became more pronounced due to the religious grants made by Ranjit Singh.[5]

After the 1840s, Western observers and some Sikhs felt that Sikhism was losing its identity and soon would disappear as a religious faith. Such assessments rested upon Western assumptions about the nature of religions and, in particular, the view that only Sikhs who maintained the outward symbols associated with Guru Gobind Singh (the five Ks, of the *keshādhārī* Sikhs) were true to the tradition. Sikhs at that time did not share either the assumptions about how religions differentiate themselves by fixed boundaries in areas such as theology, worship, and ritual, or the narrow view of a Sikhism devoid of Hindu influence.[6] Estimates vary as to the number of Sikhs who maintained the traditional symbols, as opposed to the *sahajdhārīs,* who espoused devotion to the Granth and the Gurus but saw no reason for maintaining outward symbols. At that time, however, such a differentiation did not constitute a dominant element in the social and religious life of the Sikhs. Intermarriage between Sikhs and Hindus without regard to maintenance of religious belief was common. A highly defined Sikh religion did not exist. By the end of the century such a shift toward a new orthodoxy surfaced, however, in response to pressures within the community as well as to challenges and threats associated with Western rule.

The transfer of institutions and ideology to the Punjab following annexation in 1849 created a milieu in which Sikhs were forced to reexamine their traditions, to assess their current conditions, and to plan for the future. The assortment of changes resulting from the British presence have been discussed widely, and while occasional facts and interpretations may vary, the outline of what transpired seems clear. The colonial system of government introduced a hybrid educational system that combined Western subjects with instruction in English and the vernacular. Success in the schools was the primary criterion for participation in new professions. Just as directly, official policies toward the economy and rural society helped precipitate the rise of new classes and the loss of power by at least some of the traditional elites. Perhaps more importantly, Western approaches to religion, society, and politics became integral parts of intellectual life in the Punjab and influenced how Punjabis looked at themselves and each other.[7]

Recent studies, especially those of Kenneth Jones and Harjot Singh Oberoi, have emphasized the continuities between Punjabi religious concerns in the early decades of the century and the rapid surfacing of new organizations and disputes by the 1870s.[8] Among Hindus, the students educated at Delhi College and then associated with missionary schools became involved in reform societies such as the Lahore Brahmo Samaj and Sat Sabha of Lahore. The orientalist fervor surrounding the Anjuman-i-Punjab, Dr. G. W. Leitner's forum for educational and social reform, similarly helped train Punjabi Muslims, Hindus, and Sikhs in Western-style organization and publicity. The conflict between the Sanatana Hindus, defending a Brahmanic form of tradition complete with time-honored rituals and the puranic literature, and an opposing group of Hindus, sharing a vision of a more modern religious faith, set the stage for the introduction of the Arya Samaj in 1877. The rapid growth of the Arya program involving propaganda, education, and incessant confrontation in turn helped shape the intellectual milieu of urban Punjab for decades to come.

The Sikh experience paralleled that of the Hindus and the Arya Samajists, although with somewhat different ideological and institutional concerns. By the 1860s, two sects, the Nirankaris and the Namdharis (or Kukas), already were questioning the legitimacy of many practices current among Punjab Sikhs. The founder of the Nirankari movement, Baba Dayal (?–1855), rejected idol worship and emphasized personal worship and respect for the *Ādi Granth* as essential for daily life. Ram Singh (1816–85) became a religious leader, as he and his followers (commonly called Kukas) attempted to change Sikh customs in areas such as marriage, ritual, lifestyle, and religious belief. The Kukas became known for their virulent denunciations of, and occasional attacks on, Hindu and Muslim sacred spots frequented by Sikhs. They also rejected ideas and conveniences associated with the Western presence. Although the evolving doctrines of these two sects placed them on the periphery of Sikh social and religious debate, their emphasis upon the centrality of the Granth, denunciation of Hindu-related worship, and, in the case of the Kukas, the demand for a simple orthodoxy based upon a standard *rahīt* (code of discipline) highlighted a pool of ideas and examples that influenced debates in later years.[9]

The emergence of Singh Sabhas as articulate spokesmen for a vision of Sikh tradition and change marked a turning point in the evolution of modern Sikhism. From 1873 onward, Sikhs reevaluated the history and fundamental tenets of their faith, exploring the past in order to address what were seen as pressing problems and threats. The spread of the new organizations across the province, and later beyond, was uneven, decentralized, and frequently the product of personal interests or ideological disagreement. There were two major constellations within the Singh Sabha universe. The founding Amritsar Singh Sabha (1873) was led by an assortment of traditional leaders including *gyānīs, bhāīs,* and aristocrats. As Harjot Singh Oberoi has documented, these men such as Thakur Singh Sandhawalia, Khem Singh Bedi, and Kanwar Bikram Singh shared a feeling of being under attack from the West and in competition with other Punjabis.[10] They possessed a significant network of followers and resources, and used those to promulgate education, preservation of historical documents, and other self-strengthening activities for the community. At the same time, they nevertheless recognized the existence of several traditions within Sikhism and championed the view that custom provided the answer to an increasingly asked question, "Who is a Sikh?" Those accepting the teachings of Guru Nanak were counted as Sikhs, no matter what their position on maintaining the five Ks, their worship of local saints, or their social practices. In fact, the leading publicists for the Amritsar Sabha stressed that a major problem for Sikhs was their inattention to custom and especially pollution by intermarriage. There was recognition of the divisions among Sikhs. Sikhs who adopted the *keshādhārī* discipline and underwent baptism were expected to maintain the outward symbols and other aspects of conduct associated with that tradition, but they were not seen as "true Sikhs" superior to all others.[11]

Sikhs identifying with the Lahore Singh Sabha (1879) had a radically different perspective on the nature of Sikhism. By the 1870s, a group of Sikhs sharing common interests began to provide leadership for numerous public activities in Lahore. This emerging elite drew from a variety of classes and castes, including landed aristocrats, lawyers, teachers, journalists, businessmen, and low-ranking officials.[12] They were joined by a shared experience in Anglo-vernacular education and exposure to similar currents of intellectual debate. In their quest to understand themselves and a changing world, some had joined the Anjuman-i-Punjab and participated for a few years in the Arya Samaj. Their evolving vision of Sikh tradition came to be known as Tat Khalsa, that is, Sikhism devoid of popular custom and a return to a real or imagined golden age in which Sikhs had a clear and separate identity. The Lahore Singh Sabha championed an end to caste and worship of "living *gurus,*" such as the saints or descendants of the Ten Gurus. A revival of traditional values also necessitated a new emphasis on the Granth as the major source of authority and the creation or resurrection of rituals devoid of Hindu influence as well as a cleansing of sacred space that included the removal of idols and a return of administration by the community.

The Tat Khalsa vision of a revived and purified Sikhism became dominant over the next fifty years. The struggle involved two sets of confrontations: one among differing groups of Sikhs who challenged each other for legitimacy and the right to speak for the community; another between the increasingly powerful Tat Khalsa Sikhs and Hindus who argued that Sikhs should be seen as part of a broad Hindu community. Innumerable battles took place in institutions, public associations, and particularly in the press.

Many elements contributed to the ascendancy of the Tat Khalsa interpretation of Sikh tradition and culture. British support enhanced the position of the Lahore Singh Sabha and its network of related organizations. British patronage and insistence that all Sikh troops undergo baptism and maintain the five Ks helped legitimize the Tat Khalsa arguments.[13] More importantly, individual Sikhs and associations put forth programs in such a way that over time, they came to be recognized as central to the current troubles and future prospects of the community. The Singh Sabhas, numbering close to a hundred by 1900, served as a focus of local activities. Innovative in raising money, demonstrating their commitment to the Sikh cause, and an expanding network of schools and charitable institutions, these Sabhas met a multitude of needs. These Sabhas also forged an increasingly pervasive system of communication. As noted elsewhere, this involved sending out *jathās* (organized groups with particular missions, such as preaching or raising funds), training and coordinating the work of paid preachers, routinizing festivals and meetings, and, in general, insuring that information and appeals would reach a broad audience.[14]

For several decades the results were mixed despite opposition from segments of the Sikh population, including peasants who disliked criticism of popular festivals and customary relations. The Singh Sabhas gradually built an institutional base from which they could launch new initiatives in areas such as pressuring government for concessions and gaining control of the sacred shrines. Although the zeal of individuals fueled the Tat Khalsa activities, their success ultimately resulted in large part from an ability to influence the flow of information among Sikhs. As early as the 1880s, those rallying around the Lahore Singh Sabha demonstrated appreciable talent in publishing newspapers and tracts. They quickly came to dominate those aspects of the new print culture that related to the Sikh community.

The Singh Sabhas and Their Literature

The Singh Sabha movement and its literary expression evolved in two distinct phases. The period between approximately 1880 and 1900 was characterized by decentralized activity colored by constant strife, competition, and dramatic individual effort. Projects and institutions rose and fell quickly, and the concomitant efforts to develop a viable system of printed communication also tended to be sporadic. By the end of the century, a new generation of Sikh leaders moved toward coordinating the energy and the resources of the community, especially Sikhs who shared a commitment to Tat Khalsa views. Between that time and the First World War, the Chief Khalsa Diwan tried to build a doctrinal consensus. The two main instruments for that goal were the Sikh Educational Conference and a network of tract societies, journals, and newspapers.

From the outset, Singh Sabha leaders appreciated the possibility of using printed matter as a means to broadcast a message, circulate information, and, when necessary, to raise an alarm or fight opponents. One of the first projects for the Lahore Singh Sabha was *Gurmukhi Akbhār,* a weekly journal in Punjabi owned and edited by Bhai Gurmukh Singh. Subsidized by the Maharaja of Nabha, this paper reviewed Singh Sabha activities and provided space for dialogues on history, scripture, and the personal views of its subscribers.[15] Several other newspapers and monthly journals appeared for short periods. Finally in 1886 Jawahir Singh, Attar Singh Bahadur, and editor Ditt Singh founded the *Khalsa Akhbār,* which, despite a lapse in publication (1890–93), served as the center of Sikh journalism until the end of the century. The influence of the paper far exceeded its relatively small circulation, approximately one thousand, reaching not only Sikhs dispersed across British India but small pockets of immigrants in Asia and Africa.[16] Most other newspapers tended to be short lived. Started for a particular purpose or reflecting the orientation of a publisher or sponsor, any decrease in funding generally led to collapse. These Punjabi or Urdu papers had small circulations (generally not more than four hundred) and formats similar to that of the early *Gurmukhi Akhbār.*

These journalistic efforts served a variety of functions. Some were focused on a specific cause or audience, such as *Punjābī Bhāin* (journal of domestic life and female education), *The Sikh Sepoy* (a journal for troops) or periodicals with news on one segment of the population such as the Ramgarhias. Others were more general. No matter what the purpose, however, the publications tended to be in the vernacular. Although partially due to the slow spread of English literacy among Sikhs, this pattern also derived from the Singh Sabhas' campaign to promote the use of the Punjabi language.[17]

The papers also had a common role in public affairs. They publicized events and the activities of organizations and individuals. No matter where their residence, Sikhs received information on a regular basis. Moreover, journals created a channel for *bēnāti,* appeals for financial support. At the same time, newspapers became scorecards, with funds listed regularly and annual accounts publicized. In a setting in which honor was valued, these public pronouncements of good deeds and contributions were vital in generating support. The journals also had the potential of mobilizing groups on a particular issue, either for or against a pronouncement, an event, or a cause. The spirited debates, resolutions, and occasional bursts of demonstrations among Sikhs were due largely to the new channels of communication. Finally, Sikh journalism fostered the growth of a correspondence system that tied individuals and groups together. Often newspapers had pages of special reports and commentary from secretaries of organizations hundreds and even thousands of miles away. In these and related ways, consolidation of the community was enhanced and a network created that could be used for different goals.[18]

By the turn of the century, Sikhs of the Tat Khalsa persuasion increasingly felt the need for more systematic attention to coordination of institutions, information, and the marshalling of resources. At the heart of these new efforts was the Chief Khalsa Diwan, founded in 1902. The Diwan attempted to build a consensus among Sikhs in the area of social, religious, and political goals. To do so, its leaders generated organizations such as the Sikh Educational Conference, schools, and, most importantly, two newspapers, the *Khalsa Samāchār* in Punjabi and the *Khalsa Advocate* in English. The papers represented the Diwan's views, published reports, and generally fostered dialogue and often controversy. There also grew up influential local papers, although the Diwan's journals continued to be seen as the chief spokesmen for the Singh Sabhas until the early 1920s.[19]

Although newspapers were prominent in the printed duels and controversies abundant in the Punjab, tract literature became the favored mechanism for promulgating a point of view and attacking opponents. With the exception of a handful of scholarly works and reprints of religious texts, most books and small pamphlets published by Sikhs were polemic or didactic in nature.[20] As in the case of journalism, the earlier efforts tended to be sporadic and tied to particular issues, but over time there was a move towards coordination and adoption of a common viewpoint.

The zealous members of the Lahore Singh Sabha produced the first wave of Sikh tracts. The small pamphlets were issued by their author or a patron; generally, between five hundred and one thousand were printed. Urdu and Hindi publications were common, but the growing commitment to Punjabi was soon felt in the tract material. In Amritsar, the Wazir-i-Hind Press, the Anglo-Urdu Press, and the Gurmukhi Press accounted for most of the tracts. In Lahore, their counterparts were the Sri Gurmat Press, the Khalsa Press, and the Anglo-Sanskrit Press. Prices varied from one *pice* to two *ānnās,* depending on the size of the tract (most common was the sixteen page variety, although the material occasionally exceeded two hundred pages).[21]

Commitment to producing didactic literature led to the founding of the Khalsa Tract Society in 1894. For several years, Bhai Vir Singh and a small band of supporters kept the enterprise going despite problems of finances and distribution. After 1900, the restructuring of an executive committee and improved business practices enhanced the quality and quantity of tracts. In addition to tracts sold to individuals at a price ranging from three *pice* to four *ānnās,* subscribers to the society could pay annual fees and automatically receive all its publications. By 1901, 370 Sikhs subscribed and insured steady income by pledging Rs. 12 a year. Subcommittees selected manuscripts and handled accounts. The society's activities still centered on a small group (Vir Singh and his friends such as Bhai Mohan Singh Vaid) that reviewed manuscripts carefully. Guidelines were issued to prospective authors. They had to belong to the society, write concisely in Punjabi, and avoid speaking against other religions. The authorship of the tracts remains in question, although Vir Singh apparently wrote the vast majority.[22] In 1902, an effort was made to issue Sindhi tracts as a result of the Chief Khalsa Diwan campaign in that neighboring area, and special subscriptions were raised for the project.

By 1911, the number of Sikh tracts circulating in the Punjab was staggering. The Khalsa Tract Society series, 400 in number and exceeding a million copies, consisted of original works as well as reprints of earlier tracts. The Society's effort was complemented by the output of the Sikh Book Club and the Panch Khalsa Agency, which by 1910 printed 125 tracts, mainly the one to two page variety. Moreover, the Sikh Handbill Society issued single sheets for broad distribution in the rural areas.[23] The content of the approximately 1200 tracts and small books published between 1880 and 1915 varied with the author and current issues, but, on the whole, writers associated with the Tat Khalsa message tended to dominate the printed media. The Lahore

Singh Sabha and its affiliates quickly became embroiled in tract warfare. Even before the Arya Samaj joined in the fray, Hindus were raising serious questions about Sikh tradition. In Saligram Acharya's *Srī Nānakīya Mat Nīrnayah,* (1877), for example, the head of the Vaishnava Society claimed that the Vedas and the Adi Granth reflected the same orientation toward religion. Sikhs were Hindus, and Nanak was not a god but one who considered himself low and part of the greater Hindu tradition. Maintaining long hair and outward symbols would not keep Sikhs from going to hell, and all the Gurus allegedly wore the sacred thread. In conclusion, the author suggested that Udasi *sadhūs* had special insights and were a major element within Sikhism.

The Arya Samaj and the Singh Sabhas soon locked horns in rounds of public denunciations and printed attacks. As Kenneth Jones has demonstrated, the Samaj attempted to incorporate Sikhism within greater Hinduism by a combination of persuasion and ideological attack.[24] Two tracts illustrated the nature of the encounter. In his provocative *Nūshkā-i-Granthī Fobia* (A Prescription for Granthi Phobia, 1889), Radha Kishen Mehta began with the usual "I do not want to hurt the feelings of the other religion" pledge and then proceeded to charge a Singh Sabha leader, Jawahir Singh, with opportunism and possible rape. Guru Nanak received particular criticism, including inflammatory comments about his domestic life and beliefs. A conclusion ridiculed the Granth and Sikh traditional views of medicine, science, and geography. Noting the "geographical wisdom" of Nanak in discovering new mountains and oceans, Mehta sarcastically called on Jawahir Singh to find them: "It is our view, Bhai Sahib, that you should get new maps prepared indicating these various holy places and then preach Sikhism there. It is certain that this and all similar branches of knowledge will spread over the universe. We shall raise subscriptions to meet the expenses of your travels in this regard."[25]

The corresponding Sikh tract, "Prescription for the Insanity of Dayananda's Followers," matched the earlier piece in emotion and sarcasm. Ganda Singh, president of the Guru Upkar Parcharini Sabha, Amritsar, wrote this to "refute" Lala Sahib Dyal's "Remedy for the Whims of Ditt Singh."[26] After a character sketch of Sahib Dyal, "famous" for "spitting out dirty things" (feces) on the Sikhs and the Gurus, Ganda Singh surveyed Hindu-Sikh relations and met assertations about Sikh tradition. Replying to the insinuation that Sikhs were like women because they wore hair, he asked why Aryas imitated females and shaved their faces. In typical rhetorical style, Ganda Singh replied, did the Vedas insist on men emulating women? If salvation depended on cut hair, why did Hindu women not shave their heads? If equal to Hindu men, why not wear the sacred thread? Dayananda was pictured as an uncouth braggart who spent his time dividing Indians with "daggers of bad words." In countering another charge that Sikhism and Punjabi were suitable only for rustics and uneducated men, Ganda Singh quoted foreign scholars to show that Punjabi was a viable language and that Sikhism was a separate world religion. Had it not been for Guru Gobind Singh and Sikh bravery, Hinduism and the "weak" Hindus would have been destroyed by Islam.

Internal bickering produced an increasingly large number of Sikh tracts. Individual authors or anonymous tracts frequently discussed Sikh separatism. In works such as Munshi Indar Singh's *Ākhīrī Peshwā* (1894), efforts were made to highlight the importance of Guru Gobind Singh's message and to compare Sikhism with Christianity, Hinduism, and Islam. This fifty-four page essay was conciliatory in tone compared with others that covered the same ground. Contemporary tracts championed the maintenance of hair, changes in ritual, and the links between Punjabi and Sikh prosperity.[27]

The more systematic publication of tracts by the end of the century evoked a flood of discussion of old and new topics. The Khalsa Tract Society (KTS) took the lead. Vir Singh's influence was obvious in the tone and literary quality of many tracts. The KTS series and pages of the *Khalsa Samāchār,* which he edited, serialized his stories and historical novels that later would become classics.[28] The major Tat Khalsa themes were woven into Vir Singh's historical accounts, such as Sikh heroism, maintenance of the five Ks, and respect for the Gurus and the Adi Granth as the center pieces of the faith.

Of the approximately four hundred titles published by 1910, a fourth were selections from the writings of the Gurus or tales about their lives and beliefs.[29] The remainder covered many subjects. History was a major theme. In *Gulābi* (1903) for example, the writer tells a story emphasizing the tyranny of Aurangzeb, Sikh martyrdom, and heroism. In it, a low caste couple, Gulab and Gulab Kaur, become Muslims and serve in the household of Hakim Abatarab Bamni. The three are sent as spies by Aurangzeb to observe Guru Gobind Singh. After experiencing his heroism and good deeds, they enter into religious discourse and eventually convert to Sikhism. Related to tales of Sikh bravery were accounts of military prowess and heroics in the Indian army.[30] Other booklets lectured or told stories about the current state of Sikhism. *Sādi Darāvani Dashā* (Our Dangerous State, 1900) evaluated the critical problems of Sikhs, while *Uttam Updesh* (Good Advice, 1903) noted the relevance of Japanese educational experiments and for improving Sikh health and the status of females. Similarly, historical accounts served to highlight Sikh superstitions and a general inability to cooperate and complete tasks. Didactic stories were vehicles to examine elementary ideas about Sikhism such as the existence of God and the necessity of prayer (*Sachā Bhatījā* [1900]).

Controversial topics such as conversion, rituals, and domestic affairs appeared often in KTS imprints. In *Main Ki Kita Tain Ki Kita,* a dialogue between a loyal Sikh and one who has become a sadhu, (What Have I Done, What Have you Done? 1899), the apostate is brought back to Sikhism through argument and gentle persuasion. *Main Sikh Hān* (I Am a Sikh, 1906) presents a fictional account of a Muslim conversion to Sikhism, while *Saptami Dī Bhēta* (1905) described the conversion of a family. Approximately forty tracts dealt with Hindu rituals, fasts, and superstition.[31] The Society generally did not publish reports on organizations or news, although there were exceptions.[32] The Chief Khalsa Diwan assumed that coordinating function, issuing reports either separately or as special sections of the two Tat Khalsa newspapers. In 1908, the Chief Khalsa Diwan began printing a separate *Māsik Pattar,* a monthly collection of reports and financial accounts. Increasing attempts to pull together, to standardize, affected both the publications of the Khalsa Tract Society and those of individual authors. Letters and articles attacking a tract as "unpanthic" or criticizing use of religious sources became common.

Pressure grew to set up committees that would evaluate the content of tracts claiming to reflect Sikh tradition.[33] Bhai Mohan Singh Vaid of Tarn Taran helped spearhead this development by contributing articles to the *Khalsa Samāchār* that publicized "useful" tracts and questioned the content of others. He also began his own publication series to print only Tat Khalsa material.[34]

Before attempting to assess how this outpouring of tracts, pamphlets, and books influenced individuals and ideology, a review of the works by several key writers may contribute to an understanding of the themes and milieu perpetuated by the Tat Khalsa. Although a few have been identified for discussion, the universe of dedicated Sikh publicists is far larger. These men, and their compatriots, carved out a place for themselves and their message in a transitional phase of Sikh history.

Major Contributors to Sikh Tract Literature

Many of the Sikh tracts were anonymous, but a handful of writers played a central role in the debates and controversies. They did not all think alike and, indeed, came from somewhat different backgrounds and approached issues in divergent ways. Nevertheless, their literature shared ideas and values that reveal much about the world of Punjab Sikhs at the end of the nineteenth century. Prominent prior to 1900 were Ditt Singh and Avatar Singh Vahiria, one of his primary opponents who was a member of the pro-Hindu Amritsar group. Ditt Singh's death in 1901 did not diminish the tract tradition among the Tat Khalsa. Continuing to promulgate these views were the scholarly Kahan Singh Nabha, a master of pamphleteering, Mohan Singh Vaid, and the champion of literalist interpretation of "true Sikhism," Babu Teja Singh Overseer.

Ditt Singh was at the center of public controversy for almost four decades. Born in April 1852, he studied with a *granthī* (religious teacher who played a key role in Sikh ceremonies) and then preached in the Lahore area before coming into contact with Bhai Gurmukh Singh and other Sikhs prominent in the local Singh Sabha. While trying to untangle his own personal beliefs, he debated Dayananda and later made the Arya Samaj a favorite target for tracts and articles. Ditt Singh edited journals, most notably the *Khalsa Akhbār,* and wrote approximately forty books and tracts. A Ramdasi (untouchable) frequently looked down upon by upper caste Sikhs, especially those associated with Baba Khem Singh Bedi and the neoorthodox of Amritsar Singh Sabha, he was noted for supporting programs that aimed at eliminating caste among Sikhs and converting Muslims and Hindus through a *shūddhi* ceremony. In the process of defending the Tat Khalsa doctrines and attacking both Aryas and Amritsar Sikhs, he made many enemies. Only after his death in 1901 could fresh efforts be made to consolidate the divergent groups and opinions found in Sikh public life.[35]

Ditt Singh's many tracts mirrored the energetic zeal and the issues associated with the Lahore Singh Sabha. Undoubtedly the leading publicist among Sikhs of the period, he left a trail of controversy, confrontation, and stimulating propaganda. One major theme in his writings was the separate nature of Sikhism. Whether detailing the life of Guru Nanak in *Sri Guru Nanak Prabōdh* (1890), a poetic account of the life and religious beliefs of early Sikhism, or surveying the traditions and current socioreligious ills of Sikhs in a major work, *Naklī Sikh Prabōdh* (1895), Ditt Singh emphasized the continuity of Sikh ideology and ritual. As Vir Singh was to do in subsequent novels, Ditt Singh wove insistence upon maintaining *rahīt* and the five Ks into a series of stories about Sikh martyrdom.[36]

Ditt Singh pictured Sikhism in a world beset with danger. One persistent threat was the Arya Samaj, which he lambasted with provocative attacks. In a survey of his earliest encounters with Dayananda, for example, Ditt Singh attempted to show the hollowness of the Swami's understanding of Sikhism, Vedic literature, and modern science.[37] In *Dambh Vidarān* (published posthumously in 1902), Ditt Singh examined the *Satyārth Prakāsh,* Dayananda's magnum opus, and pointed out inaccuracies about Sikh history and religion. Aggravated by what appeared to be constant Arya interference in Sikh internal problems, Ditt Singh also wrote a lampoon, "A Real Photo of the Arya Samaj," that chronicled recent events and made fun of Arya leaders.[38]

Another danger from the Tat Khalsa perspective was the continuation of popular culture and "non-Sikh" tendencies among Sikhs, especially those in the rural areas. As Harjot Singh Oberoi has demonstrated, Ditt Singh and his colleagues tried to root out attachment to Brahmans, Hindu rituals, and worship of local gods and saints. Using poetry and quotes from the Granth to convey a message, Ditt Singh issued at least ten books and tracts against elements seen as endangering Sikh progress and even survival. *Pamma Prabōdh* (written in about the 1890s), for example, is a satire directed against Brahmans; other works enjoin Sikhs to cease worshipping saints such as Miran, Sakhi Sarvar, or Gugga Gapaura (*Sultan Puārā,* 1896); *Mirān Manāut,* 2d ed. 1902; *Guggā Gapāurā* (1902). *Sultan Puārā* was an especially powerful tract that illustrated Ditt Singh's approach. In poetic detail, he presented a dialogue between Guru Ka Singh, a true Sikh, and the followers of Pir Sakhi Sarvar. The protagonists were caricatures, with the Tat Khalsa seen as intelligent and aggressive, and the others slow and conventional. The Sikhs of course decided to give up worship of the *pīr,* but only after Ditt Singh used the story to make several points. One was that pilgrimage to shrines leads to an intermixing of social codes and undercut Sikh purity and solidarity.[39] Second, the miracles of Sakhi Sarvar were not unique and often not valid. Sikh saints performed more impressive acts of faith, and therefore the *pīr* should not be revered. Moreover, worshipping a *pīr* went against the cardinal Sikh belief in one god. The clinching argument was that Sikhs should not worship a Muslim saint. In other tracts such as *Durgā Prabōdh* (1899), (a massive tome exceeding four hundred pages), Ditt Singh tried to counter the frequent charge that Guru Gobind Singh worshipped the goddess Durga and therefore was a Hindu.[40]

For Ditt Singh and his colleagues, however, the arrogance of the Amritsar clique and its alliance with Hindus presented the gravest threat. Ditt Singh lambasted Baba Khem Singh Bedi's views on pollution, ritual, and the non-separate nature of Sikh tradition. Controversial dialogue between two Sikhs in the "Cowardly Sikh" (*Darpōke Singh,* 1895), for example, attacked the notion of caste and supported the reconversion program of the Lahore Shuddhi Sabha. Most of the attacks on Baba Khem Singh Bedi and the Amritsar group came in *Khalsa Akhbār* editorials and articles, but one such piece, subsequently republished as an individual tract, led to a lengthy legal suit and public acrimony. In a play, *Svapan Nātak,* 1887, Ditt Singh lampooned the Sikh opponents through allegory and lightly disguised references. Most of the major Amritsar leaders appeared in the work, including Khem Singh, referred to as the *guru* of Satan. A subsequent lawsuit for defamation drained the resources of the newspaper and the Lahore Singh Sabha. Despite Ditt Singh's legal vindication on appeal, the incident further aggravated divisions among Sikhs and led to a five-year closure of the *Khalsa Akhbār.*[41]

One of Ditt Singh's primary opponents, Avatar Singh Vahiria, was also a noted publicist. Ditt Singh's numerous publications tended to be more systematic and less inflammatory than his opponent's.[42] Originally from Rawalpindi, Avatar Singh joined the Amritsar Singh Sabha in 1885 and became a secretary of the Amritsar Khalsa Diwan. He edited two newspapers and, in addition, wrote approximately fifteen tracts and more elaborate volumes defending Khem Singh and the Amritsar group's views on Sikhism.

In an early work, *Hornān Dharmān Nālōn Khalsa* (The Khalsa Religion is Superior, 1895), Avatar Singh argues that all religions in India had their roots in the six systems of Hindu philosophy, but Guru Nanak took earlier ideas and created a seventh, superior philosophy. This philosophy was like a school with low and high classes. Individuals could move through the various stages but still be considered Sikhs. *Sahajdhārīs* and *Udāsīs* were Sikhs because they traveled the right trail and worshipped God as revealed in the Granth. Other Sikhs had achieved the status of *Keshādhārīs* and undergone full baptism, complete with maintaining the outward symbols and obeying specific rules of conduct. He tried to show that the Gita anticipated the basic principles of Sikhism, that is, one should discard all religions and put one's self at the feet of the Supreme God. Avatar Singh avoided specificity on many points, especially on whether all Sikhs must maintain hair and specific rituals. The major themes, however, were belief in the Gurus and the Granth and personal worship as a means to salvation.

Subsequent works were more specific and probably calculated to counter Tat Khalsa positions. In *Sikh Dharam Tat Darshan, Arthāt Khalsa Dharam Kē Asūl* (1899), Vahiria elaborated on the theme of Sikhism as part of a broad religious tradition and supported the Vedas, Ramayana, and Mahabharata as important in understanding religious principles. Noting that Sikhs customarily had worshipped gods and saints, he said that such practices should be seen as an expression of individual understanding of man's relationship with the divine and not be discarded because of rigid theological arguments. Customary religion did not necessarily conflict with Sikh tradition. Similar themes could be found in *Khalsa Sūdhār Taru* (eight parts, 1900–1901), a five-hundred-page exegesis on tradition and reformation of Sikhism. Avatar Singh also helped author the large *Khalsa Dharam Shāstra* (1914), a neoorthodox code of social and religious practice that received support from many descendants of the Gurus and at least three of the *takhts* (traditional centers of authority).[43]

Avatar Singh responded to mounting pressure from opponents such as Teja Singh Bhasaur and Mohan Singh Vaid by intensifying his defense of what seemed to be the essence of Sikhism. One theme in his tracts was support for Baba Khem Singh Bedi, who claimed superiority because of lineage. In *Shōk Pattar* (1905), Vahiria lauded the life and views of his deceased leader. Similarly, he sided with Khem Singh Bedi's son, Gurdarshan Singh, who spoke at the 1910 Punjab Hindu Conference and claimed that Sikhs were Hindus (*Kūr Nā Pūjjē Sach Nūn Sau Gharat Ghariae,* 1911; *Chēhrā Dēkhān Dē Shīshā,* 1911). Teja Singh's attacks usually stung opponents, and Avatar Singh was no exception. Infuriated by the radical claims of the head of the Panch Khalsa Diwan, he uncharacteristically wrote a bitter four-page tract in 1914 that denounced the Tat Khalsa—*Chēhrā Dēkhān Dē Shīshē Dā Zamēnā* (A Supplement of the Mirror for Seeing One's Face, 1914).

Kahan Singh of Nabha served as an intellectual bridge between the first generation of Singh Sabha activists and those later associated with the Chief Khalsa Diwan. A leading theologian and scholar, Kahan Singh (1852–1938) was a major figure in supplying the facts and interpretations that permeated the Tat Khalsa message.[44] After a traditional education with *granthīs* and *pandits,* he studied in Lucknow and Delhi, arriving in Lahore in 1883 where he became immersed in controversies. Close to Gurmukh Singh, he debated with the Arya Samaj and wrote pamphlets, eventually returning to the Sikh state of Nabha as tutor for the heir apparent, Ripudaman Singh. He helped Macauliffe write *The Sikh Religion,* which remains a classic statement of Tat Khalsa interpretation of tradition, worked closely with Lahore publicists, preserved mammoth collections of notes and research material that grew into the multi-volume *Gūrūshabad Ratnākar Mahan Kōsh* (Encyclopedia of Sikh History and Literature, 1930), and served as an adviser to the Chief Khalsa Diwan and many Sikh leaders.[45]

Although he wrote pamphlets and two books (on Sikh history and drama) prior to 1890, Kahan Singh's most important scholarly cum polemical works antedating the 1930 encyclopedia were *Gurmat Prabhākar* (1898) and *Gurmat Sudhākar* (1893). The former examined the basic principles of the Sikh religion, with lengthy excerpts from the Adi Granth and commentary. The primary message was of the unity found within the thought of the Gurus, and the concomitant belief that after Guru Gobind Singh, the Granth became the Guru for the community and the source of Sikh orthodoxy. Kahan Singh also argued against continuation of the line of Gurus until the present day and pointed out Hindu accretions in Sikh ritual. The second volume discussed the Dasam Granth and the legacy of Guru Gobind Singh, again trying to reconcile teachings of the Gurus with evolving institutions and practices. The ideas in these books, plus those that Kahan Singh contributed to the program of the Lahore Singh Sabha and later the Chief Khalsa Diwan, provided much of the intellectual ammunition for the Tat Khalsa supporters.[46]

Kahan Singh was best known, however, for a tract that became the slogan for the Tat Khalsa movement, "We are Not Hindu."[47] This title summarized the thrust of many programs connected with the Lahore Singh Sabha, and the volume, as was the case with Macauliffe's *The Sikh Religion* (1909), tended to represent current opinions of specific groups rather than marking a "turning point" in the intellectual history of the Sikhs.[48] Since the work has been quoted extensively, a brief review of its contents and style seems warranted.

Originally written in Hindi and then translated into Punjabi in 1899, this tract consisted of a series of assertions, stories, and challenges interspersed between excerpts from the Granth and related historical accounts. Framed in the accepted style of debate, the dialogue began with a Hindu stating that Sikhs were ignorant of their true beliefs. They originated from Hinduism, intermarried with Hindus, mixed socially, and were citizens of Hindustan. He suggested that the Sikhs were confused about the origins of the word Hindu, supposedly meaning "one who conquers enemies and is brave." The Sikh responded with quotes from the Granth, the Rahit Nama Bhai Chaupa Singh, the Dasam Granth, and included a list of forty-one specific injunctions required after baptism. He debated with his "Hindu brother" about the origin of the word Hindu, and then undercut the reply by noting that the Hindus typically misquoted the Granth or only quoted half a phrase so as to mislead ignorant Sikhs. There followed a discussion of the differences between *qaum* and *panth,* with the Hindu arguing that the latter meant only a sect (and Sikhs were a sect of Hinduism), and that the former, akin to the concept of nation, could not be attributed to the Sikhs because they were too few in number. The introductory chapter ended a summary by Kahan Singh and a recounting of what Sikh religious books said about these issues.

The bulk of this tract covered the relationship between Vedic tradition and the faith of the Gurus, caste (particularly the role of Brahmans), *avatārs* and the oneness of God, gods and goddesses, the worship of idols, customary practices (such as ritual fasting), superstition, incantations, and symbols. With regard to the matter of ritual and symbols, the Sikh argued that the two traditions were diametrically opposed. All birth, baptism, marriage, and death ceremonies should be performed according to *gurmat,* the way of the Gurus, and without regard to Hinduism. The Hindu countered that the new Tat Khalsa practices were recent and resulted only from obstinacy, not true understanding. Faced with a deluge of quotes from the Granth and accounts about Guru Gobind Singh, the Hindu agreed to distinctions but weakly reasserted similarity in Sikh and Hindu views concerning the Vedas, the reward of sin and good action, transmigration, cremation of the dead, protection of the cow, and disdain for untouchables. The Sikh countered each argument with allegory and comparisons with other religions. He pointed out to his satisfaction that some Western faiths believed in cremation and transmigration.

In the concluding pages, the Sikh dominated this conversation and questioned why Hindus misrepresented Sikh beliefs. Supposedly most Hindus appreciated the benevolent acts of the Gurus and their efforts to protect humanity. Only a few troublemakers prompted by selfishness created conflict. If Sikhs asserted themselves, no Hindus could dominate them, and the Hindus in turn would have to earn an honest living. Benevolent British rule had made possible improvement of Sikh religious and social conditions. All Indians should cooperate and work together. Sikhs for their part must be tolerant, consider themselves part of the Sikh *qaum,* and realize that "We are not Hindus."

Kahan Singh's tract went through at least five major editions. Each was changed slightly, with new arguments added and points refined. Evidence from European sources appeared more frequently in the later editions, as in the fifth edition (1914), which incorporated quotes from the *Civil and Military Gazette* to validate Sikh separateness. Each edition also had a new introduction and a growing list of legitimizing letters from prominent Sikhs, organizations, and the *takhts.* Despite the continuing notoriety of his tract, Kahan Singh managed to avoid further involvement in bitter sectarian disputes. There are some indications, however, that he remained close to Babu Teja Singh Overseer, whose radical ideas helped focus some of the most dramatic confrontations among members of the Tat Khalsa.[49]

In the early struggles of the Lahore Singh Sabha, the courage and the zeal of Teja Singh was a wellspring of inspiration. He moved around the Punjab incessantly, giving speeches and preaching the need for baptism and a radical reform of Sikh practice. Leading in conversion of Muslims and criticism of concern over caste, he enjoined "true Sikhs" to sacrifice for their God and faith. To the next generation of Singh Sabha leaders, however, Teja Singh became first an embarrassment and then, to some, a heretic, because of his dogmatic and literalist interpretations of *gurmat.* Attempts were made to associate Teja Singh with the Chief Khalsa Diwan's programs, which rested on accommodation and widening the base of the Sikh community, but those failed. He used his small but vocal group of followers at the Bhasaur Singh Sabha to spread a message that included active proselytizing, insistence that only *keshādhārīs* were real Sikhs, abrupt changes of ceremonies that would have alienated many who considered themselves followers of the Gurus, and a demand for complete democracy including equality of women in every aspect of Sikh life. Former friends were denounced as *tankhaya* and *patīt,* apostates swerving from the true path. His obsession with rooting out non-Sikh practices eventually led to his ostracism and persecution. In 1881, news of his printing the Granth without a small section, *rāgmālā,* shook the community in 1917. Although some intellectuals sympathized with his contention about the inappropriateness of the *rāgmālā*'s inclusion in the sacred scripture, actually editing the Granth was seen as sacrilege. Teja Singh came under fierce attack, lost public funding, was imprisoned in Patiala, and banned from Sikh institutions.[50]

From the late 1890s onward, Teja Singh's organizations emitted a stream of reports and controversial tracts. A typical tract included denunciations of opponents, an account of a real or imagined public meeting at which "decisions" on specific issues were reached, and a concluding appeal for Sikhs to make these resolutions a guiding factor in their lives. In *Bhulēme* (1907) Teja Singh made several points. He maintained that the Tat Khalsa should not celebrate Hindu festivals, but should develop their own sacred calendar with holy days and birthday celebrations. Sikhs should celebrate more *gūrpūrabs,* defined not just as birthdays of the Gurus but as any major event seen as being historically important. Martyrdom days should be a time of prayer and mourning, and the completing of the Granth should be celebrated annually. Since Sikhs were separate from Hindus, they needed their own dating system based on the birth of Guru Nanak. Since Guru Nanak and Guru Gobind Singh shared the same ideas on theology and ritual, the Dasam Granth deserved more respect. That work, however, contained chapters on Durga and the psychology of women (which might arouse passions) that were not *gurmat,* and thus must be excised. Caste was to be denounced and not used as a basis for marriage or social relations, and names such as *Bedi* or *Sodhi* should be dropped, thus strengthening the equality of all Sikhs. Similar decisions and demands could be found in the annual reports and special bulletins issued from Bhasaur.[51]

Besides the tracts and actions surrounding the *rāgmālā* affair, Teja Singh's most prolonged controversy involved the nature of *rahīt* within the community. The Chief Khalsa Diwan spent several years trying to develop a compromise document that incorporated various versions of *rahītnāmās* and other guides to ritual that were circulating in the early 1900s. Beginning about 1908, they issued a series of drafts for public discussion. Teja Singh denounced the Chief Khalsa Diwan productions, and presented instead his own version of orthodox ritual, *Khalsa Rahīt Prakāsh* (1908).[52] The arguments in that volume reflected a narrow and specific view of how Sikhs should act. Not only were those who smoked sinners, but all who permitted Muslims and Hindu singers in Sikh shrines also should be treated as apostates. If individuals broke Sikh rules (a lengthy list was provided), the accepted penalty of asking forgiveness from the community was void. Instead, the sinners must do penance and be rebaptized. A Khalsa Sikh could never marry a Hindu. Women should wear turbans, be baptized with the double-edged knife, and participate fully in ceremonies, including reading the Granth and helping administer baptism. Detailed instructions on conduct in gurdwaras were provided, including where and when people should stand, type of clothes they should wear, and procedures for ceremonies. Another favorite Panch Khalsa Diwan injunction was appended: all names of officers should be changed to reflect true Sikhism, such as the president as *jathēdār,* the secretary as *sēvak,* and members as *sājan* or *sahāik.*

Had such radical ideas become legitimized, Sikhism would look quite different today. The mainstream of the Singh Sabhas and Chief Khalsa Diwan was moving in a more moderate and accommodative direction, however, and that prevailed as Sikhs began to define themselves in specific ways. The individual most representative of that spirit and, at the same time, the Singh Sabhas' most prolific tract writer, was Bhai Mohan Singh Vaid.

Born in 1881, Mohan Singh Vaid studied at local Sikh schools where he received his informal education on Sikh history and theology while participating in youth organizations and other groups linked with the Lahore Singh Sabha.[53] Despite his lack of English education, Mohan Singh taught himself and launched into a dual career of medicine and public service. He was the close associate of Vir Singh and travelled almost daily between his hometown of Tarn Taran and Amritsar to consult with leaders of the Chief Khalsa Diwan. He set up a lending library and collected virtually everything published on the Sikhs. He often rose early to write after prayers. Mohan Singh also found time to lead several social and religious reform movements in the Majha region (Amritsar and Lahore districts) and was known for his role in purifying ritual and the environs at several shrines.

Journalism and publicity, however, were his favorite tasks. He turned down an opportunity to edit the *Khalsa Samāchār,* but a year later in 1906 began his own magazine that specialized in health issues and disseminated information on the *panth.* The first issue of *Dukh Nivāran* contained articles on self-improvement, medicine, developments in foreign countries, female education, and a guide to literature useful for spreading progressive ideas among Sikhs. Unlike other papers, the monthly journal's circulation rose rapidly to four thousand copies. In his own words, being a journalist in Sikh public life was like "running a fever." Mohan Singh complemented his contributions to journalism with a seemingly endless stream of articles in Sikh papers and tracts. During one three-year period he published over forty tracts and handbills.[54] Committed to the spread of Punjabi literature, he established the Punjabi Prachar series in 1910 and a Punjabi Prachar Book Agency dedicated to providing cheap Punjabi books for the general population. Until his death in 1936, he stimulated discussion of Tat Khalsa and educational issues by continuing to write and circulate literature. His collection, and that of the *zindā shahīd,* "the living martyr" Bhai Takht Singh contain a comprehensive set of printed matter that is invaluable in understanding the Singh Sabha era.[55]

Mohan Singh wrote hundreds of books and tracts on subjects ranging from religion and social problems to health, education, morals, and contemporary fiction. His works can be broken into three categories: translations of self-help and classical literature, primarily from the West; translations or edited collections of material from South Asian writing, often paraphrased and with notes, introductory matter, and a conclusion making the material relevant to current issues; and original works, generally fiction or didactic essays. Writing in simple Punjabi, Mohan Singh was direct in supporting friends and attacking enemies. The Arya Samaj was a frequent target, evoking such works as "Exposure of the Hollowness of the Aryas" (*Arīan Dē Dhōl Dā Phōl,* c. 1914), *Dayānandī Dharam Kā Namūnā* (1900), or an edited translation of an anti-Samaj work by Pandit Jagannath Das, *Dayananda Mat Darpan* (1914). Unlike some of his contemporaries, Mohan Singh tried to be fair and conciliatory if possible. In 1903, for example, he was stung by Arya Samaj public statements and produced *Ārya Samājī Bhāīan Dē Sīkhān Par Be Jā Hamlīān Dē Ūttra.* While criticizing certain Aryas, he said that most Samajists were "peaceful" and called for unity and living together as "brothers and citizens of one nation."[56]

Concern with domestic problems prompted him to write fifty separate tracts as well as two novels and a drama on marriage. A personal experience or a newspaper report often sparked his journalistic efforts, such as those responding to the death of a nephew, contact with a widow (*Vidhvā Vilāp,* 1918), or observing the effects of illiteracy and superstition (*Punjabi Bhūtnē* [Fear of Ghosts], c. 1910). "The Widows'

Cry" was typical of his social appeal. An introductory section contained a dialogue about widowhood, followed by a review of conditions based on recent census data. Another part commented on *satī* and incorporated poems from a second tract. The work concluded with a brief life of a widow, and then a dialogue between two women on remarriage and social evils. The conflict over Anand marriage in 1907 sparked another round of tracts, the most notable being *Gurmat Vīrōdh Vināsh* (Destruction of the Opponents of Sikhism), a response to the pro-Hindu tract *Ānand Vīvāh Par Vichār.* It was not a coincidence that the Dimes and Gaur *Catalogue of Punjabi Books in the India Office Library* listed more original publications by Mohan Singh Vaid than any other recent Sikh author. His scope of interest and his commitment to promulgating Sikh tradition and progress encompassed the issues and the spirit of the Singh Sabha era.

Tract Literature and the Emergence of Modern Sikhism: A Summary

The conflict over Sikh identity and control of central institutions was not entirely resolved by the Singh Sabhas and the Chief Khalsa Diwan. Constitutional changes, first during the Morley-Minto reforms of 1909 and ten years later at the time of the Montague Chelmsford reforms, evoked fresh passion and controversy. The Akali Dal,whose members were commonly called Akalis, was an organization that successfully developed a militant nonviolent campaign to rescue Sikh shrines from Hindu control. Its strident defense of Sikh symbols and a distinct confrontational style have colored much of Sikh politics since the early 1920s. They settled key controversies in dramatic fashion, most notably, the supremacy of the *Keshādhārīs* within Sikh institutions and Tat Khalsa control of the sacred shrines. Nevertheless, the successes of the earlier initiatives had set the stage for the dramatic encounters of the 1920s. The Singh Sabha achievements were due to many things, but especially attention to financial arrangements, the ability to administer their institutions, and the quality of leadership that evoked positive responses from the Sikh community in the skills and in communicating effectively. Study of Sikh vernacular literature suggests tentative answers to the question of historical importance. In terms of evaluating the role of tracts, evidence of their ability to stir passions and generate controversy abounds in the newspapers and government reports of the period. A tract by Ditt Singh on a local saint not only created controversy, but at times led Sikh devotees to abandon a tradition of customary worship.[57] Court cases were launched and crimes committed as a result of tract warfare. Sikh publicists were aware of the potential limits of relying on the printed word for disseminating ideas and supplemented the tactic with preaching missions and district *diwāns*. However, tracts were important elements in those activities—they were read aloud in villages, discussed in open meetings, and routinely circulated by paid and volunteer missionaries.[58] Unlike newspapers, tracts and handbills could be posted and easily preserved, thus becoming part of an informal network of information linking Sikhs over time and space. Both Sikh newspapers and tracts moved back and forth between the Punjab and Sikh immigrant centers across the world, often generating funds and fostering resolutions and even deputations.[59] Tracts also influenced major turning points in Sikh history. Without question, the flood of printed matter generated by issues such as control of sacred spots and removing Hindu idols from shrines; the successful campaign to have a Tat Khalsa ritual of marriage, *anand*, recognized legally; and the sharp community reaction to alleged official sacrilege of the Rikabganj gurdwara in New Delhi molded public consciousness and led to Sikh response.

Appeal by tracts and broadsides was routinized by the Tat Khalsa publicists and became an accepted and powerful means of mobilizing the community. The most dramatic example was the popular literature surrounding the Akali movement, a wave of news, rumor, and appeals that stirred Sikhs and badly frightened the government.[60] Without the success of the Singh Sabhas in helping to define Sikhism, to undermine popular religion and the influence of traditional families, and to create a modern communication system, however, there would have been no Akali success. Tracts were an integral element in the print culture used so effectively by the Tat Khalsa and the next generation, the Akalis.

The aura of unreality, the misuse of fact and the polemical stretching of logic and argument lie at the heart of the Singh Sabha mission. The publicists were trying to define symbols and rituals, in essence, to create a reality by weaving together parts of a tangled tradition, supporting some as valid and rejecting others. The polemic and didactic tracts contributed to the growth of a new vision of the world divided into the orthodox and unorthodox, with a sense of historical consciousness in which martyrs and heroism were highlighted, producing a sense of a community united by symbols and respect for agreed-upon principles and ritual. Divisions remained after the early 1900s, but the center of Sikhism had shifted and the understanding of who was a Sikh had become more defined. The message of the tracts was accepted and took on its own reality.

The problem for Sikhs was that because of continuing internal conflict and a persistent set of problems related to their minority status, insecurities about the past, and sensitivity to real or perceived attacks from the outside remained close to the surface. In the 1920s and 1930s, growing conflict with Muslims generated a new wave of tracts stirring the community with references to past atrocities, martyrdom, and calls for united action. Sikhism was seen in danger. At a time of tension, tracts and emotional appeals could once again play a central role in arousing old tensions and opening new wounds.[61]

In recent years, there has been occasional interest in the earlier Singh Sabha movement. During the 1975 anniversary of the first Sabha at Amritsar, Singh Sabhas were portrayed as heroic saviors of the *panth,* as protectors of a tradition about to disappear. At the same time, fear of the old enemies, such as the Arya Samaj, began to surface. There was a recasting of earlier struggles and a call to defend the community.[62] Tracts and broadsides abounded. As decades earlier, many of the arguments and printed works rested upon a mixture of fact and fantasy, but in both instances, they contributed to the emergence of a new reality. The Singh Sabhas helped create a world with boundaries, ritual, and constant awareness of threats that might endanger the future of the *panth.* In fact, the dangers probably were exaggerated, but the tracts nevertheless reinforced tensions and identified dangers that became very real. Similarly, the intolerance and calls for sacrifice that permeate current Sikh tract literature contribute to an intensification of community insecurity and a minority self-consciousness. The parallels between the content and the style of Sikh tracts in the two eras are striking, as is the ability of the printed matter and symbols to stir emotions. They have made a difference in the past and, indeed, continue to do so in the present.

Bibliographic Essay

Although numerous studies discuss the importance of Indian journalism in South Asian cultural and political history, little scholarship has focused on how vernacular literature has affected communication and regional developments. This brief note will review current research on publishing in the Punjab and then assess the major sources and bibliographies that facilitate understanding of the Sikh experience during the Singh Sabha era, c. 1875–1920. General historiographic issues and recent publications on the press are discussed in N. G. Barrier, "Regional Political History: New Trends in the Study of British India," in Paul Wallace, ed., *Region and Nation in India* (Oxford and New York: 1985), 111–52. Useful introductions to new patterns of communication include Ellen Gumperz, "The Modernization of Communication," *Asian Survey* 2 (1968): 589–606; Ellen McDonald, "The Growth of Regional Consciousness in Maharashtra," *Indian Economic and Social History Review,* 5 (1968): 223–43, and Yogendra Malik, ed., *South Asian Intellectuals and Social Change* (New Delhi: 1972).

The growth of Punjab studies, both in the region and in North America, has produced new research and bibliographic guides. Within the Punjab, a network of associations and universities hold conferences, sponsor scholarly journals, most notably *Punjab Past and Present* and the *Journal of Sikh Studies,* and publish monographs. Trends in Punjab research were surveyed in N. G. Barrier, "The Evolution of Punjab Studies, 1972–1987," a paper presented at the 1987 Punjab Conference, Madison that will be published in conference proceedings by Michigan State University, 1991. American scholarship on Punjab intellectual and political history includes articles and books that have grown out of individual research or from discussions within the Research Committee on the Punjab. Complementing Dr. Ganda Singh's *Bibliography of the Punjab* (1966) has been a series of bibliographies published by Research Committee on the Punjab including Kenneth Jones and W. Eric Gustafson, *Sources on Punjab History* (New Delhi: 1975), N. G. Barrier, *The Punjab in Nineteenth Century Tracts,* South Asia Series (East Lansing, Michigan: 1969), and N. G. Barrier and Paul Wallace, *The Punjab Press, 1880–1905,* South Asia Series (East Lansing, Michigan: 1970). The extensive India Office Library holdings of Punjabi tracts now have been filmed by the South Asia Microform Project. There are several guides to that collection and complementary material in the India Office Library and British Museum relevant to Punjab studies. Bibliographies and the nature of the collection discussed in N. G. Barrier, "South Asia in Vernacular Publication," *The Journal of Asian Studies* 27 (August 1969): 803–10. The definitive guide to the India Office collection is Ganesh Gaur and Eileen Dimes, *Catalogue of Punjabi Printed Books Added to the India Office Library, 1902–1964* (London: 1975).

The primary source material for evaluating events and personalities within the Sikh community are vernacular publications. This literature was increasingly written in Punjabi after the 1890s, but much of the present research on the Sikh renaissance is in English and relies on English-language documentation. Two recent examples of English centered research are Richard Fox, *Lions of the Punjab* (Berkeley and Los Angeles: 1986) and Rajiv A. Kapur, *Sikh Separatism* (Allen and Unwin, 1986). Another broad interpretation is Harbans Singh, *Heritage of the Sikhs,* 2d rev. ed., (Manohar: 1985). The notable exceptions include dissertations and publications produced by Sikh study programs at Punjabi University, Patiala, and Guru Nanak Dev University,

Amritsar. An example of this trend is Gurdarshan Singh Dhillon, "Character and Impact of the Singh Sabha Movement on the History of the Punjab," (Punjabi University, 1973). Several journals published by these institutions contain a range of provocative articles on the Sikhs and Punjab history.

The earliest attempt to publicize Sikh tract literature and its role in Punjab religious and political history was a bibliographic guide by N. G. Barrier, *The Sikhs and Their Literature* (Delhi: 1970). In addition to identifying and often collecting an assortment of Sikh tracts, Barrier has written broadly on the communication system linking Sikhs across the world as demonstrated by "Sikh Immigration and the Transmission of Information and Values," in N. G. Barrier and Verne Dusenbery, eds., *The Sikh Diaspora* (New Delhi: 1988); "Sikh Journalism: The Early Stage and in 20th Century Punjab," in Harnam Singh, ed., *Encyclopaedia of Sikhism* (forthcoming); "The Singh Sabha and the Sikh Renaissance," in Robert Baird, ed., *Religion in Modern India* rev. ed., (Delhi: 1988). Also useful in reconstructing the tract warfare and intellectual milieu of 19th century Punjab has been Kenneth Jones's publications on the Arya Samaj and Sikh-Arya confrontation: Kenneth W. Jones, *Arya Dharm: Hindu Consciousness in Nineteenth Century Punjab* (Berkeley and Los Angeles: 1976); "Ham Hindu Nahin," *Journal of Asian Studies* 33 (1973): 457–75; "Communalism in the Punjab," *Journal of Asian Studies* 28 (1968): 39-53.

The most fruitful research on the Singh Sabhas and Sikh revitalization, however, has been produced by Harjot Singh Oberoi, currently holder of the Sikh Studies Chair at the University of British Columbia. Oberoi's dissertation, "A World Reconstructed: Religion, Ritual and Community Among the Sikhs, 1850–1909" (Australian National University, 1987), uses Sikh newspapers and tracts to demonstrate the existence of a variety of traditions and competing groups hitherto lumped together as "the Singh Sabha movement." His revised manuscript, along with several articles, "Bhais, Babas and Gyanis: Traditional Intellectuals in Nineteenth Century Punjab," *Studies in History* 2 (1980): 33-62; "A Historiographical and Bibliographical Reconstruction of the Singh Sabha in the Nineteenth Century," *Journal of Sikh Studies* 10 (1983): 108–30, should serve as a base upon which future studies rest.

With the exception of Bhai Vir Singh, none of the pamphleteers surveyed in this essay has been treated seriously. One of the best of the dozen or so studies on Bhai Vir Singh is G. S. Khosla, *Bhai Vir Singh* (New Delhi: 1984), but even that work does not place the newspaperman and intellectual within his cultural milieu. There are short and generally eulogic Punjabi accounts of Ditt Singh and Bhai Kahan Singh Nabha. Each probably will receive more critical evaluation in the forthcoming Encyclopaedia of Sikhism edited by Dr. Harbans Singh of Punjabi University. The lives and ideas of Kahan Singh and Ditt Singh are examined in the Harjot Singh Oberoi's dissertation. Examples of uncritical reviews include *Aduti Jivan Britānt Panth Rattan Bābu Teja Singh Overseer* (Bhasaur: n.d.). Also important in focusing the issues and personalities involved in Sikh pamphleteering are articles and correspondence in the three primary Sikh newspapers prior to 1920, *The Khalsa Akhbār* (Punjabi, c. 1889–1905), the *Khalsa Samāchār* (Punjabi, 1899 to the present), and the *Khalsa Advocate* (1903–23, then becoming the Punjabi *Khalsa Te Khalsa Advocate*). Mohan Singh Vaid's diary, several sections of which are reproduced in Dukhi's biography of the Vaid, provides an inside view of Sikh society as well as containing information on the production and circulation of tracts.

PART THREE

In Summary

Ten

Imagining Community: Polemical Debates in Colonial India

Barbara Daly Metcalf

Some years ago, I arrived in Agra after spending several months in Lahore. Although Lahore is in a Punjabi-speaking area, its educated classes have long shared a common language, perhaps best called by its old name of Hindustani, known across the Indo-Gangetic plain and beyond. Written in Perso-Arabic script and called Urdu, it is now an official language in Pakistan. It was that language I spoke as I checked into a hotel and chatted with the innkeeper. He graciously complimented my facility in his language. "*Āp ne itnī shuddh hindī kahān sikhī?*" he asked, taking my language to be Hindi, an official language in India. My only answer had to be that I had learned the language in Lahore—creating a juxtaposition, *shuddh hindī* and Lahore, that in today's world of politicized languages boggles the mind.

Out of what is linguistically a single language and what is, as my example indicates, even today indistinguishable in everyday life. Communalist groups—those defining and protecting the interests of specific (in this case, religious) groups—have made the choice of script and, presumably, a preferred vocabulary a rallying cry for loyalty. *Shuddh hindī* was "pure" Hindi, a language described by a Sanskrit word with charged connotations of purity in contrast to pollution; Urdu was its opposite, also a cause as much as a language to be preserved in a separate state of Pakistan.

If Hindi and Urdu can sound the same, and Hindi movies, as everyone says, are really Urdu movies—we are reminded that the bases of ideologically constituted communities, far from being primordial, are constituted in history and imagination. Even a hundred years ago in the Indian subcontinent, one would have been hard pressed to predict the shape of religious and ethnic groups whose existence today so molds every aspect of political and social life. No example is better than one currently with us, that of the Sikhs who in recent years have agitated, with tragic results on both sides, for greater autonomy. Socially integrated into every aspect of non-Sikh society, professing a religious orientation little different from many other Indic *panths* or paths, who would have predicted today's separatism?

The word "imagined" does not seem far off: imagined languages, imagined religions, imagined communities. These are "invented" communities, whose significance proves to be, to a considerable degree, arbitrary. To follow Benedict Anderson, who writes of the nationalist sentiments with which communal bonds both interact and compete, they are also "imagined" in a more fundamental way.[1] They represent the great shift, in the modern era, from an emphasis on relationships that are primarily face-to-face, based in geographically small communities, to ones that encompass groups whose members can never be known to each other—who can only be imagined. Knowing this ought to be liberating: what is imagined ought to be susceptible to being unimagined as well.

The middle and late nineteenth century in India—the so-called "heyday" of the British Empire—was a period of lively encounters carried on among Indians in public speaking and preaching, formal debates, journals, books, and tracts. Associations, some of the moment and some enduring, were formed. Spokesmen were active in defining or proclaiming matters of doctrine, worship, customs observed during life cycle or calendrical celebrations, principles of social relationships and status, and, implicitly but often explicitly, the very language a group ought to speak. Threaded through all these separate issues was the basic underlying goal of community, of defining the limits of a group which shared the correct perspective on all issues. Debaters implicitly and explicitly defined themselves against opponents, notably Christian missionaries and converts, and also against groups and individuals closer to home, including rivals who contested the interpretations of shared symbols. All operated in a context of contentiousness, challenging a variety of opponents at various removes from their own positions.

These debates, the subject of the essays included here, are to be taken neither as bad manners nor as a reflection of some other reality. They were an important element in constituting fundamental changes in Indian social, political, and cultural life. The actors, moreover, like the media, represented something new. The personalities we encounter in this book were very much products of the colonial experience, affected by the social and political changes it engendered and, in different ways, engaged in its cultural values. Through their polemics they at once created a role for themselves and forged the notion of religion, above all, as a self-conscious ideology and a primary focus for group loyalty.

To chart the differential experience of those European nations where national loyalty has dominated, in contrast to colonized areas where communal divisions have been decisive, is a significant problem for comparative history.[2] Two issues in the case of colonial India would seem to be key. First, the importance of a form of government structured on representation, in which leaders to be effective had to claim to speak for the interests of communities, cannot be underestimated: "representation" and "communalism" were indissolubly linked.[3] Second, the colonial appropriation of public and civic institutions encouraged a kind of retreat to domestic and religious space as sites where cultural values could be reworked and renewed. The importance of regulating women is clearly significant here. The temporal and causal relationship of the movements of reform and revival to enduring political shifts in India has yet to be studied in detail, but the documents of these movements, examined here, allow us to see groupings coming into existence.

The novelty of these communities is particularly illuminating when, as in most of the essays included here, those groupings are religious.[4] Whatever their spokesmen may say, the boundaries of all religious communities change, as they are changed by, the varying historical contexts they encounter. In the case of Islam, for example, there may always be shared consciousness, to varying degrees. But the salience of a Muslim identity will vary, just as the sense of the operative boundaries of community will be shaped distinctively—for example, from an implicit emphasis on the well-born to a focus on the administratively unified census category of Muslim in British India.[5] The very assumption that there even was a religion called "Hinduism," moreover, was very much a product of the colonial period, an imputation of a rarefied unity to Indic religious orientations and practices that had not previously existed.[6] "Sikhism," as noted above, also emerged as a distinctive tradition only in recent times.[7] Forms of worship and morally sanctioned patterns of social life ceased to be taken for granted and instead became foci of conscious reflection. Participants in self-conscious communities may have asserted that they were simply continuing age-old practices, but an examination of their history shows otherwise.

A key element in the creation of imaginary communities, in Europe as in Asia, has been, again to return to Anderson, the role of publications—or "print capitalism," as he calls it—in making ties possible beyond a specific locality. The publications of religio-cultural spokesmen and leaders, contesting for the loyalties of newly "imagined" communities whose characteristics they seek to define are not primarily evidence of movements, attitudes, or social change—though, of course, they are that too. They are themselves the subject of the story that has to be told.

New Leaders and New Arenas

The polemical enterprise discussed here created a new public arena in Indian social life.[8] The debates, written and oral, were part of a larger phenomenon in which leaders made political claims on the basis of a moral community and marked and claimed public space for their community through publications, associations, public rituals and, on occasion, collective actions.

Ever more important in claiming the moral leadership of communities were a new category of leaders whom we may call "lay" leaders, exemplified by most of the personalities examined in the chapters presented here. Although they became experts in the religious tradition, these people did not receive traditional teaching or initiation like the religious elites, the *'ulamā* and *pandits,* who were heirs of the historically transmitted traditional learning. They were people who utilized the new techniques of journalism, public preaching and debate, tract and book writing, and organization. Acting as debaters, journalists, and publicists, they often had some education in government or missionary schools and, occasionally, were employed in schools or government offices. The successful were able to support themselves simply by their writing and preaching activities. Sometimes teachers and translators seemed to play a significant role as people especially well prepared for interpreting and translating across or within a body of learning. They redefined the basis of religious authority. Pandit Gauri Datta, for example, gave the image of renouncer a new twist by called himself "a *sanyāsīn* for *nāgarī*" in leading the campaign for Hindi as a key to defending Hindu interests (King, 123–148). Munshi Meheru'llah (1861–1907) in Bengal, a tailor by background who never received a *madrasah* education, fits into this category; his very title, *munshī* (often used for clerk), recognized that he was educated but denied him the status of *maulānā* (Ahmed, 93–120).

The "lay" leaders profited from, and in turn stimulated, the transition from what has been called an "esoteric" paradigm of education dependent on a privileged personal relationship between a teacher and student to a more public and impersonal style of education, set in formally organized schools and furthered by the new availability of printed books. Texts once taught in a ritual setting were now available on street corners, and people once prohibited by birth from education now had access to what had been only studied by the elite. The shift was dramatically illustrated by the missionary attempt to teach the Skanda Purana (in a simplified prose version) in their own schools in order, they hoped, to demonstrate its immorality and implausibility. Arumuga Pillai (1822–79) opposed the teaching of such texts by missionaries who treated them, as he saw it, sacrilegiously (Hudson,

27–51). Texts themselves, moreover, spread reform. Thus it was at a government school that the Andhra reformer Viresalingam (1848–1919) read Brahmo Samaj texts from the first wave of reform in Bengal, inspiring him to bring socioreligious reform to Andhra; his reform opposed the traditional Brahmans (Leonard, 151–78).

The polemicists understood British institutions. Dr. Wazir Khan, the Agra debater, was trained as a medical doctor and knew English (Powell, 77–92). Sayyid Mumtaz 'Ali (1860–1935) was a "B.A. Failed" and had served as a translator for the Lahore High Court (Minault, 179–99). Many of these religious spokesmen were, in fact, directly involved in British employment or educational institutions. Viresalingam at age ten was an apprentice in a customs office, as was Vishnubawa at an early age. Pandit Gauri Datta and Munshi Sahan Prasad (the authors of the plays on the Hindi-Urdu controversy) were both school teachers, as were Viresalingam and Arumuga Pillai. The latter was also an active translator for missionaries of Christian texts into Tamil.

Many of these reformers were based in urban centers with new populations, government offices, and new educational institutions, varying in scale, to be sure, from such places as the district town of Rajahmundry to the old provincial capital of Lahore to the new colonial city of Bombay. The polemicists described here were typically mobile men. Dr. Wazir Khan, a Pathan, was educated in Calcutta and posted to Agra. Munshi Meheru'llah, born in the small town of Jessore, travelled throughout Bengal and had substantial contacts with professionals in Calcutta. Dayananda Saraswati (1824–83) was born in Gujarat but moved to Punjab (Jones, 52–74). Vishnubawa had various postings on the Konkan coast before moving first to the pilgrimage center of Pandharpur and thence to Bombay (Conlon, 5–26). Arumuga Pillai travelled from Jaffna to Madras to investigate schools there and, later, to buy a printing press; he conducted his reform activities in both Sri Lanka and India.

It was in urban settings, among people uprooted from familial contexts, that the new leaders operated. In towns and cities they found the facilities for publication and the audience for teaching and reading. Newspapers and journals, by the very audience they addressed, served to create bonds among members of that audience. In the cities the reformers found people attuned to a new cultural identity and to the new relationships offered by voluntary associations and public meetings. In these chapters we hear of a variety of movements: Muslim sectarian orientations, the Islamic Missionary Society in Calcutta, the Brahmo Samaj, the Shaiva Prakasha Samaj, the Prarthana Samaj, the Arya Samaj, the Widow Remarriage Association, the Singh Sabhas. Just as there were broad similarities in the social role of the leaders and in their institutions, so there were, generally speaking, common themes in teachings and goals behind these varied names.

New Languages and New Messages

The vernacular languages used for printing, debates, and preaching were means of communication to new groups, to the secularly educated elites, to women of educated families, and beyond to the population as a whole. Sacred texts and works about them now reached a far larger audience than that of a small, usually male elite, engaged in face to face instruction. The vernaculars, however, excluded even as they included. The use of a vernacular was a claim to the legitimacy of that language—even as it was coming into being through standardization and choices about diction and rhetoric—for a particular group at the expense of other languages. The choice of language, and the cultural meanings embedded in that choice, were themes that pervaded the writings of polemics and reform.

Regional languages in this period developed prose forms and a new capacity for expressing diverse materials. Tamil, Telugu, and Marathi, for example, became repositories of religious teachings, at once a boon for ordinary people and a means of diminishing Brahmanic prestige. Bengali in the same way came to carry Islamic teachings at the cost of those who knew Persian and Urdu, again a challenge to authority and status. In the Punjab, Punjabi became a marker of Sikh identity and Hindi of Hindu, both asserting themselves against the overwhelming preponderance of Urdu learning and publications in the Punjab (Barrier, 200–26). The differentiation between Hindi and Urdu severed the Persianate mixed culture of North Indian elites. The plays that espouse the cause of Hindi, discussed by King above, show the power of polemic associated with language in the images they chose. Both plays used female personifications of language, and hence communal identity: for the Hindu writers, Hindi was a respectable cow-and-Brahman-nurturing matron, while Urdu was nothing less than a heartless aristocratic strumpet. The new idea of the educated reformed Hindu woman and the new value placed on the Hindi language reinforced each other.

Beyond the concern with language, the texts shared other commonalities. There was in this period a very widespread dissemination of what might be called high cultural texts and textual norms. Printed texts made possible ever more detailed standards for correct knowledge and behavior: the medium permitted the message. The symbol of the book itself came to be more emphasized. Other central cultural symbols and understandings were also modified, particularly by an emphasis on what might be called high cultural normative standards and away from local cults, sacred spaces, and fixed calendrical events. Personal standards in ethics and worship were enjoined, so that religious life became more congruent with a mobile, urbanizing society; elaborate rituals tied to specific times and places were discouraged. There was a tendency to de-emphasize complex customary observations of funerals and marriages and to teach instead an internalized religion of individual responsibility. The publication of Sikh guides to conduct are an example of texts characteristic of this emphasis. This kind of change cut across what were increasingly seen to be the significant groups—Hindu, Muslim, and to a lesser extent Sikh—that defined Indian social life.

As part of these fundamental transformations of religious style, there was across the board a new emphasis on a single theistic God who was to be worshipped at the cost of appropriate devotion to local all-powerful saints (in the Muslim case) or "idols" and family deities (in the Hindu). This changed pattern awaits comprehensive study as a characteristic not specific to any one tradition. Muslims in the key pre-Mutiny movements of Tariqa-i-Muhammadiya and the Fara'idis cited pristine revelation to justify their opposition to local customs and cults; their reformist thrust was taken up in a variety of forms throughout the century. Vishnubawa, who spent three years at the great Vaishnavite pilgrimage site of Pandharpur, drew on rich themes of *bhakti* devotionalism in fostering the worship of the supreme lord, Parameshwara. Arumuga Pillai, insisting on a temple-centered deity (in contrast, for example, to the Brahmo Samaj, who opted for a more abstract theism), showed that lesser deities must be seen as manifestations or servants of Shiva. Hints of that God's characteristic were evident in tracts entitled "Crimes against the Lord" and "Grace." Viresalingam, as did Dayananda, denied the validity of the miracle-filled Puranas. Viresalingam seems to have offered instead a focus on a personal God, kind to his followers who were to live morally to please Him. Sikh reformers condemned devotion both to Muslim saints and Hindu gods. All of these teachings distinguished the reformed from the unreformed. At the same time, they posed implicitly such questions as "What does it mean to be a Hindu?" and thus they distinguished communities from each other.

Community and the Imagination of Difference

In fixing a moral standard of behavior, groups came to know not only what they were but what they were not. To imagine themselves, they had to imagine their opposite or opposites. Many reformers had multiple targets. The cases taken by Swami Dayananda in his reading of the Christian Bible are suggestive in this regard. The Arya Samajis used reform to eliminate Islamicized, Persianate characteristics common to the culture of the government classes of which so many of them were a part. In the summary of Dayananda's arguments above, it is clear that he saw the Christian Bible with eyes trained in criticism of Islam: he thus reproached the Christians for practices that, to be sure, appeared in the Old Testament but that could be, as well, hallmarks of Muslim differences with Hindus: meat eating, animal sacrifice, circumcision, and burial of the dead. By criticizing these practices, he explicitly asserted Hindu superiority over Christians in his debates, but by choosing this particular range of issues, not necessarily the obvious ones, he implicitly underlined Hindu differences from Muslims. As he did this, of course, he also targeted those who did not acknowledge his definition of being "Hindu."

The encounters between Indian spokesmen and Christian missionaries, described in several of the chapters, stimulated claims to being "Hindu" or "Muslim"; the Christian missionary assumed such identities to be prima facie significant. Ironically, however, the spectacle of the debates brought Indians of all backgrounds together. A significant dimension of the appeal of these debates lay in the opportunity to encounter Europeans on open turf, to challenge those who, in their ever intensifying political control, could not be challenged elsewhere. The fact that Dr. Wazir Khan's audience included Hindus and Sikhs, that Vishnubawa was cheered on by Parsees and Munshi Meheru'llah by Hindus suggests a general enthusiasm, not specific to community, to see Europeans held up to ridicule. Never a real threat, Christian missionaries, far from slandering Indians, would instead find themselves the subject of attack, to the general delight of the audience.[9] The party over, however, religious communities were left behind to confront each other.

One oddity of the debates was that each side invariably claimed to have won. In a sense, each did, for the goal was to stand forth to champion one's own side and foster communal self-esteem. Only rarely did a debater enter in any significant way into the frame of reference of his opponent. The choice exception to this nineteenth-century India was the encounter of the Bengali monotheist, Ram Mohan Roy, with a Baptist missionary who subsequently became, if not a Brahmo, a Unitarian. On the other side, one might place the frustrated claim of the Muslim Deobandis that their Arya Samaj opponents spoke Sanskrit, an achievement bound to impress the Hindus in the audience even as it confirms for us the lack of interest in mutual intelligibility.

Debates with Christian missionaries took place from at least the

1830s. In the 1850s, two protagonists, both the subjects of essays here, came into prominence when they not only debated, but published pamphlets and correspondence that carried their positions and provided material for later polemicists. Dr. Wazir Khan, the medical doctor who entered public disputes in pre-Mutiny Agra, was unusual in the extent to which he was able to draw his Christian opponents into his frame of argument. Literate in English, he used European higher criticism to bolster the age-old Muslim argument that only the Qur'anic text remained uncorrupted. Christianity, of course, did not historically take the biblical text as the literal word of God pronounced in a sacred tongue—Muslims did so take the Qur'an. Nonetheless, Wazir Khan, to the delight of his audience and readers, seemed able to triumph over Christian arguments and, in so doing, to leave a legacy of widely published materials subsequently utilized by both Muslims and the reformist Arya Samaj. Later in the century the Bengali Munshi Meheru'llah continued the emphasis on the corruption of the biblical text, focusing especially on the historic Muslim concern to deny the divinity of Christ. Sayyid Mumtaz 'Ali read debate literature written by Dr. Wazir Khan's partner, Maulana Rahmatu'llah Kairanawi. There was, thus, a textual tradition to illuminate Muslim-Christian difference.

Vishnubawa, the second influential polemicist, flourished in Bombay from the 1850s to the 1870s. He savored a range of issues which, taken literally, seemed to show Christians as fools. How could a virgin give birth? How could humans be made in God's image? How could the promises of Revelation be taken seriously? Other issues were adduced to show that authentic Christianity taught proper behavior—like vegetarianism—that Christians had forgotten while Hindus followed. Dayananda Saraswati built on this approach of demonstrating absurdities and revealing inconsistencies between precept and behavior. He even went so far as to call the whole ethical standard of biblical actors to account, finding that savagery dominated the Old Testament, and the foibles of a lower-caste carpenter, the New Testament. Arumuga Pillai's detailed familiarity with biblical texts, thanks to his work as a missionary translator, allowed him to find far more than neglected vegetarianism in Christian texts: the whole temple cult in Jerusalem was nothing more than Shaivism, *darshan* of images, and *prasād,* a tradition to which Christians ought to return, while Shaivites, providentially harassed by the Christians, ought to do so as well. A humble employee of the British could thus articulate not only cultural difference but superiority.

The debate with Christians offered an opportunity for asserting spiritual superiority not only by comparisons, but by assertions that Christian achievements were in fact derived from earlier unacknowledged borrowings. Nonetheless, all of these debaters (except perhaps

Dr. Wazir Khan) were concerned not only with asserting themselves against the Christians and their criticisms, but also with recognizing that in the present they strayed from the lofty teachings that had once reached to Europe. Christians did, after all, in the present evince political and technological superiority, a situation explicable only by the argument that Indian cultural life, whether Hindu, Muslim, or Sikh, did not adhere to its own high standards. As a result of this sense of crisis over current practice, there were striking similarities in the general patterns that emerged, as noted above, and in attempts to foster ethical, nonparochial norms. The interchange with Christians, so extensively discussed in this volume, influenced these changes. It is, however, more important that reformed religion offered certain affinities to the evolving society of nineteenth-century urban India and that new technologies, particularly print, both encouraged and permitted certain new emphases. Moreover, as Rafiuddin Ahmed in his chapter reminds us, in many cases reform began prior to the encounter with Christians.

The lines that marked off communities not only excluded but included. The Prarthana Samaj opposed caste and tried to educate the poor. Vishnubawa, himself a Chitpavan Brahman, would have untouchables as part of society and, in his utopia, would have hierarchy by merit but commensality among all. Viresalingam, a Niyogi Brahman, was opposed to Brahman ritual dominance. Arya Samaji professionals of different castes could marry and associate among themselves. Among the Sikh reformers discussed above, Ditt Singh, himself an untouchable, most clearly opposed caste; Teja Singh called on Sikhs to drop caste names. Deobandis (like Maulana Rahmatu'llah, Wazir Khan's collaborator) favored marriage and social relationships among more loosely defined groups of the wellborn and deplored customary untouchability. The reformers, generally speaking, sought to modify hierarchy.

Reforms related to women further modified customary hierarchy, as many were brought into education and styles of religion heretofore associated primarily with men. Of the reformers described in the present volume, Sayyid Mumtaz 'Ali's work is most centrally related to educating women, but issues concerning women—*satī,* marriage age, widow remarriage, and education—were central to nineteenth-century reform.

The importance of the family, and hence of women, as the locus of cultural values was evident throughout the reform movements. Women's role in this was not "traditional," for women had characteristically been guardians of local, not textual, norms. The inclusion of them in newly defined teachings had implications for women's status. Women were empowered with cultural skills, sometimes including literacy, but they were simultaneously constrained by male standards of cultural behavior that intruded on a variety of women's domains.[10] This emphasis also had implications for community. Elevating women and the home were, for example, at the heart of Bengali and—given the dominant position of Bengalis in cultural reformulation—of Hindu social reform. Partha Chatterjee has argued that this emphasis laid a foundation for political nationalism which, ironically, purported to be nationalist but excluded those outside the middle-class model of domestic life and those who adhered to other religions.[11]

The cultural weight placed on women and the home fostered a shared range of texts and values for women and men. It also produced an elaborate discourse on women as different, as characterized by a special nature that suited them for the domestic and the spiritual in contrast to the worldly, corrupt, and colonized outside.[12] Culturally empowering women was thus matched by a discourse that kept women in their place. The new discourse of difference is suggested by the genderization of the language of reform as Sikhs and Hindus mutually taunted each other with being effeminate. The plays about Hindi, as noted above, turned languages into symbolic women: Queen Devanagri was as much the image of the new middle-class housewife, "the Hindu woman," as of any queen; Begam Urdu was the unreformed and uncontrolled woman, projected onto a Muslim community.

We are thus reminded that if there was some de-emphasis of birth or gender as defining cultural unities, there were, far more significantly, new lines being drawn within Indian society. Even attempts to modify distinctions based on birth and gender turn out to have consequences beyond those explicitly urged. Sikhs now were called on to marry only among Sikhs. Brahmans and non-Brahmans grew more distant. Hindus and Muslims drew apart. Many of the polemics characteristic of this period were directed within: toward Brahmans seen to be mired in ritual, toward *'ulamā* or sufis who accepted historic accretions, toward women celebrating false customs. But the very process of defining what it meant to be a true Muslim or a true Hindu, whether against coreligionists or against Christians, came above all to distinguish ideally homogenized religious traditions from each other.

Reformers operating in the vernacular languages have at times been obscured by the better-known anglicized leaders. The vernacular reformers, like those considered here, took part in changes at the heart of Indian religious, social, and political life in the nineteenth century. They played a central role in the very development of the regional languages; they articulated and disseminated new standards and interpretations of religious symbols—textually based, interiorized, and theistic; and they discouraged many customary observations and social practices. They also laid a foundation, wittingly or not, for the ethnic and religious communalism that has so troubled Indian life ever since. Modern religion has been at once congruent with the demands of a more mobile and individualistic social life, fostering a diminished concern with birth, an end to parochial cults, and an emphasis on ethical teachings. At the same time, it has provided community while simultaneously challenging the larger cultural and political integration so many have long craved.

NOTES

Chapter 1

1. Research for this essay was supported in part by a fellowship of the American Institute of Indian Studies. The author acknowledges the useful comments and criticisms of earlier versions by Barbara Metcalf, Michael Fisher, and members of the University of Washington History Research Group and of the SACPAN colloquium. Typeface limitations have prevented use of conventional Marathi transliterations apart from indication of long vowels.

2. *Bombay Guardian,* (October 4, 1856), p. 316.

3. There is considerable variation in the pattern of references to Vishnubawa Brahmachari, particularly in the variant spellings of *bawa, bowa,* and *buwa,* a Marathi term of respect for elders, gurus, *samnyāssīns,* and others of spiritual attainment such as *bhajan* singers and *kīrtankars;* see J. T. Molesworth, *Marathi-English Dictionary* (reprint, Poona: Shubhada Asraswat, 1975), 557–77, 587, 595. The brahmachari designation reflected his chosen path of celibacy.

4. Cf. David Kopf, *British Orientalism and the Bengal Renaissance: The Dynamics of Indian Modernization, 1773–1835* (Berkeley and Los Angeles: University of California, 1969); D. S. Sarma, *Studies in the Renaissance of Hinduism* (Benares: Hindu University, 1944); R. C. Majumdar, ed., *The History and Culture of the Indian People,* vol. 10 of *British Paramountcy and Indian Renaissance,* Part 2 (Bombay: Bharatiya Vidya Bhavan Press, 1965).

5. Kopf, *British Orientalism,* pp. 8–9.

6. See P. Thomas, *Christians and Christianity in India and Pakistan,* (London: 1954), 150–92; S. M. Pathak, *American Missionaries and Hinduism: A Study of Their Contacts* (Delhi: 1967).

7. Ainslie T. Embree, *Charles Grant and British Rule in India* (New York: Columbia University Press, 1962), 143–57.

8. Charles Grant, "Observations on the State of Society among Asiatic Subjects of Great Britain," *Parliamentary Papers,* 1812–13, 10, no. 282, pp. 1–112, at p. 76.

9. See E. D. Potts, *British Baptist Missionaries in India, 1793–1837: The History of Serampore and Its Missions* (Cambridge: Cambridge University Press, 1967). According to the Christian-missionary newspaper *Dnyānodaya,* 15 (January 15,

1856), pp. 25–26, a Marathi New Testament was begun at Serampore in 1804 and completed in 1811. An Old Testament followed in 1815, but it was said that the production was "in such type as to be almost unintelligible and in such a dialect of the Marathi as to be utterly unfit for general use."

10. See Gordon Hall, *Anecdotes of the Bombay Mission for the Conversion of Hindoos...* (London: Frederick J. Williamson, 1836); Robert Speer, *George Bowen of Bombay* (New York: Missionary Review of 1938), p. 222.

11. A recent study of Lokahitawadi's ideas is Vasant K. Kshire, *Lokahitawadi's Thought: A Critical Study* (Poona: University of Poona, 1977), especially pp. 67–78.

12. See Siddheshvarashastri Citrav, *Bhāratavarshīya Arvācīn Caritrakosha (I. Sa. 1818–1945)* (Poona: Sh. 1868, 1946), p. 549. I am grateful to Professor Maureen L. P. Patterson for supplying me with this reference.

13. Matthew Lederle, *Philosophical Trends in Modern Maharastra* (Bombay: Popular Prakashan, 1976), p. 191.

14. Prabhakar Padhye and Sri. Ra. Tikekar, *Ājkālāca Mahārāshtra* (Bombay: Bharat Garav Granthamala, 1935), p. 110.

15. N. H. Kulkarnee, "Hindu Religious and Reform Movements in Nineteenth and Twentieth Century Maharashtra," in S. P. Sen, ed., *Social and Religious Reform Movements in the Nineteenth and Twentieth Centuries* (Calcutta: Institute for Historical Studies, 1979), p. 258.

16. N. R. Inamdar, "Political Thought of Vishnubawa Brahmachari (1825–1871)," *Journal of the University of Poona*, no. 21: *Humanities section* (1965): p. 166.

17. Ramacandra Pandurang Sastri Ajrekar, *Srī Vishnubāvā Brahmacārī yānce caritra* (Bombay: Atmaram Kanhoba Sh. 1794, A.D. 1872); Gangadhar Balkrishna Sardar, *Mahārāshtrace Upekshitā Mānkarī* (Poona: Sunanda Prakashan, 1941), pp. 88–89.

18. Vinayakrao Karmalkar, "Pahile Upekshit Hindu Mishanari," *Bharata Itihāsa Samshodhak Mandal Trimāsika* 43, 1–4 (1965): pp. 63–70. Apart from the pioneering work of Matthew Lederle cited at note 13 above, one recent historiographical recognition of Vishnubawa Brahmachari is Richard P. Tucker, "Hindu Traditionalism and Nationalist Ideologies in Nineteenth Century Maharashtra," *Modern Asian Studies* 10 (July 1976): pp. 321–48.

19. Shastri Ajrekar, *Shrī Vishnubāvā Brahmachari yānce Charita* (Bombay: Sh. 1794 [A.D. 1872]), p. 5.

20. Sardar, *Upekshita Mānkarī,* p. 75.

21. Ajrekar, *Vishnubāvā,* p. 7.

22. According to Shankar Vishnu Gokhale, writing in the *Gokhale Kulavrittānt* (Bombay?: Gokhale Kulavrittant Karyakari Mandal, Sh. 1900, A.D.

1978), 141, this was in Vishnu's twentieth year, about A.D. 1845. I wish to acknowledge the assistance of Professor Maureen L. P. Patterson in providing me with this reference.

23. Ajrekar, *Vishnubāvā,* p. 7.

24. Gordon Hall, *Anecdotes of the Bombay Mission,* pp. 96–102. For a survey of early mission activity, see George Smith, *The Life of John Wilson,* 2d ed. (London: John Murray, 1879), pp. 32–36.

25. Hall, *Anecdotes,* p. 132.

26. Hall, *Anecdotes,* p. 132.

27. Smith, *John Wilson,* p. 38ff.

28. *Dnyānodaya* 4 (1847), p. 223.

29. Smith, *John Wilson,* p. 63. For a scholarly study of further instances of polemic response, see Richard Fox Young, *Resistant Hinduism: Sanskrit Sources on Anti-Christian Apologetics in Early Nineteenth Century India* (Vienna: DeNobili Research Library, 1981). Another recent examination of polemics in Maharashtra is Richard P. Tucker,"Defence of Dharma in Maharashtra, 1840–1870," in A. G. Pawar ed., *Maratha History Seminar* (Kolhapur: Shivaji University, 1971), pp. 375–89.

30. J. C. Masselos, *Towards Nationalism: Group Affiliations and the Politics of Public Associations in Nineteenth Century Western India* (Bombay: Popular Prakashan, 1974), pp. 35–36; Ganesh G. Jambhekar, ed., *Memoirs and Writings of Acharya Bal Gangadhar Shastri Jambhekar (1812–1846)* (Poona, 1950), vol. 1, pp. xxxcii–xli; vol. 3, appendix 2, pp. 486–503; *Bombay Witness* 1 (July 1844), p. 4.

31. Jambhekar, *Memoirs,* vol. 3, appendix 3, p. 92; *Dnyānodaya* 15 (January 1, 1856), p. 1.

32. Baba Padmanji, *Arunodaya Bābā Padmanjī yānce caritra* (Bombay: Bombay Tract and Book Society, 1888), p. 100.

33. John Murray Mitchell, *In Western India: Recollections of My Early Missionary Life* (Edinburgh: D. Douglas, 1899), p. 211.

34. Robert Speer, *George Bowen,* p. 222. The impact of debate and critique is amply demonstrated in Rosalind O'Hanlon, *Caste, Conflict, and Ideology: Mahatma Jotirao Phule and Low Caste Protest in Nineteenth-Century Western India* (Cambridge: Cambridge University, 1985), pp. 50–87.

35. *Bombay Guardian* (October 4, 1856), p. 316.

36. Compare Kenneth W. Jones, *Arya Dharm: Hindu Consciousness in Nineteenth Century Punjab* (Berkeley and Los Angeles: University of California Press, 1976), p. 5 with reference to Khatris, whose ambivalent status, wealth, literacy, and search of recognition led them to roles as 'traditional innovators' who responded to and supported the Arya Samaj.

37. *Bombay Guardian* (October 4, 1856), p. 316. When during the discourse the Reverend Narayan Sheshadri emphasized the immorality of the Hindu *shāstras* in relation to differences of different punishments for different varnas, Vishnubawa retorted that Brahmans were independent of moral obligations; the audience did not seem pleased. *Bombay Guardian* (October 4, 1856), p. 317.

38. *Bombay Guardian* (October 4, 1856), p. 316.

39. *Bombay Guardian* (October 15, 1856), p. 324.

40. *Dnyānodaya* 15 (November 4, 1856), pp. 334–35.

41. *Bombay Guardian* (December 20, 1856), p. 403; Sardar, *Upekshita Mankārī,* pp. 29–30.

42. *Bombay Gazette* (16 October 1856).

43. *Dnyānodaya* (6 November 1856), p. 335. In point of fact in the actual debates, Vishnubawa faced several Christian opponents in each session, including, as noted above in note 36, Indian converts such as the Reverend Narayan Sheshadri, whose baptism had generated the great controversies of 1843–44.

44. *Bombay Guardian* (January 17, 1857), p. 17.

45. *Dnyānodaya* 15 (December 1, 1856), p. 371.

46. George Bowen, *Discussions by the Sea-Side* (Bombay: Bombay Tract and Book Society, 1857) and George Bowen, *Samudrakinārīcaā Vādavivād: Brahmacārī Bāvā anī Khristi Upadeshaka yamadhye Dharmāvishayi je vādavivād Mumbaīs jhale Tyāncī hakīkata* (Bombay: Bombay Tract and Book Society, 1872).

47. Bowen, *Discussions,* p. 176.

48. Bowen, *Discussions,* pp. 42–43.

49. Bowen, *Discussions,* pp. 54–55.

50. Bowen, *Discussions,* p. 73.

51. Bowen, *Discussions,* p. 74. *Dynānodaya* 15 (January 1, 1856), p. 1 stated that this organ had been launched specifically to "counteract the influence of Native Papers conducted by bigoted Hindus or secret infidels who were constantly reviling Christianity and demanding proofs of its truth."

52. Bowen, *Discussions,* p. 158.

53. Bowen, *Discussions,* pp. 62, 189, 192. Even in their earliest years at Bombay the American missionaries found flaws in the Serampore translations, and began translating their own versions of the New Testament in 1817, completing a revised edition in 1826. The Old Testament was not published until 1853 and was combined in 1855 with a revised New Testament. *Dnyānodaya* 15 (January 15, 1856), p. 26. Bowen at the time was serving on a committee to revise further the Marathi Bible, Speer, *George Bowen,* p. 208n.

54. Speer, *George Bowen,* pp. 28–29.

55. Speer, *George Bowen,* pp. 118–19; cf. 138–39.

56. Speer, *George Bowen,* p. 51.

57. Speer, *George Bowen,* pp. 193–94.

58. *Bombay Times* (February 18, 1857), p. 333; Bowen, *Discussions,* pp. 41–42, 113. It was also alleged that Vishnubawa coaxed away some members of the secret reformist Paramahamsa Sabha, but I have not been able to confirm the fact.

59. Bowen, *Discussions,* p. 31.

60. Bowen, *Discussions,* p. 122.

61. Bowen, *Discussions,* pp. 60, 50. Bowen asserted that Vishnubawa had raised the attack on the reputation of Mary "to please the Parsees apparently" (p. 154). I suspect that Parsis had no special interest in the questions of the story of Mary, but that this was Bowen's oblique reference to the fact that much ribald word play on the word *virgin* could be employed to amuse a public gathering.

62. Bowen, *Discussions,* pp. 199, 14.

63. Bowen, *Discussions,* p. 80.

64. *Bombay Guardian* (November 7, 1857), p. 360, quoting *Vartman Dipika* (31 October 1857).

65. Vishnubawa Brahmachari, *Srī Vedoktadharmaprakāsha* (Bombay: Sh. 1781, A.D. 1859), p. 3. A second edition (Bombay: K. B. Ranade, 1881) has also been consulted and some citations are to that source.

66. Vishnubawa Brahmachari, *Vedoktadharmaprakāsha* 2d ed., p. 30.

67. Vishnubawa Brahmachari, *Vedoktadharmaprakāsha* 2d ed., pp. 18, 231.

68. Vishnubawa Brahmachari, *Vedoktadharmaprakāsha* 2d ed., p. 237; cf. his *Sahajasthitīcā Nibandha* (Essays on Natural Condition) (Bombay: Indu Prakash Press, Sh. 1790, A.D. 1868).

69. Vishnubawa Brahmachari, *Vedoktadharmaprakāsha,* 2d ed., pp. 266–67.

70. *Bombay Guardian* (November 7, 1857), p. 354.

71. Vishnubawa Brahmachari, *Vedoktadharmaprakāsha,* 2d ed., p. 296.

72. Vishnubawa Brahmachari, *Vedoktadharmaprakāsha,* 2d ed., p. 296.

73. E.g., *Dnyānodaya* (May 15, 1861).

74. Vishnubawa Brahmachari, *Vedoktadharmaprakāsha,* 1st ed., pp. 436–50.

75. Vishnubawa Brahmachari, *Sukhadāyaka Rājyaprakarānī Nibandha* (Bombay: Indu Prakash Sh. 1789, [A.D. 1867]).

76. *An Essay in Marathi on Beneficent Government by Vishnubawa Brahmachari, translated at the desire of the author by Captain A. Phelps* (Bombay: Oriental Press, 1869).

77. S. V. Puntambekar, "Vishnu Bawa Brahmachari (1825–1871): An Utopian Socialist," *Indian Journal of Political Science* 6, iii (1945): pp. 154–61; Padhye and Tikekar, *Ājkālacā Mahārāshtra,* pp. 110–13. Cf. Inamdar, "Political Thought."

78. Vishnubawa Brahmachari, *Beneficent Government,* pp. 4–7, 10–11, 15.

79. Vishnubawa Brahmachari, *Beneficent Government,* p. 16.

80. Vishnubawa Brahmachari, *Beneficent Government,* p. 17.

81. Compare his *Sahajasthitīcā Nibandha* and his *Catuhshlokī Bhagavāta yānca artha* (Bombay: Indu Prakash, 1867).

82. Compare Sa. Ga. Date, *Marāthī Grantha Sūcī: 1800–1937* (Pune, 1943), p. 950 notes a work by Mrs. Wilson, *Greki Lokance Vrittāntkathān* (Bombay, 1838). On one debate in 1857 Vishnubawa asked about Aesop, quoted one of his fables, and asked if he was a Christian, Bowen, *Discussions,* p. 154.

83. *Gokhale Kulavrittānt* (1978), p. 141.

84. Ajrekar, *Vishnubāvā;* Kusumavati Deshpande, *Marāthī Sāhitya* (New Delhi, 1966), p. 117.

85. Mangesha Hari Nerurkar, *Srī Vishnubāvā Brahmacārīkrita Vedokta Dharmaca Vicār vā Khristimatkhandan* (Bombay: Nirnyasagar Press, 1874); *Setubandhānī Tīkā–Prākrta (Srīmadbhagavadgītā)* (Bombay: Ramchandra P. Raut, 1890).

86. M. G. Ranade, "Remarks on the Marathi portion of the *Catalogue of Native Publications in the Bombay Presidency up to 31st December 1864,*" reprinted in Ramabai Ranade, *Miscellaneous Writings of the Late Hon'ble Mr. Justice Ranade* (Bombay: Manoranjan Press, 1915), p. 4.

Chapter Two

1. To facilitate recognition of Tamil words, I have modified their transliteration in this essay to conform to their Sanskrit counterparts where appropriate and to conform to standard English usage. Their purely Tamil transliterated forms will appear in the notes. Aspects of this essay have been included in my examination of Arumuga Navalar's response to Protestant missionaries as compared to that of Vellalas who became Christians: "Tamil Hindu Responses to Protestants: Among Nineteenth Century Literati in Jaffna and Tinnevelly," in Steven Kaplan ed., *Indigenous Responses to Western Christianity.* Forthcoming.

Research for this study has been generously aided by a Fulbright Fellowship for research in Madras (1983–84), by the Committee on Faculty Compensation and Development of Smith College, and by the InterLibrary Loan Staff of the William Allen Neilson Library of Smith College.

2. For the social distinctions between Brahmans, non-Brahmans, and untouchables in Madras Presidency, see Eugene F. Irschick, *Politics and Social Conflict in South India: The Non-Brahman Movement and Tamil Separatism, 1916–1929* (Berkeley: University of California Press, 1969), pp. 5–12.

3. According to E. J. Robinson, in 1857 the inhabitants of the northern and eastern provinces totaled 184,714. *Hindu Pastors: A Memorial* (London: Wesleyan Conference Office, 1867), p. 5.

4. Robinson, *Hindu Pastors,* p. 7.

5. Robinson, *Hindu Pastors,* p. 122.

6. For the idea of the *ūr,* see E. Valentine Daniel, *Fluid Signs: Being a Person the Tamil Way* (Berkeley: University of California Press, 1984), pp. 61–104.

7. These divisions are discussed by Capapati Navalar, in "Varalaru," *Civacamavātavuraimaruppu* by Civajnana Yoki (Citamparam: Cittanta-vittiyanupalana-yantira-calai, 1893), pp. 1–6.

8. For a discussion of these monastic heads, see V. A. Devasenapathi, *Saiva Siddhānta: As Expounded in the Sivajnana-Siddhiyār and its Six Commentaries* (Madras: University of Madras, 1966), pp. 1–15.

9. For example, the first Protestant missionary to India, Bartholomeus Ziegenbalg, learned from Tamil Hindus in the early 18th century that "sin" is an immoral life and the worship of village deities rather than the One God, Shiva; and that the word "heathen" refers to anyone who does not wear the ashes of Shiva, does not recite the five-syllable mantra of Shiva, does not sacrifice and fast, and is without mercy, love, humility, and patience. See H. Grafe, "Hindu Apologetics at the Beginning of the Protestant Mission Era in India," *Indian Church History Review,* 6, No. 1,(June 1972): pp. 59–60, 65–66. See also, Dennis Hudson, "Luther's Voice in India," paper presented at Smith College, October 30, 1984, in "Martin Luther: An Interdisciplinary Symposium Commemorating the 500th Anniversary of the Reformer's Birth."

10. The Jesuit missionary in Madurai, Roberto de Nobili, responded to thirteen abuses in a work he wrote in Tamil about 1640, see Tattuva Potakar [Roberto de Nobili], *Tūsanat Tikkāram,* ed. by C. Iracamanikkam (Tuttukkuti: Tamil Ilakkiyak Kalakam, 1964). The Lutheran missionary in Tranquebar, Bartholomeus Ziegenbalg, recorded various Hindu views of Christianity in the early eighteenth century. See H. Grafe, "Hindu Apologetics," pp. 43–69.

11. John Murdoch provided a description of Tamil printing in 1865 in his *Classified Catalogue of Tamil Printed Books with Introductory Notices* (Vepery, Madras: The Christian Vernacular Education Society, 1865 [reprint ed. by M. Shanmukham and published in Madras by the Tamil Development and Research Council, Government of Tamilnad, 1968]), pp. lvii–lxxx.

12. One example is the manuscript in the British Museum by Jmamapamam Pillai, *Induc-cātiyārin-vetānta-vilakkam,* completed in 1801. The author, a Vellala, was a former Christian in Tranquebar who became a Shaiva and was hung by the British two years later for spying.

13. For a further discussion of this in the overall context of Tamil intellectual responses to the West, see Dennis Hudson, "The Responses of Tamils to Their Study by Westerners 1600–1908," in Bernard Lewis, Edmund Leites, and Margaret Case (eds.), *As Others See Us: Mutual Perceptions, East and West* (New York: International Society for the Comparative Study of Civilizations, 1985), pp. 180–200.

14. Bartholomeus Ziegenbalg, for example, circulated palmleaf writings among Tamil Hindus in 1710 which he then printed on the new Tamil press as a pamphlet in 1713. It consisted of eight chapters "in which is shown how great a horror heathenism is and how those who live in it may be saved and go to heaven." It was reprinted in 1729 and 1745. See Hans-Werner Gensichen, "'Abominable Heathenism', a Rediscovered Tract by Bartholomeus Ziegenbalg," *Indian Church History Review,* 1, no. 1 (1967), pp. 29–40.

15. Listed by Kailasa Pillai, *Ārumukanāvalar Carittiram,* (Madras: 1918 and 1955), p. 53. Robinson describes those belonging to the Wesleyan Mission in *Hindu Pastors,* pp. 7–16.

16. The decision and immediate controversy is reported in *The Second Triennial Report of the American Missionary Seminary, Jaffna, Ceylon* (Nellore, 1830), pp. 23–24, from which the following quotations come. H. R. Hoisington (1801–1858), a serious scholar of Tamil and Shaivism, was head of the seminary from 1836 to 1842 and responsible for having the *Kantapurānam* prescribed for study. See K. Meenakshisundaram, *The Contribution of European Scholars to Tamil,* Madras University Tamil Dept., Series No. 33 (Madras: University of Madras, 1974), pp. 45–46.

17. Between 1836 and 1839, H. R. Hoisington, Principal of the American Mission Seminary in Jaffna, lectured on a "List of popular objections to Christianity" called *kummi,* which probably was Muttukumara Kavirajar's poem, "Jnanakkummi." See the *Fifth Triennial Report of the American Mission Seminary, Jaffna, Ceylon, with an Appendix,* January, 1939 (Jaffna: Press of the American Mission, 1839), p. 12. This "Jnanakkummi" was attacked by a Christian in a poem called *Ajjnānakkummi* which in turn was attacked by Cilampunata Pillai in *Ajjnānakkummi Maruppu.* See Ci. Kanecaiyar in his *Īlanāttut Tamilppulavar Caritam* ([N.P.]: Na. Ponnaiya, 1939), p. 44.

18. The two poems are contained in the collection of Muttukumara Kavirajar's poems in the volume commemorating the centenary of his death, *Muttukkumārakavirācar Pirapantattirattu,* ed. Cunnakam Ku. Muttukkumaracuvamip Pillai (Mayilani/Cunnakam: Pulavarakam, 1952).

19. Arumuga Tambiran of the Dharmapuram Atinam was baptized in Madras as Wesley Abraham in 1836. His "Jnanakkummi" (also listed as *Ajj-*

nānakkummi) was published in Madras in 1837 according to the *Second Supplementary Catalogue of Tamil Books in the British Library* by Albertine Gaur (London: The British Library, 1980), p. 1b. See also Cu. A. Iramacamip Pulavar, *Tamilppulavar Varicai,* vol. 6 (Cennai: Tirunelveli Tennintiya Caivacittanta Nurpatippuk Kalakam, Ltd., 1958), pp. 27–29, where it is listed as *Ajjnānakkummi.*

20. Published in Madras in 1840 and reprinted at the American Mission Press in 1850 and again in 1862. The 1840 publication date is given by Murdoch, *Catalogue,* p. 21.

21. It went by the Sanskrit name Catur Veda Siddhanta Sabha and was also called the Salay Street Society from its location. See George Pettitt, *The Tinnevelly Mission of the Church Missionary Society* (London: Church Missionary Society, 1851), pp. 255–257; and R. Suntharalingam, *Politics and Nationalist Awakening in South India, 1852–1891* (The Association for Asian Studies: Monographs and Papers, No. XXVII) (Tucson: University of Arizona Press, 1974), pp. 42–43.

22. *Vētavikarpa* was composed by Ponnampala Cuvami of Purusavakkam and *Vēta vikarpa tikkāram* by Muttucami Pillai of Pondichery. The latter died in 1840 and the response may actually have been written by the head Tamil teacher at the College of Fort St. George, Tantavaraya Mutaliyar. See Chengalvaraya Pillai, *History of the Tamil Prose Literature* (Madras, 1966 [1904]), pp. 58–59; and Simon Casie Chitty, *The Tamil Plutarch* (Jaffna, 1859), pp. 55–56.

23. *The Utayatārakai—Morning Star,* Vol. 1 (1841), (Jaffna: American Mission Press), p. 1. Henry Martyn edited the English and Seth Payson the Tamil sections.

24. *Morning Star,* vol. 3, (1843), pp. 114–15.

25. *Morning Star,* vol. 2, (1842), p. 287.

26. *Morning Star,* vol. 2, (1842), p. 272.

27. Reported by Atdinarayana Cettiyar Shivaprakashan in *Supplement to the Utayatārakai—Morning Star,* Thursday, October 20, 1842 (vol. 2, No. 20), p. 249, with response from the editor on p. 250. A very different version of the meeting is given by a disenchanted Shaiva, "S. Tannayerperagasan," in vol. 2, pp. 284–87 together with editorial comments.

28. From the English version of the letter by A. Shivaprakashan in *Morning Star* 2, (1842), p. 271b.

29. *Morning Star,* 2, (1842), p. 271a. According to Robinson, *Hindu Pastors,* p. 119, the school was at Vannarpannai and did not survive.

30. Another connection between the school and Arumuga Pillai was the priest Arunacala Gurukkal, known commonly as Vedakutti Aiyar. He was present at the meetings in 1842 and about ten years later Arumuga Pillai's brothers tried to use his influence to talk Arumuga Pillai into getting married. See

Morning Star, vol. 2, (1842), p. 270–71; and Kailasa Pillai, *Ārumukanāvalar Carittiram,* p. 17.

31. *Nayana-sāstra* according to *Nāvalar nūrrāntu malar 1979,* p. 299. The following biographical information on Arumuga Navalar comes from "Navalar valkkaiyil mukkiya campavankal" in *Nāvalar nūrrāntu malar 1979 (Navalar Centenary Souvenir 1979),* ed. by K. Kailasapati (Colombo and Kottavil, 1979), 299–304, and from three biographies: Ve. Kanakarattina, *Ārumukanāvalar carittiram* (Jaffna 1882, reprinted 1968); T. Kailasa Pillai, *Ārumukanāvalar carittiram* (Madras, 1918, with an expanded edition in 1955); and V. Muttucumaraswamy, *Sri La Sri Arumuga Navalar, The Champion Reformer of the Hindus (1822–1879) A Biographical Study,* new rev. ed. (N.p., 1965).

32. *Caivan kumāran nanmatarapētcan.* His letter appeared in its Tamil original with an English translation in the *Supplement to the Utayatārakai—Morning Star,* January 26, 1843 (vol. 3, No. 2), pp. 21–23. The editors' lengthy reply to it is included in vol. 3, Nos. 3–6.

33. His father was P. Kanta Pillai of Nallur and the drama was *Irattinavalli Vilācam.*

34. "*manam unarcci ataintu.*"

35. The quotations follow the English translation which I have amended with reference to the Tamil original for greater accuracy. The translator omitted some sentences and phrases and used "Shivas" instead of "Shaivas".

36. *Supplement to the Utayatārakai—Morning Star,* vol. 3, no.3 (February 1843), p. 1a.

37. Kanakarattina, *Ārumukanāvalar Carittiram,* pp. 8–10.

38. They included Sadashiva Pillai, Swaminatha Aiyar, Nataraja Aiyar, Vishvanatha Aiyar, Arumuga Pillai, Kantaswami Pillai, and Arumuga Cettiyar, according to Kanakarattina, *Ārumukanāvalar Carittiram,* p. 10.

39. One was Mu. Tillainatha Pillai who had studied English with Arumuga Pillai and was now a teacher in Percival's English school; the other was Cu. Cinnappa Pillai. According to Kanakarattina, because they refused baptism, the one lost his teaching job and the other did not receive one. *Ārumukanāvalar Carittiram,* pp. 13–15.

40. The companion was Ambalavana Mutaliyar. See *Nāvalar Malar,* p. 299. Kailasa Pillai reports a story that as a young boy he went to Nagappattinam and expounded a portion of the *Skanda Purāna.* See Kailasa Pillai, *Ārumuganāvalar Carittiram* (1955), pp. 36–37.

41. See Kanakarattina, *Ārumukanāvalar Carittiram,* p. 16. In 1875, for example, he published three pamphlets addressed to the officials of the temple, contained in *Srī La Srī Ārumukanāvalar Perumānin Pirapantattrattu,* ed. T. Kailasa Pillai, 2 vols. (Cennai: Arumuka Navalar Vittiyanupalana Accakam, 1954), vol. 2, pp. 1–97.

42. He resigned when he found that the Shaivas would not let him teach the Bible as English literature. The school then became totally Tamil and many students returned to the mission school. See Robinson, *Hindu Pastors,* pp. 119–21.

43. Robinson, *Hindu Pastors,* p. 123.

44. Robinson lists the topics as Richard Watson recorded them for twenty-nine sermons between February 18 to November 17, 1848, in *Hindu Pastors,* pp. 124–25. Kanakarattina gives examples in *Ārumuka Nāvalar Carittiram,* p. 20, which Muttucumaraswamy repeats in *Srī La Srī,* p. 20.

45. Kanakarattina, *Ārumukanāvalar Carittiram,* p. 18.

46. For examples, see Kanakarattina, *Ārumukanāvalar Carittiram,* pp. 20–24.

47. Kanakarattina, *Ārumukanāvalar Carittiram,* pp. 18–19; Muttucumaraswamy, *Srī La Srī,* p. 19.

48. Sabapathy Kulandran, "The Tentative Version of the Bible or 'The Navalar Version'," *Tamil Culture,* vol. 7 (1958), pp. 229–50, especially p. 239. Kulandran also discussed Arumuga Navalar's work with Percival in Catapati Kulentiran, *Kiristava Tamil Vētākamattin Varalāru* (A History of the Tamil Bible) (Bangalore: The Bible Society of India, 1967), pp. 117–49.

49. Kulandran, "The Tentative Version of the Bible," p. 249. On the British and Foreign Bible Society in India, see D. Rajarigam, *The History of Tamil Christian Literature,* Studies in Indian Christian Theology, no.2 (Madras: The Christian Literature Society, 1958), pp. 27–28.

50. His statement is reprinted by Kailasa Pillai, *Ārumukanāvalar Carittiram,* pp. 19–21.

51. This was probably a form of the "shifting matri-uxorilocal pattern" typical among Tamils on the east coast of Sri Lanka. See Dennis B. McGilvray, "Mukkuvar vanniasmi: Tamil caste and matriclan ideology in Batticaloa, Sri Lanka," *Caste Ideology and Interaction* (Cambridge Papers in Social Anthropology, No. 9), (Cambridge: Cambridge University Press, 1982), pp. 34–97, especially pp. 43–46.

52. Kanakarattina, *Ārumukanāvalar Carittiram,* pp. 25–28.

53. Charles E. Gover described this system in "Pyal Schools in Madras," *The Indian Antiquary,* vol. 2 (February 1873), pp. 52–56. Other literature commonly taught included *Krishmantūtu, Pancatantra, Kampar Rāmāyanam,* and *Katā Cintāmani.* Grammar was learned from *Nannūl* and vocabulary from a *Nikantu,* usually the *Cūtāmani Nikantu.*

54. Gover, "Pyal Schools in Madras," p. 536.

55. Gover, "Pyal Schools in Madras," p. 551.

56. On the *matha* in south India as an educational institution, see S. Gurumurthy, *Education in South India (Ancient and Medieval Periods)* (Madras: New Era Publications, 1979), pp. 13–25. Contemporary *mathas* are described briefly in "Maths in South India," *The Vedanta Kesari,* vol. 44, No. 4 (August 1957), pp. 148–81. For an example of a nineteenth-century householder teacher at a *matha,* see the English versions of U. V. Swaminatha Aiyar's autobiography, *The Story of My Life by Dr. U. V. Swaminathaiyer,* trans. S. K. Guruswamy, ed. A. Rama Iyer (Madras: Mahamahopadhyaya Dr. U. V. Swaminathaiyar Library, 1980), and his biography of his teacher, *A Poet's Poet: Life of Maha Vidwan Srī Meenakshisundaram Pillai: Based on the Biography in Tamil by Mahamahopadhyaya Dr. U. V. Swaminathaiyer* (Madras: Mahamahopadhyaya Dr. U. V. Swaminatha Iyer Library, 1976).

57. Kailasa Pillai, *Ārumukanāvalar Carittiram,* p. 16.

58. The first ten parts contain about eleven thousand words and they constitute the section Navalar appears to have published. It was republished five times before the last two parts were added. See S. Vaiyapuri Pillai, "History of Tamil Lexicography," *Tamil Lexicon,* vol. 1 (Madras: University of Madras, 1982 [1936]), pp. xxv–xliv, especially pp. xxi–xxviii; and *Cūtāmani Nikantu mūlamum uraiyum,* 1–10 tokutikal Yalppanam Nallur *Srī La Srī Ārumukanāvalar Avarkal Paricotittanu;* Ponnampala Pillai, *Avarkal Paricotittanu* (Cennai: Arumukanavalar Vi. Accakam, 1966).

59. Virai Kaviracapantitar, *Cauntariyalakari: Ikatu Caiva Ellappa Nāvalar ceyta uraiyutan* (Nunkampakkam [Madras], 1864).

60. Vannarpannai A. Arumuga Cettiyar. See Kanakarattina, *Ārumukanāvalar Carittiram,* p. 31.

61. Robinson, *Hindu Pastors,* p. 125. "Traitor-sepoys of the press" he called them.

62. Kailasa Pillai, *Ārumukanāvalar Carittiram,* p. 32.

63. Following the date given in the *Nāvalar Malar,* p. 300.

64. At the end of volume one he included Auvaiyar's *Ātticāti* and *Konraivēntan,* and in volume two his own commentaries (*urai*) on them. See Kanakarattina, *Ārumukanāvalar Carittiram,* p. 31.

65. This dating is given in *Pālapātam: Nānkām Puttakam,* Yalppanam Nallur Arumukanavalar Avarkal ceytatu (Cennai: Sri Arumukanavalar Vittyanupalana Accakam, 1969), p. i. The *Pāla Pātam* has been reprinted numerous times and its three volumes are now four: Navalar's third volume has become the fourth and K. C. Ponnambalam Pillai has compiled a new third volume. Today the lessons are considered appropriate up through the sixth and seventh classes.

66. Robinson, *Hindu Pastors,* p. 125.

67. Tirutturaiyur Cantalinkacuvamikal, *Kolaimaruttal (Tirupporūr Citamparacuvāmikal arulicceyta uraiyutan),* 7th ed. published by Vicuvanatapillai (Cennapattanam: Vittyanupalana Yantiracalai, 1924).

68. The *Tiruccenti-nirōttaka-yamaka-v-antāti* by Turaimankalam Civaprakacacuvamikal, 5th ed. published by Catacivapillai, (Cennapattanam: Vittiyanupalana Yantiracalai, 1882).

69. Pavananti, *Nannūlum—Viruttiyuraium* (Nannul with the Virttiyurai by Cankaranamaccivayappulavar as corrected by Civajnanacuvamikal of the Atinam), ed. Arumukanavalar (Cennapattanam: Vittiyanupalana Yantiracalai, 1902). A tenth edition appeared in 1974.

70. Arumukanavalar, *Civālayataricanaviti,* 5th ed.(Cennapattanam: Vittyanupalana Yanttiracalai, 1882).

71. Noted by Kailasa Pillai, *Ārumukanāvalar Carittiram* (1955 ed.), p. 75. I have not located these small printed pieces; they may have become part of his later and larger publications.

72. See Dennis Hudson, "Violent and Fanatical Devotion Among the Nayanars: A Study in the *Periya Purānam* of Cekkilar," *Criminal Gods and Demon Devotees,* ed. by Alf Hiltebeitel. Forthcoming.

73. Arumukanavalar, *Civālayataricanaviti* (1882), p. 40.

74. Arumuka Navalar, *Tiruttontar Periyapurānam...kattiya rūpamākac ceytu* (1852), p. 5.

75. Kanakarattina, *Ārumukanāvalar Carittiram,* p. 34. The *Nūrrāntu Malar,* p. 300, places this publication in 1854. I have not been able to locate this pamphlet; the British Library's *Second Supplementary Catalogue of Tamil Books* (1980), p. 16, lists Kiristumata Kanana Kutari, *Vajratankam* ("Vajra Dankam, The Diamond Axe.") A Tamil pamphlet for the use of Hindus against Christianity. (Madras, 1888), p. 24.

76. Based on that of Naccinarkkiniyar. See Nakkirar, *Tirumurukārruppatai mūlamum...Ārumuka Nāvalar...putturaiyum,* 19th ed. (Cennai: Sri Arumuka Navalar Vi. Accakam, 1967).

77. For a sympathetic discussion of the story, see David Dean Shulman, *Tamil Temple Myths: Sacrifice and Divine Marriage in the South Indian Saiva Tradition* (Princeton: Princeton University Press, 1980), pp. 275–85. For a discussion of the festivals in Sri Lanka that celebrate the story, see Gannanath Obeyesekere, *The Cult of the Goddess Pattini* (Chicago: The University of Chicago Press, 1984), pp. 470–74, and *Medusa's Hair: An Essay on Personal Symbols and Religious Experience* (Chicago: University of Chicago Press, 1981).

78. *Cupirapōtam* (1853), reprinted in *Ārumukanāvalar Pirapantattirattu,* vol. 1, Nallur T. Kailasa Pillai, ed., 3d ed., published by C. Ponnusvami (Cennapattanam: Vittyanupalana Yantiracalai, 1954), pp. 3–16.

79. Kailasa Pillai, *Ārumukanāvalar Carittiram,* p. 55.

80. According to C. Ponnusvami in *Civa. Cankarapantitar Pirapantattirattu,* C. Ponnusvami, comp. 2d ed. (Cennai: Vittiyanupalana Accakam, 1957 [1882]). The pamphlets are *Kiristumata Kantanam, Carpiracānkam,* and *Milēccamata Vikarpam.* See also Kailasa Pillai, *Ārumukanāvalar Carittiram,* p. 55.

81. As he notes in his letter to John Walton of January 18, 1856, reprinted in Kailasa Pillai, *Ārumukanāvalar Carittiram,* p. 102.

82. He adds hopefully: "...but it was one of those victories which are equivalent to defeats, a suicidal advantage prompting to devout research persons who might never otherwise have been led to examine the Scriptures, and conducting inquirers beyond such limits as the apologists would have allowed." Robinson, *Hindu Pastors,* pp. 127–28. The immediate response to the booklet, including letters exchanged between Navalar and the missionary John Walton, are contained in the appendix to Kailasa Pillai, *Ārumukanāvalar Carittiram,* pp. 101–108.

83. Navalar, *Caivatūsana Parikāram* (Cennai: Vittiyanupalana Accakam, 1956). The India Office Library lists the 1868 edition and the British Library lists the 1890 edition.

84. The Hindu Church of the Lord Jesus founded by Arumanayagam, known commonly as Sattampillai among the Christian Nadars in Tinnevelly District. See Hudson, "Responses of Tamils to Their Study," pp., 189–90.

85. He names specifically "Blind Way" (*Kuruttuvali*), "Attributes of the Hindu Triad" (*Mūmūrtti Laksanam*), and "News of Depravity" (*Turācāravirut-tāntam).*

86. Arumuga Navalar, *Caivatūsana Parikāram,* p. 9.

87. Navalar, *Caivatūsana Parikāram,* p. 10.

88. Navalar, *Caivatūsana, Parikāram,* p. 11.

89. D. Carroll, *Cuppiratīpam: Ikatu Caivatūsanaparikāra Nirākaranam* (Jaffna: Ripley and Strong, 1857).

90. Kanakarattina, *Ārumukanāvalar Carittiram,* p. 36, note.

91. Arumuga Navalar was initiated into the worship of his own quartz *linga (spatika lingam)*, the *utaiyavar pūcai,* and Sadashiva Pillai was initiated into the worship of the impermanent *linga, the ksanikalingam pūcai.* Kanakarattina, *Ārumukanāvalar Carittiram,* pp. 38–39; Kailasa Pillai, *Ārumukanāvalar Carittiram,* pp. 81–82.

92. I am working on a long-range study of him tentatively entitled, *For the Love of Shiva: Arumuga Navalar and Hindu Reform in the Nineteenth Century.*

93. Listed in *Malar,* pp. 308–15.

94. Damodharam Pillai in particular continued this work, himself having been a Christian who became a Shaiva because of Navalar. Tiru. Vi. Kaliyanasundaram says that Arumuga Navalar dug the foundations for the recovery of Tamil classics, Damodharam Pillai built its walls, and Swaminatha Aiyar roofed it and made it into a temple. The temple is in Tamil literature the house of Shiva. See Tiru. Vi. Ka. Valkkaik Kurippukkal, *Autobiographical Notes of Tiru. Valkkaik Kurippukkal,* vol. 1 (1944; reprint, Madras: South Indian Saiva Siddhanta Works Publishing Society, 1969), p. 160.

95. Kamil Zvelebil, *The Smile of Murugan: On Tamil Literature of South India* (Leiden: E. J. Brill, 1973), p. 259.

96. Mayuram and Vedaranyam. See Muttucumarswamy, *Srī La Srī,* p. 35.

97. It lasted from 1874 to 1878 in Vannarpannai. See Kailasa Pillai, *Ārumukanāvalar Carittiram,* pp. 52–53; and Muttucumarswamy, *Srī La Srī,* pp. 83, 86, 101.

98. K. M. de Silva, ed., *Sri Lanka: A Survey* (Honolulu: The University Press of Hawaii, 1977), p. 389.

99. Muttucumaraswamy, *Srī La Srī,* pp. 97–99.

100. Navalar's student's student, N. Katirvel Pillai of Jaffna (d. 1907), was influential on Tiru. Vi. Ka. in Madras. In his youth, Maraimal Adigal (formerly Swami Vedachalam) participated in the Shaiva Siddhanta Sabha in Nagapattinam led by a friend of Navalar's, Virappa Cettiyar. See Tiru Pulavar Aracu, *Tiru. Vi. Kaliyānacuntaranār* (Madras: South India Saiva Siddhanta Works Publishing Society, 1982), pp. 21–22; and Tavattiru Alakaratikal, *Maraimalaiyatikalar Varalāru Mātci* (Madras: South India Saiva Siddhanta Works Publishing Society, 1977), pp. 185–91.

101. Pulavar Ira. Ilankumaran, *Kalaka Ātciyar V. C. Varalāru* (Madras: South India Saiva Siddhanta Works Publishing Society, 1981), p. 112.

102. Capapati Kulentiran, *Kiristava Tamil Vētākamattin Varalāru,* pp. 148–49.

103. See Irschick, *Politics and Social Conflict in South India,* pp. 292–94.

104. For Sri Lanka, see Gananath Obeyesekere, *The Cult of the Goddess Pattini,* p. 599, n. 7.

Chapter 3

1. Ganga Prasad Upadhyaya, *The Light of Truth, English Translation of Swami Dayananda's Satyārth Prakāsh* (Allahabad: 1956), p. 684. For the Hindi text, see Shri Paramahansa Vrajat Acharya and Shri Maddayananda Saraswati, *Satyārth Prakāsh* (Ajmer: Vedic Yantralaya, 1947), pp. 458–59. Both the English and Hindi texts are cited for each quote. A second translation by Durga

Prasad, *An English Translation of the Satyārth Prakāsh* (Delhi: 1970), was used to compare unclear passages.

2. Upadhyaya, p. 689–90 and Dayananda, p. 462.

3. Upadhyaya, p. 686 and Dayananda, p. 460.

4. This is the version of God's attributes given in the Hindi text: *Ishvar sarvavyapāk, anant guna karma, svabhāv yukt, sacchidān, svarūp, nitya, shūddh, buddh, sukta svabhāv, anādi, anantādi, lakshanaykti Vedon me kahā hai.* Upadhyaya, p. 687–88 and Dayananda, pp. 461–462.

5. Upadhyaya, pp. 689–90 and Dayananda, p. 462.

6. Upadhyaya, p. 691 and Dayananda, p. 463.

7. Upadhyaya, p. 693 and Dayananda, p. 464.

8. Upadhyaya, p. 721 and Dayananda, pp. 483–84.

9. Upadhyaya, p. 697 and Dayananda, pp. 466–67.

10. Upadhyaya, p. 695–96 and Dayananda, p. 466.

11. Upadhyaya, p. 699 and Dayananda, p. 468.

12. Upadhyaya, p. 702 and Dayananda, p. 470.

13. The Biblical quote, from Leviticus 4: in Upadhyaya, page 716–717 was garbled and so I replaced it with a quote from the translation by Shri Durga Prasad, p. 478. For the Hindi text see Dayananda, p. 480.

14. Upadhyaya, p. 717 and Dayananda, p. 480.

15. Upadhyaya, p. 703 and Dayananda, p. 470.

16. Upadhyaya, p. 712 and Dayananda, pp. 475–76.

17. Upadhyaya, p. 713 and Dayananda, p. 477.

18. Upadhyaya, p. 701 and Dayananda, p. 469.

19. Upadhyaya, pp. 705–6 and Dayananda, pp. 472–73.

20. Upadhyaya, p. 698 and Dayananda, p. 467.

21. Upadhyaya, p. 722 and Dayananda, p. 485.

22. Upadhyaya, pp. 728–29 and Dayananda, p. 489.

23. Upadhyaya, p. 734 and Dayananda, p. 493.

24. Upadhyaya, p. 742 and Dayananda, p. 498.

25. Upadhyaya, p. 734 and Dayananda, p. 493.

26. Upadhyaya, p. 734 and Dayananda, p. 493. Note that I translated *Wah*

Ji īsa as "Bravo Honored Sir!" since this is closer to the Hindi and has the flavor of contempt that was intended.

27. Upadhyaya, p. 725 and Dayananda, p. 487.

28. Upadhyaya, p. 732 and Dayananda, pp. 491–92.

29. Upadhyaya, pp. 727–28, and Dayananda, p.488–89.

30. Upadhyaya, p. 755 and Dayananda, p. 508.

31. Upadhyaya, p. 732 and Dayananda, p. 492.

32. Upadhyaya, p. 733 and Dayananda, p. 492.

33. Upadhyaya, p. 738 and Dayananda, p. 495.

34. Upadhyaya, p. 730 and Dayananda, pp. 490–91.

35. Upadhyaya, p. 731 and Dayananda, p. 491.

36. Upadhyaya, p. 736 and Dayananda, p. 494.

37. Upadhyaya, p. 745 and Dayananda, p. 501.

38. Upadhyaya, p. 758 and Dayananda, p. 510.

39. Upadhyaya. p. 759 and Dayananda, p. 510.

40. Upadhyaya, p. 750 and Dayananda, p. 504.

41. Upadhyaya, p. 756 and Dayananda, p. 508.

Chapter 4

1. C. G. Pfander, "Wage der Wahrheit oder Untersuchung uber das Evangelium und den Koran," MS 1829; published as *Mīzān al-Haqq* (Persian translations: Schusha, 1835; Calcutta, 1839; Agra, 1849; Urdu translations: Mirzapur, 1843; Agra, 1850).

2. *Selections from the Records of Government, N.W.P.*, pt. 31 (Calcutta, 1858), p. 9; S. A. A. Rizvi, ed., *Freedom Struggle in Uttar Pradesh,* Vol. 5 of *Western Districts and Rohilkhand, 1857–59,* pp. 381, 437.

3. Muhammad Salim, *Ek mujāhid me'mār* (Mecca, 1952); Imdad Sabri, *Asar-i-Rahmat* (Delhi, 1967).

4. Rev. T. G. Clark, Agra, May 22, 1854, *Home and Foreign Record of the Free Church of Scotland* (October 1854), p. 66.

5. Wazir al-Din, *Taqrīr-i-dilpazīr* (Khairabad, 1875), p. 3.

6. Dr. John Murray, Civil Surgeon, Agra, Vaccine Report for 1852–53, May 1853, Letters written to the Commissioner of Agra, 1854, Agra (Judicial), Uttar

Pradesh State Archives.

7. C. G. Pfander, Agra, May 1, 1854; T. G. Clark, Agra, May 22, 1854.

8. Rahmat Allah Kairanawi to Pfander, April 13, 1854.

9. Wazir Khan to Pfander, postcript to letter of July 8, 1854.

10. Wazir al-Din, *Taqrīr-i-dilpazīr* (Khairabad, 1875), pp. 1–19. There is no missionary account, and the Muslim account was only published after an interval of twenty-one years.

11. Sayyid 'Abd-Allah Akbarabadi, *Pahlā hissa mubāhasa-i-mazhabī kā* (in Urdu) (Agra, A.H. 1270 [A.D. 1854]); (in Persian) (Agra, A.H. 1271 [A.D. 1854–55]); Wazir al-Din, *Al-bahs al-sharīf fi asbāt al-naskh wal tahrīf,* (in Persian) (Delhi, A.H. 1270 [A.D. 1854]).

12. Sayyid 'Abd-Allah Akbarabadi, *Murāsalat-i-Mazhabī: Dusrā hissa mubāhasa-i-Mazhabī Kāz* (in Urdu) (Agra, A.H. 1271 [A.D. 1854–55]). Pfander published one of the letters in *Ikhtitām dīnī mubāhasa kā* (Agra, 1855), pp. 125–52.

13. Pfander to Wazir Khan, May 29, 1854; Wazir Khan to Pfander, June 1, 1854 Akbarabadi, *Murāsalat,* pp. 10–14.

14. Wazir Khan to Pfander, June 9, 1854, Akbarabadi, *Murāsalat,* p. 31.

15. Pfander to Wazir Khan, August 14, 1854, Akbarabadi, *Murāsalat,* pp. 91, 95; *Ikhtitām,* pp. 126, 129.

16. Muslim scholars distinguish *tahrīf-i-lafzī* (corruption of the *words* of a text) from *tahrīf-i-ma'nawī* (corruption of the *meaning* of a text). See H. A. R. Gibb and J. H. Kramers, ed., *Shorter Encyclopaedia of Islam* (Leiden and London, 1961), pp. 560–61, for a historical review of the context of the charge.

17. Wazir Khan listed the works of Paine and Voltaire among those of *mulhidīn* (atheists) he had consulted. He claimed Spinoza too as a legitimate source, on the grounds (disputed by Pfander) that he had abandoned Judaism for Christianity. His most heavily used pre-nineteenth-century critical source was the "Six Treatises" of the Deist, Thomas Woolston (1690–1733) who had interpreted the Biblical miracles in an allegorical sense.

18. In that period recently published commentaries by "believing" clerics included, *A Commentary upon the Holy Bible* extracted from Henry and Scott, Religious Tract Society, 6 vols. (London, 1834); N. Lardner, *Works,* 10 vols. (London, 1827); G. D. D'Oyly and R. Mant, *Notes, Explanatory and Practical to the Holy Bible* (London, 1848). An American nonconformist work of commentary cited by the Muslims was Andrews Norton's, *The Evidence of the Genuineness of the Gospels,* 3 vols. (Boston, 1837–44).

19. "Willful corruptions, in order to serve the purposes of a party, whether orthodox or heterodox, are another source of various readings," T. H. Horne, *Introduction to the Critical Study and Knowledge of the Holy Scriptures,* 3d ed., vol. 2 (London, 1822), p. 331.

20. Among others, Intizam Allah Shahabi refers to Wazir Khan's visit to Europe, *Īst Indiyā Kampanī aur bāghī 'ulamā* (Delhi, n.d.), p. 28. But the known dates of his admittance to the Bengal Medical College (1843) and his first Indian appointment (1845) render any such visit unlikely. His name appears neither in lists of medical students going to London, nor in teaching hospital records.

21. "One of those our opponents has been brought up in the Calcutta Government College, knows English well, and got there already acquainted with English infidel writers," Pfander to Venn, Agra, June 12, 1854.

22. *Catalogue of English, Oriental and Translated Works in the Library of the Agra College at the close of 1854,* 3d ed. (Agra, 1855), pp. 76–79, 107–9.

23. In his eighth letter to Pfander (July 26, 1854) Wazir Khan gave page references to Horne's citations of other critics' works. In his reply Pfander objected to second-hand references (July 27, 1854). In the tract which he appended to the published correspondence Wazir Khan allowed that he had not actually seen all the books whose authors' views he had earlier cited. Akbarabadi, *Murāsalat,* pp. 83, 120.

24. Akbarabadi, *Murāsalat,* pp. 122–23.

25. D. F. Strauss, *The Life of Jesus, critically examined,* 3 vols. trans. Marian Evans (George Eliot) from *Das Leben Jesu, Kritisch bearbeitet,* 4th ed. (London, 1846).

26. Akbarabadi, *Murāsalat,* p. 121.

27. Akbarabadi, *Murāsalat,* pp. 163–64; Horne, *Introduction to the Critical Study,* vol. 4, pp. 249–54.

28. Wazir al-Din, *Al-bahs al-sharīf,* pp. 31–32.

29. Pfander to Wazir Khan, August 14, 1854, Akbarabadi, *Murāsalat,* p. 94; Pfander, *Ikhtitām,* p. 128.

30. *Al-bahs al-sharīf,* p. 31; Pfander to Wazir Khan, August 14, 1854, Akbarabadi, *Murāsalat,* pp. 96–97; Pfander, *Ikhtitām,* pp. 131–32.

31. Syud Ahmud, *The Mohomedan Commentary on the Holy Bible,* pt. 1 (Ghazipur, 1862), 7th discourse, "What is the opinion entertained by the Mohomedans regarding the corruption of the sacred Scriptures?"

32. Akbarabadi, *Murāsalat,* p. 202.

33. Wazir Khan to Pfander, June 9, 1854, Akbarabadi, *Murāsalat,* pp. 32–34.

34. Akbarabadi, *Murāsalat,* pp. 32–34.

35. Akbarabadi, *Murāsalat,* p. 41.

36. Pfander to Wazir Khan, June 22, 1854; August 14, 1854, Akbarabadi, *Murāsalat,* pp. 50–51, 104, 181–88; Pfander, *Ikhtitām,* p. 142.

37. Wazir Khan to Pfander, June 9, 1854, Akbarabadi, *Murāsalat,* p. 42. In a report to his society Pfander explained that Muslims find Paul's status unacceptable because he was not one of the twelve disciples, thus "his writings are called only common letters much as Divines and Muhammedan doctors or Mujtahids are in the habit of writing." Church Missionary Society Archive, CI 1/0227/52/1.

38. Wazir Khan to Pfander, May 20, 1854, Akbarabadi, *Murāsalat,* pp. 8–9.

39. Wazir Khan to Pfander, June 1, 1854, *Ibid.*, pp. 15–18.

40. Pfander to Wazir Khan, June 2, 1854, *Ibid.*, p. 23.

41. Pfander to Wazir Khan, June 22, 1854; Wazir Khan to Pfander, July 8, 1854, *Ibid.*, pp. 53–55, 71–75.

42. Publication of *Das Leben Jesu, kritisch bearbeitet,* 2 vols. (1835–36) had resulted in the hounding of Strauss from his post at Tubingen, and the withdrawal in 1839 of the offer of a professorship at Zurich. At the time of the Agra controversies Strauss was still in enforced academic retirement, engaged instead in political writing and local government. The bitter arguments over his view of Christ continued to disturb Protestant Europe.

43. The concept of myth was already known in German theology as Strauss's own introduction makes clear. He considered that although there was a historical framework to the life of Jesus as recorded in the gospels, it had been overlain and mythically rewritten in order to fulfill the Old Testament prophecies. He concluded not that Christianity was untrue, but that it should be understood symbolically rather than historically, as the manifestation of the Hegelian Absolute Spirit in man.

44. "Davidical descent of Jesus, according to the genealogical tables of Matthew and Luke," in Pfander, *The Life of Jesus,* trans. Marian Evans, vol. 1, pp. 108–12.

45. Pfander to Wazir Khan, June 22, 1854, Akbarabadi, *Murāsalat,* pp. 53–54.

46. Wazir Khan to Pfander, July 8, 1854, Akbarabadi, *Murāsalat,* pp. 71–75, 193–94.

47. Wazir Khan to Pfander, August 15, 1854 and August 17, 1854; Pfander to Wazir Khan, August 16, 1854, *Murāsalat,* pp. 113–16. Between May and August Wazir Khan had written fifteen letters and Pfander eleven.

48. Wazir Khan to J. Murray, Civil Surgeon, Agra, September 27, 1854, COA–1, Agra (Judicial), no. 20, Uttar Pradesh State Archives.

49. Among others, there were debates in Amritsar (1867), Shahjahanpur

(1875 and 1876), Roorki (1878), Bareilly (1879), and Delhi (1869 and 1892). The Shahjahanpur debates were three-cornered controversies, participated in by Muslims, Arya Samajists and Christian missionaries.

50. Participating in the Keshabpur debates on the Sunni side, besides the Munshi, were men like Maulana Maniruzzaman Islamabadi of Chittagong and Shaikh Muhammad Zamiruddin. The Deobandi, Muhammad Qasim, and Muhammad Abu al-Mansur both used the corruption charge against the Bible at the second Shahjahanpur debate of 1876. Barbara D. Metcalf, *Islamic Revival in British India: Deoband, 1860–1900* (Princeton: 1982), p. 226. E. M. Wherry noted in 1911 that, "this characteristic has marked the Muslim method of controversy ever since," *The Muhammedan Controversy* (Madras, 1911), p. 1. It seems that it was not until the turn of the century that the Arya Samaj polemicists began to draw on western writers who were critical of Christianity. See Ken Jones, "Hindu-Christian polemics in 19th-Century Punjab," paper presented at the Association for Asian Studies, Philadelphia, March 23, 1985.

51. Imad al-Din, *A Muhammedand brought to Christ, being the autobiography of a native clergyman in India* (London, 1869).

52. Imad al-Din, *Hidāyat al-Muslimīn* (Lahore, 1868), pp. 378–91.

53. Safdar 'Ali, *Niyāz Nāmah* (Allahabad, 1867).

54. *Izhar al-Haqq* (Constantinople, A.H. 1284 [A.D. 1867]).

55. Translations include Turkish, Urdu, Gujerati, English, and French: e.g., Rahmat-Ullah Efendi de Delhi, *Idh-Har-ul-Haqq ou Manifestation de la Verite,* ed. P. Carletti, 2 vols (Paris, 1880); *Ijaharul Hakk or Truth Revealed* (Surat, 1915).

56. Recent re-editions include an Urdu translation published in Karachi in 1968 and Arabic editions published in Morocco and Egypt (1978).

Chapter 5

1. See for details, Rafiuddin Ahmed, *The Bengal Muslims 1871–1906: A Quest for Identity* (New Delhi: Oxford University Press, 1981), especially chapters 2 and 3; also Muin ud-Din Ahmed Khan, *History of the Fara'idī Movement in Bengal 1818–1906* (Karachi: Pakistan Historical Society, 1965), introduction and chapters 1 and 2.

2. Maulana Keramat 'Ali along with Maulanas Inayet 'Ali (1794–1858) and Wilayet 'Ali (1791–1835) were the leading personalities in the Tariqah-i-Muhammadiya movement in Bengal at the early stage. The question of India's legal status under alien British rule proved crucial for many *'ulamā* to choose their ways. See *Abstract Proceedings of the Mahomedan Literary Society in Calcutta* (Calcutta: Mahomedan Literary Society, 1871), p. 6 for Maulana Keramat 'Ali's views in this regard.

3. Christian missionary activity was centered in the districts of Jessore, Khulna, Maldah, and the 24-Parganahs, while the Islamic reformists were active in Faridpur, Backergunj, Naokhali, Dhaka, Myemsingh, Tipperah, and Murshidabad in West Bengal.

4. For a fuller picture on the situation, see Ahmed, *The Bengali Muslims,* pp. 48–49.

5. See Annemarie Schimmel, *Islam in the Indian Subcontinent* (Leiden-Cologne: E. J. Brill, 1980), p. 206.

6. Schimmel, *Islam,* p. 205.

7. Ahmed, *The Bengal Muslims,* pp. 95–97.

8. Ahmed, *The Bengal Muslims,* pp.95–97; also The *Sudhākar,* December 5, 1890, in *Bengal Native Newspaper Reports* (hereinafter *BNNR*), 1890, p. 1137.

9. *The Mihīr o Sudhākar,* June 30, 1899 in *BNNR* 1899, p. 786.

10. *The Moslem World* 4 (1914): p. 17.

11. See William H. Hart, *Everyday Life in Bengal and other Indian Sketches* (London: Charles H. Kelly, 1906), p. 125; *The Moslem World* 21, no. 14 (October 1931): p. 374; also Muhammad Mohar 'Ali, *The Bengal Reaction to Christian Missionary Activities 1833–1857* (Chittagong: Mehrub Publications, 1965), pp. 203–5.

12. See *Census of India,* 1891, vol. 3, p. 152; 1901, vol. 6: 1, p. 164.

13. *Census of India,* 1891, table 6, pp. 36–38.

14. *Ibid.*, p. 147. For a better appreciation of the situation, see. T. W. Arnold, *The Preaching of Islam,* 2d edition (London: Constable & Co., 1913), pp. 282–88.

15. Shaikh Muhammad Zamiruddin, *Meher Charīt* (Calcutta, 1909), p. 47.

16. For an interesting discussion on the question, see Peter McNee, *Crucial Issues in Bangladesh: Making Missions more Effective in the Mosaic of Peoples* (South Pasadena: William Carey Library, 1976), p. 137; also Zamiruddin, *Meher Charīt,* p. 47.

17. The Bengal district gazetteers of the period contain some details about the enormity of these programs. See, for example, J. H. E. Garrett, *Nadia* (Calcutta: Bengal Secretariat Book Depot, 1910), pp. 143–47; L. S. S. O'Malley, *24-Parganas* (Calcutta: The Bengal Secretariat Book Depot, 1914), pp. 80–81.

18. Muhammad Meheru'llah, *Kshrīstīya Dharmer Asāratā* (Calcutta: Reazul Islam Press, 3d edition, 1315 BS [A.D. 1909]), pp. 1–2.

19. *The Moslem World* 2, no. 14 (October 1931): p. 374; see also *The Calcutta Christian Observer,* 13 (October 1844): pp. 606–7, which has a very interesting paper on the "difficulties of preaching the Gospel to Muhammadans."

20. *The Calcutta Christian Observer,* 1844, p. 607.

21. Reverend G. H. Rouse, *Tracts for Muhammadans* (Madras, Allahabad, and Calcutta: The Christian Literature Book Society of India, 1913) (first published in Musalmani Bengali in the 1870s), pp. 64–65; also The Calcutta Christian Tract and Book Society, *Allahtālār Nabi Haibēr Dalīl* (Bhowanipur: The Saptahik Sambad Press, 1871), p. 26.

22. Rev. G. H. Rouse, *Tracts for Muhammadans,* p. 67; also The Calcutta Christian Tract and Book Society, *Hazrat Isā Masihēr Ilāhiyāt O Insaneyāter Dalil* (Bhowanipur: The Saptahik Sambad Press, 1876), p. 109.

23. Rouse, *Tracts for Muhammadans,* p. 75.

24. *Allahtālār Nabi,* p. 26; also The Calcutta Christian Tract and Book Society, *Muhammadī Dharmer Vīsayē Kathabārtā* (Bhowanipur: The Saptahik Sambad Press, 1870), p. 2.

25. See Ahmed, *The Bengal Muslims,* pp. 84–95.

26. *The Moslem World* 4 (1914): p. 18.

27. Mohar 'Ali, *The Bengali Reaction to Christian Missionary Activities,* pp. 204–5.

28. Mohar 'Ali, *The Bengali Reaction to Christian Missionary Activities,* p. 203.

29. *Hazrat Isā Masiher Ilāhiyāt O Insaneyāter Dalil* (1876), pp. 1–26.

30. Throughout the later half of the nineteenth century, sectarian controversies caused great tension in the Bengali Muslim society prompting James Wise to warn about a real possibility of it "being split into rival creeds." See James Wise, "The Muhammadans of Eastern Bengal," *Journal of the Asiatic Society of Bengal* 63 (1894): p. 64. The Muslim-Christian debate added a new dimension to the situation.

31. Muhammad Asiruddin Pradhan, *Meheru'llāhr Jivanī* (Jalpaiguri: Islam Mission Society, 1914), p. 9 and Zamiruddin, *Meher Charīt,* pp. 6–7.

32. Pradhan, *Meheru'llahr Jivanī,* p. 9.

33. Describing this attitude of the *'ulamā,* the Reverend Mr. Tackle wrote in 1914: "He is so bigoted that he tries to dispense with Bengali, his mother tongue, and many a man we have met who, though born and bred in a Bengali village, has protested his ignorance of the language." Reverend John Tackle, "Islam in Bengal," *The Moslem World* 4 (1914): p. 14; see also Asim Roy, "The Social Factors in the Making of Bengali Islam," *South Asia,* 3 (1973): pp. 23–26.

34. See Zamiruddin, *Meher Charīt,* pp. 7–8.

35. Munshi Meheru'llah never discused these theological questions in any of his writings and seemed rather unconcerned about their implications for the Muslims of the subcontinent.

36. Meheru'llah, *Kshrīstīya Dharmer Asāratā,* p. 1.

37. *Hazrat Isā Masiher Ilāhiyāt O Insaneyāter Dalil* (1876), p. 1.

38. Rev. W. Goldsack, *Islamē Kor'an* (Calcutta: The Christian Literary Society, 1931), pp. 2–5.

39. Meheru'llah, *Kshrīstīya Dharmer Asāratā,* p. 14.

40. Meheru'llah, *Kshrīstīya Dharmer Asāratā,* p. 15.

41. *The Islam Prachārak,* 2 *Baisākh* and 27 *Jaīstha* 1299 BS (A.D. 1891); also Muhammad 'Abu Talib, *Mūnshī Muhammad Meheru'llāh: Dēsh, Kāl, Samāj* (Dhaka: The Islamic Foundation, 1893), pp. 44–45.

42. *The Sudhākar,* 2 *Baisākh* and 17 *Āsār,* 1300 BS (A.D. 1892).

43. Meheru'llah, *Kshrīstīya Dharmer Asāratā,* p. 13.

44. Zamiruddin, *Meher Charīt,* p. 50.

45. See Muhammad 'Abu Talib, *Mūnshī Muhammad Meheru'llāh,* pp. 183–203.

46. *The Sudhākar,* 19, 26, *Chaītra* 1299 BS (A.D. 1892), and 2 *Baisākh* and 27 *Jaīstha,* 1300 BS (A.D. 1892); also Zamiruddin, *Meher Charīt,* p. 36.

47. See Ahmed, *The Bengal Muslims,* pp. 75–82; also Muinud-Din Ahmed Khan, *The Farā'idī Movement in Bengal,* chapters 3 and 4 and following.

48. *The Islam Prachārak,* vol. 1, no. 1, *Bhādra* 1298 BS (A.D. 1891); also Zamiruddin, *Meher Charīt,* p. 11.

49. Muhammad Meheru'llah, *Jawābunnāsarā* (1897; reprint, Dhaka Muslim Anushilan Sangstha, 1976).

50. Zamiruddin, *Meher Charīt,* p. 56.

51. Cited in the *Report of the Census of India 1901,* vol. 6: 1, p. 175.

52. See Muhammad 'Abu Talib, *Mūnshī Muhammad Meheru'llāh,* chapter 4. 'Abu Talib has collected a number of interesting examples of the nature of questions raised in these *bahās* meetings. These were quite different from the serious theological issues that were debated in sectarian *bahās.* A similar pattern emerges from Barbara Metcalf's discussion of *bahās* in northern India in the later nineteenth century, in Barbara D. Metcalf, *Islamic Revival in British India: Deoband, 1860–1900* (Princeton: Princeton University Press, 1982), pp. 215–33.

53. Zamiruddin, *Meher Charīt,* p. 63.

54. *Akhlāq-ī-Ahmadīyā* (Noakhali: 1899), pp. 38–40.

55. Hart, *Everyday Life in Bengal,* pp. 124–25; also Zamiruddin, *Meher Charīt,* p. 7.

56. Ill treatment of Muslim widows was most severe in Nadia, Hugli, Mednipur, Bankura, Birnbhum, Burdwan, and Murshidabad disticts.

57. Muhammad Meheru'llah, *Vidhabā Ganjanā O Vishād Bhandār,* 6th ed. (Calcutta: Reazul Islam Press, 1907), p. iii. This was also the theme of many of his *waz mahfils.* Zamiruddin mentions that in one such *mahfil,* the *sharīf* (upper class) Muslims rebuked Meheru'llah for his advocacy of widow remarriage and suggested that the Syeds and Sheikhs (supposedly two higher social classes among the Bengali Muslims) could not go against their long established tradition in this regard. In reply, the Munshi pointed out that even the Prophet of Islam married a widow as his first wife and added, in verse,

> Who amongst us is more respectable, and learned than the Prophet. Tell me, my aristocrat brothers, then how do you consider yourselves to be members of the *sharīf* class (while denying what the Prophet of Islam himself did!). (Zamiruddin, *Meher Charīt,* pp. 74–78.)

58. Zamiruddin, *Meher Charīt,* p. 73.

Chapter 6

1. Radha Krishna Das, "Hindi-Urdu," in *Saraswati* 3 (1902), p. 359.

2. The term *Urdu script* refers to a modified version of the Persian script, which in turn is a modified version of the Arabic script. Thus the Urdu script includes characters for sounds (e.g., the retroflex consonants), which do not occur in Persian. During our period the terms *Persian script* and *Urdu script* were largely interchangeable.

3. The term *Nagari* often referred to not only the Nagari script, also used to write Sanskrit, but also the Hindi language. The connection between script and language, though arbitrary from a linguistic point of view, appeared inseparable to many partisans of Hindi. Interview with Shri Ray Krishna Das, Banares, May 12, 1972.

4. Amrit Rai, *A House Divided: The Origin and Development of Hindi/Hindavi* (Delhi: Oxford University Press, 1984), pp. 226–64.

5. Christopher R. King, "Forging a New Linguistic Identity: The Hindi Movement in Banaras 1868–1914," in Sandria B. Freitag, ed., *Culture and Power in Banaras: Community, Performance and Environment 1800–1980* (Berkeley and Los Angeles: University of California Press, 1989), pp. 109–202.

6. Shiva Prasad, *Memorandum: Court Characters, in the Upper Provinces of India* (Benares: n.p., 1868).

7. Prasad, *Memorandum,* p. 5–6.

8. Prasad, *Memorandum,* p. 5–6.

9. Government of India, *Report of the Indian Education Commission* (Calcutta: 1883), pp. 630–31, 635, 639, appendix C.

10. Christopher R. King, "The Nagari Pracharini Sabha (Society for the Promotion of the Nagari Script and Language) of Benares 1893–1914: A Study in the Social and Political History of the Hindi Language" (Ph.D. diss., University of Wisconsin, 1974), pp. 114–22, 135–36, 377–83, 416–21.

11. See the Bibliographic Essay for an explanation of these dates.

12. For a discussion of *swāng,* see Kathryn Hansen, "The Birth of Hindi Drama in Banaras (1868–1885)," in Sandria B. Freitag, ed., *Culture and Power in Banaras,* pp. 62–92.

13. See note 3.

14. This organization, founded some time before 1882, espoused the cause of Nagari in the western North-Western Provinces and Oudh. By 1889, the Sabha had founded a school, the Devanagari Pathshala, in which children received a primary education in Hindi. The Sabha also held frequent public meetings to celebrate auspicious occasions or to award prizes and certificates to graduates of the Pathshala. During some of these meetings, the Sabha presented memorials and addresses in favor of Hindi and the Nagari script and expressed loyalty to the British government. See, Government of India, *Selections from the Vernacular Newspapers Published in the Panjab, North-Western Provinces and Oudh* (Allahabad: 1898–99), *Devanagari Gazette* (Meerut), June 25, 1898, p. 641; *Devanagari Gazette,* June 1889, pp. 403–4.

15. Ram Chandra Shukla, *Hindī Sāhitya kā Itihās* (The History of Hindi Literature) (Banaras: Nagari Pracharini Sabha, 1968), pp. 462–63.

16. I have used *mime* to translate *swāng.*

17. The word *play* has been used to translate *nātak.*

18. This refers to the Hunter Education Commission of 1882. See pages 3–4.

19. The terms *dohā, Chauvolā, athvolā, rāganī,* and *bhairavī* refer to various metrical forms in Hindi verse which I have attempted to capture as far as possible in rhyme and number of lines, if not in meter.

20. The Hindi words are: *parabrahma paramātmā.*

21. In translating the verse sections of this play, I have in most cases kept the rhyme scheme of the original to give its flavor. In a number of cases this has forced me to add words or phrases which are not in the original. Nevertheless, I have added nothing that significantly distorts the meaning of the original verse.

22. In Hindu mythology, Chitragupta is the scribe of the court of Yama, lord of the underworld, who continuously records all the good and evil deeds of all mankind. He is also the patron deity of the Kayasths, a caste cluster

renowned for its writing and literary skills, many of whose members earned their living through government service in our period.

23. The Hindi for "true lady" is *satyavatī*. Satyavati was the wife of the sage Richik, and the mother of the sage Vedavyas who put the Vedas in order. In this context, the word probably means an exceptionally righteous and truthful woman.

24. Kashi is one of the names of Banaras. More strictly speaking, the term refers to one of the several roughly concentric sacred zones of Banaras. See Diana Eck, *Banaras: City of Light* (New York: Alfred Knopf, 1982), pp. 350–53.

25. Again, the word for 'lady true' is *satyavatī*.

26. The Hindi word here is *Kaliyug*, the last and worst of the fourfold Hindu cycle of eras.

27. The Hindi word here is *Satyug*, the first and best of the fourfold cycle of eras.

28. Although the word Nagari does not actually occur in the text, the context makes it clear that Begam Urdu's lawyer must be speaking about the difficulty of reading names and places in the Nagari script. Urdu supporters did not hesitate to criticize the Nagari script of being illegible, just as Hindi supporters frequently levelled the same charge against the Urdu script.

29. Government of India, *Selections from the Vernacular Newspapers Published in the Panjab, North-Western Provinces and Oudh, Prayag Samachar* (Allahabad), June 24, 1885, p. 434; *Bharatendu* (Brindaban), October, 1885, p.783; *Dinkar Prakash* (Lucknow), p. 784; *Hindustani* (Lucknow), November 18, 1885, p. 831, and *Najmu-i-Akbar* (Etawah), November 24, 1885, p. 839.

30. In the translation of Prasad's verses, as in those of Datta's, I have kept the rhyme and tried to imitate the meter of the original. See note 21.

31. Sohan Prasad, *Hindī aur Urdū Kī Larāī* (A Fight between Hindi and Urdu) (Gorakhpur [?]: n.p., 1886), verse 45.

32. Prasad, *Hindī aur Urdū*, verse 86.

33. Prakash Tandon, *Punjabi Century: 1857–1947* (Berkeley and Los Angeles: University of California Press, 1968), p. 69.

34. Tandon, *Punjabi Century*, p. 70.

35. During the period covered by this essay, the term *Nagari* usually included both language and script. From here on, I will use *Hindi/Nagari* as a convenient term to refer to the chief character of both plays.

36. Sohan Prasad, *Hindī aur Urdū Kī Larāī*, verse 111.

37. Prasad, *Hindī aur Urdū*, verse 22.

38. Prasad, *Hindī aur Urdū,* verse 251.

39. Prasad, *Hindī aur Urdū,* verse 120.

40. Prasad, *Hindī aur Urdū,* verse 122.

41. Government of India, *Report of the Indian Education Commission,* pp.3–4.

42. Government of India, *Report of the Indian Education Commission,* p. 201.

43. During our period the term *Nagari* often included both the Nagari script and the Hindi language, as did the term *Hindi.* Interview with Shri Ray Krishna Das, Banaras, May 12, 1972.

44. Prasad, *Hindī aur Urdū,* verse 137.

45. See note 34.

46. The author consistently uses the term *turk* to refer to Muslims.

47. Prasad, *Hindī aur Urdū,* verse 182.

48. Prasad, *Hindī aur Urdū,* verse 242.

49. Prasad, *Hindī aur Urdū,* verse 115.

50. Prasad, *Hindī aur Urdū,* verse 121.

51. The Roman script was explicitly rejected by both sides of the Hindi-Urdu controversy.

52. Prasad, *Hindī aur Urdū,* verses 332–334.

53. Prasad, *Hindī aur Urdū,* verses 398–399.

54. Prasad, *Hindī aur Urdū,* verse 280.

55. Prasad, *Hindī aur Urdū,* verse 289.

56. Prasad, *Hindī aur Urdū,* verses 162–178.

57. Prasad, *Hindī aur Urdū,* verse 180.

58. We learn from one of the stanzas spoken by English, that Hindi is a widow (*vidhvā*). Prasad may have intended to connect Hindi with the abolition of child marriage in this way.

59. Prasad, *Hindī aur Urdū,* verse 381.

60. Prasad, *Hindī aur Urdū,* verses 359–61.

61. Prasad, *Hindī aur Urdū,* verse 40.

62. Prasad, *Hindī aur Urdū,* verse 55.

63. Government of India, *Selections from the Vernacular Newspapers Published*

in the Panjab, North-Western Provinces and Oudh, 1889, p. 284.

64. Babu Ratnachand, *Hindī Urdū kā Nātak* (A Play about Hindi and Urdu) (Allahabad: Hindu Press, 1890), pp. 1–3.

65. Christopher R. King, "Hindu Nationalism in the 19th Century U. P. and the Dramas of Bharatendu Harishchandra," in Dhirendra Vajpeyi, ed., *Boeings and Bullock Carts* (Leiden: E. J. Brill, 1989).

66. King, "The Nagari Pracharini Sabha," pp. 290–92.

67. For example, the Nagari Pracharini Sabha (Society for the Promotion of Nagari) of Banaras, the leading Hindi organization of the late nineteenth and early twentieth centuries, received close to Rs. 40,000 from various Hindu princes during its first thirty years, approximately 12 percent of its total income for the period.

68. King, "The Nagari Pracharini Society," pp. 457–59.

69. Marshall Singer, *Intercultural Communication: A Perceptual Approach* (Englewood Cliffs, N. J.: Prentice-Hall, 1987), p. 9; emphasis mine.

Chapter 7

1. The other two are Rayalaseema, a slightly less populated dry area northwest of Madras (most of the present Nellore District), and Telangana, separately administered as part of the Nizam's Dominions until 1948 and of Hyderabad State until 1956.

2. Cilukurvi Virabhadra Rau, *Rajamendra Pura Caritra* (Rajahmundry: 1915), pp. 33–34; F. R. Hemingway, *Godavari* (Madras: Madras District Gazetteer, 1915), 1, p. 247; Digavalli Venkata Siva Rau, ed., *Kasi Yātra Caritra,* 3d ed. (Bezwada, 1941), pp. 344–45.

3. K. A. Nilakanta Sastry, *A History of South India,* 3d ed. (Madras: Oxford University Press, 1966), p. 406.

4. Henry Morris, *A Descriptive and Historical Account of the Godavary District in the Presidency of Madras* (London: Madras District Manual, 1878), pp. 244, 303–4.

5. Morris, *Godavary District,* p. 22.

6. For comparisons between Rajahmundry and Madras, see John G. Leonard, "Urban Government Under the Raj," *Modern Asian Studies* 7, no. 2 (April 1973), pp. 227–51 and Susan J. Lewandowski, "Urban Growth and Municipal Development in the Colonial City of Madras, 1860–1900," *Journal of Asian Studies* 34, no. 2 (February 1975), pp. 341–60.

7. Government of India, *Census of India,* 1891–92 (Madras, 1893), vol. 13, p. 181.

8. This was a precipitating cause of the Andhra movement—only in the Circars region did Telugus outnumber Tamils in government positions. See John G. Leonard, "Politics and Social Change in South India: A Study of the Andhra Movement," *Journal of Commonwealth Political Studies* 5, no. 1 (March 1967), pp. 60–77.

9. Government of India, Indian Education Commission, *Report of the Madras Provincial Committee* (Calcutta, 1884), p. 38; Government of Madras, *Report on Public Instruction in the Madras Presidency for 1880–1881* (Madras, 1881), pp. 65–67.

10. Government of Madras, *Madras Financial Proceedings,* no. 58 (10 January 1884), India Office Library.

11. Morris, *Godavary District,* p. 24; Martin Luther Dolbeer, Jr., *A History of Lutheranism in the Andhra Desh, 1842–1920* (New York: Board of the Foreign Missions of the United Lutheran Church in America, 1959), p. 14; Martin Luther Dolbeer, Sr., *The Andhra Evangelical Lutheran Church: A Brief History* (Rajahmundry: Department of Religious Education, Andhra Evangelical Church, 1951), pp. 27–30.

12. Government of Madras, *Report on Public Instruction in the Madras Presidency for 1876–77* (Madras, 1877), p. 135.

13. Government of Madras, *Report on Public Instruction for 1876–77,* p. 136. This ratio is best understood with the help of data drawn from later sources: it seems to approximate the proportion of Tamils to Telugus in Madras City, which was 2.7 to 1; see Government of India, *Census of India,* 1891–2 (Madras, 1893), vol. 14, pp. 137, 139. The ratio of Tamils to Telugus in Madras Presidency was 1.1 to 1; see Government of India, *Census of India,* 1911, vol. 12, pt. 2 (Madras, 1912), p. 140 for details.

14. J. Gurunatham, *Viresalingam, the Founder of Telugu Public Life* (Rajahmundry: S. Gunnesworao Bros., 1911), pp. 165–66.

15. Tanguturi Prakasam, *Nā Jīvita Yātra* (Rajahmundry: Kalahastri Tamma Rao and Sons, 1957), p. 48; Kandukuri Viresalingam, *Svīya Caritramu* (Rajahmundry: Hitakarini Samaj, 1954), vol. 1, pp. 1–2, 8–9, 17; A. Ramapati Rao, "Jivitamunandali Konni Mukhya Ghattamulu," in *Yuga Purusudu Vīrēsalingam* (Hyderabad, n.d.), p. 223. Viresalingam's father and uncle were revenue officials for the Government of Madras.

16. The following information about family life comes from Viresalingam's recollections in *Caritramu,* vol. 1, p. 18 *passim,* pp. 30–34, and about his wife, pp. 10–11 (but he gives no details of their early years together).

17. Kandukuri Viresalingam, "Stri Vidya," *Vivēka Vardhani* (hereafter abbreviated *VV*), February 1875 in *Kandukūri Vīrēsalingam Kavikrta Granthamulu* (hereafter abbreviated *KVKG*), 8 (Rajahmundry, 1951–52), pp. 330–32.

18. Smarta Brahmans are followers of Sankara (c. 788–820), believers in

monistic or Advaita Vedanta who are supposed to conform to Smrti traditions. Viresalingam expressed devotion by repeating the Gayatri from one hundred to one thousand times each day and visiting the river Godavari and the various Saivite and Vaishnavite temples for prayer. His only recollections of specific practices were of fasting on Shivaratri (fast day of the God Shiva) and of putting the three horizontal stripes of Shiva on his chest, upper arms, and face while he was praying: Viresalingam, *Caritramu,* vol. 1, pp. 19, 56.

19. Viresalingam, *Caritramu,* vol. 1, pp. 15, 17. For *pyal* schools, see *The Foreign Missionary* (Philadelphia), 10, no. 2 (February 1889), p. 11, and "South Indian Pyal Schools," *Christian Mission Intelligencer* 10, n.s. (September 1874): pp. 287–88.

20. Viresalingam, *Caritramu,* vol. 2, p. 138.

21. A. Ramapati Rau, "Pantulu Gari Grantha Racana Mudranamula Vivaramulu (A Bibliography of Viresalingam's Writings), in *Yuga Purusudu Vīrē-salingam* p. 206; Viresalingam, *Caritramu,* vol. 2, p. 146.

22. Viresalingam first stated that he passed the Matriculation examination in 1871 but later gave 1870 as the date: Viresalingam, *Caritramu,* vol. 1, p. 66 and vol. 2, p. 146. Although his claim was accepted by his biographers (*The Hindu,* January 19, 1893; Gurunatham, *Viresalingam,* pp. 26–27; V. R. Narla, *Veeresalingam* [New Delhi: Sahitya Akcademi, 1968], p. 18), examination of several contemporary sources does not show his name in the lists of students who passed the Matriculation; see Government of Madras, *Godavary District Gazette,* 1869–1871; Government of Madras, *Fort St. George Gazette,* 1869–1871; *Madras Times,* 1870.

23. Viresalingam, *Caritramu,* vol. 1, p. 60. At this time Keshav Chandra Sen had broken with the older Brahmo Samaj members led by Devendranath Tagore and had organized his own association; in contrast to Tagore's stress on the gradual changing of Hinduism, Sen emphasized the necessity of more drastic uprooting of old customs. S. Natarajan, *A Century of Social Reform in India* (Bombay: Asia Publishing House, 1959), pp. 48–49; The Brahmo Samaj, "Jesus Christ: Europe and Asia" (a lecture given on May 5, 1877), *Keshub Chunder Sen's Lectures in India,* 3d ed. (Calcutta, 1899), pp. 30–31.

24. Kandukuri Viresalingam, "Satyamu," *VV,* November 1874, in *KVKG,* vol. 8, pp. 313–20.

25. He began in 1871 as an assistant teacher in the Rajahmundry Provincial School, then passed a government examination qualifying him to practice in the lower courts. In 1872 he accepted a job as headmaster of a village school. That same year he passed a translator's examination in English and Telugu, but he continued to teach and in 1874 became headmaster of a school in Dowleshwaram, a large village near his Rajahmundry home. He lived in the village but walked to town frequently to participate in the activities of the Provincial School Club. In 1875 he passed an English precis writing examina-

tion that qualified him for a sub-magistrate's position. Viresalingam, *Caritramu,* vol. 1, pp. 66–77.

26. He first had his journal published in Madras and then persuaded six men to finance the purchase of a press which was set up in his Rajahmundry home. After a quarrel with the Dowleshwaram school management, he left there in 1875 and began a printing business in Rajahmundry. A rupture with his partners followed and he bought them out, using funds from his books. Viresalingam, *Caritramu,* vol. 1, pp. 88, 92–95, 99.

27. Viresalingam, *Caritramu,* vol. 1, pp. 88, 94.

28. Viresalingam, *Caritramu,* vol. 1, p. 99.

29. Viresalingam, *Caritramu,* vol. 1, pp. 77, 92. Viresalingam refused a government job when one was offered to him: Viresalingam, *Caritramu,* vol. 1, p. 137. He attacked government service as the "meanest" of jobs: Kandukuri Viresalingam, "Aikamatyamu," *VV,* July 1875 in *KVKG* vol. 8, p. 366.

30. Viresalingam, *Caritramu,* vol. 1, p. 59.

31. For details of Viresalingam's life and career, especially his later career, which cannot be covered here in outline, see John G. Leonard, "Kandukuri Viresalingam, 1848–1919: A Biography of an Indian Social Reformer" (Ph.D. diss., University of Wisconsin, 1970).

32. Members of the educated elite in the 1870s had difficulty following some of these essays: Nidudavolu Venkata Rau, *Āndhra Vacana Vāngmayamu* (Madras, 1954), p. 147; G. V. Sitapati, "Telugu," in Nagendra, ed., *Indian Literature* (Agra: Lakshmi Narain Agarwal, 1959), pp. 53–55, 63–65; Rayasam Venkata Sivudu, *Srī Vīrēsalinga Samsmrti* (Guntur: R. V. Sirudu, 1931); Konda Venkatappayya, *Svīya Caritra,* vol. 1 (Vijayawada: Andhra Rastra Hindi Pracara Sangham, 1952–55), I, p. 60. Classical Telugu, or the poetic dialect, differed from spoken Telugu and had a highly Sanskritized vocabulary and syntax. Poetry was the only approved form of literary creation until the last part of the nineteenth century, with grammar and rhetoric recognized as subsections of poetry. Prose was used for business or government purposes in the spoken dialect and was considered "village" or crude Telugu. Not only did poetry have a particular structure and dialect, it was also confined to particular subject matter, much of it erotic in nature. This posed a problem to scholars looking for texts for classroom use in the new educational systems. The initial formulation of a solution to this problem for educators in Telugu had come from one of Viresalingam's scholarly predecessors, Cinnaya Suri (1809–62). This non-Brahman became head of the Department of Telugu at Madras Presidency College and standardized many of the rules for classical Telugu as applied to prose.

33. A. Ramapati Rau, "Viresalingamu Pantulu Savimarsa Parisilanamu," (Ph.D. diss., Osmania University, 1964), pp. 37–38; A. Ramapati Rau, "Mukhya Ghattamulu," in *Yuga Purusudu,* p. 223.

34. Following the visit of the famous Bengali Brahmo Samaj leader, Keshav Chandra Sen, a Brahman in Madras started a Veda Samaj in 1864; many members were non-Brahmans, however. The founder was Rajagopalacharlu; his friend, Subbarayalu Chetty, a non-Brahman, seems to have been the principal leader. The Veda Samaj limited its activities to preaching, although it started a Tamil journal, *Tattvabodhini,* to propagate the view of the association's leaders. Sridharulu Naidu, a non-Brahman in charge of the association from 1867 until 1874, changed the name to the Southern India Brahmo Samaj and framed regulations more in keeping with Brahmo traditions in Calcutta: Sivanatha Sastri, *History of the Brahmo Samaj,* vol. 2 (Calcutta: R. Chatterjee, 1912), pp. 456–65. After Naidu's death in 1874 the association was dormant until 1878 when a Telugu Brahman, Mannava Buccayya, teacher at a girls' school in Madras, revived it and associated it with the Sadharan Brahmo Samaj in Calcutta. Viresalingam, *Caritramu,* vol. 1, pp. 93–94. For its anti-Brahman character, see Sivudu, *Samsmrti,* p. 38; *The Madras Mail,* November 24, 1881, p. 3.

35. According to R. Srinivasan, the Brahmo movement "has been wholly forgotten by the Tamils." He was unable to find books or pamphlets on it in Madras libraries, Brahmo characters in Tamil novels, or more than one Tamil Brahman in the Madras chapter of the Southern Indian Brahmo Samaj. In contrast, he noted the prominence of Telugus in it and the involvement of Telugu *zamīndārs* in funding it and of Telugu school teachers in popularizing Brahmo and reformist ideals in Andhra. Citing a 1912 source, he listed six samajs in the Tamil region and twenty in the Telugu-speaking region. (The Madras Presidency had 17,038,000 Tamil speakers and 15,782,000 Telugu speakers in 1911 [*Census of India,* 1911, vol. 12, pt. 2 (Madras, 1912), p. 140].) Finally, he remarked on the appearance of missionaries in Tamil novels in the proselytizing roles given to Brahmos in Bengali literature (and, we add, Telugu literature) of that period: R. Srinivasan, "The Brahmo Samaj in Tamilnadu," *Journal of the University of Bombay,* arts nos., 44–45 (1975–76), pp. 80–81, 213–25.

36. Viresalingam, *Caritramu,* vol. 1, pp. 138–139; Sastri, *Brahmo Samaj,* Vol. 2, pp. 494–95. Despite its name, this association was not derived from the Prarthana Samaj movement in western India.

37. One's occupation was unknown. Viresalingam, *Caritramu,* vol. 1, pp. 135, 159.

38. *The Madras Mail,* October 27, 1880, p. 2.

39. *The Hindu* (Madras), November 19, 1885, and December 1, 1884, p. 5.

40. *The Madras Standard,* November 17, 1879, p. 3, and June 13, 1881, p. 3.

41. Viresalingam, *Caritramu,* vol. 1, p. 79.

42. Viresalingam, *Caritramu,* vol. 1, pp. 79–80.

43. Viresalingam contributed several early articles to journals in Masulipatnam and Madras, but his earliest surviving writings are from *VV,* the articles

which he reprinted in the volumes of his collected works: Viresalingam, *KVKG,* vol. 8, pp. 313–447.

44. Viresalingam, *VV,* February 1875, in *KVKG,* vol. 8, p. 335.

45. Although Viresalingam attacked contemporary "false" scholars as early as January 1875, he began criticizing ancient Indian scholars in April 1875, and he accentuated this criticism in October 1875, and July 1876. See the following articles by him: *VV,* January 1875, in *KVKG,* vol. 8, pp. 325–29; *VV,* April 1875, in *KVKG,* vol. 8, pp. 347–48; "Brahmanavicaramu," *VV,* October 1875, in *KVKG,* vol. 8, pp. 400–1; "Brahmanulunu, vari vrttulunu," *VV,* July 1876, in *KVKG,* vol. 8, p. 431.

46. Viresalingam, *VV,* January 1875, in *KVKG,* vol. 8, p. 326; Viresalingam, *VV,* July 1875, in *KVKG,* vol. 8, pp. 363–68; Viresalingam, "Pramanavicaramu," *VV,* October 1875, in *KVKG,* vol. 8, pp. 392–404.

47. Viresalingam, *VV,* April 1875, in *KVKG,* vol. 8, pp. 348–49.

48. Viresalingam, *VV,* July 1876 in *KVKG,* vol. 8, pp. 428–38.

49. The one-act farce "Brahma Vivahamu" he published in his journal's supplement, *Hāsya Sanjīvani,* in July 1876 and he republished this in 1878 as a separate piece. It ridiculed the logic used to justify Brahman marriage customs: Ramapati Rau, "Pantulu Gari Grantha Racana," in *Yuga Purusudu,* p. 207; Viresalingam, "Brahma Vivahamu," in *KVKG,* vol. 2, pp. 1–67. He developed the farces to attack social evils: Viresalingam, *Caritramu,* vol. 1, p. 140. His use of colloquial speech offended critics: letter of G. V. Appa Rao, June 2, 1912, as quoted in Vedamu Venkataraya Sastri, *Vēdamu Vēnkatarāya Sastrulavāri Jīvita Caritra Sangra* (Madras, 1949), p. 121. In Madras, however, attacks on Brahmans were deprecated by social reformers: *Athenaeum and Daily News,* June 3, 1874.

50. Viresalingam, *VV,* July 1876, in *KVKG,* vol. 8, pp. 428–38.

51. Viresalingam, *VV,* January 1875, in *KVKG,* vol. 7, p. 329; Viresalingam, *VV,* April 1875, in *KVKG,* vol. 8, pp. 347–49; Viresalingam, *VV,* July 1875, in *KVKG,* vol. 8, p. 364; Viresalingam, "Aikamatyamu," in *KVKG,* vol. 7, pp. 8, 9.

52. Viresalingam, *VV,* July 1876, in *KVKG,* vol. 8, pp. 431–39.

53. Viresalingam, *VV,* April 1875, in *KVKG,* vol. 8, pp. 343–49.

54. Viresalingam, *VV,* July 1875, in *KVKG,* vol. 8, pp. 363–71; Viresalingam, "Aikamatyamu," in *KVKG,* vol. 8, pp. 4–13.

55. Viresalingam, *Caritramu,* vol. 1, p. 69.

56. Viresalingam, *Caritramu,* vol. 1, pp. 143–45. Burial rather than cremation prevailed among Telugu Brahman Virashaivites of the Aradhya sect.

57. Viresalingam, *Caritramu,* vol. 1, pp. 140–43.

58. A detailed comparison of the Andhra and Madras social reform movements is in John G. Leonard, "Viresalingam and the Making of Modern Andhra: Social Reform in Rajahmundry and Madras, 1874–1891." (MS, 1968) A summary appears in Karen I. Leonard and John G. Leonard, "Social Reform and Women's Participation in Political Culture: Andhra and Madras," in Gail Minault, ed., *The Extended Family: Women and Political Participation in India and Pakistan* (Columbia, Mo.: South Asia Books, 1981), pp. 19–45.

59. Viresalingam, *Caritramu,* vol. 1, pp. 152–58, 277. Kandukuri Viresalingam, "Rajahamahendravara Stri Punar Vivaha Caritramu," in *KVKG,* vol. 7, pp. 6–8. The latter was an unofficial report presented to the Rajahmundry Widow Marriage Association by Viresalingam on June 9, 1885. It contained a description of the widow marriage campaign and Viresalingam included it in his collected works. Hereafter it will be cited as "Vivaha Caritramu." For an example of an orthodox Hindu argument, see Vedamu Venkataraya Sastri, *Strī Punar Vivāha Durvāda Nirvāpanamu,* 2d ed. (Madras, 1924).

60. Viresalingam, *Caritramu,* vol. 1, pp. 163–66; *Indian Law Review* 6 (Madras Ser.): pp. 382–83.

61. Viresalingam, *Caritramu,* vol. 1, p. 159; Viresalingam, "Vivaha Caritramu," in *KVKG,* vol. 7, pp. 11–12.

62. Viresalingam, *Caritramu,* vol. 1, pp. 159, 161–62. D. V. Prakasa Row, "The Widow Marriage Movement in Madras," *Kāyastha Samāchar* (Allahabad) vol. 7, no. 6 (1903): p. 540.

63. Sivudu, *Samsmrti,* pp. 2–4, 135–43; Subba Rao, *Memories,* pp. 19–25; *Sundara Rao,* pp. 3–13; C. Cilakamarti Laksminarasimham, *Svīya Caritramu* (Vishakapatnam, 1957), p. 51; Valluri Suryanarayana Rau, *Sūryanārāyanīyamu,* (Kovvuru, 1936), p. 165.

64. Viresalingam, *Caritramu,* vol. 1, pp. 166–68, 170, 252–54; Venkatappayya, *Caritra,* vol. 1, p. 36.

65. Suryanarayana Rau, *Sūryanārāyanīyamu,* pp. 166–67; Viresalingam, *Caritramu,* vol. 1, pp. 158–62, 171; Viresalingam, "Vivaha Caritramu," in *KVKG,* vol. 7, p. 11; Prakasa Row, "Widow Marriage," p. 540.

66. Suryanarayana Rau, *Sūryanārāyanīmu,* pp. 166–67.

67. A Deputy Tahsildar found a mother willing to have her widowed daughter remarried and Viresalingam sent a college student to go to the village and bring the girl in the night to his home. Then Viresalingam found a bridegroom, a young man who had been educated for many years in his house, was enthused about widow marriages, and was of the right sect. Viresalingam, *Caritramu,* vol. 1, pp. 158–59, 181–84, 188; Viresalingam, "Vivaha Caritramu," in *KVKG,* vol. 7, p. 17; Prakasa Row, "Widow Marriage," p. 542.

68. Intimidation from the orthodox Hindu side resulted in Viresalingam's cook and family priest ceasing their services, and many reformers did not

attend the wedding because of such threats: Viresalingam, *Caritramu,* vol. 1, pp. 189, 191; Viresalingam, "Vivaha Caritramu," in *KVKG,* vol. 7, pp. 20–22.

69. Viresalingam, *Caritramu,* vol. 1, pp. 190, 196; Viresalingam, "Vivaha Caritramu," in *KVKG,* vol. 7, p. 23. Prakasa Row, *Kāyastha Samāchar* 7, no. 4 (1903): pp. 294–96.

70. Viresalingam, *Caritramu,* vol. 1, pp. 160–61; Viresalingam, "Vivaha Caritramu," in *KVKG,* vol. 7, p. 11; Prakasa Row, *Kāyastha Samāchar* 8, no. 5 (1903): p. 413.

71. Venkataraya Sastri, *Vēdamu Vēnkatarāya Sāstrulavāri Jīvita Caritra Sangrahamu,* pp. 36–37; Viresalingam, *Caritramu,* vol. 1, pp. 152–58.

72. Viresalingam, *Caritramu,* vol. 1, pp. 172, 184–85, 187, 197–99; Viresalingam, "Vivaha Caritramu," in *KVKG,* vol. 7, p. 12; Prakasa Row, "Widow Marriage," p. 542; Venkatappayya, *Caritra,* vol. 1, p. 61.

73. Viresalingam, *Caritramu,* vol. 1, pp. 197–99, 281–82; Viresalingam, "Vivaha Caritramu," in *KVKG,* vol. 7, pp. 18–20, 23–24, 25; Prakasa Row, *Kāyastha Samāchar* 8, no. 4 (1903): pp. 296–97.

74. Prakasa Row, *Kāyastha Samāchar* 8, no. 4 (1903): pp. 298–301, 294; Viresalingam, *Caritramu,* vol. 1, pp. 204–09.

75. Viresalingam, *Caritramu,* vol. 1, pp. 215–19, 230, 242, 246; Viresalingam, "Vivaha Caritramu," in *KVKG,* vol. 7, p. 31; Prakasam, *Yatra,* p. 89; Venkatappayya, *Caritra,* vol. 1, p. 36; Prakasa Row, *Kāyastha Samāchar* 8, no. 4 (1903): pp. 299–301.

76. *The Madras Mail,* September 12, 1882, p. 3.

77. *Indian Law Review* 6 (Madras Ser.): pp. 381–96; Viresalingam, *Caritramu,* vol. 1, p. 235; Prakasa Row, *Kāyastha Samāchar* 8, no. 4 (1903): p. 298.

78. *Hindu Dēsābhimāni* in *Madras Native Newspaper Reports,* October 1882; *Vizag Observer,* no. 20, and *Purushārthapradāyini,* nos. 4, 5, and 6, in *Madras Native Newspaper Reports,* July 1883.

79. *The Madras Standard,* April 27, 1883, p. 3; *The Madras Mail,* April 25, 1883, p. 2, and April 26, 1883, p. 3.

80. Viresalingam, *Caritramu,* vol. 1, pp. 196–266; Prakasa Row, *Kāyastha Samāchar* 8, no. 5 (1903): p. 414.

81. Five percent of Hindu girls in Madras Presidency, but 11 percent of Brahman girls, married before the age of ten; and 3.3 percent of Brahman girls ten to fourteen were widowed, compared to less than 1 percent of all girls ten to fourteen. The marriage percentages before the age of ten are from 1881: *Imperial Census of 1881* (Presidency of Madras) (Madras: Government of India, 1883), vol. 1, pp. 70–73, and the widow percentages from 1891: *Census of India,* 1891 (Presidency of Madras) (Madras: Government of India, 1893), XIII, pp. 146–47.

82. Gurunatham, *Viresalingam,* p. 101; Viresalingam, "Vivaha Caritramu," in *KVKG,* vol. 8, pp. 41–42.

83. Viresalingam had given many of the bridegrooms allowances in their college days to permit them to continue their educations, and the marriages themselves usually cost more than they ordinarily would have for boys of that status—thus expectations were raised but the benefits after marriage were not very great. Viresalingam mentioned only a few bridegrooms who were dissatisfied but the situation was obviously more serious. The old reform association was dissolved, and a new one was constituted specifically to exclude some bridegrooms and to counter the demands of the married couples. Viresalingam, *Caritramu,* vol. 1, pp. 278–79; Gurunatham, *Viresalingam,* pp. 116–17.

84. Viresalingam, *Caritramu,* vol. 1, pp. 326–75; Gurunatham, *Viresalingam,* pp. 104–12; Prakasa Row, *Kāyastha Samāchar* (Allahabad) 8, no. 5 (1903): pp. 416–17. For the satire Viresalingam published, see Kandukuri Viresalingam, "Dambhacarya Vilasanamu," *VV,* March 13, 1886, and Ramapati Rau, "Grantha Racana," in *Yuga Purusudu,* p. 211. Lakshminarasimham's initial reaction was to burn *Viveka Vardhani* at a public demonstration, although he later apologized for this outburst; see Viresalingam, *Caritramu,* vol. 1, pp. 347–54.

85. *The Indian Social Reformer* 16 (1905): pp. 548, 560.

86. Gurunatham, *Viresalingam,* pp. 180–81. In the 1880s, journals were still the main outlet for Telugu authors, and Viresalingam published scholarly works on Telugu poetry in his journal until he was forced to discontinue it in 1890 because of competing journals and government pressure. Then he and his friend Nyapati Subha Rao started a monthly journal which Viresalingam edited, *Cintamani.* From 1891 on this journal featured novels published serially, and although a few novels had been published just prior to this time (including one by Viresalingam), Telugu novels really originated with this journal's encouragement (Venkata Rau, *Andhra Vacana,* pp. 139–41). Telugu journals founded in 1885 in Madras competed with *Viveka Vardhani* in its last years: *Andhra Prakasika* was closely allied with the Madras Mahajana Sabha, a political association formed in 1884, and the Brahmo Samaj leader in Madras, Mannava Buccayya, began *Hindu Jana Samskaram,* which represented the interests of social reform in Madras. Other specialized journals began in 1885 and 1891. The type of men who edited these journals changed for most Telugu journals from 1885 to 1891, a change coinciding with the decline of social reform. The new editors were not Western-educated Telugu scholars but members of the educated elite who practiced journalism as a profession. Educated as lawyers or teachers, these men were more attuned to the new currents in politics than the older editors. The Madras Mahajana Sabha got publicity for its efforts from the English language *The Hindu,* but *Andhra Prakasika* (Telugu) and *Swadesamitra* (Tamil) became regional language journals allied with the Sabha: *The Hindu,* January 21, 1885, p. 5; *The Madras Mail,* September 18, 1885, p. 4. *Andhra Prakasika* soon outstripped *Viveka Vardhani* and the *Andhra Bhasha Sajivani* in circulation, but it concentrated solely on political issues. Buccayya was a friend of Viresalingam, and his *Hindu Jana Samskaram* combined political and social

comment and equalled *Viveka Vardhani's* circulation: *Madras Native Newspaper Reports*, January to December 1885 (Madras Record Office). The literary journal *Amrta Granthamali* of Nellore began in 1885 and the Rajahmundry Prarthana Samaj journal *Satya Samvardhani* began in 1891: *Amudrta Grandha Cintamani* (Nellore), no. 9 (1887); Sivudu, *Samsmrti*, p. 31. For the new editors, *The Hindu*, April 8, 1895, p. 4; Sivudu, *Samsmrti*, p. 31.

87. Prakasam, *Yatra*, p. 252.

88. Much later, in the beginning of the twentieth century, this process stimulated an interest in a political guarantee—an Andhra state—for the continuation of the Telugu cultural revival. See John G. Leonard, "Andhra Movement" *Journal of Commonwealth Political Studies* 5, no. 1 (March 1967), pp. 60–77.

89. Viresalingam, *VV*, July 1880, in *KVKG*, vol. 8, p. 485; Kandukuri Viresalingam, "Desabhimanamu," *VV*, July 1881, in *KVKG*, vol. 8, p. 555; Kandukuri Viresalingam, "Sangha Duracara Nivaranamunaku Stri Vidya Yavasyakamu," *VV*, March 1885, in *KVKG*, vol. 8, pp. 639–40.

90. Kandukuri Viresalingam, "Stri Punar Vivaha Visayakopanyasamu," in *KVKG*, vol. 7, pp. 13, 48.

91. Viresalingam, "Stri Punar...," in *KVKG*, vol. 7, pp. 5, 48, 56.

92. Kandukuri Viresalingam, "Desabhimanamu," *VV*, July 1880, in *KVKG*, vol. 8, pp. 482–83.

93. Viresalingam, "Desabhimanamu," *VV*, July 1880, in *KVKG*, vol. 8, p. 482.

94. Viresalingam, "Stri Punar...," in *KVKG*, vol. 7, pp. 6–16.

95. Kandukuri Viresalingam, "Hindu Matamulu," in *KVKG*, vol. 7, p. 3.

96. Kandukuri Viresalingam, "Kalamu Yokka Viluva," *VV*, March 1880, in *KVKG*, vol. 8, p. 460; Kandukuri Viresalingam, "Vaidyulu," *VV*, February 1881, in *KVKG*, vol. 8, p. 510; Viresalingam, *VV*, October 1881, in *KVKG*, vol. 8, p. 562.

97. Kandukuri Viresalingam, "Isvara Datta Pustakamulu," in *KVKG*, vol. 7, p. 22; Viresalingam, "Stri Punar...," in *KVKG*, vol. 7, pp. 6, 11.

98. Viresalingam used the phrase "common folk" or "ordinary people" (*samanya janulu*) which has a vulgar connotation in Telugu. Our use of "the masses" expresses the social distance which Viresalingam felt separated him from the masses of illiterate people.

99. Kandukuri Viresalingam, "Rajakiya Pathasalalu," *VV*, March 1881, in *KVKG*, vol. 8, p. 526; Kandukuri Viresalingam, "Kulina Brahmana Vivahamulu," *VV*, August 1885, in *KVKG*, vol. 8, p. 647; Viresalingam, *VV*, July 1880, in *KVKG*, p. 489.

100. Viresalingam, *VV*, July 1880, in *KVKG*, vol. 8, p. 485; Kandukuri Viresalingam, "Desabhimanamu," *VV*, July 1881, in *KVKG*, vol. 8, p. 555.

101. Kandukuri Viresalingam, "Sangha Duracara Nivaranamunaku Stri Vidya Yavasyakamu," *VV*, March 1885, in *KVKG*, vol. 8, pp. 639–40.

102. Viresalingam, "Isvara Datta Pustakamalu," in *KVKG*, vol. 7, p. 22.

103. Kandukuri Viresalingam, "Desa Bhasalu," *VV*, October 1881, in *KVKG*, vol. 8, pp. 556–66.

104. Kandukuri Viresalingam, "Desabhivrddhi," *VV*, January 1883, in *KVKG*, vol. 8, p. 597.

105. Kandukuri Viresalingam, "Patupaduta," *VV*, November 1884, in *KVKG*, vol. 8, p. 633.

106. Kandukuri Viresalingam, "Vidyadhikula Yokka Krtyamulu," *VV*, June 1883, in *KVKG*, vol. 8, p. 607.

107. Viresalingam, *VV*, October 1881, in *KVKG*, vol. 8, p. 566.

108. Kandukuri Viresalingam, "Vidyadhikula Yokka Krtyamulu," *VV*, March 1882, in *KVKG*, vol. 8, pp. 577–78; Kandukuri Viresalinga, "Andhra Bhasabhivrddhi," *VV*, June 1882, in *KVKG*, vol. 8, pp. 580–81.

109. Viresalingam, *VV*, November 1886, in *KVKG*, vol. 8, p. 667; *The Hindu*, January 12, 1885, p. 6.

110. Viresalingam, *VV*, March 1882, in *KVKG*, vol. 8, pp. 577–78; Kandukuri Viresalingam, "Desa Bhasa," *VV*, November 1886, in *KVKG*, vol. 8, p. 670.

111. Viresalingam, *VV*, June 1882, in *KVKG*, vol. 8, pp. 580–81; Viresalingam, "Vidyadhikula Yokka Krtyamulu," *VV*, March 1882, in *KVKG*, vol. 8, pp. 577–78; Viresalingam, *VV*, January 1883, in *KVKG*, vol. 8, p. 600.

112. Kandukuri Viresalingam, "Stri Vidyabhyasamu," *VV*, February 1884, in *KVKG*, vol. 8, p. 624; Viresalingam, *VV*, November 1886, in *KVKG*, vol. 8, p. 667.

113. Viresalingam, *VV*, June 1882, in *KVKG*, vol. 8, p. 667.

114. Viresalingam, *VV*, November 1884, in *KVKG*, vol. 8, p. 633; Viresalingam, *VV*, November 1886, in *KVKG*, vol. 8, p. 667.

115. Viresalingam, *VV*, July 1881, in *KVKG*, vol. 8, p. 554; Kandukuri Viresalingam, "Janmantaramu," in *KVKG*, vol. 7, pp. 9–10.

116. Viresalingam, *VV*, March 1882, in *KVKG*, vol. 8, p. 577; *The Hindu*, January 12, 1885, p. 6; Kandukuri Viresalingam, "Desiya Mahasabhalu, Dani Yuddesamulunu," in *KVKG*, vol. 8, p. 1–6.

117. Viresalingam, *VV*, November 1884, in *KVKG*, vol. 8, p. 633; Kandukuri Viresalingam, "Kulacara, Matacara Samskaranamu," *VV*, April 1887, in *KVKG*, vol. 8, pp. 674–77; Viresalingam, "Desiya Mahasabha...," in *KVKG*, vol. 8, pp. 21–46.

118. Viresalingam, *VV,* November 1886, in *KVKG,* vol. 8, p. 667.

119. Viresalingam, "Desiya Mahasabha...," in *KVKG,* vol. 8, p. 8–17.

120. Viresalingam, *VV,* November 1886, in *KVKG,* vol. 8, p. 667.

121. *The Hindu,* July 15, 1893, p. 3; Government of Madras, *General Index to Proceedings, Government of Madras, 1894* (Madras, 1895), p. 339.

122. Cilakamarti Laksminarasimham gives an amusing description of the educated elite travelling from one district conference to another: *Caritramu,* pp. 127, 165–75.

123. *The Hindu,* July 3, 1895, p. 6; *The Madras Times,* June 10, 1895, p. 4; for a description of how social reform issues were treated in the different conferences, see Viresalingam, *Caritramu,* vol. 2, pp. 86–88.

124. *The Hindu Weekly Edition,* April 11, 1907, pp. 9–10; *The Indian Social Reformer,* 15 (1905): pp. 436–37.

Chapter 8

1. The term "vernacular" is used here in the sense of a modern Indian language, as opposed to classical or ritual languages such as Sanskrit, Arabic, or Persian, or a modern foreign language such as English. Some have objected to the term as a pejorative, implying a spoken dialect rather than a literary language. That is not the implication here. The Indian languages discussed in this volume are literary languages of considerable range and subtlety that also have the advantage of being spoken in their respective regions. With the advent of the printing press, these languages became the media of communication between those who were literate and those who had access to the printed word through various forms of community readings or public performances. For a discussion of this phenomenon in rural Bengal, see Rafiuddin Ahmed, *The Bengal Muslims, 1871–1906: A Quest for Identity* (Delhi: Oxford University Press, 1981), pp. 72–105; for a parallel in early modern Europe, see Natalie Zemon Davis, "Printing and the People," in her *Society and Culture in Early Modern France* (Stanford: Stanford University Press, 1975), pp. 189–226.

2. There is no biography of Mumtaz 'Ali. The following account is pieced together from: Sayyid Mumtaz 'Ali, "Tahzib un-Niswan," *Tahzīb un-Niswān* (hereafter *TN*) 21, Jubilee no. (July 6, 1918): pp. 424–33; Abul Athar Hafiz Jalandhari, "Maulvi Sayyid Mumtaz 'Ali," *TN,* 38 (6, July 1935): pp. 607–17 (originally published in *Makhzan* in 1927, this article was reprinted in *Tahzīb un-Niswān* as an obituary); MS biography in Urdu of Muhammadi Begam, Mumtaz 'Ali's second wife, by her sister, Ahmadi Begam (Begam S. Wahid 'Ali), kindly lent to me by Naim and Yasmin Tahir of Lahore; Interviews in Lahore in 1977 with Naim and Yasmin Tahir (S. Mumtaz 'Ali's granddaughter) and Hijjab Imtiyaz 'Ali (daughter-in-law of S. Mumtaz 'Ali). I would like to

express my gratitude to the Tahirs, without whose cooperation this research would not have been possible.

3. Sayyid Ahmad Dehlawi started the biweekly *Akhbār un-Nissa* (Women's Newspaper) in Delhi in 1887, but it closed after a very brief run. Another journal for women, the monthly *Mu'allim-i-Niswān* (Women's Guide), edited by Maulvi Muhibb-i-Husain, appeared in Hyderabad in the 1890s but closed in 1901. *Tahzīb un-Niswān* ran from 1898 into the 1950s.

4. *Purdah* and *zanāna: purdah* is the custom of veiling and seclusion of women. *Zanāna* is the women's quarters of a household, usually an inner courtyard. For studies dealing with these concepts, see Hanna Papanek and Gail Minault, eds., *Separate Worlds: Studies of Purdah in South Asia* (Columbia, Mo.: South Asia Books; Delhi: Chanakya Publications, 1982).

5. For a history of the school and its reformist intellectual tradition, see Barbara D. Metcalf, *Islamic Revival in British India: Deoband, 1860–1900* (Princeton: Princeton University Press, 1982).

6. Rafiuddin Ahmed emphasizes the importance of religious disputations, or *bahās,* as social events in his *Bengal Muslims,* pp. 75–82.

7. The adversary of the missionary, Pfander, in Agra in the 1850s. See A. A. Powell, "Maulana Rahmat Allah Kairanwi and Muslim-Christian controversy in India in the mid-19th Century," *Journal of the Royal Asiatic Society* (1976) (hereafter *JRAS*): 42–63; Christian W. Troll, *Sayyid Ahmad Khan: A Reinterpretation of Muslim Theology* (Delhi: Vikas, 1978), pp. 68–70.

8. The leading Muslim spokesman in the Shahjahanpur debates among Christians, Muslims, and Arya Samajis in 1875 and 1876. See Metcalf, *Islamic Revival in British India,* pp. 221–30.

9. Babu Chandranath Mitter later became Registrar of Punjab University.

10. It is worthwhile mentioning that Sir Sayyid, too, was a student of Maulana Mamluk 'Ali Nanautawi in pre-Mutiny Delhi, and hence partook of the same Waliu'llahi intellectual tradition as did the Deoband '*ulamā.* For an intellectual biography of Sir Sayyid that emphasizes his theological contribution, see Troll, *Sayyid Ahmad Khan.*

11. Jalandhari, "Maulvi Sayyid Mumtaz 'Ali," *TN* (July 6, 1935): p. 612; Metcalf, *Islamic Revival,* pp. 212–13.

12. Metcalf, *Islamic Revival,* pp. 141–43; Troll, *Sayyid Ahmad Khan,* pp. 140–43; Sayyid Mumtaz 'Ali, *Huqūq un-Niswān* (Lahore: Dar ul-Isha'iat-i-Punjab, 1898), pp. 22–30.

13. Jalandhari, "Maulvi Sayyid Mumtaz 'Ali," *TN* (July 6, 1935): 615–16.

14. Mumtaz 'Ali, "Tahzib un-Niswan," in *TN* (July 6, 1918): 425.

15. See Metcalf, *Islamic Revival,* pp. 198–234.

16. Metcalf, *Islamic Revival,* pp. 1–15.

17. *Fatāwa:* rulings on points of Islamic law (Singular, *fatwa*).

18. Metcalf, *Islamic Revival,* p. 146. Barbara Metcalf, "Islam and Custom in Nineteenth-Century India: The Reformist Standard of Maulana Thanawi's *Bihishtī Zēwar,*" *Contributions to Asian Studies* 17: pp. 62–78.

19. Sir Sayyid felt that concerns for women's education were premature, given the then current backward state of men's education among Muslims. Mumtaz 'Ali quotes a letter from Sir Sayyid to this effect in *Huqūq un-Niswān,* pp. 57–59.

20. Mumtaz 'Ali, "Tahzib un-Niswan," *TN* (July 6, 1918): p. 425; Jalandhari, "Maulvi Sayyid Mumtaz 'Ali," *TN* (July 6, 1935): 614–15.

21. For the Victorian ideal of domesticity, see Walter E. Houghton, *The Victorian Frame of Mind* (New Haven: Yale University Press, 1957), pp. 341–93.

22. Mumtaz 'Ali, *Huqūq un-Niswān,* p. 55.

23. *Mirāt ul-'Arus* has been translated into English by G. E. Ward as *The Bride's Mirror* (London: Henry Frowde, 1903); for a quick summary of the plot, see C. M. Naim, "Prize-Winning *Adab:* A Study of Five Urdu Books Written in Response to the Allahabad Government Gazette Notification," in Barbara Metcalf, ed., *Moral Conduct and Authority: The Place of Adab in South Asian Islam* (Berkeley and Los Angeles: University of California Press, 1984), pp. 290–314; specifically, pp. 301–2.

24. The MS biography uses the term *chōtī khāla* (mother's younger sister) to refer to Zulfiqar 'Ali's daughters, but this may have been a fictive relationship.

25. This account is taken from the ms. biography written by her sister, Ahmadi Begam.

26. Though she had many duties, it was a nuclear household, nor had she a mother-in-law, always the biggest trial for any new bride.

27. According to her sister's account, S. Hamid 'Ali was a particularly difficult child who also had a skin condition that required bandaging. He would allow no one but Muhammadi to change his dressings.

28. Mumtaz 'Ali, "Tahzib un-Niswan," *TN* (July 6, 1918): p. 424.

29. His phrase is *Angrēzon kī Taqlīd.*

30. Metcalf, *Islamic Revival,* pp. 11–12.

31. Mumtaz 'Ali, *Huqūq un-Niswān,* pp. 3–4; the rest of this section summarizes *Huqūq un-Niswān,* pp. 3–42.

32. The Urdu word used to describe his style is *salīs:* easy, simple, clear, not abstruse. At one point, Mumtaz 'Ali uses the term *maulwiāna* to describe

difficult Urdu style, as contrasted with the style he wished to achieve. Mumtaz 'Ali, "Tahzib un-Niswan," *TN* (July 6, 1918): p. 430.

33. This translation is by A. J. Arberry, *The Koran Interpreted,* vol. 1 (New York: Macmillan, 1955), p. 105.

34. For a complete summary of the text, see my article "Mumtaz 'Ali and *Huqūq un-Niswān:* An Advocate of Women's Rights in Islam in the late 19th Century." Forthcoming.

35. Mumtaz 'Ali, "Tahzib un-Niswan," *TN* (July 6, 1918): 424–33.

36. Zohra Fyzee, "Muhammadi Begam," *TN* 33 (July 14, 1930): 585–87.

37. Shaista Akhtar Banu Suhrawardy (Begam Ikramullah), *A Critical Survey of the Development of the Urdu Novel and Short Story* (London: Longmans, 1945), pp. 123–30; Muhammadi Begam, *Safiya Bēgam: ya'nī Bachpan kī Mangnī kā 'Ibratnāk Qissa* (Lahore: Dar ul-Ishā'iat-i-Punjab, 1930).

38. Muhammadi Begam, *Khānadarī: ya'nī Asā'ish aur Tahzīb-o- Kafāyat-ī-Sh'ari sē Rahnē-Sahnē kē Qā'idē* (Lahore: Dar ul-Isha'iat-i-Punjab, 1933).

39. Muhammadi Begam, *Ādāb-i-Mulāqāt* (Lahore: Dar ul-Isha'iat-i-Punjab, 1935).

40. This too is a refrain in reformist literature for women issuing from Deoband at this time, as Barbara Metcalf's study of Maulana Ashraf 'Ali Thanawi's *Bihishtī Zēwar* makes clear. Metcalf, "Islam and Custom in Nineteenth-Century India"; Barbara Metcalf, "Islamic Reform and Islamic Women: Maulana Thanawi's *Jewelry of Paradise,* in Metcalf, ed., *Moral Conduct and Authority,* (Berkeley and Los Angeles: University of California Press, 1984), pp. 184-95.

41. This summary of *Tahzīb un-Niswān*'s contents is based on reading files of *TN* from before 1908.

42. These sisters were highly educated and visible members of the extended Tyabji clan of Bombay. They were leading advocates of Muslim women's education and of lowering the barriers of *purdah.*

43. Urdu novelist, later the wife of Sayyid Sajjad Hyder and mother of Qurratulain Hyder, the well-known contemporary Urdu novelist.

44. Educator and member of the politically influential Suhrawardy family of Calcutta.

45. For a good summary of novels by early women writers in Urdu, see Begam Ikramullah's *A Critical Survey of the Development of the Urdu Novel and Short Story* (London: Longmans, Green, 1945), pp. 123–65.

46. She married Muhammad Yaqub (Later Sir Muhammad Yaqub) of Moradabad. Wahida died in 1917.

47. The wife of S. Hamid 'Ali, Mumtaz 'Ali's son by his first wife.

48. Also an author of Urdu short stories and novels, and the first Muslim woman to obtain a pilot's license.

49. This rapid survey is based on reading files of *TN* from 1914 into the 1940s.

50. Mumtaz 'Ali, *Huqūq un-Niswān,* pp. 168–69; John L. Esposito, *Women in Muslim Family Law* (Syracuse, N.Y.: Syracuse University Press, 1982), p. 78.

Chapter 9

1. Particularly illustrated in Ellen Gumperz, "The Modernization of Communication," *Asian Survey,* 2 (1968), pp.589–606; Ellen McDonald, "The Growth of Regional Consciousness in Maharashtra," *Indian Economic and Social History Review,* 5 (1968), pp.223–43; essays in Yogendra Malik, ed., *South Asian Intellectual and Social Change* (New Delhi: Heritage, 1972).

2. Themes discussed in this volume. Background on the press drawn from *Statements of English, Foreign, Anglo-Vernacular and Vernacular Newspapers Published in India and Burma during the Year 1905,* Confidential police report, Indian Home Department, 1907. Background on press and politicalization in N. G. Barrier, *Banned* (Columbia, Missouri: University of Missouri Press, 1974).

3. Press trends and tracts treated in the following: N. G. Barrier and Paul Wallace, *The Punjab Press, 1880–1905,* South Asia Series (Michigan State University, 1970); N. G. Barrier, *The Punjab in Nineteenth Century Tracts,* South Asia Series (Michigan State University, 1969); Eric Gustafson and Kenneth Jones, *Sources on Punjab History* (Delhi: Manohar, 1975); Emmett Davis, *Press and Politics in British Western Punjab, 1836–1947* (New Delhi: Academic, 1983).

4. Sources quoted in footnote 3, and N. G. Barrier, "Punjab Politics and the Press, 1880–1910," in Margaret Case and N. G. Barrier, eds., *Aspects of India* (Manohar,1985), pp. 118–33; N. G. Barrier, "Sikh Immigrants and Their Homeland: The Transmission of Information, Resources and Values in the Early Twentieth Century." Forthcoming; N. G. Barrier, "Sikh Politics in British Punjab Prior to the Gurdwara Reform Movement." Forthcoming.

5. This primarily is based upon the essays and recent dissertation by Harjot Singh Oberoi, "A World Reconstructed: Religion, Ritual and Community among the Sikhs, 1850–1909" (Ph.D. diss., Australian National University, 1987). Also relevant is Harjot Singh Oberoi, "A Historical and Bibliographical Reconstruction of the Singh Sabha in 19th Century Punjab," *Journal of Sikh Studies,* 10 (August 1983), pp. 108–30; N. G. Barrier, *The Sikhs and Their Literature* (New Delhi: Manohar Book Service, 1969). The problems in eighteenth-century Sikh history are discussed in W. H. McLeod, *The Evolution of the Sikh Community* (Oxford: Oxford University Press, 1976).

6. Reviewed in Oberoi, "A World Reconstructed." Also background in Harbans Singh, *Heritage of the Sikhs,* rev. ed. (Delhi: Manohar, 1984); Rajiv

Kapur, *Sikh Separatism* (London: Allen and Unwin, 1986); Richard Fox, *The Lions of the Punjab* (Berkeley and Los Angeles: University of California, 1986).

7. Background in Kenneth Jones, *Arya Dharm* (Berkeley and Los Angeles: University of California Press, 1975); N. G. Barrier, *Sikhs and Their Literature;* Kenneth Jones, "Communalism in the Punjab," *Journal of Asian Studies* 28 (1968), pp. 39–53; N. G. Barrier, "The Punjab Government and Communal Politics," *Journal of Asian Studies* 27 (1967–68), pp. 523–39. A recent scholarly assessment of early British administration is J. Andrew Major, "Return to Empire: The Sikhs and British in the Punjab, 1939–72" (Ph.D. diss., Australian National University, 1981).

8. Also the discussion of Oberoi's research by Sikh scholars at the Toronto and Berkeley Sikh conferences, 1987. On the early intellectual milieu and orientalism, Jeffrey Perrill, "Anjuman-i-Panjab as a Common Interest Association and Symbol of Social Change in Nineteenth Century Punjab," *Panjab Past and Present* 16 (1982), pp. 343–70. Several articles by Sulakhan Singh in the *Journal of Regional History* (1980–83) summarize the institutional legacy and continuities of Udasi practices.

9. Namdharis assessed in Oberoi dissertation; W. H. McLeod, "The Kukas, a Millenarian Sect of the Punjab," in G. A. Wood and P. S. O'Connor, eds., *W. P. Morrell: A Tribute* (University of Otago, 1973), pp. 85–103. Relevant documents in Nahar Singh, ed., *Gooroo Ram Singh and the Kūkā Sikhs,* 3 vols. (Nahar Singh, 1965–67); on the Nirankaris, John Webster, *The Nirankārī Sikhs* (Delhi: Macmillan India, 1979).

10. Oberoi's dissertation and his article "Bhais, Babas and Gyanis: Traditional Intellectuals in Nineteenth Century Punjab," *Studies in History* 2 (1980), pp. 33–62. Also useful as background is Gurdarshan Singh Dhillon, "Character and Impact of the Singh Sabha Movement on the History of the Panjab" (Ph.D. diss., Punjabi University, 1973).

11. Illustrated in the tracts of Avtar Singh Vahiria, to be discussed in a later section. Differing perspectives outlined in Oberoi dissertation and "Bhais."

12. Tat Khalsa perspective is reviewed in Oberoi dissertation; Fox, *Lions of the Punjab,* and Kapur, *Sikh Separatism.* It should be emphasized that there was a variety of opinion on specific issues, even among the most aggressive Sikh reformers associated with the Lahore Sabha and later the Chief Khalsa Diwan.

13. Diversity of Sikh opinion discussed in N. G. Barrier, *The Sikhs and Their Literature,* and my forthcoming monograph on the emergence of modern Sikhism. On the divergence of opinion, Ian Kerr, "British Relationships with the Golden Temple, 1849–90," *The Indian Economic and Social History Review* 21 (1984), pp. 139–51.

14. N. G. Barrier, "Sikh Migration" in *The Sikh Diaspora.* Also Oberoi's treatment of Singh Sabha innovations in communication and constructing linkages, "A World Reconstructed."

15. Based on data in Barrier and Wallace, *The Punjab Press.*

16. Information network analyzed in Barrier, "Sikh Migration."

17. Discussion of the emphasis on Punjabi in Barrier, *The Sikhs;* the newspaper and tract material was filled with references to the issue, and before each commission, Sikh petitioners would plead for additional support for Punjabi.

18. Background in Oberoi dissertation; Barrier, "Sikh Migration" and "Sikh Politics."

19. The following are the most recent studies on the Chief Khalsa Diwan: Barrier, "Sikh Politics"; Surjit Singh Narang, "Chief Khalsa Diwan," in Paul Wallace and Surendra Chopra, eds., *Political Dynamics of Punjab* (Amritsar: Guru Nanak Dev University, 1981), pp. 67–81; Narotam Singh, "Chief Khalsa Diwan in the Field of Education," *Journal of Sikh Studies* 8, nos. 1–2 (1981), pp. 118–29; Kapur, *Sikh Separatism.* Articles in *Panjab Past and Present* and *Journal of Sikh Studies* regularly survey various dimensions of Sikh politics and history.

20. Based upon comprehensive files on Sikh publications gathered from the British quarterly list of books from the Punjab, India Office Library, 1875–1920. Supplementary information in Ganesh Gaur and Eileen M. Dimes, *Catalogue of the Panjabi Printed Books Added to the India Office Library, 1902–1964* (Foreign and Commonwealth Office, 1975) and the various earlier catalogues to the Punjabi collections in the IOL and British Museum. Background on collections in N.G. Barrier, "South Asia in Vernacular Publications," *Journal of Asian Studies* 28 (1968–69), pp. 803–10.

21. Sources in last footnote and advertisements in Sikh papers of the period. See, for example, the agency ads of the Khalsa Store, the Khalsa Agency, the Sri Arjan Dev Agency, the Sri Gurmati Pustak Bhandar, the Sikh General Store, and the large stock of titles of Ram Ditta Mal, a Lahore dealer.

22. *Report of the Khalsa Tract Society,* 1901 (Amritsar: Wazir Hind Press, 1902), *Report of the Khalsa Tract Society,* 1902 (Wazir Hind Press, 1903). Almost 100,000 tracts were shipped out in 1902, frequently to individual Singh Sabhas such as Bhasaur and Amritsar, which in turn circulated the material.

23. Lists of tracts in the Punjab Book catalogue, 1911; reports of the agencies for 1910 and 1912; background on the various institutions in Munsha Singh Dukhi, *Jīvan Bhāī Sāhīb Bhāī Mohan Singhjī Vaid* (Amritsar: Munsha Singh Dukhi, n.d.), especially pp. 186–89, 222; Oberoi, "A World Reconstructed," pp. 303–5.

24. Kenneth W. Jones, *Arya Dharm: Hindu Consciousness in Nineteenth Century Punjab* (Berkeley and Los Angeles: University of California Press, 1976); Kenneth W. Jones, "Communalism in the Punjab," *Journal of Asian Studies* 28 (1968), pp. 39–53. Also relevant are the essays in Gustafson and Jones, *Sources.*

25. Radha Krishna Mehta, *Nūshkhā-Granthī Fobia* (Lahore: Aurora Bans Press, 1889), p. 39.

26. *Ilāj-i-Wahmat-i-Dītt Singhīā.* Local Sikh and Arya papers frequently quoted from these and similar tracts, thus broadening the controversies.

27. Tracts listed and annotated in Barrier, *Sikhs and Their Literature.*

28. On Vir Singh's life and literary works, Harbans Singh, *Bhai Vir Singh* (New Delhi: Sahitya Akademi, 1972); G. S. Khosla, *Bhai Vir Singh, An Analytical Study* (Heritage, 1983).

29. Based on author's file of Khalsa Tract Society publications. Background on tracts in Barrier, *Sikhs and Their Literature* and Ganesh Gaur and Eileen Dimes, *Catalogue of Panjabi Printed Books Added to the India Office Library, 1902–1964* (Foreign and Commonwealth Office, 1965).

30. Ram Singh, *Paltan no. 15 Sikh: Surbirta Ate Kadardani* (1897), reviewed in *Khalsa Akhbār* (December 14, 1897), *Saragarhī Dā Jūdh* (1899), and subsequently reprinted in a Sindhi edition, 1905. Sikh bravery and recruitment efforts during the First World War stimulated another round of tracts on the same topic.

31. Examples of this literature include *Nūnh Sas Dā Sambad* (KTS, 1900), a dialogue between a woman and her daughter-in-law; *Prem Patola* (KTS, 1904), a collection of sacred songs for the moral and social instruction of women, two thousand copies printed; *Ehtān Garkī Āī* (No Longer Endurable) (KTS, 1899), on wearing provocative dresses; *Bībī Bhāīn Arthāt Rusevē Dē Augan* (To my Sister, or the evils of petty family quarrels) (KTS, 1900), which condemned ornaments and showy dresses and emphasized the need for performing household duties. *Nai Ni Merā Nak Nahīn Rahndā, Arthāt Siāpe Pallē Te Phūrian Dē Dūkh* (People Will Cease to Have Regard For Me, or the Evils of the Siapa) (1900) against female mourning; *Aj Mangal Wār* (1900), a condemnation of fasts and related customs; *An Ishwar Parthae, Gūrū Jī Dē Updēsh* (1900) verses from the Granth against idol worship; *Srī Gūrū Granth Sahib Vichchon Chalanē De Shabad* (1898), funeral verses from the Adi Granth; and *Srī Gūrū Granth Sahib Jī cīchchōn Lānwān* (1907), the marriage ceremony as set forth by the Granth, with commentary. Proper care for children, including warnings not to scare them with superstitions and not to put ornaments on them (*Haua Āyā,* 1903; *Bālān Nūn Gahnē Pahnawānē Dē Āugan,* 1900) were frequent themes, as were quarrels among women, the wearing of inappropriate clothes, and female education to strengthen Sikhism

32. For example, *Khalsa Barādarī Unnatī Āshram Dīan Kūnjīan* (Khalsa Tract Society, 1909), "The keys to the advancement of the ashram of the Khalsa Biradari," background on a missionary program and plans for a worldwide campaign to spread Sikhism.

33. Discussion in *Khālsā Akhbār* (August 2, 1901). Teja Singh Bhasaur pressured the Chief Khalsa Diwan to initiate special review committees, and there are some indications that Bhai Vir Singh played such a role in deciding what material would be reviewed for this journal and published in the Khalsa Tract Society. Discussion in Dukhi, *Mohan Singh Vaid,* p. 113.

34. Background in Dukhi, *Mohan Singh Vaid.*

35. Life and works reviewed in Oberoi, "A World Reconstructed" and Giani Amar Singh, *Giānī Ditt Singhjī* (Kirpal Singh, 1962).

36. For example, *Bhai Botā Singh Dī Shahīd* (Khalsa Press, 1901); *Sikh Bachchē Dī Sachchī Shahīdī* (Khalsa Press, 1898); *Singhānīān Dē Sīdak* (Khalsa Press, 1898, on torture and cruelties Sikh women endured after refusing to accept Islam).

37. *Mērā Atē Sādhu Dayānand Dā Sambhad* (Khalsa Press, 1900). Dating some of Ditt Singh's tracts is difficult because many were reprints or had inaccurate dates on the title page. Several were published after his death. A list of his publications is found in Oberoi, "A World Reconstructed," p. 210, and Amar Singh, *Giānī Ditt Singhjī* pp. 93–96.

38. *Tā'lim Satyārth Prakāsh Kā Aslī Fōtō* (Lyallpur: Hari Chand, 1910).

39. Excellent analysis in Oberoi, "A World Reconstructed," pp. 219–20.

40. Ditt Singh, *Durga Prabodh* (Lahore: Baldev Singh, 1899). Central to the argument was insistence on reinterpreting terms and phrases, such as taking references about Bhagauti and relating that to the symbol of the sword instead of worship of Durga.

41. Background in Oberoi, "A World Reconstructed," pp. 287–88; Amar Singh, *Giānī Ditt Singhjī,* pp. 66–68.

42. Several sections of Oberoi's dissertation evaluate his role as a publicist. Lists of publications found in Barrier, *Sikhs and Their Literature* and the India Office/British Museum Catalogues of Punjabi books.

43. Oberoi, "A World Reconstructed," pp. 282–84.

44. Life surveyed in Shamsher Singh Ashok, *Bhai Kahan Singh Nabha* (Ashok Pustak Mala, 1966).

45. *Ham Hīndu Nahīn,* first published in Hindi, c. 1879, with first Punjabi edition, 1899. Last critical edition approximately 1915, with various reprints thereafter. The following based on the introductions to each edition and the background and notes in *Sikhs—We Are Not Hindu,* a translation of the tract by Jarnail Singh (Amritsar: Sikh Social and Educational Society, 1985). Also see discussion and partial translation in W. H. McLeod, *Sikhism* (New York: Barnes and Noble, 1984), pp. 133–36.

46. Ashok, *Kahan Singh Nabha,* p. 27–28, and discussions of the tract between 1898–1907 in local newspapers and tracts.

47. From Introduction, p. 1.

48. References to Kahan Singh in the various publications of the Panch Khalsa Diwan, background in Lal Singh Sangrur's, *Ītīhas Dā Panch Khālsā*

Diwan and *Kalmī Tasvīr.* Several opponents of Kahan Singh also suggest the links with the Bhasaur group.

49. Interviews with Nahar Singh, M.A., New Delhi, 1969, and several tracts attacking Kahan Singh, c. 1914–20.

50. Based on the two volumes by Lal Singh, the reports of the Panch Khalsa Diwan and Bhasaur Singh Sabha, and a short biography, *Adūti Jīvan Brītaint Panth Ratan Bābu Tejā Singhjī Sahīb* (Amritsar: Guru Khalsa Press, n.d.). A useful discussion of Teja Singh's role is in Harbans Singh's essay on Teja Singh and the Bakapur incident, *Panjab Past and Present,* 9 (1975), pp. 322–32.

51. Listed in Barrier, *Sikhs and Their Literature.*

52. Background in Barrier, "Sikh Immigrants" and the Chief Khalsa Diwan executive committee proceedings, c. 1907–17.

53. The best source on Mohan Singh Vaid is a set of diaries reprinted in Dukhi's life of the Singh Sabha activist.

54. List and discussion in Dukhi, *Mohan Singh Vaid,* pp. 133–34, 222.

55. Described in Barrier, *Sikhs and Their Literature.* The Takht Singh collection remains at the Sikh Kanya Mahavidyala, but the Mohan Singh Vaid library now is preserved at Punjabi University, Patiala.

56. Dukhi, *Mohan Singh Vaid,* pp. 47–48.

57. The effect of tracts on customary practice discussed in detail in Oberoi, "A World Reconstructed." Incidents of former devotees of Sakhi Sarvar undergoing Khalsa baptism and renouncing earlier practices reviewed in Oberoi, p. 221. Sikh missionaries kept records of such conversions, and Tat Khalsa journals commented on the impact of specific tracts.

58. Summarized in Barrier, "Sikh Immigrants" and a constant theme in the diaries of Bhai Mohan Singh Vaid, Dukhi.

59. For example, stories in *Khalsa Samāchār,* August 7, 1913, p. 6; January 8, 1914, p. 7.

60. Surveyed in N. G. Barrier, "The British and Controversial Publications in Punjab," *Panjab Past and Present,* 8 (1974), pp. 32–60. On the Akali material, Barrier, *Banned,* pp. 195–99.

61. Tract literature, newspapers and the spiral of conflict between Muslims and Sikhs treated in Prem Uprety, *Religion and Politics in Punjab in the 1920s* (New Delhi: Sterling, 1980) and Sarfraz Khwaja, *Sikhs of the Punjab* (Lahore: Modern Book Depot, 1985).

62. Events and particularly the role of the mass media ably evaluated in Robin Jeffrey, *What's Happening to India* (London: Holmes and Meier, 1986).

Chapter 10

1. Benedict Anderson, *Imagined Communities: Reflections on the Origin and Spread of Nationalism* (London: Verso, 1983).

2. For explorations of these themes, see Sandria B. Freitag, University of California, Berkeley, "Popular Culture in the Rewriting of History: An Essay in Comparative History and Historiography" (TS, 1989).

3. For a case study that shows the relationship of this mode of government and its sociological implications, see Douglas Haynes, *Rhetoric and Ritual in Colonial India: The Shaping of Public Culture in Surat City 1852–1928* (University of California Press, 1991). It is inspired by the essays of Bernard S. Cohn, notably "Representing Authority in Victorian India," in Eric Hobsbawm and Terrence Ranger, eds., *The Invention of Tradition* (Cambridge: Cambridge University Press, 1984), pp. 155–210.

4. The implicit issue here is the orientalist mode of essentializing or reifying religious traditions whose texts are taken to be timeless and transparent. The locus classicus for elaboration of that mentality from the position of power of European colonizers is Edward Said, *Orientalism* (New York: Pantheon, 1978).

5. David S. Lelyveld, *Aligarh's First Generation: Muslim Solidarity in British India* (Princeton: Princeton University Press, 1978).

6. See Arjun Appadurai, "Hinduism," *Encyclopedia of Asian History* 2 (New York: Charles Scribner's Sons, 1988), pp. 56–59.

7. Richard Fox, *Lions of the Punjab* (Berkeley and Los Angeles: University of California Press, 1987).

8. For the concept of "public arena," see Sandria B. Freitag, "Ambiguous Public Arenas and Coherent Personal Practice: Kanpur Muslims, 1913–1931," in Katherine Ewing, ed., *Shari'at and Ambiguity in South Asian Islam* (Berkeley and Los Angeles: University of California Press, 1988), pp. 143–64, as well as her *Collective Action and Community: Public Arenas in the Emergence of Communalism in North India* (Berkeley and Los Angeles: University of California Press, 1990).

9. Elsewhere I have argued that these debates took on a ritualized form: participants proclaiming reluctance to participate; high judicial officials, even Englishmen, in attendance; a cultivation of wit and specious scientism in the rhetoric; a claim on every side that the opponents retreated in silence or fled in dismay. Barbara D. Metcalf, *Islamic Reform in British India: Deoband 1860–1900* (Princeton: Princeton University Press, 1982), Chapter Six.

10. See my introduction to *Perfecting Women: Maulana Ashraf 'Ali Thanawi's Bihishti Zewar* (Berkeley and Los Angeles: University of California Press, 1990).

11. Partha Chatterjee, "Colonialism, Nationalism and Colonised Women: The Contest in India" (Paper delivered at Symposium no. 107 of the Wenner

Gren Foundation for Anthropological Research, "Tensions of Empire: Colonial Control and Visions of Rule," Mijas, Spain, November 5–13, 1988).

12. See Hannah Papanek, "Afterword," in Rokeya Sakhawat Hossain, *Sultana's Dream and Selections from the Secluded Ones,* ed. and trans., Roushan Jahan (New York: The Feminist Press, 1988), pp. 78–79, 61–62.

CONTRIBUTORS

RAFIUDDIN AHMED, MacArthur Fellow and visiting professor of History,
Cornell University

N. GERALD BARRIER, professor, Department of History,
University of Missouri

FRANK F. CONLON, professor, Department of History,
University of Washington

D. DENNIS HUDSON, professor of World Religions, Department of Religion,
Smith College

KENNETH W. JONES, distinguished professor of South Asian History,
Department of History,
Kansas State University

CHRISTOPHER R. KING, associate professor,
Department of Communication Studies,
University of Windsor

KAREN LEONARD, professor, Department of Anthropology,
University of California, Irvine

BARBARA DALY METCALF, professor, Department of History,
University of California, Davis

GAIL MINAULT, associate professor, Department of History,
University of Texas

AVRIL A. POWELL, lecturer, School of Asian and African Studies,
University of London